STATEMENT ON THE STAFF STUDIES

The Commission was directed to "go as far as man's knowledge takes" it in searching for the causes of violence and the means of prevention. These studies are reports to the Commission by independent scholars and lawyers who have served as directors of our staff task forces and study teams; they are not reports by the Commission itself. Publication of any of the reports should not be taken to imply endorsement of their contents by the Commission, or by any member of the Commission's staff, including the Executive Director and other staff officers, not directly responsible for the preparation of the particular report. Both the credit and the responsibility for the reports lie in each case with the directors of the task forces and study teams. The Commission is making the reports available at this time as works of scholarship to be judged on their merits, so that the Commission as well as the public may have the benefit of both the reports and informed criticism and comment on their contents.

Dr. Milton S. Eisenhower, *Chairman*

For sale by the Superintendent of Documents, U.S. Government Printing Office
Washington, D.C. 20402 - Price $1.50 (paper cover)

Task Force on Historical and Comparative Perspectives

Co-Directors

Hugh Davis Graham
Ted Robert Gurr

Secretaries

Carol Voit
Frances Adams

Commission Staff Officers

Lloyd N. Cutler, *Executive Director*
Thomas D. Barr, *Deputy Director*
James F. Short, Jr., Marvin E. Wolfgang, *Co-Directors of Research*
James S. Campbell, *General Counsel*
William G. McDonald, *Administrative Office*
Ronald Wolk, *Special Assistant to the Chairman*
Joseph Laitin, *Director of Information*

National Commission on the Causes and Prevention of Violence

Dr. Milton S. Eisenhower, *Chairman*

VIOLENCE IN AMERICA:

HISTORICAL AND COMPARATIVE PERSPECTIVES

VOL. II

A Report to the
National Commission on
the Causes and Prevention of
Violence

by
Hugh Davis Graham
and
Ted Robert Gurr

8CL

June 1969

Library of Congress catalog card number: 76-601931

PREFACE

From the earliest days of organization, the Chairman, Commissioners, and Executive Director of the National Commission on the Causes and Prevention of Violence recognized the importance of research in accomplishing the task of analyzing the many facets of violence in America. As a result of this recognition, the Commission has enjoyed the receptivity, encouragement, and cooperation of a large part of the scientific community in this country. Because of the assistance given in varying degrees by scores of scholars here and abroad, these Task Force reports represent some of the most elaborate work ever done on the major topics they cover.

The Commission was formed on June 10, 1968. By the end of the month, the Executive Director had gathered together a small cadre of capable young lawyers from various Federal agencies and law firms around the country. That group was later augmented by partners borrowed from some of the Nation's major law firms who served without compensation. Such a professional group can be assembled more quickly than university faculty because the latter are not accustomed to quick institutional shifts after making firm commitments of teaching or research at a particular locus. Moreover, the legal profession has long had a major and traditional role in Federal agencies and commissions.

In early July a group of 50 persons from the academic disciplines of sociology, psychology, psychiatry, political science, history, law, and biology were called together on short notice to discuss for 2 days how best the Commission and its staff might proceed to analyze violence. The enthusiastic response of these scientists came at a moment when our Nation was still suffering from the tragedy of Senator Kennedy's assassination.

It was clear from that meeting that the scholars were prepared to join research analysis and action, interpretation, and policy. They were eager to present to the American people the best available data, to bring reason to bear where myth had prevailed. They cautioned against simplistic solutions, but urged application of what is known in the service of sane policies for the benefit of the entire society.

Shortly thereafter the position of Director of Research was created. We assumed the role as a joint undertaking, with common responsibilities. Our function was to enlist social and other scientists to join the staff, to write papers, act as advisers or consultants, and engage in new research. The decentralized structure of the staff, which at its peak numbered 100, required research coordination to reduce duplication and to fill in gaps among the

vii

original seven separate Task Forces. In general, the plan was for each Task Force to have a pair of directors: one a social scientist, one a lawyer. In a number of instances, this formal structure bent before the necessities of available personnel but in almost every case the Task Force work program relied on both social scientists and lawyers for its successful completion. In addition to our work with the seven original Task Forces, we provided consultation for the work of the eighth "Investigative" Task Force, formed originally to investigate the disorders at the Democratic and Republican National Conventions and the civil strife in Cleveland during the summer of 1968 and eventually expanded to study campus disorders at several colleges and universities.

Throughout September and October and in December of 1968 the Commission held about 30 days of public hearings related expressly to each of the Task Force areas. About 100 witnesses testified, including many scholars, Government officials, corporate executives as well as militants and activists of various persuasions. In addition to the hearings, the Commission and the staff met privately with scores of persons, including college presidents, religious and youth leaders, and experts in such areas as the media, victim compensation, and firearms. The staff participated actively in structuring and conducting those hearings and conferences and in the questioning of witnesses.

As Research Directors, we participated in structuring the strategy of design for each Task Force, but we listened more than directed. We have known the delicate details of some of the statistical problems and computer runs. We have argued over philosophy and syntax; we have offered bibliographical and other resource materials, we have written portions of reports and copy edited others. In short, we know the enormous energy and devotion, the long hours and accelerated study that members of each Task Force have invested in their labors. In retrospect we are amazed at the high caliber and quantity of the material produced, much of which truly represents, the best in research and scholarship. About 150 separate papers and projects were involved in the work culminating in the Task Force reports. We feel less that we have orchestrated than that we have been members of the orchestra, and that together with the entire staff we have helped compose a repertoire of current knowledge about the enormously complex subject of this Commission.

That scholarly research is predominant in the work here presented is evident in the product. But we should like to emphasize that the roles which we occupied were not limited to scholarly inquiry. The Directors of Research were afforded an opportunity to participate in all Commission meetings. We engaged in discussions at the highest levels of decisionmaking, and had great freedom in the selection of scholars, in the control of research budgets, and in the direction and design of research. If this was not unique, it is at least an uncommon degree of prominence accorded research by a national commission.

There were three major levels to our research pursuit: (1) summarizing the state of our present knowledge and clarifying the lacunae where more or new research should be encouraged; (2) accelerating known ongoing research so as to make it available to the Task Forces; (3) undertaking new research projects within the limits of time and funds available. Coming from a university setting where the pace of research is more conducive to reflection and quiet hours analyzing data, we at first thought that completing much meaningful new research within a matter of months was most unlikely. But the need was matched by the talent and enthusiasm of the staff, and the Task Forces very early had begun enough new projects to launch a small university with a score of doctoral theses. It is well to remember also that in each volume here presented, the research reported is on full public display and thereby makes the staff more than usually accountable for their products.

One of the very rewarding aspects of these research undertakings has been the experience of minds trained in the law mingling and meshing, sometimes fiercely arguing, with other minds trained in behavioral science. The organizational structure and the substantive issues of each Task Force required members from both groups. Intuitive judgment and the logic of argument and organization blended, not always smoothly, with the methodology of science and statistical reasoning. Critical and analytical faculties were sharpened as theories confronted facts. The arrogance neither of ignorance nor of certainty could long endure the doubts and questions of interdisciplinary debate. Any sign of approaching the priestly pontification of scientism was quickly dispelled in the matrix of mutual criticism. Years required for the normal accumulation of experience were compressed into months of sharing ideas with others who had equally valid but differing perspectives. Because of this process, these volumes are much richer than they otherwise might have been.

Partly because of the freedom which the Commission gave to the Directors of Research and the Directors of each Task Force, and partly to retain the full integrity of the research work in publication, these reports of the Task Forces are in the posture of being submitted to and received by the Commission. These are volumes published under the authority of the Commission, but they do not necessarily represent the views or the conclusions of the Commission. The Commission is presently at work producing its own report, based in part on the materials presented to it by the Task Forces. Commission members have, of course, commented on earlier drafts of each Task Force, and have caused alterations by reason of the cogency of their remarks and insights. But the final responsibility for what is contained in these volumes rests fully and properly on the research staffs who labored on them.

In this connection, we should like to acknowledge the special leadership of the Chairman, Dr. Milton S. Eisenhower, in formulating and supporting the principle of research freedom and autonomy under which this work has been conducted.

We note, finally, that these volumes are in many respects incomplete and tentative. The urgency with which papers were prepared and then integrated into Task Force Reports rendered impossible the successive siftings of data and argument to which the typical academic article or volume is subjected. The reports have benefited greatly from the counsel of our colleagues on the Advisory Panel, and from much debate and revision from within the staff. It is our hope, that the total work effort of the Commission staff will be the source and subject of continued research by scholars in the several disciplines, as well as a useful resource for policymakers. We feel certain that public policy and the disciplines will benefit greatly from such further work.

* * *

To the Commission, and especially to its Chairman, for the opportunity they provided for complete research freedom, and to the staff for its prodigious and prolific work, we, who were intermediaries and servants to both, are most grateful.

James F. Short, Jr.   Marvin E. Wolfgang

Directors of Research

x

INTRODUCTION

By Hugh Davis Graham* and Ted Robert Gurr†

Many unique aspects of our society and politics have contributed to the individual and collective violence that troubles contemporary America, among them the psychological residues of slavery, the coexistence of mass consumption with pockets and strata of sullen poverty, the conflict among competing ethics that leaves many men without clear guides to social action. Other sources of violence in our national life are inheritances of our own past: a celebration of violence in good causes by our revolutionary progenitors, frontiersmen, and vigilantes; immigrant expectations of an earthly paradise only partly fulfilled; the unresolved tensions of rapid and unregulated urban and industrial growth. Yet many societies as well as our own have experienced violent disorder as a consequence of such conditions at different times in their national development, in some cases disintegrating in a welter of blood and shattered institutions, in others emerging as stronger and more satisfying communities. Examination of our development as a nation provides a sense of understanding of the historical genesis of our present situation. Comparison with the historical experiences of other societies helps identify the points at which our cultural experience differed from that of more—and less—orderly societies. Contemporary comparisons provide a mirror that can tell us, without favor or rancor, how far we have fallen from our self-anointed status as the most favored of nations. By these comparisons we also begin to identify some of the general conditions, processes, and outcomes of violence, and ultimately to anticipate the effects of what we do now and tomorrow on the creation, maintenance, and destruction of political community.

Men often are accused of being blinded by the immediacy of contemporary events to the lessons of history. A difficulty of American scholarship is that those lessons are only partly studied and partly understood. Historians

*Hugh Davis Graham is associate professor of history and Assistant Director of the Institute of Southern History at the Johns Hopkins University. His publications include *Crisis in Print: Desegregation and the Press in Tennessee* (Nashville: Vanderbilt University Press, 1967); "The Storm Over Black Power," *Virginia Quarterly Review,* XLII (Fall 1967); an edited volume, *Huey Long* (Englewood Cliffs, N.J.: Prentice-Hall, 1969); and *Since 1954, the Supreme Court and the Schools* (New York: *New York Times* and Harper and Row, forthcoming).

†Ted Robert Gurr is assistant professor of politics, faculty associate of the Center of International Studies, and Associate Director of the Workshop in Comparative Politics at Princeton University. He is author of *Why Men Rebel* (Princeton University Press, 1969); *The Conditions of Civil Violence: First Tests of a Causal Model,* with Charles Ruttenberg (Princeton: Center of International Studies, 1967); *American Welfare,* with Alfred de Grazia (New York: New York University Press, 1961); and a number of articles.

interested in the differential inclinations of a people or of groups within a society to resort to violence face four basic obstacles. The first is a familiar one: insufficient or inadequate evidence. To be sure, evidence of violence per se is abundant, sure as newspaper accounts of civil commotion, though few of them have been closely examined. But many kinds of precise data that contemporary social scientists require—e.g., consistent and reliable crime statistics, participant profiles, public opinion surveys—are generally unavailable to historians. Others, such as the results of systematic content analysis of documents and evaluation of court records, are only occasionally used by American historians.

A second barrier to historical understanding has been the lack of a general theoretical framework with which to order our perceptions of the motives and attitudes that impel groups toward violence and the social conditions conducive to it. Until fairly recently, American historians have been inclined to regard economic motives as paramount, and to explain violence either sympathetically as the protest of the have-nots or unsympathetically as a byproduct of the defense of privilege. Sociologists and political scientists have usually focused on the tension-generating characteristics of incompatible social values and maladaptive institutions that lead to violent conflict among groups. Some social scientists have employed psychological instruments of analysis, such as frustration-aggression and cognitive dissonance theories, attempting to take into account social and political as well as economic motives, psychological dispositions as well as class cleavages. The variety of theoretical approaches reflected in this volume by no means exhausts the repertory, nor are all of them consistent in their assumptions or conclusions. But all assume that civil commotion has many causes, not just one, and that those causes have to do with both the nature of man and his social circumstances.

Ironically, professional specialization itself has in some ways impeded our understanding of the role of violence in our past. As the grand sweep of the multivolume historical surveys of the 19th century have given way to the penetrating but narrow monographic studies of the 20th, the quantity of American historical knowledge had been accumulating, but at the expense of synthesis. While the historians have been specializing by era, or through a process of professional tunneling that creates long but narrow channels of inquiry—diplomatic, constitutional, labor history—other social scientists have largely eschewed the study of violence in America and have concentrated almost exclusively on the peaceful and institutional processes of our social and political life. "Violence" does not even rate an entry in the new *International Encyclopedia of the Social Sciences.* We are not suggesting that the students of man add yet another specialty to their atomized ranks. But more of them should become more acutely aware of the bellwether function of civil strife. It is worth examining not only in its own right but as evidence of the character and social processes of the times and societies from which it rises. As Charles Tilly observes in chapter 1, violence is normal in political life, and changes in its form tell us that something important is happening in the political system. Not only may a closer attentiveness to the dynamics of civil turmoil increase our understanding of political and social life; it may be a healthy corrective to our habit of looking at society from the top down.

A fourth impediment to understanding our violent past has been the powerful strain of optimistic parochialism that has variously equated the growth of the American nation with the New Jerusalem, Manifest Destiny, and inelectably progressive Darwinian evolution. Historians have been perhaps less guilty of this ethnocentrism than have been chambers of commerce, but even historians who have eschewed flag waving have tended to focus their research so exclusively on American behavior that they have been denied the insights of the comparative dimension. Yet so disturbing is today's civil commotion and its attendant widespread disillusionment that it invites a reaction against the comfortable old certitudes. Contemporary Americans, confronted as they are with overseas war and domestic turmoil, may be tempted to overcompensate for past patriotic excesses by equating the American experience instead with slavery and imperialism, Indian genocide, and Judge Lynch. Similarly, some contemporary European intellectuals, such as Jean-Paul Sartre, have come to regard "that super-European monstrosity, North America" as a bastard child or satanic mutation of degraded Europe.[1] Clearly, this era of discontent demands a more careful and sober analysis, both historical and comparative, of the dimensions, antecedents, and consequences of violence. The borrowing by historians of the insights and, to a lesser extent, the methods of the other social sciences has considerably enriched historical understanding in recent years. But American historians in their traditional intranational inquiries have generally reflected the powerful strain of parochialism and ethnocentrism that has suffused the national character. If the essence of social science is comparison, American historians and, to a lesser extent, behavioral scientists are only beginning systematically to explore the rich comparative dimension. This volume represents less a triumphal synthesis than, we hope, a promising step toward exploring that fruitful conjunction between the vertical dimension of historical inquiry and the horizontal dimension of comparative analysis.

The organization of this volume reflects the questions to be answered by historical and comparative inquiry. Few of these questions are answered in any definitive sense, but our contributors provide much evidence and partial answers for most of them. The first is a descriptive, historical question: What have been the patterns and extent of violence by private individuals and groups in the United States, and what, by comparison, have they been in Western Europe? The papers by Tilly and Richard Maxwell Brown in part I offer some general historical answers with special reference to collective violence. The appendix to part I reports a sample study of 150 years of violence as reported in the American press. Together these studies suggest two summary judgements: one, that group violence has been chronic and pervasive in the European and American past; and second, that both Europeans and Americans have a noteworthy capacity to forget or deny its commonality. The chapters of part V provide some of the meager information we have on historical trends in violent crime in the United States.

The second general question is an analytic one: What are the historical conditions that have contributed to different kinds of violence in the American past and present? The chapters in part II suggest the relevance of the immigrant experience, the frontier and vigilante traditions, and the portrayal of violence in American literature and folklore. Parts III through VI sketch the sources and character of specific kinds of protest and private violence: labor and working-class strife, racial conflict, individual aggression, and antiwar protest.

The third general question is the contemporary, descriptive one: How do group protest and violence in the United States compare with similar activities elsewhere in the world? Part VII provides some of the most systematic answers now available. These answers are sought not solely for the purpose of descriptive comparison but in an attempt to answer a fourth question: What are the general conditions of group violence? The quantitative comparisons in this part and the case studies in part VII provide evidence that makes it possible to identify some of the general political and social circumstances and patterns of change that are likely to lead to violence.

The final question is: What are the processes of violence, and what are some alternatives to it? The chapters in parts VIII and IX examine this question in some specific cases; it is a peripheral or central issue of many other chapters. Taken in its entirely, this report provides a wealth of examples of the conditions that give rise to violence and of the extent to which private violence, public force, concession, and nonviolent group responses to discontent can lead to the resolution of those conditions.

Another issue, the definitional one, must be dealt with as a prelude to description and analysis of violence. All of us—citizens, officials, and scholars—look at "violence" from perspectives colored by our beliefs and cultural experience. In common usage the term is pejorative. We use it as a label to categorize, and implicitly to condemn, acts of which we disapprove, whether or not all of them are violent or illegal. If we are sympathetic with the motives underlying collective violence, we are likely to call it "protest." When violence is used by public individuals, such as police and soldiers, we typically refer to it as "legitimate force" and as such praise it. These are emotion-laden words whose customary users are as likely to contribute to acrimonious debate as to understanding: "violence," "force," "protest," "legality," "legitimacy." A clear understanding of the phenomena discussed in this report requires not that we abandon such terms or the perspectives that underlie them, but that we distinguish among them and say what we mean by them.

"Violence" is narrowly defined here as behavior designed to inflict physical injury to people or damage to property. Collectively, and individually, we may regard specific acts of violence as good, bad, or neutral, depending on who engages in it and against whom. "Force" is a more general concept: we define it here as the actual or threatened use of violence to compel others to do what they might not otherwise do. Force, like violence, can be judged good or bad. Sixty years ago most Americans condemned workers' resort to strikes and picketing to gain union recognition and wage increases, but praised the forceful efforts of employers and state militias to break the strikes. By these definitions, force and violence are closely linked concepts. Force necessarily involves the threat if not the actuality of violence; violence is forceful if it is used with the intent to change others' actions. "Protest" does not have necessary implications of force or violence. We mean by protest the expression of dissatisfaction with other people's actions. It can take individual or collective, verbal or physical, peaceful or violent forms. The forms of protest that most concern Americans are the collective and physical ones, but collective, public protest does not by definition include the use of force or violence, nor do public protestors in contemporary America frequently use them.

"Legality" and legitimacy" are words that we use to pass judgement on the desirability of violence, force, and protest, as well as other acts. The "legality" of acts is determined by formal procedures of community decision making. Acts are "legitimate," in the sense meant here, if members of a community regard them as desirable or justifiable. We have laws that proscribe most uses of violence by private citizens, others that permit law officers to use forceful violence to deter private violence, and still others that regulate various kinds of protest. But the judgement that an act is legal or illegal is a formal one, made and enforced by a small segment of the community. In the perfect social order all acts judged legal would be regarded as legitimate by the community, all illegal acts would be illegitimate. No such clear-cut distinction holds in the United States so far as violence, force, and protest are concerned, nor has it ever. Our nation was founded in a revolutionary war that was illegal but widely regarded as legitimate. It survived a civil war whose competing causes most Northerners and most Southerners thought both legal and legitimate. Americans deplored the assassination of President John F. Kennedy, yet years earlier many had appaluded the abortive attempt on the life of Adolph Hitler. Hundreds of vigilante movements grace the pages of American history: most of them entailed violence by private individuals that was technically illegal but popularly regarded as legitimate. On the other hand, such institutions and practices as de jure racial segregation and civil rights demonstrations have been technically legal in various regions and eras, but have been widely regarded as illegitimate.

The complexity of the American conflict between legitimacy and legality of actions is apparent in an analysis of the demonstrations and riots that accompanied the 1968 Democratic National Convention.[2] Some of the demonstrations were technically legal, others were not, by fiat of municipal authority. In other American cities all might have been approved, in some all might have been ruled illegal. Most demonstrators regarded their actions as legitimate, whatever their legality or their violence. Many Chicagoans, and perhaps a majority of Americans, had directly opposing perceptions: they apparently regarded the demonstrations as illegitimate, whatever their legality and whether or not they were violent. Some police actions in response to the demonstrations were technically legal, some not. The police and—according to opinion polls—the majority of Americans throught the police action in its entirety was legitimate, the demonstrators obviously did not.

These distinctions are not merely an exercise in semantics. They are intended to demonstrate the Americans historically have not agreed, and do not now agree, on the propriety of different kinds of force, violence, and protest. One group's legitimate protest has been another group's illegal violence throughout our history. This report is not designed to persuade the reader about the rightness of the views of any of these groups in conflict. It does try to provide a sense of understanding of three critical contemporary issues: how some of our differences of opinion over goals and means came into being, what some consequences of our failures to resolve them have been for civil peace, and what we and other peoples have done in the past to overcome such devisive disagreements. We are a diverse nation, linked together most fundamentally by our common desires for way of life both civil and satisfying. To attain them we must cooperate with one another, all of us, for violent antagonisms expressed violently destroy peace, and men, and ultimately community. One blunt sentiment of our rebellious forefathers, voiced by Benjamin Franklin, is as applicable to life in the United States today as it was nearly two centuries ago: "We shall all hang together, or assuredly we shall all hang separately."

References

1. Preface to Frantz Fanon, *The Wretched of the Earth,* (New York: Grove Press, 1963), p. 22.
2. See Daniel Walker, *Rights In Conflict,* a report submitted to the National Commission on the Causes and Prevention of Violence (Washington: The Commission, 1968).

ACKNOWLEDGMENTS

The editors want to thank the Commissioners and staff of the National Commission on the Causes and Prevention of Violence, first, for recognizing the importance of historical and comparative studies for public understanding of violence, second for their consistent support and counsel in the task of compiling this report. We are especially grateful to Profs. Morris Janowitz and Richard Wade of the University of Chicago, James Q. Wilson of Harvard, and Benjamin Quarles of Morgan State College, whose criticisms and suggestions as members of the Commission's Advisory Panel helped strengthen the final report—as did the guidance and advice of the Commission's Co-Directors of Research, Dr. James F. Short, Jr., and Dr. Marvin E. Wolfgang. Similarly, the initial strategic guidance of several colleagues not officially associated with the Commission greatly facilitated our task: Profs. David M. Potter, John Hope Franklin, Harry Eckstein, David Donald, Carl Degler, and Paul Bohannan.

Most of all we are indebted to our contributors, who promptly set aside their other obligations to communicate to the Commission and to Americans generally some of what has been learned in the last several generations of scholarship on violent conflict. They proved willing not only to summarize the knowledge of their special fields but to make available many new findings and interpretations, and to do so within severe time constraints. In addition to their contributions per se, the critical advice they provided one another and to us added immeasurably to the report. Of course, responsibility for the interpretations we have placed on their findings in the part introductions and conclusion is ours, not theirs.

Appreciation also is due to Prof. Sheldon Levy of Brandeis University for his permission to include in our report a revised version his statistical study by newspaper sample of the past 150 years of American violence, and to Prof. Michael Hudson of Brooklyn College for an unpublished background paper comparing the American incidence of violence with its frequency in other nations.

Some members of the Commission staff deserve special recognition: James Campbell for his sustained and infectious enthusiasm for our work, Ronald Wolk for his valiant efforts to make sense of our prose, and finally the Commission's administrative and clerical staff, under the energetic direction of William McDonald, especially Carol Voit, Susan Lipsitch, and Frances Adams. Lastly we are indebted to our wives, Ann Graham and Erika Gurr, for providing moral and clerical support far beyond the call of duty.

Hugh Davis Graham
Ted Robert Gurr
Codirectors, Task Force on
Historical and Comparative Perspectives on Violence in America

CONTENTS

FIGURES

TABLES

PART IV

PATTERNS AND SOURCES OF RACIAL AGGRESSION

The history of white aggression against American Negroes has been so thoroughly documented that there is no need to elaborate further upon it here. What is probably most remarkable about the "American Dilemma" of which Gunnar Myrdal and others wrote is that for most white Americans, who have been living with the dilemma since the 17th century, its quotient of frustration has been so minimal. If a dilemma is defined as a situation requiring a choice between two equally undersirable alternatives, one wonders, since the contradiction between the equalitarian American Creed and oppressive behavior has never been resolved, whether Charles Silberman wasn't closer to the mark when he observed that "the tragedy of race relations in the United States is that there is no American Dilemma."[1]

Or perhaps there has been an American dilemma, but one which has more accurately characterized the plight of black Americans, for surely the undesirability of the two alternatives has always been more apparent to them. To acquiesce in slavery and caste meant enduring misery and degradation. But to strike out against the status quo was to invite the rope and faggot. Today, Negro Americans are at long last sharpening the twin horns of the white dilemma, and thereby forcing its resolution. That it will be resolved in favor of the equalitarian creed is by no means certain, for it is possible that under extreme stress American society will choose security over freedom and order over justice.

Whatever the outcome, the contemporary effusion of black militancy poses two closely related questions: What has been the sequence of events

that in the 20th century has transformed the
Negroes' response to oppression from a defensive
to a retaliatory one? And how can we explain the
paradox that so many generations of black Americans were relatively quiescent during the epochs
of slavery and formal caste, only to explode in
wrathful protest just as the physical conditions of
life were ostensibly improving?[2]

Racial violence in the 20th century has under-
gone a fundamental transformation. Interracial
riots in the early years of the century were essentially pogroms in which the Negroes were victims
of white aggression. In the 1960's the Negroes
have been the aggressors; however, in contrast to
the earlier riots, deaths have been few, the attacks
being concentrated on property rather than persons.
Deaths have occurred primarily as the result of conflict between police and Negro civilians, rather than
between Negro and white civilians, as had been the
case in the early-20th century.

Although black retaliatory violence has been essentially a characteristic only of recent racial rioting,
Profs. August Meier and Elliott Rudwick demonstrate in chapter 9 that neither the rhetoric nor the
practice of black retaliation is new. They argue
that tendencies toward retaliatory violence are correlated to a considerable extent with periods of
generally heightened militance among Negroes, and
that the reasons for this relationship—as well as for
the absence of retaliatory violence during the initial
period of growing militance after World War II—are
to be found less in external circumstances than in
the changing expectations of the black population
of the United States.

The historical analysis of Meier and Rudwick is
supplemented in chapter 10 by Morris Janowitz's
sociological analysis of the transformation of collective racial violence through three stages. First, 50
years ago, the typical race riot in American cities
was an interracial clash on the boundaries of expanding black neighborhoods, one in which whites
more often than Negroes took offensive action. Second, during World War II, these communal clashes
began to give way to large-scale riots, wholly within
the black community. Often triggered by a police
incident, the outbursts resulted in clash between

the local population and officers and agents of the larger society, with implied overtones of political protest. Because the outbursts resulted in widespread looting, they can be described as commodity riots. Third, by the summer of 1968, however, this form of racial violence appeared to be in decline, being replaced by a new form: a more selective, terroristic use of force against whites by small, organized groups of blacks with crude ideological motives.

Each stage in the transformation of racial violence in the United States has carried with it elements of the next stage. Each stage is an expression of the social structure of the United States and the position of the Negro in this social structure. In other words, Janowitz's basic orientation is that the agencies of social change and social control are crucial in accounting for the occurrence and form of urban racial outbreaks. The impact of two such agencies is examined: the patterns of intervention and the consequences of law enforcement crucially condition the sequence and extent of the riot; while the mass media have both an immediate impact on the contagion of riot behavior and a long-term effect on the social structure.

In chapter 11 James P. Comer, a psychiatrist, addresses himself to the paradoxical recent venting of black anger in the face of the demonstrable economic and educational gains made by Negro Americans since 1960. Clearly, the concurrence of accelerated socioeconomic mobility and violence cannot be explained on the basis of any objective and measurable criteria such as the number and quality of jobs and the level of employment or income. The coincidence of black progress and black rage suggests that the latter is in part a legacy of an earlier form of violence: the severe psychic damage wrought by the powerlessness of enslavement and subsequently of caste.

The chronic psychological trauma of slavery and later of caste forced the powerless black community to adapt avoidance and denial mechanisms, which resulted in ignoring or turning anger inward against the self in self-destructive acts, or in projecting or displacing it onto group members and acting aggressively against them rather than toward members of the oppressive group. But social conditions of the past few years have permitted these feelings to be turned outward and directed toward the perceived oppressor. Dr. Comer's psychoanalytical analysis of the relationship of the oppressor and the oppressed over time suggests that the analogy of individual development may largely resolve the apparent paradox.

References

1. Charles E. Silberman, *Crisis in Black and White* (New York: Random House, 1964), p. 10.
2. In addition to the historical, sociological, and psychological answers proposed in the following three chapters, a comparative interpretation is advanced by James C. Davies in chapter 19.

Chapter 9

BLACK VIOLENCE IN THE 20th CENTURY: A STUDY IN RHETORIC AND RETALIATION

By August Meier and Elliott Rudwick*

For most Americans, the increasingly overt talk of retaliatory violence among Negro militants, and the outbreaks in the urban ghettos over recent summers, signify something new and different in the history of Negro protest. Actually, retaliatory violence has never been entirely absent from Negro thinking. Moreover, advocacy of retaliatory violence, and actual instances of it, have tended to increase during periods of heightened Negro protest activity.

Thus the past decade of rising Negro militance has been no stranger to the advocacy of retaliatory violence. For example, as far back as 1959, Robert F. Williams, at the time president of the Monroe, North Carolina, branch of the NAACP, came to public attention when the Union County Superior Court acquitted two white men of brutal assaults on two Negro women, but sentenced a mentally retarded Negro to imprisonment as a result of an argument he had with a white woman. Williams angrily told a reporter, "We cannot take these people who do us injustice to the court, and it becomes necessary to punish them ourselves. If it's necessary to stop lynching with lynching, then we must be willing to resort to that method." The NAACP dismissed Williams as branch president, but he remained a leader of Monroe's working-class Negroes, who for several years had been using guns to protect their homes from white Klansmen. In 1961, falsely charged with kidnaping a white couple, he fled from the country. Williams became the most famous of that group of militants existing at the fringe of the civil-rights movement, who in their complete alienation from American society articulated a revolutionary synthesis of nationalism and Marxism.[1] From his place of exile in

*August Meier is the university professor of history at Kent State University. He is author of *Negro Thought in America, 1880–1915* (Ann Arbor: University of Michigan Press, 1963), and coauthor with Elliott Rudwick of *From Plantation to Ghetto: An Interpretive History of American Negroes* (New York: Hill & Wang, 1966).

Elliott Rudwick is professor of sociology at Kent State University. His publications include *Race Riot at East St. Louis, July 2, 1917* (Cleveland and New York: Meridian Books, 1966), and *W. E. B. Du Bois: Propagandist of the Negor Protest* (New York Atheneum, 1968).

Professors Meier and Rudwick are senior research fellows at Kent State University's Center for Urban Regionalism.

Havana, Cuba, Williams undertook the publication of a monthly newsletter, *The Crusader.* In a typical issue, he declared:

> Our only logical and successful answer is to meet organized and massive violence with massive and organized violence. . . . The weapons of defense employed by Afro-American freedom fighters must consist of a poor man's arsenal. . . . Molotov cocktails, lye, or acid bombs [made by injecting lye or acid in the metal end of light bulbs] can be used extensively. During the night hours such weapons, thrown from roof tops, will make the streets impossible for racist cops to patrol. . . . Yes, a minority war of self-defense can succeed.[2]

Subsequently Williams was named chairman in exile of an organization known as the Revolutionary Action Movement (RAM),[3] a tiny group of college-educated people in a few major northern cities, some of whose members have been recently charged with plotting the murder of Roy Wilkins and Whitney Young.

Williams, RAM, and the better known Black Muslims[4] were on the fringes of the Negro protest of the early 1960's. More recently violence and the propaganda for violence have moved closer to the center of the race relations stage. Well over 200 riots have occurred since the summer of 1964. The incendiary statements of the Rap Browns and the Stokeley Carmichaels became familiar TV and newspaper fare for millions of white Americans. The Oakland, California, Black Panthers and toehr local groups espousing a nationalist and revolutionary rhetoric thrived and received national publicity. As has been often pointed out, there is no evidence that the race riots of the 1960's have any direct relations to the preachings of Williams, of these various groups, even of the SNCC advocates of armed rebellion and guerrilla warfare. Yet both the statements of these ideologists, and the spontaneous actions of the masses, have much in common. For both are the product of the frustrations resulting from the growing disparity between the Negroes' status in American society and the rapidly rising expectations induced by the civil-rights revolution and its earlier successes.

Historically, this doctrine of retaliatiory violence has taken various forms. Some have advocated self-defense against a specific attack. Others have called for revolutionary violence. There are also those who hopefully predicted a general race war in which Negroes would emerge victorious. Though seldom articulated for white ears, and only rarely appearing in print, thoughts of violent retaliation against whites have been quite common. For example, Ralph Bunche, in preparing a memorandum for Gunnar Myrdal's *American Dilemma* in 1940, noted that "there are Negroes, too, who, fed up with frustration of their life, here, see no hope and express an angry desire 'to shoot their way out of it.' I have on many occasions heard Negroes exclaim, 'Just give us machine guns and we'll blow the lid off the whole damn business.' "[5]

In surveying the history of race relations during the 20th century, it is evident that there have been two major periods of upsurge both in overt discussion by Negro intellectuals concerning the desirability of violent retaliation against white oppressors, and also in dramatic incidents of actual social violence committed by ordinary Negro citizens. One was the period during and immediately after the First World War. The second has been the period of the current civil rights revolution.

W. E. B. Du Bois, the noted protest leader and a founder of the NAACP, occasionally advocated retaliatory violence, and somewhat more often predicted intense racial warfare in which Negroes would be the victors. In 1916, inspired by the Irish Rebellion, in an editorial in the NAACP's official organ, *The Crisis,* he admonished Negro youth to stop spouting platitudes of accommodation and remember that no people ever achieved their liberation without an armed struggle. He said that "war is hell, but there are things worse than hell, as every Negro knows."[6] Amid the violence and repression that Negroes experienced in the postwar world, Du Bois declared that the holocaust of World War I was "nothing to compare with that fight for freedom which black and brown and yellow men must and will make unless their oppression and humiliation and insult at the hands of the White World cease."[7]

Other intellectuals reflected this restless mood. The postwar years were the era of the militant, race-conscious New Negro of the urban North, an intellectual type who rejected the gradualism and conciliation of his ancestors. The tone of the New Negro was recorded by Claude McKay, who in 1921 wrote his well-known poem, "If We Must Die": "If we must die/let it not be like hogs; hunted and penned in an accursed spot!/ . . . . If we must die; oh, let us nobly die/dying but fighting back." A. Philip Randolph, editor of the militant socialist monthly, *The Messenger,* organizer of the Brotherhood of Sleeping Car Porters, and later leader of the March on Washington Movements of 1941 and 1963, also advocated physical resistance to white mobs. He observed that "Anglo-Saxon jurisprudence recognizes the law of self-defense . . . . The black man has no rights which will be respected unless the black man enforces that respect. . . . We are consequently urging Negroes and other oppressed groups concerned with lynching or mob violence to act upon the recognized and accepted law of self-defense."[8]

The legality of retaliatory violent self-defense was asserted not only by A. Philip Randolph, but also by the NAACP, which Randolph regarded as a moderate, if not futile organization, wedded to the interest of the Negro middle class. In 1925, half a dozen years after *The Messenger* article, the NAACP secured the acquittal of Dr. Ossian Sweet and his family. The Sweets were Detroit Negroes who had moved into a white neighborhood, and fired on a stone-throwing mob in front of their home, killing one white man and wounding another.[9] More than a quarter of a century later, at the time of the Robert Williams episode, the NAACP in clarifying its position, reiterated the stand that "The NAACP has never condoned mob violence but it firmly supports the right of Negroes individually and collectively to defend their person, their homes, and their property from attack. This position has always been the policy of the NAACP."[10] The views of intellectuals like Du Bois, McKay, and Randolph during World War I and the early postwar years paralleled instances of Negro retaliatory violence which actually triggered some of the major race riots of the period.

The East St. Louis riot of 1917, the bloodiest in the 20th century, was precipitated in July when Negroes, having been waylaid and beaten repeatedly by white gangs, shot into a police car and killed two white detectives. On the darkened street a Negro mob of 50 to 100 evidently mistook the Ford squad car for the Ford automobile containing white "joyriders" who had shot up Negro homes earlier in the evening. The following morning the riot began.[11]

In Houston, several weeks later, about 100 Negro soldiers broke into an Army ammunition storage room and marched on the city's police station. The troops, mostly Northerners, were avenging an incident which occurred earlier in the day, when a white policeman used force in arresting a Negro woman and then beat up a Negro soldier attempting to intervene. A Negro provost guard was pistol whipped and shot at for asking the policeman about the wounded soldier. Even before these events, the Negro soldiers nursed a hatred for Houston policemen, who had attempted to enforce streetcar segregation, frequently used the term "nigger," and officiously patrolled the Negro ghetto. The Houston riot was not only unusual because it involved Negro soldiers, but also because white persons constituted most of the fatalities.[12]

By 1919 there was evidence that the Negro masses were prepared to fight back in many parts of the country, even in the Deep South. In an unpublished report to the NAACP Board of Directors, a staff member, traveling in Tennessee and Mississippi during early 1919, noted that "bloody conflicts impended in a number of southern cities." Perry Howard, the leading colored attorney in Jackson, and R. R. Church, the wealthy Memphis politician, both reported that Negroes were armed and prepared to defend themselves from mob violence. Howard detailed an incident in which armed Negroes had prevented a white policeman from arresting a Negro who had become involved in a fight with two white soldiers after they had slapped a colored girl. In Memphis, R. R. Church, fearing armed conflict, privately advised the city's mayor that "the Negroes would not make trouble unless they were attacked, but in that event they were prepared to defend themselves."[13]

The Chicago race riot of 1919 grew out of Negro resentment of exclusion from a bathing beach dominated by whites. One Sunday, while Negroes and whites scuffled on the beach, a colored teenager drowned after being attacked in the swimming area. That attack was the most recent of a long series of assaults against Negroes. A white policeman not only refused to arrest a white man allegedly involved in the drowning, but actually attempted to arrest one of the two complaining Negroes. The officer was mobbed and soon the rioting was underway.[14]

The Elaine, Arkansas riot of 1919 was precipitated when two white law officers shot into a Negro church, and the Negroes returned the fire, causing one death. The white planters in the area, already angered because Negro cottonpickers were seeking to unionize and obtain an increase in their sharecropping wages, embarked upon a massive Negro hunt to put the black peons "in their place."[15]

The Tulsa riot of 1921 originated when a crowd of armed Negroes assembled before the courthouse to protest the possible lynching of a Negro who had just been arrested for allegedly attacking a white girl. The Negroes shot at white police and civilians who attempted to disperse them.[16]

In each of these conflagrations, the typical pattern was initial Negro retaliation to white acts of persecution and violence, and white perception of this resistance as an organized, premeditated conspiracy to "take over," thus unleashing the massive armed power of white mobs and police. In the Southern communities, Negro resistance tended to collapse early in the riots. After the church incident in the rural Elaine area, most Negroes passively accepted the planters' armed attacks on their homes. At Tulsa, Negroes retreated from the courthouse to the ghetto, and throughout the night held off by gunfire the assaults of white mobs. But after daybreak, many Negroes fled or surrendered before the white onslaught burned down much of the ghetto.[17] One exception to this pattern was the Washington riot of 1919, where it appears that Negroes did not retaliate until the third and last day of the riot.[18]

Negro resistance generally lasted longer in Northern riots than in Southern ones, but even in East St. Louis and Chicago the death toll told the story: in East St. Louis, 9 whites and at least 39 Negroes were killed. In Chicago, 15 whites and 23 Negroes lost their lives. Negroes attacked a small number of whites found in the ghetto or on its fringes. Negro fatalities mainly occurred when victims were trapped in white-dominated downtown areas or residential sections. Negroes were also attacked on the edges of their neighborhood in a boundary zone separating a colored residential district from a lower class white area.[19] In the face of overwhelming white numerical superiority, many armed Negroes fled from their homes, leaving guns and ammunition behind. In East St. Louis, for example, there was a constant rattle of small explosions when fire enveloped a small colored residential district. Perhaps psychological factors contributed to the terrified inactivity of some Negroes. Despite the wish to meet fire with fire, over the years they had become so demoralized by white supremacy and race discrimination that effective armed defense could exist only in the realm of psychological fantasy.

During World War II, the most important race riot erupted in 1943 in Detroit, where nine whites and 25 Negroes were killed. In many respects the riot exhibited a pattern similar to East St. Louis and Chicago. The precipitating incident involved an attack on whites at the Belle Isle Amusement Park by several Negro teenagers who, a few days earlier, had been ejected from the white-controlled Eastwood Park. In the mounting tension at Belle Isle, many fights between Negroes and whites broke out, and the violence spread to the Negro ghetto where patrons at a night club were urged to "take care of a bunch of whites who killed a colored woman and her baby at Belle Isle." Although there had been no fatalities at the park, the night club emptied and revengeful Negroes stoned passing cars driven by whites. They began smashing windows on the ghetto's main business street, where the mob's major attention was directed to destroying and looting white-owned businesses.[20]

It was this symbolic destrution of "whitey" through his property that gave the Detroit holocaust the characteristic of what we may call the "new-style" race riot. It may be noted that in all the riots discussed above, there were direct clashes between Negroes and whites, and the major part of the violence was perpetrated by the white mobs. The riot pattern since the summer of 1964, however, has involved Negro aggression mainly against white-owned property, not white people. This "new style" riot first appeared in Harlem in 1935 and 1943.[21] The modern riot does not involve white mobs at all, and policemen or guardsmen constitute most of the relatively small number of casualties.

One can identify perhaps two major factors responsible for this contrast between the old-style and the new-style riot. One is the relatively marked shift in the climate of race relations in this country over the past generation. On the one hand, whites have become, on the whole, more sensitive to the Negro's plight, more receptive toward Negro demands, and less punitive in their response to Negro aggression. The black masses, on the other hand, have raised their expectations markedly and, disillusioned by the relatively slow pace of social change which has left the underprivileged urban Negro of the North scarcely, if at all, better off than he was 10 or 15 years ago, have become more restless and militant than before.

In the second place, there is an ecological factor. From South to North, the migration of the World War I period was a mere drop in the bucket compared to what it later became. The migration to the North in each of the decades since 1940 has been equal to or greater than the migration of the whole 30-year period, 1910 to 1940. At the same time, owing to the Supreme Court's outlawing of the restrictive covenant in 1948, and the tearing down of the older slums through urban renewal, the Negro population has been dispersed over a wider area, thus accentuating the trend toward the development of vast ghettos. Indeed, compared to the enormous ghettos of today, the Negro residential areas of the World War I period were mere enclaves. Today, of course, Negroes are close to becoming a majority in several of the major American cities.

The character of American race riots has been markedly affected by these demographic changes. Even if white mobs were to form, they would be unable to attack and burn down the Negro residential areas; even in the 19th- and early-20th-century riots, white mobs did not usually dare to invade the larger Negro sections, and destroyed only the smaller areas of Negro concentration. Nor, since the Negroes are such a large share of the population of the central city areas, would white mobs today be in a position to chase, beat, and kill isolated Negroes on downtown streets. More important, from the Negroes' point of view, the large-scale ghettos provide a relatively safe place for the destruction and looting of white-owned property; it is impossible for local police forces to guard business property in the farflung ghettos; even State police and federal troops find themselves in hostile territory where it is difficult to chase down rioters beyond the principal thoroughfares.

It is notable that during the 20th century, both the overt discussion of the advisability of violent retaliation on the part of Negroes, and also actual incidents of violence were prominent in the years during and after World War I, and again during the 1960's. While there have been significant differences between the outbreaks characteristic of each era, there have been also important similarities. In both periods retaliatory violence accompanied a heightened militancy among American Negroes—a militancy described as the "New Negro" in the years after World War I, and described in the sixties, with the phrase, "the Negro Revolt." In neither case was retaliatory violence the major tactic, or the central thrust, but in both periods it was a significant subordinate theme. However, in both periods a major factor leading Negroes to advocate or adopt such a tactic was the gap between Negro aspiration and objective status. The rapid escalation of the aspirations of the Negro masses who shared Martin Luther King's "dream" and identify vicariously with the success of the civil-rights revolution, while their own economic, housing, and educational opportunities have not improved, is a phenomenon of such frequent comment that it requires no elaboration here.

A comparable situation occurred during and shortly after the First World War. The agitation of the recently founded NAACP, whose membership doubled in 1918-19, the propaganda of fighting a war to make the world safe for democracy, and especially the great Negro migration to the Northern cities which Southern peasants and workers viewed as a promised land, all created new hopes for the fulfillment of age-old dreams, while Negro soldiers who had served in France returned with new expectations. But the Negro's new hopes collided with increasing white hostility. Northern Negroes assigned to southern army camps met indignities unknown at home. They rioted at Houston and came so close to rioting in Spartanburg, South Carolina, that the army hastily shipped them overseas. In the northern cities like East St. Louis and Chicago, Negroes found not a promised land, but overcrowded ghettos and hostile white workers who feared Negro competition for their jobs. The Ku Klux Klan was revived beginning in 1915, and grew rapidly in the North and South after the war ended. By 1919 economic opportunities plummeted as factories converted to peacetime operations. For a while Negroes resisted, protested, fought back, in the South as well as the North; but the superior might of the whites proved overpowering and the Southern Negroes retreated into old paths of accommodation where they generally remained until the momentous events of the past decade.

There has been no systematic research on Negro advocacy of violence prior to the First World War, but the available evidence supports the thesis that increased overt expression of this tendency accompanies peaks in other kinds of protest activity. For example, it appears likely that Negro resistance to white rioters was minimal in the riots at the turn of the century—at Wilmington, North Carolina, in 1898, and at New Orleans, Akron, and New York in 1900[22]— which took place in a period when the sentiment of accommodation to white supremacy, epitomized by Booker T. Washington, was in the ascendency.

Again, during the ante-bellum period, one can cite two noted cases of incendiary statements urging Negroes to revolt—*David Walker's Appeal* of 1829, and Rev. Henry Highland Garnet's suppressed *Address to the Slaves of the United States of America,* delivered at the national Negro convention of 1843.[23] Both coincided with periods of rising militant protest activity on the part of the northern free Negroes. *Walker's Appeal* appeared on the eve of the beginning of the Negro convention movement, and at the time of intensified Negro opposition to the expatriation plans of the American Colonization Society.[24] Garnet's speech was made at a time when free Negro leaders were disturbed at the prejudiced attitudes of white abolitionists who refused to concern themselves with obtaining rights for the free people of color, or to allow Negroes to participate in the inner circles of the leadership of the antislavery societies. Consequently they had revived the Negro national convention movement which had been inactive since 1836. (Garnet's speech was also in part a product of disillusionment with the lack of actual progress being made by the antislavery societies toward achieving abolition.)

We lack any careful analysis of race riots during the 19th century. Some certainly were pogrom-like affairs, in which the Negroes were so thoroughly terrorized from the beginning that they failed to fight back. (Perhaps the Draft Riots, and some of the Reconstruction riots as in Mississippi in 1876 were of this sort.) Yet other riots were characterized by some degree of Negro retaliatory violence, such as the Snow Hill riot in Providence, in 1831, and the Cincinnati riots of 1841. Both appear to have been, like the Chicago and East St. Louis riots, the climaxes to a series of interracial altercations. In the Providence riot, a mob of about 100 white sailors and citizens advanced on a small Negro section; a Negro shot a sailor dead, and within a half hour a large mob descended upon the neighborhood, damaging many houses.25 In the Cincinnati riot, a pitched battle was fought on the streets; the blacks had enough guns and ammunition to fire into the mob such a volley that it was twice repulsed. Only when the mob secured an iron six-pounder and hauled it to the place of combat and fired on the Negroes were the latter forced to retreat, permitting the rioters to hold sway for 2 days without interference from the authorities.26 A careful study of interracial violence during Reconstruction will undoubtedly produce evidence of comparable situations. These riots occurred at a time of high Negro expectations and self-assertiveness, and seem to have been characterized by a significant amount of fighting back on the part of Negroes.

One period of marked and rising Negro militance, however, was not accompanied by a significant increase in manifestations of Negro retaliatory violence. This was the one following the Second World War. Indeed, the Second World War itself witnessed far less Negro violence than did the First World War. The reason for this would appear to be that the 1940's and early 1950's were years of gradually improving Negro status, and a period in which the expectations of the masses did not greatly outrun the actual improvements being made. In fact, from 1941 until the mid-1950's the relative position of the Negro workers, as compared to the white wage earners, was generally improving and it was not until the recession of 1954-55, for example, that the Black Muslims, with their rhetoric of race hatred and retaliatory violence, began to expand rapidly.

It would appear that both in the World War I period, and today—and indeed during the ante-bellum era and at other times when manifestations of violence came to the fore—there has been a strong element of fantasy in Negro discussion and efforts concerning violent retaliation. Robert Williams talked of Molotov cocktails and snarling up traffic as devices for a largely poverty-stricken ethnic minority to engineer a revolution. The Black Muslims talk of violence, but the talk seems to function as a psychological safety valve; by preaching separation, they in effect accommodate to the American social order and place racial warfare off in the future when Allah in his time will destroy the whites and usher in an era of black domination. Similarly, in view of population statistics and power distribution in American society, Du Bois and others who have spoken of the inevitability of racial warfare and Negro victory in such a struggle were engaging in wishful prophesies. And Negroes have been nothing if not realistic. The patterns of Negro behavior in riots demonstrate this. In earlier times, as already indicated, those who bought guns in anticipation of the day when self-defense would be necessary usually did not retaliate. And Negro attacks on whites occurred mainly in the early stages of the riots before the full extent of anger and power and sadism of the white mobs became evident.

Negroes of the World War I era resisted white insults and attacks only as long as they had hopes of being successful in the resistance. It should be emphasized that one of the remarkable things about the riots since 1964, in spite of their having been marked by particular resentment at police brutality, is the fact that Negro destruction was aimed at white-owned property, not white lives, even after National Guardsmen and policemen killed scores of Negroes. And in those cases where retaliatory violence has been attempted, Negroes have retreated in the face of massive white armed force. Economically impoverished Negroes press as far as they realistically can; and one reason for the explosions of recent years has been the awareness that whites are to some degree in retreat, that white mobs in the North no longer organize to attack, and that to a large degree the frustrated Negroes in slums like Watts, Detroit, Washington, or Newark, can get away with acts of destruction.

It is impossible of course to make any foolproof predictions for the future. Yet, judging by past experience and present conditions, it is our view that, despite all the rhetoric of engineering a social revolution through armed rebellion and guerrilla warfare, of planned invasions of downtown business districts and white suburbs, the kind of violence we are likely to witness will, at most, continue to be the sort of outbreaks against the property of white businessmen such as those we have witnessed in recent years. The advocacy and use of violence as a deliberate program for solving the problems of racial discrimination remains thus far, at least, in the realm of fantasy; and there it is likely to remain.

References

1. For accounts, see Julian Mayfield, "Challenge to Negro Leadership," *Commentary* Vol. XXXI (Apr. 1961), pp. 297–305; "The Robert F. Williams Case," *Crisis,* Vol. LXVI (June–July–August–September, 1959), pp. 325–329; 409–410; Robert F. Williams, *Negroes With Guns* (New York: Marzani & Munsell, 1962).
2. *Crusader,* Vol. V (May–June, 1964), pp. 5–6.
3. See the RAM publication *Black America* (Summer–Fall, 1965); *Crusader,* (Mar. 1965).
4. C. Eric Lincoln, *The Black Muslims in America* (Boston: Beacon Press, 1961), p. 205.
5. Ralph Bunche, "Conceptions and Ideologies of the Negro Problem," memorandum prepared for the Carnegie-Myrdal Study of the Negro in America, 1940, p. 161.
6. *Crisis,* Vol. XII (Aug. 1916), pp. 166–167; Vol. XIII (Dec. 1916), p. 63.
7. W. E. B. Du Bois, *Darkwater* (New York, 1920), p. 49.
8. A Philip Randolph, "How To Stop Lynching," *Messenger,* Vol. III (Apr. 1919), pp. 8–9.
9. Walter White, "The Sweet Trial," *Crisis,* Vol. XXXI (Jan. 1926), pp. 125–129.
10. "The Robert F. Williams Case," *Crisis,* Vol. LXVI (June–July 1959), p. 327.
11. Elliott M. Rudwick, *Race Riot at East St. Louis* (Cleveland and New York: Meredian Books, 1968), pp. 38–39.
12. Edgar A. Schuler, "The Houston Race Riot, 1917," *Journal of Negro History,* Vol. XXIX (Oct. 1944), pp. 300–338.
13. *NAACP Board Minutes,* Secretary's Report for June 1919.
14. *The Negro in Chicago* (Chicago, 1922), pp. 4–5.
15. *Crisis,* Vol. XIX (Dec. 1919), pp. 56–62.
16. Allen Grimshaw, *A Study in Social Violence: Urban Race Riots in the U. S.,* University of Pennsylvania unpublished doctoral dissertation, 1959, pp. 42–47.
17. *Ibid.*
18. Constance M. Green, *Washington, Capital City, 1879–1950* (Princeton: Princeton University Press, 1962), pp. 266–267; John Hope Franklin, *From Slavery to Freedom* (New York: Alfred A. Knopf, 1947), p. 473; *New York Times,* July 20–22, 1919.
19. Rudwick, *op. cit.,* pp. 226–227; *Negro in Chicago, op. cit.,* pp. 5–10.
20. Alfred McClung Lee and Norman D. Humphrey, *Race Riot* (New York, 1943), pp. 26–30.

21.   Roi Ottley, *New World A-Coming* (Boston: Beacon Press, 1943), pp. 151–152;
      Harold Orlansky, *The Harlem Riot: A Study in Mass Frustration* (New York,
      1943), pp. 5–6, 14–15; New York *Age*, Mar. 30, 1935, and Aug. 7, 1943.
22.   In the New York riot, however, the precipitating incident was a physical altercation
      between a white policeman and a Negro; see Gilbert Osofsky, *Harlem: The Making
      of a Ghetto* (New York: Harper & Row, 1966), pp. 46–52.
23.   Herbert Aptheker, *A Documentary History of the Negro People in the United
      States* (New York: Citadel, 1951), pp. 93–97, 226–233.
24.   Founded in 1817 by a group of prominent white Americans, the American
      Colonization Society officially encouraged colonization as a means of furthering
      the cause of antislavery. Most Negores, even most of those who themselves at
      one time or another advocated emigration to Africa or the Caribbean as the only
      solution for the Negro's hopeless situation in the United States, denounced the
      society as a cloak for those attempting to protect slavery by deporting free
      Negroes.
25.   Irving H. Bartlett, "The Free Negro in Providence, Rhode Island," *Negro History
      Bulletin*, Vol. XIV (Dec. 1950), p. 54.
26.   Carter G. Woodson, The Negroes of Cincinnati Prior to the Civil War," *Journal of
      Negro History*, Vol. I (Jan. 1916), pp. 13–15.

Chapter 10

PATTERNS OF COLLECTIVE
RACIAL VIOLENCE

By Morris Janowitz*

Race riots are the dramatic hallmark of the injustices of race relations in
the United States. They have an explosive, destructive, and amorphous
character which makes generalization very difficult. As a form of "collective
behavior," their natural history is not easily recorded or analyzed. Students
of race relations believe that one of the most adequate and comprehensive
studies of a particular race riot still remains that prepared by the Chicago
Commission on Race Relations on the Chicago rioting of 1919—the result of
the careful work of the late Charles S. Johnson, which was done under the
supervision of Robert E. Park of the University of Chicago.[1] Nevertheless, it
is the purpose of this paper to present a sociological interpretation of changed
patterns of collective racial violence in the United States over the last century.
The history of race riots reflects not only the expanded aspirations of the
Negro but also the techniques that have been used to maintain his inferior
social position. The history of race relations in the United States has been
grounded in a system of law enforcement that has denied to Negroes due process and equal protection, and that therefore has weakened the legitimacy of
the agents of law enforcement, especially in the lowest Negro income areas.

The purpose of this paper is to trace the transformation in the patterns of
collective racial violence in urban areas over the last 50 years through three
different phases. First, the typical race riot of the period of World War I and
thereafter, the communal riot, was an interracial clash, an ecologically based
struggle at the boundaries of the expanding black neighborhoods. Second,
during World War II, communal riots began to give way to large-scale outbursts within the black community. These riots represented a form of collective behavior against the agents and symbols of the larger society. They can
be described as commodity riots because of the extensive looting that gives
symbolic meaning to these outbursts. Third, the commodity-type riots that
reached a high point during the period of 1964-67 have shown signs of being

*Morris Janowitz is professor of sociology at the University of Chicago and has written
on many aspects of social and political change. Two of his numerous books are
Social Change and Prejudice, with Bruno Bettelheim (New York: The Free Press, 1964),
and *The Military in the Political Development of New Nations* (Chicago: University
of Chicago Press, 1964).

replaced by a new form of racial violence, a more selective, terroristic use of force with political overtones, again mainly against whites, by small organized groups of blacks.

The form and extent of collective racial violence, it is assumed, are expressions of the social structure and the agencies of social change and social control. Therefore, in particular, the role of the police and law enforcement agencies and of the mass media in fashioning patterns of collective urban violence will be explored.

A central "sociological assumption" supplies a point of departure. There is a considerable body of evidence to support this assumption, but it is best to consider it as an assumption. Social tensions generated by discrimination, prejudice, and poverty offer essential but only partial explanations of Negro mass rioting in the urban centers of the United States. Social conditions conducive for collective violence have been much more widespread than the actual selective outbursts. Allen Grimshaw, one of the most careful students of race riots, concluded in 1962 that "there is no direct relation between the level of social tension and the eruption of social violence."[2]

It is not necessary to accept all that this proposition implies because the evidence is not that solid, and more important, because significant "indirect relations" may well have operated. It is enough to reemphasize the obvious fact that, in the United States, social tensions exist where riots break out, and to accept his alternative formulation that "in every case where major rioting has occurred, the social structure of the community has been characterized by weak patterns of external control."[3] Because of the widespread potentials for racial violence, in the language of sociology, the agencies of social change and social control are crucial in accounting for actual urban racial outbreaks. Moreover, the manner in which outbursts are handled and controlled deeply influences race relations and subsequent patterns of violence. It is well to keep in mind that the supporting evidence for this basic assumption rests on the events before the mid-1960's, when a new and intensified wave of urban racial violence broke out in the United States.

On the whole, statistical studies designed to account for which cities have been struck by riots have not been highly rewarding. However, one carefully matched comparison of riot and nonriot cities by Stanley Lieberson and Arnold R. Silverman of 76 race riots between 1913 and 1963 confirms and amplies this perspective.[4] For the period before the new wave of riots of the mid-1960's, they found (a) no support for the contention that rapid population change accompanies riots; (b) no confirmation for the hypothesis that unemployment level is a direct factor, but rather that encroachment of Negroes on the white occupational world evidently tends to increase chances of riots; and (c) no support for the notion that race riots are a consequence either of low Negro income or relatively large Negro-white discrepancies in income. Nor, for that matter, does poor Negro housing serve to distinguish riot cities from nonriot cities.

However, their evidence supports "the proposition that the functioning of local government is important in determining whether a riot will follow a precipitating incident." Thus, (a) cities with more racially integrated police forces had fewer riots; (b) cities which had more representative forms of local government (e.g., citywide election of councilmen versus district elections) had fewer riots; and (c) cities were less riot prone that had a large percentage of Negroes who were self-employed in retail trade, such as store, restaurant, or tavern owners—that is, cities that had stronger independent middle-class business groups. In short, these measures were indicators of the articulation of the Negro into the social and political fabric of the metropolitan community, reflecting stronger and more viable patterns of social control.

In addition, if one is interested in the institutional aspects of race riots, it is necessary to focus attention on (a) the professional and organizational limitations of law enforcement agencies, and (b) the impact of the mass media. The record of law enforcement agencies over the last half century has been one of inadequate equal protection for minorities and limited capacity for dealing with urban disorders, with noteworthy exceptions and with slowly and definitely increasing levels of professionalization. Likewise, the growth of the mass media, especially television, has not been accompanied by increased standards of performance. The impact of the mass media, in its lack of a constructive role in describing problems of social change, plus its imagery of violence and its treatment of riots and law enforcement agencies, has made a positive contribution to violence.

FROM "COMMUNAL" TO "COMMODITY" RIOTS

Racial violence has a history as old as the nation itself. The institution of slavery was rooted in ready resort to violence. After the Civil War, the political control of the freed Negro was enmeshed in a variety of illegal forms of resort to violence. For the purposes of this analysis, however, the particularly devastating and explosive outbreak of collective mass racial riots can be thought of as a distinct phenomenon, although any effort at categorization is a tricky and elusive intellectual effort. The draft riots of the Civil War had clear racial overtones. But "modern" riots can be traced to the racial outbreaks that were generated during the period of World War I and again during World War II. There were, of course, riots during the interwar period, but the heaviest concentration was during wartime years. The riots of this historical era need to be distinguished from the outbursts that took place during the 1960's.

During World War I and its aftermath, the modern form of the race riot developed in Northern and border cities where the Negro was attempting to alter his position of subordination. These outbreaks had two predisposing elements. First, relatively large numbers of new migrants—both Negro and white—were living in segregated enclaves in urban centers under conditions in which older patterns of accommodation were not effective. The riots were linked to a phase in the growth and transformation of American cities. Second, the police and law enforcement agencies had a limited capacity for dealing with the outbreak of mass violence and often conspired with the white rioters against the Negro population. The historical record indicates that they did not anticipate such happenings.

The riots of this period could be called "communal" riots or "contested area" riots. They involved ecological warfare, because they were a direct struggle between the residents of white and Negro areas. The precipitating incidents would come after a period of increasing tension and minor but persistent outbursts of violence. For example, the Chicago riot of 1919 was preceded by 2 years of residential violence in which more than 27 Negro dwellings were bombed. Typically, the precipitating incident would be a small-scale struggle between white and Negro civilians—often in a public place such as a beach or in an area of unclear racial domain. In the major riots of the large cities, tension and violence would spread quickly throughout various parts of the larger community. Thus, deaths and injuries were the result of direct confrontation and fighting between whites and Negroes.

Within a few hours the riot was in full swing, and continued intermittently with decreasing intensity for a number of days. Whites invaded Negro areas and very often the riot spread to the central business district where the white population outnumbered the Negroes. Much of the violence took place on main thoroughfares and transfer points as Negroes sought to return to their homes or sought some sort of refuge. Symbolically, the riot was an expression of elements of the white community's impulse to "kick the Negro back into his place."

Despite the wide areas that were engulfed and the number of casualties inflicted, the whites involved were limited to very small groups or nuclei of activists, often encourage by vocal bystanders to take the initiative. White youth gangs and their leaders were in the forefront in a number of cities. The Negroes fought back in time, but they seldom invaded white areas. According to available documentation, the whites were mainly armed with bricks and blunt sticks, and they fought with their fists. There were a limited number of handguns (pistols) and rifles. On occasion, Negroes were better armed because they had more of these weapons and knives as well. These riots had many incidents of direct, personal, and brutal struggle between the contestants. The personalized aspect of the violence can be inferred from reports such as that of the Chicago Commission report, which stated that "Without the spectators, mob violence would probably have stopped short of murder in many cases."[5]

Gunshots were directed at specific and visible targets, often where one side had the overwhelming superiority. Nevertheless, deaths by beating and mauling greatly outnumber those from gunshots. Newspaper reports of snipers were exaggerated. In the East Chicago riots of 1917, there was only one case of repeated gunfire, and in Chicago in 1919, the Commission found one such serious incident and a number of more scattered occurrences, as Negroes sought to retaliate against white marauders passing by in automobiles. In fact, instead of the term "sniper" fire, the reports of the period around World War I speak of occasional "volley firing."

During these riots, rumors about specific incidents of racial strife were spread by word of mouth. Newspapers contributed to racial tension by frequently and repeatedly publishing inflammatory reports such as one that Negroes slaughtered a defenseless white child. Since the riots often lasted for several days, news reports served to recruit white activists from other parts of the city and even from out of town. Editorial efforts to calm public opinion and to demand effective law enforcement developed slowly and hardly balanced the presentation in news columns.

The restoration of civil order required the police to separate the two groups and to protect the enclaves of Negroes from whites. Frequently the police were very deficient in their duties and occasionally assisted the white rioters. In any case they were not prepared for such outbreaks. The state militia or federal troops were used repeatedly and generally displayed a higher level of professional standards. Without overlooking the casualties that were caused by the police themselves, the fundamental anatomy of these riots was a communal clash between Negroes and whites.

During World War II, the pattern of rioting underwent a transformation which took full form with outbreaks in Harlem and Brooklyn in 1964, in Watts in 1965, and in Newark and Detroit in 1967. For lack of a better term, there has been a metamorphosis from "communal" riots to "commodity" riots.[6] The Detroit riot of 1943 conformed to the communal or contested area pattern. It involved concentrations of recently arrived Negro migrants, and the precipitating incident occurred in a contested area, Belle Isle. The violence spread rapidly and produced clashes between Negroes and whites. However, the Harlem riots of 1943 contained features of the new type of rioting. The Negro population was composed of a higher concentration of long-term residents in the community. Most important, it was a riot that started within the Negro community, not at the periphery. It did not involve a confrontation between white and Negro civilians. It was an outburst against property and retail establishments, plus looting—therefore the notion of the commodity riot in the Negro community. These establishments were mainly owned by outside white proprietors. The deaths and casualties resulted mainly from the use of force against the Negro population by police and National Guard units. Some direct and active participation by white civilians may take place in such a riot, as was the case in Detroit in 1967, but this is a minor element.

THE NATURAL HISTORY OF COMMODITY RIOTS

There have been repeated efforts to describe the various stages in the natural history of race riots, especially the commodity-type riots.[7] Two considerations need to be held in mind in pursuing this goal. The style of intervention by the law enforcement officers has deeply influenced the anatomy of race riots in the United States. During the period of the initial communal riots, the effectiveness of local police forces varied greatly, reflecting their high degree of decentralization. The increased ability of local police to seal off contested areas reduced the prospect of communal riots. Since the riots of World War I, there has been a gradual growth in the capacity of local police to prevent riots at the periphery of the Negro community, but not without conspicuous exceptions. The use of radio communications and motorized local police forces have been the essential ingredients of control. Most Northern cities have witnessed a steady and gradual expansion of the Negro residential areas, accompanied by bitter resentment and continuous minor outbreaks of violence, including bombings. But the police almost daily contain these tensions, which could explode into communal riots if there were defects in their performance. But the capacity of local enforcement agencies to deal with "border" incidents has not been matched with a capacity for controlling the resort to violence within the Negro community. The outbreak of commodity riots produced very different police responses in various communities, ranging from highly effective and professional behavior to weak and irresponsible action that exacerbated rioting and prolonged tension. Thus, the stages of a riot are not predetermined but reflect the pattern of intervention of law enforcement agencies.

Second, it is, of course, very difficult to assemble accurate documentation in order to describe the natural history of a riot and especially the behavior of rioters in a commodity riot. The riots of the 1960's have produced a number of official inquiries and a variety of private studies, but there are few adequate analyses in depth.[8]

The President's Advisory Commission on Civil Disorders (Kerner Commission) sponsored a variety of social research studies that focused mainly on the attitudes of the public and the rioters. The methodology of the sample survey was emphasized, which does not make possible a full analysis of the dynamics of the "collective behavior" of a racial riot. While teams of investigators are required to collect basic documentation, the natural history and anatomy of a riot is still best assessed by a single person who is concerned with cross-checking sources. Brig. Gen. S. L. A. Marshall has demonstrated how a single investigator can reconstruct a complex and fluid battle by after-action group interviews. This procedure has not generally been applied to race riots. Perhaps the most analytic account of a commodity riot was presented by Anthony Oberschall, a Yale University sociologist.[9]

From all sources, one conclusion emerges, namely the absence of organized conspiracy in commodity riots. However, the absence of organized conspiracy does not mean the absence of a pattern of events. Thus, Jules J. Wanderer's analysis of 75 riots during the period 1965-67 demonstrates the pattern of events in these outbursts. By means of the Guttman scale techniques, he demonstrated the consistent cumulation of a very similar configuration of violence from low to high intensity.[10] The difference from one outburst to another involved the extent to which each one proceeded through the various stages of increased and intensified collective behavior.

The motivation of contemporary commodity riots is clearly not desperation generated by the anticipation of starvation, such as in food riots in India during famine times. One is struck by the repeated reports of the carnival and happy-day spirit that pervades the early stages of a commodity riot. The new type of rioting is most likely to be set off by an incident involving the police in the ghetto where some actual or believed violation of accepted police practice has taken place. The very first phase is generally nasty and brutish: the police are stoned, crowds collect, and tension mounts. The second stage is reached with the breaking of windows. Local social control breaks down and the population recognizes that a temporary opportunity for looting is available. The atmosphere changes quickly, and this is when positive enthusiasm is released. But all too briefly. If the crowds are not dispersed and order restored, the third stage of the riot is the transformation wrought by arson, firebombs, and sniper fire and the countermeasures taken by police and uniformed soldiers.

There can be no doubt that the countermeasures employed deeply influence the course of rioting—even in some cases prolonging the period of reestablishing order. One is, of course, struck by the great variation in local response to escalated rioting and in the skill and professionalism of the forces in their counterefforts. Differences in police strategy have been partly accidental and partly the result of conscious policy, because law enforcement officials have a past record to draw on, and are continuously alerted to the possiblity of riots. Thus, for example, there were wide differences in response patterns to early manifestations of disorder by local police in the 1960's. In

Detroit, Ray Girardin, a former police reporter who became police commissioner, explicitly acknowledged that he followed a loose policy in the early
phase of the Detroit rioting, assuming that local civilian Negro leadership
would contain the disorder. He cited his previous experience in which this
approach worked effectively. In his theories of riot behavior, he made frequent recourse to "sociological" terms.

By contrast, the operational code of the police in New York City under
Commissioner Howard Leary and in Chicago has been to intervene with that
amount of force judged to be appropriate for early stages of the confrontation.
The objective was to prevent the spread of contagion. Special steps were
taken to prevent routine police performance from developing into incidents
which might provoke tension. However, if an incident became the focal point
for tension and the collection of a crowd, the police responded early and in
depth in order to prevent the second stage from actually expanding. Numerous police were sent to the scene or kept in reserve nearby. The police sought
to operate by their sheer presence, not to provoke further counteraction.
They sought to prevent the breaking of windows and the starting of looting
that would set the stage for an escalated riot. If actual rioting threatened, one
response was the early mobilization of local National Guard units and their
ready reserve deployment in inner city garrisons. In part, this was designed
to reduce the time required for their deployment on city streets and in part
it was policy that enables the local police to commit their reserves with the
surety of having a supporting force available.

Whereas the communal riot involved a confrontation between the white
and the black community, the commodity riot, especially as it entered into
the third and destructive phase, represents a confrontation between the black
community and law enforcement officials of the larger society. The question
of the extent of the exchange of gunfire emerged as one of the most problem-
atic dimensions. The reports in the mass media of the use of weapons during
and immediately after the riots by the rioters were exaggerated, according to
the investigations of the Kerner Commission.[11] In fact, the deaths inflicted
by sniper fire were few. For example, it is reported that 5 of 43 deaths during
the Detroit disorder were linked to sniper fire, and in Newark, 2 of 26 deaths.[12]
These observations did not involve comparisons with earlier riots or an assessment that the gunfire contributed to conditions in which extensive arson developed. In fact, direct comparisons with the communal type riots underline
the greater dispersal of firearms and the much more intense use of firepower.
They are escalated riots because of the more extensive but still scattered use
of weaponry.

A distinguishing characteristic of commodity riots is not only the widespread dispersal of small arms and rifles among the rioters, and correspond-
ingly, the increased capacity of the local police to concentrate armed personnel in a given area. There are no adequate statistics on the distribution
of weapons in the hands of participants before any particular riot started.
However, there is clear evidence that, over the years, the sale and home storage of firearms has continually increased, made possible by affluence, the
absence of adequate gun control legislation, and stimulated by fears of racial
violence. These trends have taken place both in the white and in the Negro
community. As Zimring has demonstrated in the case of personal violence,
the sheer availability of weapons has tended to escalate racial conflict.[13] In

addition to the already available arms, a significant stock of weapons appears
to have been accumulated during the actual rioting in particular areas. Important sources of supply have been looted including sporting goods stores,
general merchandise establishments, and pawnshops.

Available documentation indicates that during the third phase of the commodity riots, when sniper fire developed, it usually involved single individuals,
occasionally groups of two or three persons. There is little evidence of fore-
thought by rioters in the deployment of weapons for effectiveness or mutual
fire support. Supporting fire by such snipers could render them much more
destructive. In isolated cases, there is evidence of limited coordination and
planning of firepower. But these cases are of minor importance in accounting
for the firepower involved or its destructiveness. The crucial impact of the
sniper fire derived from its interplay with arson activities. Sniper fire im-
mobilized firefighting equipment, which permitted widespread destruction
by fire, which in turn contributed to more rioting and sniper fire. In this sense,
the commodity riots were escalated in intensity and sheer destruction as compared with the communal outbreaks. They were escalated also in the sense
that the mass media rapidly disseminates the image and reality of mass fires
and widespread looting on a scale not found in the earlier ones. The spread
of fire was frequently facilitated by various incendiary bombs of a homemade
nature. These firebombs have been used as antivehicle bombs, but generally
with little effectiveness.

The phase of scattered sniper fire is, in some respects, a type of quasi-mili-
tary situation, but the notion of an insurrection has little meaning, for snipers
had no intention or capability for holding territory, nor were they part of a
scheme to do so even temporarily. Frequently the sniper fire exposed police
officers and National Guard units without experience to dangers with which
they were not accustomed. Personal risk was clearly present. The scattered
source of fire often enveloped the law enforcement units. It was this envelop-
ment fire, especially from behind, which has led to the use of the term "guerrilla tactics," but the guerrilla concept is also not relevant since guerrillas are
part of an organization, proceed with a plan, prepare paths of withdrawal, and
develop sanctuaries.

Overresponse and excessive use of firepower by police and National Guard
units in turn contributed to the escalation of the rioting.[14] The police were
at times surrounded and, in the absence of effective command and control,
were exposed to an environment that most had not previously experienced.
Their behavior was conditioned by the sheer feeling of the unreality of the
rioting situation and the physical disruption that takes place. They often responded with indiscriminate and uncontrolled fire. The immediate result was
that they exposed numerous civilians to danger. Such fire does not suppress
snipers, who can only be eliminated by carefully directed fire and counter-
sniper procedures. In fact, the initial counterfire actually mobilized new
rioters.

The summers of 1964 through 1967 demonstrated wide variations in the
capacity of National Guard units to respond to and assist local police. On the
whole, National Guard units had received little specific training in riot control
and the content of any such training did not appear to have been particularly
germane to actual problems. The level of National Guard effectiveness derived
from their military preparedness in general. The performance of National

Guard units in Newark and in Detroit has been judged by expert observers to be deficient. By contrast, the behavior of the National Guard units in Maryland and in Wisconsin (Milwaukee) has been reported to be much more in accordance with the requirements of the constabulary function; namely, the minimum use of force to restore civil law and due process. The basic question is fire control and an effective communications network. By contrast, federal troops used in Detroit were highly professional units with extensive training, who clearly displayed a higher degree of unit control and were less prone to employ unnecessary fire. The superiority of the federal troops reflects past, experience and indicates that more effective military training per se (even without additional civil disorder training), and more effective officers, produces more appropriate responses.

There is some evidence that one index to National Guard effectiveness is the extent of integration of units. Because of its fraternal spirit, most National Guard units have been able to resist Federal directives and Negroes accounted for less than 2 percent of its personnel in 1967. In those cases where integration took place, it meant that the units were seen as more legitimate by the local population. Moreover, units that were forced to integrate were more likely to be concerned with problems of conflict in the unit and developed an officer corps concerned with these issues. For example, units in Detroit and Newark were not integrated while Chicago-based units that were employed during the summer disturbances of 1965 were integrated and had Negro officers.

PARTICIPATION IN COMMODITY RIOTS

The extent of participation and the social characteristics of the riots are revealing indices of underlying factors in the social structure that condition these collective outbursts. There is every reason to believe that in the commodity riots of the 1960's, a larger number of Negroes and a greater percentage of the population of riot-torn communities actively participated in the outbursts than was the case during the older, communal-type confrontations. The commodity-type riots take place within the confines of the black ghettos, which have grown greatly in size and population since World War I. Within these massive ghettos during the hours of the most intensive outbursts, it appears as if social controls were momentarily suspended. The sheer size of the ghettos and the greater remoteness of the outer community contribute to this breakdown and to the "mobilization" of numbers. It is understandable that in the second phase of milling and looting, many residents were swept up by the sheer contagion of events, especially where law officers stood by passively while stores and shops were being entered.

It is also necessary to emphasize that the societal context had radically changed during the period of transition to commodity riots. Through the mass media, the demands of the Negro population had received widespread and favorable publicity and there was considerable sympathy in the nation for their plight. The civil-rights movements had achieved strong legitimacy. Within the black community there was strongly increased sensitivity about minority status. All these factors contributed to the intensity and participation during actual rioting.

The size of the groups rioting and their percentage of the available population, as well as their social characteristics, became matters of public debate.

The Kerner Commission devoted efforts to probing these questions and refuting the claim that only a very tiny percentage—for example, less than 1 percent—of the Negro population was involved in riot-torn communities.[15] The Commission argued that the riots included a much larger active group who were generally representative of lower class slum dwellers and therefore could not be characterized as a tiny criminal element. The size of the rioting group could be estimated from direct observation, a most hazardous approach; from extrapolations from arrest data—a technique that probably underestimated the number of the activists; or from self-reports gathered by sample surveys after the riots—an approach that grossly overstated the case. On the basis of different sources, it was estimated that between 10 to 20 percent of the potential population was involved in the riots of 1967. The lower figure of 10 percent appears to be more accurate, although even this estimate is open to serious question. Aside from the reliability of the data, the question hinges on the differing definitions of participation. To speak of even 10 percent participation is to include those persons who were caught up in the collective processes of the riot as the contagion spread.

Although there are numerous statistical and methodological weaknesses in the various analyses of the arrest data and sample surveys, the findings are relevant for describing the social characteristics of the rioters. All sources agree that women were a significant minority of the activists in the commodity riots, reflecting a broadening of the base of involvement as contrasted with the communal riots, which were mainly a men's affair. Interestingly enough, the police tended to arrest few women, either because their infractions of the law were minor or because they believed that women were not at the core of the riot.

As expected, the bulk of the rioters were young males between the ages of 15 and 34 whose skill levels were low. In a social profile of the 496 Negro males arrested in Detroit, the typical participant has been characterized as "a blue collar worker in a manufacturing plant where he earned about $120.00 a week. Although currently employed, he had experienced more than 5 weeks of unemployment in the past year. He had not participated in a government training or poverty program." In some groups of arrested Negro youths, the unemployment level reached almost 40 percent.[16] In addition, among samples of those caught up in the riots and arrested in 1967, previous arrest records comparable to the equivalent age groups in the black population at large were found. The explanation for this finding is that it is very common for young Negro males to have an arrest record—in some categories, a majority.

Clearly, these data indicate that the activists were not a tiny minority of chronic law offenders nor highly unrepresentative in terms of selected social background characteristics. The full personal and social dynamics will probably never be adequately described, for involvement relates not merely to the demographic and social characteristics but to the patterns of primary and informal group structures of the ghetto community, as well as social personality and attitude. Some clues can be drawn from the observation of various surveys that the participants over-represented single men, who frequently lived outside of family units. These were persons who were less subject to the informal group structure linked to family life and more to informal street and community life. Anthony Oberschall is one of the few analysts who sought to probe the role of youth gangs in riots, in his case, Watts:

Another informant who has been close to some of the gangs in South Los Angeles reported, however, that gang members, in an effort to prove their claims upon leadership in a certain territory and in competition with each other, were vying for leadership over the crowds during the riots, and this meant among other things actively participating in the skirmishes against the police, breaking into the stores and setting them on fire.[17]

In other cities, especially in Chicago in 1968, gang leaders were active in seeking to dampen tensions and violent outbursts. Fogelson reports on the social difference between those arrested as disorderly persons—who tended to be younger, unemployed, and native born in the locality—and the looters, who tended to be older, less unemployed, and Southern born.[18] In other words, the looters, who joined the riots after they were underway, were more integrated into the adult occupational world.

In contrast to the criminal interpretation, the alternative formulation of the commodity riots as a form of political insurrection appears equally inadequate, if by insurrection is meant an armed social movement with an explicit set of goals. The very absence of evidence of prior planning—either rightist or leftist—would weaken such an interpretation. In 23 disorders studies by the Kerner Commission, none were "caused by, nor were they the consequence of any plan or conspiracy."[19] But more important, it is striking that during the riots of 1964 to 1967, there was a remarkable absence of visible leadership—either existing or emergent—that sought to press for collective demands. It is, of course, clear that the leadership and support of the civil-rights movement were not centrally involved in the riots. The emphasis of the civil-rights leaders on issues such as school integration, access to public accommodation, and voting rights were less directly relevant to the immediate lives of slum dwellers, who were mainly concerned with the welfare system and with immediate employment opportunities. The impact of the riots of 1967 on the civil-rights movement was drastic in that it made the movement's demands more militant. But clearly the leaders of the civil-rights movement were not activists in these outbursts. If anything, they occurred because of the inability of the civil-rights movement to accomplish sufficient social change in the slums, although the movement made a decisive contribution in intensifying aspirations and group consciousness.

Many participants, after the riots, could consciously verbalize their social and economic dilemmas and link their situation to their behavior. In interviews, they had a tendency to highlight "police brutality" as the underlying cause. Of course, many who participated merely took the events as a given fact of life and offered little explanation for their involvement.

In contrast to the communal riots, where the Negro response was a direct and primitive struggle for survival, the commodity riots had overtones which might be called parapolitical, in the sense that group consciousness pervaded this particular form of collective behavior. In balance it can be said that the commodity riot by 1967 was a form of collective action, which on occasion was large scale and included a broadly representative segment of the lower socioeconomic class of the urban community. Regardless of the amount of sympathetic interest they mobilized among middle-class Negroes, the commodity riots were a "violent lower class outburst."[20]

A final aspect of participation has been the active involvement of those in the Negro community who sought to dampen or inhibit the spread of the riot. In official reports, they have come to be described by the awkward and unfortunate term, "counterrioters." In the communal riot, such a role was not possible and, paradoxically, such behavior by Negroes during a riot was a consequence of an increase in integration of the Negro into the larger social structure as compared with the period of communal rioting. Already in the Harlem riot of 1943, more than 300 Negroes were given Civilian Defense insignias and armbands, and used as deputies. For the summer of 1967, the Kerner Commission reported that in all but 6 of 24 disorders they investigated, Negroes were actively on the streets attempting to control rioters.[21]

In some cities, political and community leaders sought to address gathering crowds. On other occasions, religious leaders and community workers walked the streets urging persons to disperse, while still other local residents assisted police and firemen in their tasks. Some of these activities were officially recognized and even sanctioned by the local authorities, but the bulk of the efforts seem to have been without official sponsorship. It is very difficult to evaluate the effectiveness of these efforts, especially in communities where extensive rioting broke out. However, it does appear that such activities had the greatest effect in communities which were on the verge of rioting and in which rioting was avoided.

SUMMER RIOTS OF 1968

It will remain for future historians to assess whether the summer of 1968 was in fact a turning point in the era of communal riots. The trend in racial conflict from 1964 to 1967 was one of continued, and even expanded, outbreaks that appeared to reach one high point with the massive destruction of Newark and Detroit.

In the winter and sping months of 1968, the outlook for the summer of that year was bleak. Racial tensions remained high. Extremist and even moderate leaders anticipated even higher levels of violence, and a variety of analysts were thinking in the same direction. One of the writers for the Kerner Commission, assessing public opinion polls, stated "on the eve of the summer of 1968, these responses are anything but reassuring."[22] The tensions of the Vietnam crisis continued. There was no new massive national response to the social and economic needs of the black community, except in the important employment sector where industrial corporations started to abandon rigid recruitment and training procedures and to engage an increasing number of inner city personnel who would develop their qualifications on the job. Community relations were made more difficult by extremist statements by some individual police officers, who spoke of the necessity of a "tough" policy and of their plans to use heavier hardware for control purposes. The tragic assassination of Dr. Martin Luther King, Jr., served as a final element in the prelude to the summer of 1968.

However, race relations during the summer had a different character from these anticipations. In October 1968, the Department of Justice released a report by Attorney General Ramsey Clark which revealed a decline in the scope and intensity of racial riots. Quantitative measures of riots are difficult to construct, but these appear to be of relatively high validity. The definitions were carefully worked out and the same data collection procedures used to compare the months of June, July, and August, 1967, with the same months of 1968. The results showed a decline in "major" disturbances from 11 to 7, and of "serious" ones from 35 to 18, while minor outbursts increased slightly from 92 to 95. The most dramatic indicator of the decline was the drop in deaths from 87 to 19. To some degree, these data understate the full decline from 1967 to 1968, since the category "major" riots included all riots which lasted longer than 12 hours and included more than 300 persons. The very large-scale riots such as Newark and Detroit were absent in 1968. This is reflected in part in the marked decline in estimated property damage, from $56 million in 1967 for three riots in Cincinnati, Newark, and Detroit to $4 million for all damage during June, July, and August of 1968. It is, of course, very possible that no new long-term trend was at work. One hypothesis to account for the short-term and immediate pattern was the development of new tactics and new organizations that permit more effective expression of black interests and black solidarity. Another hypothesis is that improved police-community relations and higher levels of police professionalism contributed to the decline. These data seem to indicate that, while minor outbreaks continued, interaction between the police and the black community was able to reduce and contain larger and more widespread riots.

Under pressure of political and community leadership, many police took initial steps to improve communications with the Negro community through devices such as special conferences, the assigning of special officers of community relations, and improved police training. The criticism of the police in some communities and the relative success in other areas led to more professional behavior. The advocates of deescalation had more and more influence; the slogan became "manpower and not firepower." Older doctrines of riot control, which emphasized weaponry and technical characteristics, gave way to new and more flexible approaches. Police departments sought to improve their internal communications and their ability to mobilize manpower. They sought to strengthen supervision and control in the field and emphasized the need for restraint. There was a much more professional response to the problem of sniper fire, in that police were instructed not to respond with indiscriminate firepower. There was some progress toward deescalation of police response to more appropriate levels. Despite the publicity given to those few police officers who spoke about the need for tanks and Mace, the major trend in local police work was in the opposite direction.

National Guard and federal troops were deeply involved in the events of the summer of 1968. The lack of professional competence on the part of the local police to deal with problems of urban racial violence in part reflects the particular system of law enforcement that developed in the United States. Deeply influenced by British institutions, the nation did not develop a national police force that had responsibility for the control of civil disorder, in contrast to France for example. However, the United States has had extensive civil disorders throughout its history and the country found its equivalent to a gendarmerie in the state militia and later in the National Guard. The National Guard especially was organized and trained for national defense purposes, so that it seldom developed professional standards for local police support. The result has been that in both labor disputes and in race riots, federal troops have performed with high levels of effectiveness, not because of their specialized training for the task but because of generally higher organizational effectiveness.

But the division of responsibility between local, state, and federal agencies greatly complicates the conditions under which federal troops will intervene in a riot. In the Detroit riots of July 1967, federal troops were not deployed on the basis of the request of State and local authorities, but only after the Presidential representative, former Assistant Secretary of Defense Cyrus Vance, had personally inspected the city and certified the need for federal troops. There was local criticism that this procedure unduly delayed the dispatch of necessary troops. The office of the President has had to struggle to avoid premature commitment of federal troops whenever local authorities feel under pressure, but at the same time maintain the credibility of swift federal intervention if required. As a result, the Department of the Army established a Directorate for Civil Disturbance Policy and Operations to oversee such involvements. Greater use was made of federal troops in 1968 than in 1967. These troops underwent specialized training, but it was their general organizational effectiveness and command structure that enabled them to operate with the greatest restraint. They very seldom made use of their weapons; their sheer presence was mainly responsible for limiting riot behavior. (For example, in the Washington, D.C., operation, at most 15 bullets were fired.) In fact, there were numerous occasions in which the local population welcomed the arrival of federal troops, with the clear implication that they preferred not to be policed by local personnel.

With reliance placed on the National Guard, it became abundantly clear during the summer of 1967 that racial integration in these units had to be pressed with much greater vigor. It had been federal policy to encourage such integration, and in fact all Negro units were disbanded, but the recruitment of Negroes into the National Guard lagged. Where integration of the Negro into the National Guard had taken place, it was the result of state and local political leadership. Therefore, on August 10, 1967, the President's Commission on Civil Disorders unanimously issued a set of recommendations to produce short-term improvements in riot control. These recommendations called for increased recruitment of Negro personnel into the National Guard, the establishment of standards for eliminating inferior officers, and greater reliance on specialized training. During the next year, these federal policies began to have an effect, especially in the area of improved training.

NEXT STAGE: POLITICAL VIOLENCE

Each stage in the transformation of racial violence already carries with it the elements of the next stage. In the midst of the mass rioting of 1967, there was anticipated marked decline in such outbursts and an emergence of a more selective, more delimited form of violence.[23]

The social position of the Negro in American society was changing, with an effect on patterns of racial tension. In our open society, it is necessary to underline that the commodity rioting of 1964-67 bears a parallel to one explanation of the outbursts of militancy in the trade union movement in the 1930's. The unions displayed their vigor not during the depth of the depression but during 1936 and 1937, a period of halting but increasing prosperity. It may well be that the ghetto outbursts, especially of 1965-67, were linked to the first stages—slow and incomplete—in new levels of opportunity and achievement for the Negro community. If social and economic progress were to continue, the conditions conducive to tension would then start to decline.

Although the topic is outside the scope of this paper, continued improvement of the relative socioeconomic position of the Negro in American society depends on a variety of elements of social change. Much social learning has taken place since the initial phase of the "war against poverty." The main lines of effective innovation are beginning to emerge: federal assistance in family planning, radical modification of the present welfare system including a negative income tax, special youth work training enterprises, and decentralization, plus improved quality of public education. Of special importance are the efforts to locate employment opportunities in depressed areas. Experience to date indicates that such industrial establishments become training stations that serve to incorporate youngsters into the labor market for the first time and that, after a period of work experience, they develop incentives to seek additional training or better employment in the wider labor market. No doubt, regardless of their limited immediate impact, some of the community organizations being developed in Negro areas with foundation, trade union, and federal funds serve as a learning experience for training new leadership.

Any anticipation of a continued decline of commodity riots is also based on the assumption that a more professional police force would both extend more equal protection and would be more effective and more humane in avoiding collective outbursts. Likewise there would be a more equitable judicial system that would accord more due process to the Negro community. Thus the likelihood of destruction on the level of Newark and Detroit declines, although the escalated riot remains a possibility in any area of heavy Negro population concentration. Likewise, as Negro enclaves develop in suburban areas, forms of communal riots between Negroes and whites become a reality in these areas.

However, the essential trend was that escalated rioting and the rioting of commodity looting appeared in 1967 to be giving way to more specific, more premeditated, and more regularized uses of force. It was as if the rioters learned the lesson emphasized in the mass media, that mass destruction achieves too few tangible benefits. New outbursts appeared to be more goal directed—a diffuse goal at time, at other times a very specific one. It is almost appropriate to describe these outbursts as political violence or political terror, or even conspiratorial violence. It is not inaccurate to describe this shift as one from expressive outburst to a more instrumental use of violence. Those involved were persons who came to believe that white society cannot be changed except with violence.

The participants were likely to be persons who have taken part in previous outbursts. There was an element of organization, at least to the extent that activists are concerned with personal survival and avoidance of the police. There was an element of organization to the extent that the target seems to be selected, and the patterns repeated for a specific purpose. The local school was a particular target. The form of violence can be the harassment of a group of white schoolteachers active in union work, an assault on teacher picket lines during a strike, or a small-scale outburst at the neighborhood schoolyard and on occasion sniper fire against the police. Housing projects, especially integrated housing projects, were repeatedly subject to rifle fire and fire bombing. These incidents are created for the purpose of developing solidarity in local gangs and in paramilitary groups. The United Automobile Workers Union reported the use of terror tactics, including knifings and physical assault, against both white and black workers in the Detroit area. The union identified a group, League of Revolutionary Black Workers, in its documentation.[24]

The object seems to be to establish a vague political presence. Conspiratorial overtones are involved and the assaults spill over against social agencies and local political leaders. The line between random outbursts and these forms of political violence or political terror is difficult to draw. However, these outbursts often take place with the explicit appeal of Black Power. Traditional youth gang activities tend to resist political orientations, but signs of conscious political orientation become more visible.

Dramatic manifestations of the third phase of political violence, or conspiratorial violence, were the shootouts which occurred with police personnel during the summer of 1968 in New York City, Cleveland, Pittsburgh, Oakland, Los Angeles, and elsewhere. The amount of prior planning is difficult to ascertain, but focused selection of police personnel as specific and delimited targets is obvious. In some cases the action appears to have been a response to presumed harassment by the police. In other cases the police were responding to a call for help. In still other cases police cars were attacked without warning. For example, on September 29, 1968, a man wearing a "black cape lined with orange walked up to a police car in Harlem early yesterday and without provocation, opened fire on two patrolmen, wounding them both. . . ."[25] Other incidents developed around a police action such as the removal of a disabled vehicle. Generally these incidents seem to involve loosely and informally organized groups. It is much rarer but perhaps indicative of emerging trends that a formal organization such as the Black Panthers finds itself in repeated gun battles with the Oakland police. The shootout in Cleveland on July 26, 1968, created such community tension that Mayor Carl B. Stokes responded by the unprecedented withdrawal of white police officers and deployment of Negro officers and 500 black community leaders to maintain peace. This procedure was rapidly terminated.[26]

Such activities appear to be a new form of "defiance" politics. In the past, organized racketeers, including groups which penetrated political party organizations, made use of violence to extract a financial toll from slum communities. These traditional groups confined violent outbursts to the maintenance of their economic privilege. Practitioners of political violence and political terror are now more open in advocating violence and opposition to the larger society. They represent an effort to achieve goals much broader and vaguer than those of the racketeer. There are crude ideological overtones and especially a desire to carry violence into the white community.[27]

It is very difficult to contain terroristic eruptions of political violence. The toll is small at a given point and therefore does not produce a violent public reaction. The tactics and organizational plans are more secret and only official surveillance and covert penetration supplies an effective technique of management. The forms of organization are those of a combination of a conspiratorial and predatory gang and a paramilitary unit with overtones of a "liberation" outlook. The more secret and cohesive the group, the greater the problems of surveillance. Even though many of these paramilitary groups will break into factions, the task of control will become extremely difficult. It bodes ill when it is necessary to rely on covert operators. The control of secret operations is at best difficult; in the United States, it is very difficult.[28] The task becomes even more complex and troublesome when these surveillance agencies develop the conception, as they often do, that to collect information is not enough. They begin to believe that they must act as active agents of control, particularly in spreading distrust within these organizations. The task become endless and dangerous if the operators play a game without an end or develop an interest in maintaining the groups whom they are supposed to be monitoring.

The failure of the larger society to meet the needs of the black community would contribute to an environment in which conspiratorial violence will continue to flourish. However, such violence has a life of its own. Small groups of terrorists have on historical occasion been able to achieve important goals and political objectives. It is hazardous to even speculate about the conditions under which they are able to succeed. In the past, they appear to have succeeded when they were struggling against a political elite that ruled by terror and without a broad base of support. They have also succeeded when terror is merely an opening step in a broad political campaign. Neither of these conditions seems applicable. Instead it may well be the case that political violence will have counterproductive features. Only limited amounts of political violence can be employed before a point of diminishing return is reached for both the user and the social order in which it is applied.[29]

THE IMPACT OF THE MASS MEDIA

Another important institution of social control that has special relevance for collective racial violence is the mass media. A debate on this issue has raged among social scientists since the early 1930's when the Payne Foundation underwrote a group of University of Chicago social scientists in the first large-scale study of the impact of the mass media, in this case, the consequences of movies for young people.[30]

The mass media both reflect the values of the larger society and at the same time are agents of change and devices for molding tastes and values. It is a complex task to discern their impact because they are at the same time both cause and effect. Controversies about the mass media focus particularly on the issue of their contribution to crime and delinquency and to an atmosphere of lawlessness. Among social scientists, it is generally agreed that consequences of the mass media are secondary as compared with the influence of family, technology, and the organization of modern society. But differences in the meaning and importance attributed to this "secondary factor" among social scientists are great. "Secondary" can mean still important enough to require constructive social policy, or "secondary" can mean that a factor is trivial and unimportant.

Two separate but closely linked issues require attention. First, what are the consequences of the mass media, with its high component of violence, on popular attitudes toward authority and on conditioning and acceptance of violence in social relations? Second, what have been the specific consequences of the manner in which the mass media have handled escalated riot-

ing since the period of Watts? The managers of the mass media run their
enterprises on a profit basis and one result has been that the content of
channels of communication, especially television, in the United States have
a distinct "violence flavor" as contrasted with other nations. This content
emphasis continued to persist as of the end of 1968 despite all the public
discussion about this standard of the mass media.[31] In this respect, self-
regulation of the mass media has not been effective except to some extent
in the comic book industry.

In my judgment, the cumulative evidence collected by social scientists
over the last 30 years has pointed to a discernible, but limited, negative impact
of the media on social values and on personal controls required to inhibit individual disposition into aggressive actions. Other students of the same data
have concluded that their impact is so small as not to constitute a social
problem.

Many studies on media impact are based on limited amounts of exposure,
as contrasted to the continuous expose of real life. Other studies made use of
ex post facto sample surveys that are too superficial to probe the psychological depths of these issues. More recent research employing rigorous experimental methods has strengthened the conclusion that high exposure to violence content in the mass media weakens personal and social controls.[32]
These new findings are based on probing fantasy and psychological responses
of young people after exposure to violence content. They have special importance for lower class groups because of the high exposure of these groups
to television. These lower class groups have less involvement in printed
media, which has less violence material.

The issue runs deeper than the concentration of materials on violence in
the mass media. It involves as assessment of the mass media's performance
in disseminating a portrayal of the Negro and social change in depth. It
also involves the access that the mass media extends to the creative talent of
the Negro community. The Kerner Commission emphasized the lack of
effective coverage of the problems of minority groups by the mass media
and the absence of minority group members, especially Negroes, in operating and supervisory positions in these enterprises. The events of the riots
and the recommendations of the Kerner Commission on this aspect of the
mass media produced "crash" programs to recruit and train minority group
personnel. The contents of the media have become more integrated, including advertising, and a long-run impact on public opinion is likely to be felt,
especially in younger persons.

It is also necessary to assess the coverage of the riots themselves by television and the impact of this coverage on social control. For example, the
National Advisory Commission on Civil Disorders sought to probe the immediate impact of the mass media coverage of the riots of the summer of
1967 both on the Negro community and on the nation as a whole. They
commissioned a systematic content analysis study which, despite its quantitative approach, did not effectively penetrate the issue or even satisfy the
Commission itself. The content study sought to determine if "the media
had sensationalized the disturbances, consistently overplaying violence and
giving disproportionate amounts of time to emotional events and militant
leaders."[33] The conclusion was negative because of findings that, of 837
television sequences of riot and racial news examined, 494 were classified

as calm, 262 as emotional, and 81 as normal. "Only a small proportion of all scenes analyzed showed actual mob action, people looting, sniping, setting fires or being killed or injured." In addition, moderate Negro leaders were shown on television more frequently than were militant leaders. Equivalent findings were reported for the printed media.

But such a statistical balance is no indicator of the impact of the presentation. Even calm and moral presentations of the riots could have had effect on both black and white communities; more certainly, persistent presentation of "hot" messages, even though they constitute only a part of the coverage, would have an impact. Therefore, the Commission modified and in effect rejected its own statistical findings and more appropriately concluded that (1) "there were instances of gross flaws in presenting news of the 1967 riots;" and (2) the cumulative effect was important in that it "heightened reaction." "What the public saw and read last summer thus produced emotional reactions and left vivid impressions not wholly attributable to the material itself." The Commission concluded that "the main failure of the media last summer was that the totality of its coverage was not as representative as it should have been to be accurate."

The national crisis produced by escalated riots warranted massive coverage according to existing standards of mass media performance. The coverage was so extensive that there was an imbalance in presentation of the total scene in the United States, and in particular, a failure to cover successful accomplishments by community leaders and law enforcement agencies. In fact, there were overtones in the coverage of racial violence which conformed to the "crime wave" pattern of news. The result was to bring into the scope of coverage violent events that would not have been reported under "normal" circumstances.

Television has served as the main instrument for impressing the grim realities of the riots onto the mass consciousness of the nation. On-the-spot reportage of the details of the minor riots and their aftermath was extensive and was buttressed by elaborate commentaries. If the fullest coverage of these events is deemed to be necessary as a basis for developing constructive social policy, the costs of such media coverage should not be overlooked. It is impossible to rule out the strong contention that detailed coverage of riots has had an effect on potential rioters. Such a contention does not rest on the occasional instance in which the television camera focused on the riot scene and led either rioters or police to play to the television audience. Of greater importance is the impact of pictures of the rioting on a wider audience. Again we are dealing with a process of social learning, especially for potential participants. Rioting is based on contagion, the process by which the mood and attitudes of those who are actually caught up in the riot are disseminated to a larger audience on the basis of direct contact. Television images serve to spread the contagion pattern throughout urban areas and the nation. Large audiences see the details of riots, the manner in which people participate in them, and especially the ferment associated with looting and obtaining commodities which was so much at the heart of riot behavior. Television presents detailed information about the tactics of participation and the gratifications that were derived.

A direct and realistic account of the tactical role of the mass media, in particular television, can be seen from specific case studies, such as reported in depth by Anthony Oberschall on the Watts riot. He writes:

The success of the store breakers, arsonists, and looters in eluding the
police can in part be put down to the role of the mass media during the
riot week. The Los Angeles riot was the first one in which rioters were
able to watch their actions on television. The concentration and movements of the police in the area were well reported on the air, better
than that of the rioters themselves. By listening to the continuous
radio and TV coverage, it was possible to deduce that the police were
moving toward or away from a particular neighborhood. Those who
were active in raiding stores could choose when and where to strike,
and still have ample time for retreat. The entire curfew area is a very
extended one.[34]

The media disseminate the rationalizations and symbols of identification
used by the rioters. The mass media serve to reenforce and spread a feeling
of consciousness among those who participate or sympathize with extremist
actions, regardless of the actions' origins. In particular, television offers them
a mass audience far beyond their most optimistic aspirations. Knowledge of
the riot would spread in any case, but immediate extensive and detailed
coverage both speeds up the process and gives it a special reality. On balance,
I would argue that these images serve to reenforce predispositions to participate and even to legitimate participation. To be able to generate mass media
coverage, especially television coverage, becomes an element in the motivation
of the rioters. The sheer ability of the rioters to command mass media attention is an ingredient in developing legitimacy. In selected highbrow intellectual
circles in the United States, a language of rationalization of violence has developed. The mass media serve to disseminate a popular version of such justification. The commentaries on television were filled with pseudo-sociological
interpretations and the rioters themselves given ample opportunity to offer a
set of suitable rationalizations.

In the past, when rioting was of the contested area variety, the newspapers
were the major mass media. In many areas they developed an operational
code, informally and formally, to deal with news about rioting. The practice
was to apply an embargo on news about a riot during the actual period of
the riot. After the event, it would be covered. The goal was to prevent the
newspapers from serving as a means for mobilizing rioters, as was the case
in the riots of Chicago in 1919. With the growth of television and the intensification of competition between the press and television, this practice broke
down.

It is difficult to estimate the short- and long-term effects of the mass media
portrayal of riots on white and Negro opinions. However, the riots projected
a new element in the mass media imagery of the Negro, if only for a limited
period of time. In the past, the mass media served to reenforce the system of
segregation by casting the Negro exclusively in a minority position as well as
by describing and characterizing him as weak. The portrait of the Negro as
weak in the mass media served to mobilize and reenforce aggressive sentiments
and emotions against these groups. The extremely prejudiced person is more
disposed to release his aggression if he believes that the object of his aggression
is too weak to respond to his hostile feelings and emotions.[35]

Since the end of World War II, the mass media have been helping to modify
the imagery of the Negro and thereby to weaken the prejudiced symbolism.
The advances of the Negro in economic, social, and political life have supplied

a basis by which the mass media could project a more realistic and more favorable picture of the Negro. The reasoned and moral arguments in defense of racial equality by black and white leaders provide the subject for extensive editorial commentary in the mass media. Mass media images of the Negro were enhanced by the role of Negro troops in the Korean conflict and by the increasing presentation of the Negro as policemen. Regardless of Negro leadership opinion on the war in South Vietnam, the Negro soldier's role has served to modify in a positive direction the image of the Negro in both white and Negro communities. The early phase of the civil-rights movement, with its emphasis on orderly and controlled demonstrations, served also to alter the symbolism of the Negro from that of a weak, powerless figure. The climax of this phase of change, as presented by the mass media, was the dramatic March on Washington led by the late Dr. Martin Luther King, Jr. As an event in the mass media, it was unique. The national media were focused on a predominantly black assemblage moving in an orderly and powerful fashion. In a real sense, it was a symbolic incorporation of the Negro into American society, because of the heavy emphasis on religion and the setting in the nation's capital.

In the elimination of prejudiced imagery, the Negro in the United States obviously has had to face much greater psychological barriers than any other minority group. Hostility and prejudice formed on the axis of color runs deep. Nevertheless, the secular trend in negative stereotypes toward the Negro from 1945 to 1965 has showed a dramatic decline, and the mass media have had an effect in this trend.

Even in the absence of adequate psychological studies in depth, some speculation is possible about the image projected by the riots. The view of Negroes as a group growing in strength and direction was for the moment shattered. Instead, a partial image of explosive irrationality has been dramatized. The use of sheer strength for destructive purposes rather than to achieve a goal that the white population could define as reasonable and worthwhile has served only to mobilize counter hostility and counteraggression. No doubt these images fade away as the mass media focus on reporting in depth the realities of the black community and the processes of social change that are at work.

Thus, in conclusion, the history of the race riot is more than an account of the change from communal to commodity type conflict. It is more than the history of the gross inadequacies of the system of law enforcement the limitations in the performance of the mass media. It is in part an answer to the question posed by Ralph Ellison, the Negro novelist, "But can a people live and develop for over three hundred years simply by reacting?"[36] The Negro outbursts have been more than a reaction to police brutality and a double standard of legal justice. In a symbolic sense, they are expressions of energies to participate in and transform the larger society. In all phases of life, the Negro is not merely reacting but acting.

References

1. Chicago Commission on Race Relations, *The Negro in Chicago: A Study of Race Relations and a Race Riot* (Chicago: The University of Chicago; 1922). For another riot that has been documented in depth, see Elliott M. Rudwick, *Race Riot at East St. Louis* (Carbandale: Southern Illinois University Press, 1964).
2. Allen D. Grimshaw, "Factors Contributing to Color Violence in the United States and Great Britain," *Race*, May 1962, p. 18. See also Robin M. Williams, "Social Change and Social Conflict: Race Relations in the United States, 1944-1964," *Social Inquiry*, Apr. 1965, pp. 8-25.
3. Allen D. Grimshaw, "Actions of Police and Military in American Race Riots," *Phylon*, Fall 1963, p. 288.
4. Stanley Lieberson and Arnold R. Silverman, "Precipitants and Conditions of Race Riots," *American Sociological Review*, Dec. 1965, pp. 887-898.
5. The Chicago Commission on Race Relations, *op. cit.,* p. 23.
6. See also Allen D. Grimshaw, "Lawlessness and Violence in the United States and their Special Manifestations in Changing Negro-White Relationships," *Journal of Negro History*, Jan. 1957, pp. 52-72.
7. See for example, Hans Mattick, "The Form and Content of Recent Riots," *Midway*, Summer 1968, pp. 3-32.
8. See Allen A. Silver, "Official Interpretations of Racial Riots," *Urban Riots: Violence and Social Change, Proceedings of the Academy of Political Science*, vol. XXIX, No. 1, July 1968, pp. 146-158.
9. Anthony Oberschall, "The Los Angeles Riot of August 1965," *Social Problems*, pp. 322-334.
10. Jules J. Wanderer, "1967 Riots: A Test of the Congruity of Events," *Social Problems*, Fall 1968, pp. 193-198.
11. National Advisory Commission on Civil Disorders, *op. cit.,* p. 180.
12. Arnold Katz, "Firearms, Violence and Civil Disorders," Stanford Research Institute, July 1968, p. 10.
13. Frank Zimring, "Is Gun Control Likely to Reduce Violent Killings?" *The University of Chicago Law Review*, Summer 1968, pp. 721-737.
14. Louis C. Goldberg, "Ghetto Riots and Others: The Faces of Civil Disorder in 1967," *Journal of Peace Research*, p. 120.
15. Robert M. Fogelson and Robert B. Hill, "Who Riots? A Study of Participation in the 1967 Riots," *Supplemental Studies for the National Advisory Commission on Civil Disorders*, July 1968, pp. 221-248.
16. *The Detroit Riot: A Profile of 500 Prisoners*, Department of Labor, Mar. 1968, 28 pp.
17. Anthony Oberschall, *op. cit.,* p. 335.
18. National Advisory Commission on Civil Disorders, *Supplemental Studies*, p. 239.
19. *Ibid.,* p. 89.
20. Anthony Oberschall, *op. cit.,* p. 329.
21. The National Advisory Commission on Civil Disorders, p. 73.
22. *Ibid.,* p. 243.
23. Morris Janowitz, *The Social Control of Escalated Riots* (Chicago: The University of Chicago Press, 1967).
24. *New York Times*, Mar. 13, 1969, p. 22.
25. *New York Times*, Sept. 29, 1968.
26. For a list and analysis of 25 reported sniping incidents in July and August 1968, see *Riot Data Review* (Lemberg Center for the Study of Violence), No. 3 (Feb. 1969), pp. 1-38.
27. See Harold Cruse, *The Crisis of the Negro Intellectual* (New York: William Morrow, 1967), pp. 347-401, for an analysis of the ideologies of violence in the black community.
28. Paul Blackstock, *The Strategy of Subversion* (Chicago: Quadrangle Books, 1964).
29. Paul Blackstock, "Anarchism, Manipulated Violence and Civil Disorder," unpublished manuscript, 1968.
30. See W. W. Charter, *Motion Pictures and Youth* (New York: Macmillan, 1933).
31. See *Christian Science Monitor*, Oct. 4, 1968 for details of a survey conducted by that newspaper's staff.

32. Leonard Berkowitz, Ronald Corwin, and Mark Heironimus, "Film Violence and
     Subsequent Aggressive Tendencies," *Public Opinion Quarterly*, vol. XXVII
     (Summer 1963), pp. 217-229.
33. National Advisory Commission on Civil Disorders, p. 202.
34. Oberschall, *op. cit.,* pp. 335-336.
35. For a discussion of this psychological mechanism, see Bruno Bettelheim and
     Morris Janowitz, *Social Change and Prejudice* (New York: The Free Press, 1964).
36. Ralph Ellison, *Shadow and Act* (New York: Random House, 1964), p. 315.

Chapter 11

THE DYNAMICS OF BLACK AND WHITE VIOLENCE

By James P. Comer, M.D.*

When black and white violence again struck urban America in the early 1960's, social scientists and government leaders looked around hurriedly for a quick solution. The obvious cause, to many, was the low social and economic conditions of black Americans. In spite of multiple efforts to improve this situation, violence mounted to a frightening peak in 1967. While interracial violence decreased sharply in 1968, the polarization of the races pointed up in the *Report of the National Advisory Commission on Civil Disorders* is continuing to take place. Thus the possibility of future and even more malignant violence, such as guerrilla tactics, remains a possibility, if not a probability.

If the social and economic conditions of a group are the primary determinants of group violence and potential violence, civil disorder on the part of blacks is a paradox.[1] While the irrelative economic position remains low, social and economic gains directly experienced by black Americans from 1960 through 1968 have been more rapid and substantial than ever before in American history.[2] The number of nonwhites, 92 percent black, at the poverty level as defined by the Social Security Administration has declined from 10.9 million in 1964 to 8.3 million in 1967. The unemployment rate for blacks has declined from 12.4 percent of the labor force in 1961 to 6.8 percent for the first 6 months of 1968. A 31 percent drop in underemployment was recorded between 1966 and 1967, compared with a 17 percent decline for whites.

In 1960 there were only 3 million blacks in the better job categories, while 46 million whites held such jobs. Between 1960 and 1967 there was a 47 percent increase in the number of blacks in white-collar jobs, craftsmen, and operatives (the better jobs), compared to a 16 percent increase by whites. There was an 80 percent increase in the number of black professional and technical workers between 1960 and 1967, compared with a 30 percent increase among whites. There was a 77 percent increase in the number of black clerical workers as compared to a 23 percent increase for whites; a 49 percent increase in

---

*James Comer is assistant professor of psychiatry at the Yale Child Study Center. His publications include "The Social Power of the Negro." *Scientific American* (Apr. 1967), and "Black Rebellion and Individual Development: Some Parallels," *Midway* (Summer 1968).

craftsmen and foremen in the nonwhite category, compared with 13 percent of whites. There was a corresponding decline in private household workers, 17 percent for nonwhites compared with 23 percent among whites; a 7 percent decline was registered among black nonfarm laborers, compared with a 2 percent decline among whites. Because so few blacks held relatively good occupational positions prior to 1960, these changes are not as dramatic as they appear, yet represent substantial improvement.

During the summer of 1967, it became clear that the socioeconomic explanation for black and white violence was inadequate.[3] Observations made after the disorders following the assassination of Dr. Martin Luther King, Jr., suggest the same. A *Wall Street Journal*[4] report read:

> Arrest records suggest that the adults who looted were for the most part Negroes with comparatively good education who held jobs and had not been arrested before. Few expressed a conscious desire to revenge Dr. King's slaying. . . . In many cities, the violence apparently originated with Negroes in their early teens, or even all the way down to kindergarten age—those who had the least reason to revere, or even know of, Dr. King, and those who scorned the moderate civil rights approach Dr. King espoused.

A black militant in Baltimore responded to the question of what sparked the riots with this comment, "You did, Whitey. You did it by treating us like animals. The black man in Baltimore is tired of his life, tired of his low pay, tired of being kicked about. King was just an excuse." The National Advisory Commission of Civil Disorders, while stating the problem differently, agreed that white racism was the basic cause of black and white violence. Both explanations—racism and poverty—view intergroup violence as a simple reaction to an unhappy set of circumstances.

A third explanation of black and white violence is of even more limited value. Some social scientists have contended that persons with impulse-control difficulties as a consequence of black family disintegration have been heavily involved in precipitating urban violence.[5] Recent studies have both challenged the notion of black family disintegration and shown that such persons are just as likely to be nonparticipants as they are to be participants.[6] The complexity of intergroup violence is further revealed in some of the incongruous events which occurred during several 1967 disturbances. A group of black youngsters in Washington, D.C., escorted their white teacher out of the danger area, but hurried back to throw rocks at the passing cars of "white honkies." In Detroit, blacks and whites sat together in a friendly atmosphere and bid on the plunder recovered in disturbances which occurred only a few months before.

Obviously there is no simple explanation. Racism, poverty and personal-control problems are not enough to explain the complexities and incongruities of current black-white conflict—although all three factors are involved. A more useful approach is to recognize intergroup violence as primarily a product of specific social system malfunctioning. It is a natural and predictable phenomonon—although largely preventable—related to the nature of man and his basic human tasks. It occurs and recurs when an individual or group is denied the opportunity to meet their basic and man-made needs.

The human animal is born with drives and needs which conflict with those of other human beings.[7] Some form of social organization that will regulate the manner in which these drives are expressed and needs are met have always been necessary. In all societies, parents, caretakers, and socializers of one kind or another are charged with the responsibility of meeting the child's basic needs and helping the young convert drive energy into "tools" which will help them cope with the demands of an adult society. Libidinal energy becomes "the stuff" of exploration, learning, and work.[8] Without satisfactory transformation, these energies may result in a variety of troublesome forms of personal behavior, including self-destructive action and unwarranted conflict and violence against people and property. When the young are adequately developed and socialized and are able to cope as adults, they enjoy a sense of adequacy and security. Being able to cope and as a result receiving the respect and acceptance of significant peers is the primary way an individual meets basic and man-made needs. When a sufficient number of members of a society feel relatively adequate and secure, a high level of peace and stability can exist in families and the society without force and repression of individuals or groups.[9]

It is the task of the leaders of a society to establish social policy that facilitates optimal individual development and adequate socialization of the young. Failure to do so constitutes social violence, resulting in damage to individuals, groups, and the society, which is far more harmful and lasting than overt physical violence. In a representative society where groups must organize and participate in the political and administrative system in order to obtain opportunities that will facilitate the optimal development of their members, the obstructive and unjust exercise of power—physical or social—by another group constitutes a crippling form of violence. The victimized group, when healthy, struggles against the unjust and oppressive situation. This struggle in the face of resistance frequently results in overt physical violence. In addition, when the leaders of a society sanction social exploitation of a group, they concommitantly encourage physical violence toward that group. Thus the historical American situation of slavery or legal social violence toward blacks; white physical violence and relatively little black retaliation;[10] finally a legal and non-violent struggle now punctuated with black violence is an understandable sequence.[11]

There is an aspect of the pattern—black restraint—which, on the surface, is difficult to explain. Given the level of social violence toward blacks, the logical question now should not be "Why black violence?" but "Why has black initiated and retaliatory violence been so little and so late?" The record of provocation certainly is extreme.

During slavery, whippings and other abusive acts were frequent. Because of the economic value of the slave, it was usually only after abortive slave revolts or "unpardonable" offences that the killing of slaves took place. Freedmen, North and South, who found themselves in economic competition with whites frequently fared less well. After slavery when the 4 million blacks in the South came into direct economic competition with the 5-1/2 million poor whites and were no longer of value to the white planters, the severity of violence toward blacks increased. Beatings, torture, and murder in order to disfranchise blacks, decrease economic competition, and maintain a caste system for economic and psychological advantage became the pattern of the day.

It has been estimated that between 1865 and 1955 over 5,000 blacks were lynched by white mobs.[12] Official U. S. Census Bureau statistics show that over 3,000 were lynched between 1882 and 1935.[13] Legal lynchings, "kangaroo court" action, and unreported murders are not included in these totals. Black schools and homes were frequently burned in the early postslavery period. Between 1865 and 1940, over 500 blacks were killed in race riots and massacres. Many more were injured and abused. Relatively few whites were killed in these disturbances. Finally, the burning and bombing of black property and the murder and intimidation of blacks and their white supporters involved in civil-rights activities since the early 1950's is well known.

Despite this abusive and oppressive pattern, black reaction was generally not violence but nonviolence. Aptheker and other historians have pointed out that there were slave uprisings and rumors of uprisings, but they certainly did not approximate the frequency or severity of black slave uprisings in South America. Even after slavery there was generally an under response to the level of oppression. Historians and revolutionaries have often puzzled over and despaired about this situation.

Certainly the overwhelming power of the dominant group is a factor. But it is not enough to explain the phenomenon. Often slaves and freedmen greatly outnumbered their masters and sometimes did attack and kill them, but not very often. Subsequent events have demonstrated that inherent docility and passivity and the other explanations for extreme black restraint were inaccurate. This is evidenced by the remarkable change in black reaction to white control efforts in a short period of time. Only 15 years ago a black family stood fearful and powerless as whites, without legal authority, dragged their black youngster from his home and murdered him. Today the arrest of a black man by a white policeman in a black neighborhood carries with it the risk of touching off a violent disturbance. Obviously there are important psychosocial forces at play in black and white violence which go beyond simple unhappiness and reaction to racism or poverty. These forces can best be delineated through a review of the critical aspects of black and white reaction over time.

Slavery, the initial contact of most blacks and whites in America, set the stage for continuing conflict. Many students of slavery have been preoccupied with the question of whether it was largely a harsh and cruel or pleasant and humane system. This is an interesting but relatively unrewarding focus. The most important consideration here is the effect of the system on the social and psychological development of individual blacks and whites and on the functioning of the respective groups in the society at large. The effects of the system were enormous indeed and still "haunt" us over 100 years since the demise of the "peculiar institution."

The issue of who was to blame, the black chiefs or middlemen in Africa or slavers, is likewise not important here. The point which is critical to this discussion is that established social systems were interrupted and new and traumatic ones were imposed on the victims. Socialization, which was meaningful and enabled individuals to meet basic needs and prepare to cope as adults in the African society, was no longer useful nor possible. The socialization which was necessary to cope as a slave was traumatic and harmful to the psychological and social development of blacks—an extreme form of social violence.

In West Africa, blacks were socialized in a way to meet the needs of individuals and the respective societies.[14] Children were provided with nurturance and physical care in a family or kinship system which oriented them to their immediate world of kin, the community, society and to their own feelings. Cultural and subcultural goals and values were transmitted to the children and interpersonal skills, modes of feeling, thinking, and working were developed. Contact with parents, elders, chiefs, warriors, medicine men, traders, etc.—one of which they were destined to become—gave the children a sense of direction, purpose, and meaning.

Ritual and ceremony deepened the meaning of individual existence and gave testimony to the importance of societal functions. The circumcision and naming ceremonies of the Dogon tribe were very important exercises with life-long significance to the individual. Indeed it is only through the naming ceremony that a member of that tribe became a part of the society. In the Ibo, Zulu, Dogon, and other tribes of West Africa, children were brought into the adult cultural milieu through age-group organizations. Every function in the society brought these groups together and a sense of belonging and participation resulted. The transference from age group to age group was marked by meaningful ceremony.

Specific expectations and responsibilities were laid down and had to be met before a young person could receive additional responsibilities and privileges. The individual received approval and acceptance from important people in his society through the accomplishment of societal tasks and developed a sense of adequacy and self-respect for his achievement. The universal outcome of adequate socialization which permits one to cope as an adult is a sense of security. This is not to say that there were no injustices, insecurity, or uncertainty within the African system. But in general the operation of the tribes and tribal nations fostered the development of a sense of security and a positive self and group concept. Slavery radically changed this situation.

The objective of socialization in slavery was not to develop the individual to a point that he or she might perform as a fully adequate, competent, full participant in adult society. The socialization and management of slaves was designed to maintain the master's power and control over them and to increase his benefits. Even humane treatment had its "master's twist." An ex-slave from Louisiana said, "Marse always say being mean to the young-uns make them mean when they grows up and nobody gwine to buy a mean nigger."[15]

The slaves were powerless for two major reasons. Their legal status was that of chattel without rights in court and without the protection of any institution. The master was all-powerful and had the right to control every aspect of slave life from birth to death, from sex to settling disputes. His power was enhanced by additional factors. Black slaves in a predominantly white controlled land were readily identifiable. The slaves were not of a single tribal origin with a long group history and a resultant cohesive bond. They were far from home and generally unwanted except for economic exploitation. They were not able to maintain the organizational elements of their respective previous cultures—kinship ties, family organization, religion, government, courts, etc.[16] Thus they were not able to run away en masse; to turn in on their own culture for psychological support or to effectively organize to attack their oppressors.

Economic and social policies were not determined by the slaves. The provision of food, clothing, and shelter for a family was not the task of the black male. Often a family structure or kinship structure did not exist at all. Protecting the family and tribe from assault was not the role of a black warrior, groomed from childhood for the task and honored for his feats by ritual and ceremony. The naming ceremony meant nothing any more. Males were often referred to by the master they worked for and the woman they had a sexual liaison with. . . . Mr. Barber's boy or Sophie's man. The master provided for basic human needs and regulated basic human functions. For everything the slaves were forced to look to the master.

Obviously the slavemaster functioned as "father," ruler, and God. Indeed slaves were often taught to "obey thy master as thy God." Even when the slave resisted, he was relating to a master, for it was not resistance in the name of a people or a tribe or a tribal nation. It was one to one, slave to master. The condition of total power and complete powerlessness, with the master providing and regulating basic needs—thus providing all the security a black slave could know—resulted in an intense emotional bond or tie between the black slave and the white master. Because slaveholdings in this country averaged 5 to 15 persons, this bond was much more intense than in South American countries where the slaveholdings were much larger and a greater degree of black self-identity and culture were maintained.

After the first generation, children were born into the system and prepared from birth for a life of subservience. Nurturance and physical care came from an adult but not in the interest of a family, kinship group, or tribe, but in the interest of a master. (This is probably the reason that so many adults cared so little for children—a point which confounded slaveowners and observers.) Children were not destined to become elders, chiefs, warriors, traders, etc. Their future was that of a despised slave. Ritual and ceremony did not give testimony to the importance of their own lives and that of their people. The master, or parents doing his bidding, set expectations. Approval and acceptance from fellow slaves was based on the degree to which the child achieved goals acceptable to the master.

Children were taught what they could and could not do in relation to whites. They were taught to obey and respect whites. The Bible and the whip reinforced their parent's teaching. Frequent references in the literature of slavery indicate that black children were taught to knuckle under to the little white tyrant of the same age, one in training to become the master and the other to become the slave. There could be no black-group goals for children to inculcate. Blacks did not exist as a group with goals of their own. They were given organization, goals, and direction by the master. They existed for his benefit and by his permission.

Some ran away to the Indians, to Canada, and to freedom in the North.[17] But most could not. Most had to adjust to the circumstances, for man does not exist in groups without some form of social organization. Some led a passive-aggressive existence in relationship to whites—working as little as they could without being punished, sabotaging property, and generally provoking the master. Some used religion to establish a relationship and existence in which they had an importance and purpose beyond the master and their lowly slave position. Some established a life style which was a carbon copy of the master. Some adjustments were extremely harmful to individual development and others were less so. All, however, had to identify and relate to the master or the white power group. This led to an identification with the agressor or oppressor—an adaptive mechanism of generally adverse consequences to blacks.[18]

It is understandable under the condition of powerlessness, dependency and rejection inherent in the nature of American slavery that wisdom and adequacy became associated with the master. Eventually these attributes were extended to all white persons. All whites had the right to abuse and exploit blacks without fear of serious censure or consequences. Blackness was associated with inadequacy and subservience and the notion was transmitted to black and white children during their earliest developmental years. The message was driven home well. Benjamin Botkin's collection of slave narratives shows many instances of slave guilt for not working hard or disobeying the master. This suggests that the values of the master were internalized by the slaves. Slave narratives also indicate very clearly that they were rendered dependent on the powerful master and many developed feelings and attitudes toward him parallel to the parent-child relationship. The large number of slaves who could not or would not leave the plantation after slavery indicates the degree of psychological dependency that was developed.

Identification with the master was of serious psychological consequence to the slaves. Attitudes about blacks held by whites became the feelings or attitudes blacks held for themselves and each other as a group. Hatred of self, anger toward the self, presumption of black incompetence, etc., are a legacy of slavery reinforced by residual and later social practices—segregation and exclusion. Independent black achievement was almost nonexistent during slavery.[19] Success was being like whites, being with whites, or being white. Often the black ideal or goal was to be white or to become white.[20] Students of behavior have repeatedly documented the adverse psychological effect of these "impossible strivings.[21]

Given the circumstances, dependency and identification with the master is an understandable outcome. But such a relationship is always an ambivalent one. Man in such situations enjoys the security of dependency but rebels against the price, external control. He despises the person of power but attempts to be a part of him. The goals and ideals of the powerful can easily become those of the powerless. In such a relationship, anger or action against the powerful and protective person or group is a blow against part of the self of the dependent and powerless person or group. It is not surprising then that many blacks would have some difficulty expressing anger toward whites during slavery and for a long period thereafter. The psychological tie of powerless blacks to powerful whites was as important a deterent of black retaliation as the probable physical consequences.

Had blacks become an acceptable part of the total society after slavery, the significance of racial differences would have been greatly changed. Race would not have remained as a symbol or a sign of goodness and badness, success or failure. Blacks would not have been denied employment, education, ownership and entreprenurial opportunities. The masses could have received a basic sense of adequacy by simply providing for their families and receiving recognition as desirable parents and citizens. The talented could have moved to positions of leadership and registered high-level achievement. Without the atmosphere of white rejection of blacks at every level, the latter could have

identified with achievers, leaders, goals, and values which were American
rather than black or white. Black children would have aspired to a wide range
of goals rather than those open to blacks. But blacks were not accepted into
the total society and the consequential psychological outcome was different.

After slavery, blacks were immediately closed out of the economic, political, and educational mainstream of American life.[22] The program of federal
Reconstruction failed to provide blacks with a solid economic base and was,
as a consequence, gradually eroded as an adjustment tool. None of the organizational aspects of the African culture remained to provide a basis for group
stability and direction. Only remnants of previous African life styles and behavioral residuals remained, greatly modified by the American experience and
of little value in promoting adjustment in the postslavery period. As a result
of these factors, blacks remained economically, socially, and psychologically
dependent on whites who retained almost complete economic and social control. Over 50 percent of the black population remained in a condition of
serfdom until the early part of the 20th century. While some were able to
directly express anger and advocate rejection of and attacks on the perceived
oppressor—as some did in slavery—most were not able to do so. Not only had
their training been effective but to express hostility toward whites on which
many were dependent was to risk the loss of a major source of a sense of
security.

The circumstances reflected an extremely unhealthy state of affairs. As a group,
blacks were unable to obtain opportunities which would facilitate the optimal
development of large numbers of their members. Public education was long
delayed and often inadequate. They were employed at the lowest level of
the job market. They were rapidly closed out of business and government.
Yet because many had been trained to accept white control, their lack of
education and skills, the level of antagonism toward blacks, and their dependency tie to whites with power, many blacks—although woefully oppressed—
were unable to struggle against the unjust exercise of power they experienced.
This combination of circumstances did not exist for any other excluded group
in America.

Although powerless after slavery with still little sense of community other
than being a despised, rejected part of a larger community, blacks were forced
to turn in on themselves anyway. Segregation, which rapidly developed as a
social policy after slavery, made this necessary. With the end of the control
and exploitation of blacks by their masters, legislation, judicial and extralegal control (intimidation, violence, economic reprisals) were established.
Control and authority had now been extended to all whites, most of them
more economically vulnerable and in need of psychological scapegoats than
the more wealthy slaveowning class.[23] Whites outside the planter class were
more likely to act in an unjust and violent fashion toward blacks. Black parents had to prepare their children to live in such a setting. Aggressive styles
had to be crushed least they lead to conflicts with whites. Such socialization
led to the destruction and/or diminution of the capacity for exploration,
learning, and work in many blacks.

A strict social etiquette developed which symbolized white privilege and
black subservience.[24] Children learned the rules of the game through subtle
and overt ways. In the 1930's when a black youngster in Texas was beaten
by white adult males for entering a bus before a white woman, his father did

not protect or console him but angrily counseled, "You ought to know better than to get on the bus before the white folks."

The implication of segregation, as it was practiced, was clear: blacks are inferior and incapable of participation in the total society. This rejection occurred to a people generally trying desperately to belong. Denied the tools and opportunity for personal achievement and the resultant sense of adequacy and security achievement brings, belonging to a group which met these needs was most important. Blacks made various adaptations to meet adequacy and security needs in a society in which they were now "free" but still rejected and abused.

Blacks who had used religion as an adaptive mechanism during slavery now embraced it more firmly. The church became a substitute society.[25] "Walking and talking with Jesus" was more than a metaphor. It was an important method of being a valued person. In many black communities, a sense of relatedness born of the need for mutual support necessary to survive in a threatening society began to develop. Sharing and mutual aid became a style of life for many. Many informal and formal Afro-American mutual support organizations developed after slavery, reflecting the great need. Other blacks became paid employees of their former masters and maintained a carbon-copy style of life and identified strongly with whites. Some wandered disorganized and hopeless for several years after slavery. Some were without social organization, goals, and direction, and were largely pleasure oriented, responding to their inadequately controlled sexual and aggressive drives in a way that led them into conflict with the larger society. Such behavior was not viewed as a failure of the society to establish social policy which promoted adequate social and psychological development but was seen as "the way the niggers are." Similar behavior among whites was not viewed as "white behavior."

Because blacks did not respond to oppression with violent retaliation did not mean that they did not experience anger. It was generally turned against the self or others like the self.[26] Passive, self-destructive modes of behavior are, in part, a product of the reaction to self-hate and low self-esteem. The excessive use of drugs and alcohol are but a few examples. Violent behavior against other blacks—often a displacement of anger toward whites—is a familiar pattern. The assault on "a friend" over a dime or a bottle of wine is an indication of the low self-esteem. The disproportionately high violent crime rate of blacks is, in part, a manifestation of displaced anger. A black student at an Ivy League school angrily contested a black professor after it was obvious that the student was in error. He readily accepts similar comments from whites. Low aspiration level and high family-conflict rates among some blacks is often a byproduct (or partially so) of anger against the self. Because many blacks have very little power to effect change, overwhelming obstacles and hopeless surrender produce high social and psychological depression rates. Only occasionally and only recently has rage and anger been turned against whites.

The circumstances of black and white interaction has also had an impact on the white psyche.[27] Until recent years, many whites have felt justified in their abuse and exploitation of blacks. Leaders of the society—a U.S. Congressman as late as the early 1900's—threatened greater violence toward blacks if favorable legislation for them was passed. During Reconstruction, many white leaders urged the white masses to attack blacks and often joined in the fun. It is small wonder that a cavalier attitude (indeed a collective superego

defect) developed with regard to white abuse of black. It was wrong to murder unless it was a nigger out of his place—his place being determined by
whites.

Inherent superiority was taught and is still taught to white youngsters
through denial and by ignoring the accomplishments of blacks in the face of
overwhelming obstacles. Institutional denial—exclusion of blacks from text-
books, communications media, and white institutions—facilitated individual
denial. White youngsters were taught white superiority and black inferiority
through direct and inadvertent means. A white youngster of marginal intelligence had learned from his father that he should be nice to blacks, otherwise
they would not want to work for him when he grew up—an assumption of a
superior status in spite of the fact that the youngster was less prepared to be
a high-level achiever than many blacks. A golf caddy who wanted to work
for two black physicians without taking his turn asked them to tell the pro
in charge that they worked for his father. A white suburban child looked at
a black youngster in town and said, "Look Mommy, a baby maid!" White
people act consciously and unconsciously on these feelings in relationship
to blacks. These attitudes and conditions are clearly changing under the pressure of new social forces but many undersirable conditions still exist. Such
attitudes and reactions are, in part, a basis for continued black and white
conflict.

In spite of the many psychological and social forces which inhibited normal black reaction to oppression, the basis for such a reaction has been gradually developing for a long time. It began when slavery was ended and the
policy of racial segregation forced white leaders to prepare or permit some
blacks to prepare themselves to take care of their own. This "crack" in the
pattern of forced dependency was the beginning of the development of a
positive black group identity and eventually a normal reaction to oppression.
Many blacks, as preachers, teachers, physicians, and other professional service
people, began to develop skills which gave them a sense of adequacy and the
capacity to cope. In the South in particular, successful business communities
developed. Black youngsters were able to identify with people like themselves
in positions of leadership and respect. Obviously the level of respect was
limited by the implications of a segregated system, but nonetheless it was of
value in enhancing black self-esteem. More among the black masses were
better able to earn enough money to take care of their families and as a result were able to develop a sense of personal adequacy. Involvement in two
world wars and achievement in entertainment, athletics and other areas, and
the exposure facilitated by mass migration began to change the black American's feelings toward the self. A positive sense of self began to replace the
previous negative self concept.[28]

Today's young adult blacks and teenagers grew up observing the heroics
of Jackie Robinson and Jimmie Brown. They watch Sidney Poitier and listen
to Aretha Franklin. They observe better trained blacks achieve and move to
positions of high responsibility. They test themselves against white youngsters
on the gridiron, in the military service, and occasionally in the classroom, and
often find that they can perform just as well. When this is not the case, it is
often clear that limited opportunity and not a lack of ability is the probable
cause. The black nurse's aide and practical nurse often realize that with the
same educational development and training, they could hold the nurse's job,
more often held by whites.

For good reasons, blacks began to raise critical questions. Why is the White American entitled to special opportunity and privilege? Why have we been denied political, economic, and educational opportunity? Why should we despise blackness, indeed, hate aspects of ourselves? Having rejected notions of inferiority, there is no good answer. In spite of this, blacks continue to experience excessive white resistance to pressure for justice and opportunity.

Many of the young black leaders of today were part of the sit-in movement of a decade ago. Many attended racially integrated schools while being harassed, intimidated, and attacked by white hoodlums while "responsible authorities" turned their heads. Many watched "Bull" Connor bring out the dogs to interfere with the peaceful protest of unjust laws and practices. Many looked in vain for action by the legislative, judiciary, and executive branches of government to remove obstacles to first-class citizenship. Most troublesome, they watched white public officials, clearly violating the law, be elected to offices of high trust and responsibility because they stood for the unjust exercise of power against blacks.

The reaction to resistance could now be different. Blacks are no longer largely employed in Southern agriculture and consequently vulnerable to economic reprisal for any self-interest activities—political, economic, or social. Black adequacy and comptence is now built on more than white approval and assurance of acceptance as a child of God with a reward in heaven. A significant number of black parents on longer teach their children to accept white authority, right or wrong. Many whites, now economically more secure and better educated, no longer need or approve of the scapegoating of blacks. The tie that bound—black social, economic, and psychological dependence on an almost totally rejecting white community—has now been broken.

With the breaking of the dependency bond came expected responses. A greater number of blacks could experience anger and rage in response to denial and injustice.[29] In addition, blacks could now seek an identity free of the implications of the aggressor and/or oppressor (the white power structure which denied opportunity to blacks on the basis of a rationalization—inferiority). An intense search for a positive black identity followed.

The breaking of the dependency bond, acceptance of blackness, and a sense of outrage is an energizing and potentially explosive set of psychological developments. The potency is increased by the fact of a continued high level of resistance. The black American experiences intense and ambivalent feelings as a result and is confronted with numerous questions and conflicts. Should he attempt to become a part of the mainstream of his society—now changing but once so abusive and rejecting—or is he obliged to retaliate and/ or reject it? Indeed, does manhood require retaliation and rejection? Can he trust a white America which has never before demonstrated itself trustworthy with regard to recognizing and protecting the human rights of black Americans? These developments and circumstance have created the tension and potential for black violence, retaliatory and black initiated.

The ambivalence and uncertainty is reflected in the wide range of black community responses. The shooting of a black man in connection with a jay-walking traffic violation in Washington, D.C., recently prompted a violent, retaliatory black community mood, necessitating a massive police confrontation. In St. Louis, black churchmen made angry demands for an apology when a white cashier referred to the group of men as "boys." Any expression of white superiority or excessive control evokes a strong reaction from many blacks. Obviously new ground rules for black and white interaction are being established and blacks are sensitive to violations.

A black student was ordered off the lawn at his predominantly white college campus by a white policeman. To be a man—a black man—he had to hit the policeman, a symbol of oppression. But it was a "minor incident" and to avoid difficulty he had to hold back. In fury, rage, and confusion he smashed his arm through a plateglass window a few minutes later. Such feeling occasionally results in a loss of control after "trigger incidents" (reflecting white superiority and black helplessness) with attendent burning of property. With a breakdown in personal control, blacks, employed and unemployed, loot and plunder the "symbolic enemy." Such reactions on the part of oppressed groups have been reported throughout human history.

In the one-to-one black and white relationship where mutual respect exists, interaction is less difficult, perhaps better than ever before. It is the battle against the symbolic enemy that permits black youngsters to escort their white teacher to safety and stone the cars of passing white strangers a few minutes later.

Black reactions are manifest in other ways. A distinguished banker in New York has said that "I am a black man first and an American second." The new black bank president in Chicago identified himself in reverse order. Both accept the values and styles of the total society but want to change the society to meet the needs of more among the black masses. On the other extreme are blacks so angry and aliented that they advocate the establishment of a separate state. One group has already emigrated to Africa. Two black Olympic athletes raised their fists in a symbolic black power salute and another waved an American flag. Black militants and intellectuals ponder the question of whether entrance into the American mainstream is possible or desirable, whether constructive modification of the American system is a realistic aim or whether revolution is necessary, possible, or suicidal.

Some black college students are so "hungup" on these issues that they are unable to concentrate on course work which is irrelevant by comparison. The feelings have filtered down to youngsters, as young as 3 or 4 years of age. Just as young members of the Klan are taught that it is permissible to abuse blacks, some young blacks are being taught that it is permissible to abuse whites. The level of awakening and concern is now so pervasive and reaches such a young age group that one can only anticipate growing pressure for justice—the fair exercise of power. This level of uncertainty, ambivalence, anger and confusion, and resistance cannot persist for long without a drift toward a more malignant reaction—guerrilla warfare and vigilante-type responses.

There is no easy answer to the problem of black and white conflict and violence. The energy released by black awakening and the development of a positive group concept is profound. If channeled, it can be a powerful force for black community development, pride and forceful but nonviolent (or minimally violent) pressure for constructive change within the present social system. But before it can be channeled, it must be clear to blacks that support of the present system and participation in it is in the interest of justice for the black masses. To support a social system that continues to formulate social policy which does not permit adequate development of individual blacks as well as the community and permits blatant disregard for the rights of blacks is to support the conditions that promote intolerable rage and anger.

The nation is a race against time. Constructive attitudinal and economic changes have been made. In many places, members of the white power structure have shown an unprecedented interest in facilitating black entrance into the mainstream of American life. The interaction is establishing new and more healthy ground rules for black and white relations. But often the complex factors related to emergence from a dependent, despised position to full participation in the society are not well understood—nor are the many subtle forms of resistance and racism.

Only when blacks are competent performers in much more significant numbers with access to every area and level of human endeavor within the society will the impression of white power, superiority, and independence and black powerlessness, inferiority, and dependence be destroyed. One alternative now is to attempt to achieve these ends within the society, as a part of the society and through methods deemed acceptable by the society. Another, most likely to develop if white resistance to full black participation persists, is to move against the society—violently. Logic or concern for the consequences cannot stay passion generated by the desire to satisfy basic human needs. Government, industry, educators, and every group responsible for establishing social policy must make it clear through rapid and enlightened action that manhood, respect, adequacy, and security are possible within this society or black and white conflict and violence will become more malignant.

References

1. In an analysis of the feelings, attitudes, and behavioral interaction between black and white Americans, a basic methodological problem exists. Primary documents relating conditions and reactions from the loss of the organizational elements of the original black culture through subjugation are generally available from the slaver and master and not the slaves—save a limited number of narratives. Yet behavior under certain conditions is somewhat predictable and understandable even in retrospect. Combining historical, sociological, and psychological data can give us a greater depth and breadth of understanding of current behavior than documentable historical evidence alone. After all, to say that what cannot be completely documented did not happen is to limit progress in understanding critical problems. I have combined my backgrounds in social science, public health, child, adult, and social psychiatry as well as a vast amount of work in disorganized and low-income black community areas to develop the thesis presented in this paper.
2. U.S. Department of Labor and U.S. Department of Commerce, *Recent Trends in Social and Economic Conditions of Negroes in the United States,* Current Population Reports, Series P-23, No. 26 BLS Report No. 347, July 1968.
3. U.S. Riot Commission Report, *Report of the National Advisory Commission on Civil Disorders,* Mar. 1968
4. *The Wall Street Journal,* Apr. 10, 1968, p. 1.
5. Richard Komisaruk and Carol Pearson, "Children of the Detroit Riots: A Study of their Participation and Mental Health," Lafayette Clinic and Wayne State University, unpublished.
6. Gerald Caplan, "A Study of Ghetto Rioters," *Scientific American,* vol. 219:12 (August 1968), pp. 15-21.
7. Anna Freud, *Normality and Pathology in Childhood* (New York: International Universities Press, Inc., 1965).
8. Albert J. Solnit, "Some Adaptive Functions of Aggressive Behavior," *Psychoanalysis—A General Psychology* (New York: Interational Universities Press, Inc., 1966).
9. Theodore Lidz, *The Family and Human Adaptation* (New York: International Universities Press, Inc., 1963).

10. See Morris Janowitz, "Patterns of Collective Racial Violence," in this report.
11. See August Meier and Elliott Rudwick, "Black Violence in the Twentieth Century: A Study in Rhetoric and Retaliation," in this report.
12. Tuskeegee Institute Report, Tuskeegee, Ala., Apr. 1959.
13. Bureau of the Census, *Historical Statistics of the United States, Colonial Times to 1957* (Washington, D.C.: U. S. Government Printing Office, 1960), p. 218.
14. James L. Gibbs, Jr. (ed.), *Peoples of Africa* (New York: Holt, Rinehart & Winston, Inc., July 1966).
15. Benjamin A. Botkin, *Lay My Burden Down, A Folk History of Slavery* (Chicago: The University of Chicago Press, 1945), p. 126.
16. Stanley M. Elkins, *Slavery* (Chicago:, the University of Chicago Press, 1959), pt. III.
17. George Frederickson and Christopher Lasch, "Resistance to Slavery," *Civil War History* (Fall 1967), pp. 293-329.
18. Urie Bronfenbrenner, *Child Development,* 1960, 31, pp. 15-40
19. Kenneth B. Clark, *Prejudice and Your Child* (Boston: Beacon Press, 1955).
20. Bertram P. Karon, *The Negro Personality* (New York: Springer Publishing Co., Inc., 1958).
21. Mary Ellen Goodman, *Race Awareness in Young Children* (Reading, Mass.: Addison-Wesley Press, 1952).
22. John Hope Franklin, *Reconstruction After the Civil War* (Chicago: The University of Chicago Press, 1961).
23. C. Vann Woodward, *The Strange Career of Jim Crow* (Oxford: Oxford University Press, 1955), pp. 44-60.
24. John Dollard, *Caste and Class in a Southern Town* (New York: Oxford University Press, 1938).
25. E. Franklin Frazier, *The Negro Church in America* (New York: Schocken Books, 1963).
26. Alvin F. Poussaint, "The Negro American: His Self-Image and Integration," *Journal of the National Medical Association ; vol. 58, No. 6* (Nov. 1966), pp. 419-423.
27. Dollard, *op. cit.*
28. Thomas F. Pettigrew, *A Profile of the Negro American* (Princeton, N.J.: D. Van Nostrand Co., Inc., 1964), pt. III.
29. William H. Grier and Price M. Cobbs, *Black Rage* (New York: Basic Books, Inc., 1968).

PART V

PERSPECTIVES ON CRIME IN THE UNITED STATES

Whether the stark assertion that violence is "as American as cherry pie" has any historical validity, the recent spate of political assassination, urban rioting, and a crime wave of allegedly epidemic proportions has clearly convinced many Americans that their persons and property are endangered to an unprecedented degree. While the wave of assassination and ghetto rioting that has plagued the 1960's is manifestly unsettling to our restive society, it is probable that the fear of personal assault—the dark spectre of the stranger lurking in the night—currently instills the greatest sense of terror in the collective American psyche.

The essays in this section are addressed to three broad clusters of questions concerning the magnitude of violent crime in America. First, how unprecedented is the contemporary upsurge of violent assault? How valid is the apparently popular assumption that the curvilinear ascent of violent crime reflects the evolution of American society from a relatively stable and quiescent agrarian order to our present metropolitan disarray? Central to this view is a pervasive strain of agrarian suspicion and mistrust of the sinister city. This instinctive animosity owes much of its respectability to the romantic naturalism of Crevecoeur, Franklin and Jefferson, Emerson and Melville, but it has persisted even in the cosmopolitan thought of such urbane figures as Henry James, John Dewey, and Theodore Dreiser. Frank Lloyd Wright wanted to demolish the city. Henry Ford explained that "We shall solve the City Problem by leaving the City."[1] How much historical validity is there to the defeatist

corollary implicit in this intellectual antiurbanism—
that spiraling crime is an inevitable companion to
metropolis?

If criminologists, like most students of contemporary society, are burdened today by a surfeit of
statistical evidence, historians of American crime
have been severely hindered by the scarcity of data.
There is simply insufficient evidence available from
which to reconstruct a complete historical model
of national trends in violent crime. Whatever the
social and political virtues of a federal system
which has historically vested the police power in
state and local government, the implication for
historians has been that a definitive history of American crime remains impossible of achievement. Even
so, sufficient if fragmentary records have been kept
by a variety of local and state jurisdictions to permit a cautious generalization from a defensible sample. Possibly the best such state sample is the Commonwealth of Massachusetts, which during the 19th
century experienced in microcosm the great American transition from an agrarian-commercial to an
urban-industrial society. Roger Lane's analysis in
chapter 12 brings sharply into question the conventional American assumption that spiraling criminal
disorder is inherently a child of the city.

A second concern, one imminently more com-
pelling to our generation, is whether the alarm expressed over the current crime wave is warranted
by the facts. Writing in 1960, the sociologist Daniel
Bell concluded after "a somber look at the problem"
that "there is probably less crime today in the
United States than existed a hundred, or fifty, or
even twenty-five years ago, and that today the
United States is a more lawful and safe country than
popular opinion imagines."[2] This reassuring view
was reaffirmed as recently as 1968 by Robert M.
Cipes, a lawyer and consultant to the President's
Commission on Crime in the District of Columbia.
Cipes concluded that "in fact there is no crime
wave," but rather that "current statistics simply reflect the fact that we are digging into the reservoir
of unreported crimes."[3] Academic criminologists
have generally shared this optimistic assessment.
They have periodically debunked the rising crime
index of the Federal Bureau of Investigation. How

can we reconcile this analysis with the frenetic outcry of an aroused public, and that of the politicians
who echo their alarm?

Criminal statistics have been collated nationally
only since 1933, when the Federal Bureau of Investigation began systematic publication of its crime
index. Far from bringing consensual order to the
statistical void—or chaos—the FBI's crime index
has provoked a running controversy over its credibility. Critics have argued that the Bureau had a
vested interest in magnifying the magnitude of
criminal activity in order to substantiate its bureau-
cratic demands for increased appropriations. Furthermore, the Bureau's system of statistical collection has suffered from the decentralized and multi-
form nature of the American police function. Some
police jurisdictions rewarded their districts and pre-
cincts for reporting a high rate of criminal activity,
which might substantiate demands for greater manpower; others rewarded low reporting, which allegedly reflected police efficiency. Finally, "crime"
was reported according to no uniform criteria.

Although the FBI has periodically revised and
tightened its data-gathering system, critics continued
into the late 1960's to insist that the FBI's peren-
nially soaring Uniform Crime Reports (UCR) largely
reflected self-serving "paper crime waves." Fred P.
Graham, an attorney and legal correspondent for
the Washington Bureau of the *New York Times,*
weighs the evidence in a critical analysis in chapter
13 that concludes on a somber note.

The final question concerns regional variations in
patterns of criminal violence. Whether the aggregate national crime rate has been rising or falling,
it is clear from even the static evidence that there
have been significant variations in regional patterns
of criminal violence in the United States. What
light can an analysis of this regional variation shed
on the origins of criminal violence? More specifically, can a purely sociological analysis of regional
violence suffice to account for these differences,
in the absence of a historical analysis of the evolution of what may be called distinctive regional
subcultures?

Although historical analysis of national trends in
violent crime has been retarded by a lack of data,

and the contemporary calculus of crime is rendered
problematical by the uses to which the relative abundance of data is put, the studies of Lane and Graham
suggest that while rising crime is not an inevitable
concomitant of urbanization, rapid urbanization
may be accompanied by alarmingly spiraling rates
of crime, depending upon the form that urbanization takes. Whereas latter-19th-century urbanization
was accompanied by a vast industrial expansion
which provided a channel for upward socioeconomic mobility, contemporary urbanization has
crowded young males, often Negro migrants from
the rural South, into deteriorating inner cities from
whence whites and an increasingly automating industry are fleeing.

Since violent crime, while not inevitably a by-
product of urbanization, is clearly accelerated by
the ghettoization of the nation's inner cities, logic
would suggest that rates of criminal assault would
be highest in the more rapidly urbanizing North
and West than in the more rural South. Such a pre-
diction would be reinforced by a corollary to the
frontier hypothesis—that rates of personal assault
should decline as the frontier's environment gives
way to a more settled and ordered civilization.
Yet the data reveal a somewhat contrary pattern:
of all regions in America, the traditional Southeast
manifests substantially the highest incidence of personal assault, followed by the post-frontier Southwest. In chapter 14, Sheldon Hackney seeks to explain this paradox by bringing both sociological and
historical analysis to bear on the persistence of violence in the South.

References

1. For a lucid analysis of this tradition, see Morton and Lucia White,
   The Intellectual Versus the City (Cambridge: Harvard University
   Press, 1962).
2. Daniel Bell, "The Myth of Crime Waves: The Actual Decline of
   Crime in the United States," ch. 8 of *The End of Ideology*
   (Glencoe: The Free Press, 1961), p. 151 of the Collier edition.
3. Robert M. Cipes, *The Crime War* (New York: New American
   Library, 1968).

Chapter 12

URBANIZATION AND CRIMINAL VIOLENCE IN THE 19th CENTURY: MASSACHUSETTS AS A TEST CASE*

By Roger Lane

America is now an urban nation, but Americans are still afraid of cities. There are many dimensions to this fear, but one of them is especially direct, and starkly physical. The current concern with "safety in the streets" echoes a belief, as old as the Republic, that the city is dangerous, the breeding ground of vice and violence. Observers of varying sophistication have pointed out that dark streets hide dark deeds, and that the anonymity and freedom of urban society, its temptations and frenzied pace, all contribute to encourage criminal behavior. From this it is easy to conclude that with metropolitan growth and the multiplication of all these conditions, the rate of violence crime is inexorably multiplied also.

But constant repetition of a myth is no substitute for proof. Under some circumstances it does in fact seem clear that migration to the metropolis has been accompanied by disruption and violence. This does not mean that there is a necessary or inevitable connection between the growth of cities and the growth of crime. In fact the existing historical evidence suggest the very reverse, that over a long-term urbanization has had a settling, literally a civilizing, effect on the population involved.

The statistical evidence for such a long-term trend is necessarily fragmentary and local. But for this purpose local studies may well be more reliable than national. Figures for the United States as a whole, compiled by the Federal Bureau of Investigation, have been available only since 1930. Based on the records of police departments with widely varying standards of accuracy, these have provided a generation of criminologists with material for argument.[1] Analyses of crime rates in individual urban areas, on the other hand, are less complicated by discrepancies in definition and in police practice. While few of these reach back to any period before the FBI's Uniform Crime Reports, these few are significant. None points to any clear proportional increase in

*This chapter is copyrighted by the *Journal of Social History*, 1968; reprinted by permission of the copyright owner.

Roger Lane is associate professor of history at Haverford College. His publications include *Policing the City: Boston, 1822-1855* (Cambridge, Mass.: Harvard University Press, 1967), and "Crime and Criminal Statistics in Nineteenth Century Massachusetts," *Journal of Social History, vol. II* (December 1968). This article is reprinted here in revised form by permission of the *Journal of Social History*.

serious crime within particular cities. And the more recent suggest, on the contrary, a sometimes striking proportional decrease.[2]

Both the decrease and some of the explanation for it may be demonstrated since it is necessary to choose a single area to represent the whole—by an examination of 19th-century Massachusetts. A stable Eastern state, with one growing metropolis and a number of thriving smaller cities, this Commonwealth had a fairly typical experience with industrial urbanization. As a result of the legislature's enormous appetite for statistical information, its official records, including all those relating to criminal behavior, are probably better than any kept elsewhere.[3] And while criminal statistics are notoriously difficult to deal with, and by themselves offer no firm conclusions, the history of the Commonwealth has been abundantly studied, and may be used to help interpret the raw numerical data. Together, the statistics and the social record can illuminate several aspects of the history of criminal violence in America. These include: the changing incidence of disorder itself, the relation of this change to urban growth, the special conditions which may upset this relation, and lastly the problem of public attitudes or concern.

While all criminal statistics are subject to some doubt, the central conclusion about the figures from Massachusetts may be stated with confidence: serious crime in metropolitan Boston has declined sharply between the middle of the 19th century and the middle of the 20th. This often ragged downward trend does not, of course, apply equally to all offenses, but it does to most of the more serious common-law crimes. Three independent studies, by a lawyer, a historian, and a sociologist, confirm this basic direction.[4] While the three cover different periods, and employ somewhat different methods, they do fit together, and all are based essentially on police arrest statistics, the index most widely used by contemporary criminologists.[5] The most comprehensive, covering the years from 1849 to 1951, shows a drop of nearly two-thirds in those crimes which the FBI classifies as "major."[6]

But only half the story, at best, can be told through the figures from the metropolis alone. Our concern is with the whole society. And it has been argued that the difference in crime rates between urban and nonurban areas may be great enough so that a drop in the incidence of criminality in the cities is more than offset by the fact that a continually greater percentage of the population is living in them.[7] It is necessary, to meet this problem, to look at the statistics for Massachusetts as a whole.

For most of the 19th century, the use of police records is neither possible nor desirable on a statewide basis.[8] But other indices of real criminal activity are available. And four of them may be used to establish the changing incidence of "serious" crime, defined as that which involves real injury to persons or loss of property.[9] These four are lower court cases, jail commitments, grand jury cases, and state prison commitments, all involving the major common-law offenses against persons or property. The first date for which two of these indices were published in trustworthy form is 1834; the first year for which all four were compiled is 1860. The figures for these periods, expressed in 3-year averages, may be compared with those for the end of the century in the table 12-1:[10]

The decline in the officially recorded crime rate is unmistakable here. And it is strongly probable that the real decline is greater than the statistics indicate. The key problem in the interpretation of criminal statistics is posed by "the dark figure," representing those illegal activities or incidents which never come

Table 12-1—*Average yearly incidence of cases per 100,000 population*

	1834-36	1860-62	1899-1901
Lower Court cases		777	707
Jail commitments		333	163
Grand jury cases	89	117	63
Imprisonments	16.8	11.9	5.9

to the light of official attention. But since in later years, as will be discussed
below, there was both an increasing intolerance of criminal activity and a great
growth in the numbers of police and investigative agents, all evidence suggests
that this "dark figure" was growing proportionately smaller as the century
progressed. Thus table 12-1 considerably understates the real decline.

For purposes of explanation, it is almost equally important to note the pattern of this decline. The table lists offenses in the order of their severity:
lower court cases generally involve the least important crimes, jailings the next,
indictments next, and imprisonments the most. And with one exception—the
relative rise in indictments between the 1830's and the 1860's, which will be
considered later—it is especially notable that the recorded drop in the crime
rate is directly proportional to the seriousness of the offense. This is generally true also when the four indices used are examined further and broken
into subcategories. Thus for example the combined rate of commitments for
homicide, rape, armed robbery, and arson in 1860-62 was 6.8 per 100,000; by
1900 it has dropped to 2.9 per 100,000.[11] Most of the other data point in
the same direction—not only a fall over time but a fall most marked in the most
serious categories.

Meanwhile, however, while the serious crime rate was falling, the total
crime rate—or the officially recorded total—was actually rising. This apparent
paradox results from the fact that the downward curve described above may
be wholly reversed simply by adding a third official category, "Crimes Against
Public Order," to the two above. When these offenses are added in—drunkenness is by far the largest of them—the results for the lower courts may be indicated as follows:[12]

Table 12-2—*Yearly incidence of cases per 100,000 population.*

	1840	1860	1900
Total lower court cases	595	1,869	3,317

The pattern for these minor crimes is the obverse of that for serious offenses,
in that the more trivial the degree of the offense the larger its proportional increase over time. While virtually no indictments or imprisonments resulted
from third-class offenses, their addition makes less difference in the case of
jailings than of lower court cases:[13]

Table 12-3—*Yearly incidence of cases per 100,000 population.*

	1841	1860	1900
Total jail commitments	419	548	969

This upward curve in total offenses does not have the same importance as
the other, downward curve in the incidence of serious crime. The latter represents the basic statistical conclusion, in that it reflects a real situation, a real
decline in the rate of criminal activity. But the former, while it is merely

statical, is nonetheless important. There is a complementary relationship between the two trends, and the nature of this relationship helps account for much that underlies the numbers.

The entire increase in the criminal statistics of Massachusetts, during the period covered, may in fact be attributed wholly to the rise in cases of drunkenness. Indeed this one offense, together with simple assault, its constant companion, may serve as a focus for much more. To understand the reasons for the rise in drunk arrests is to understand much about the social changes occurring in the 19th century, changes which affected all of its criminal patterns.

It is clear, first, that the mounting total of cases fed into the official machinery of justice does not reflect a real increase in the consumption of alcohol. The misuse of drink was throughout the 19th century a problem of enormous dimensions. The continuing debate about the nature of drunkenness, although some of it anticipated the best of current thinking, was on the whole punitive, and tended to blame the use of alcohol for virtually every individual and most social evils.[14] But even the most ardent spirits in the temperance movement did not usually suggest that there was any long-term rise in drunken behavior. They and their opponents generally united in agreeing that the situation, in ragged fashion, was improving with time.[15] Because much of the alcohol was made and sold illegally, especially in the countryside, it is difficult to investigate this statistically. But certainly in the metropolis and probably elsewhere the evidence does suggest a decline. Early in the century even ministerial ordinations, to say nothing of less grave occasions, were frequently bibulous affairs.[16] By the 1830's a substantial portion of the middle class had renounced the use of hard liquor. The prohibition was extended later to all drinks, and its champions carried on a continuous political and educational campaign against it. In the 1830's, and again in the 1850's, law enforcement officers estimated that 1 in every 65 inhabitants of Boston—men, women, and children—were selling alcohol for a living, in the latter period in defiance of a state law which prohibited all private sales.[17] Certainly neither this proportion nor this widespread evasion of the law was matched later in the century; by about 1880 the ratio was down to 1 seller in 150 and rising fast.[18]

On one level, the rising statistics of drunk arrests simply reflect an increase in the numbers of professional police and in the penal apparatus. It was not until 1837 that Boston organized a squad of full-time professionals, and for many years these were the only ones in the Commonwealth. But by 1860 all of the larger cities had organized forces of varying sizes, and these had grown and spread to the smaller towns well before 1900.[19] The effect of this, and of a proportionate increase in the rest of the agents of justice, is easily demonstrated. In the absence of police, ordinary citizens were expected to make complaints on their own, and to call on constables only to execute warrants already sworn. But while private individuals may make the effort to initiate the processes of justice when directly injured, professionals are required to deal, in number, with those whose merely immoral or distasteful behavior hurts no one in particular. It takes real cops, in short, to make drunk arrests.

Again on this level, the relative shortage of official agents of law enforcement accounts for one of the most striking characteristics of table 12-1 above. The farther back the figures go, as noted, the higher is the relative proportion of serious crimes. The authorities, with limited resources, obviously had to deal with felony first, indictable crime next, and misdemeanor only when resources permitted.

Conversely it is notable that as time advanced and it became easier for injured citizens to complain to a policeman, the tables indicate that proportionately fewer such complaints were being made. In the city of Boston, at least, the result was a progressive decrease in the number of annual arrests made by each patrolman: in 1855, the average was 71 per man, while by 1885 this had dropped to 37.[20]

Drawn as a model, this development may explain the only apparent anomaly in table 12-1, already referred to. This is the fact that between the 1830's and the 1860's the figures show both a fall in prison commitments and a rise in grand jury indictments. Perhaps—the subject will be investigated further—there is no great paradox at all. District attorneys in the 1830's, faced with a high incidence of truly violent criminal behavior, may have had to concentrate on the more important prisonable offenses, to the neglect of others, even indictable ones. As their resources were increased, and as the real crime rate fell, they would be able by the 1860's to catch up on lesser indictments.

But there remains a more fundamental level of explanation. To account for the rise in lesser offenses or the drop in more serious crimes simply in terms of the expansion of police, courts, and prosecutors is to misplace the emphasis. The expansion is not cause but symptom. The machinery of justice was increased because of a felt need, a growing intolerance of behavior which had earlier been tolerated, coupled with a belief that the state and not the individual citizen was required to do the necessary job.

This process is most evident in Boston itself. Leading citizens and governmental officials were always proud of their reputation for maintaining a tidy and well-governed "order" in the city. But the definition of what constituted "order" changed considerably with time.

Josiah Quincy, one of Boston's first mayors, was also the first to boast that in no other city "of equal population, are there fewer instances of those crimes, to which all populous places are subject."[21] He had in fact assumed charge, in 1823, of a newly incorporated city of about 45,000 inhabitants, which officially issued some 697 liquor licenses and ignored the existence of a large number of illegal sellers. Relatively little attention was paid to such common offenses as simple drunkenness and assault. The night watch, largely concerned with the danger of fire or arson, was afraid to enter some of the more notorious neighborhoods. No one patrolled anywhere in the daytime. Quincy's several terms of office were marked by frequent battles between rival gangs of firemen, whose hunger for looting threatened the whole institution of fire insurance. When, after one of the city's numerous "riots, routs, and tumultuous assemblies" had spluttered on for a full week during the long hot summer of 1825, Quincy was forced to take personal charge of a posse of citizens to put it down. This was clearly an unusual action, and the mayor refused later opportunities to risk his limbs and authority in physical combat, preferring to let mob violence burn out by itself. Nevertheless, neither he nor the voters were unduly alarmed by the prevailing level of disorder. Citizens were traditionally supposed to take care of themselves, with the help of family, friends, or servants when available. An organized professional police would certainly be expensive and might be a threat to valued freedoms. And Quincy was proud to point out, at the end of his official career, that he had not added a single constable or watchman to Boston's part-time corps of peace officers.

By the 1880's, when an aldermanic committee echoed Mayor Quincy's earlier claim that Boston was the most orderly of America's larger cities,

the situation had changed considerably.[22] In 1837, after three major riots in
4 years, the city had acquired a police force.[23] Since then it had been growing
steadily, at a rate faster than the population. By the Civil War, the citizens
had abandoned their objection to uniforms, with their paramilitary connotations, and the patrolmen had begun to carry guns.[24] By the 1880's the force
had acquired most of its familiar modern characteristics and functions.[25] And
the demand for more men continued—despite the fact that the crime rate had
been dropping for some time, and with it the workload for each man on the
force.

The demand for more men, then, reflected not a worsening situation but
higher standards, a change in attitude. Really violent crime brought more
severe retribution than formerly; the same offenses which had earned 2-year
sentences in the 1830's were now punished by 3 to 4 years or more in the
state penitentiary, and the average was still going up.[26] While the police stations were still being built for "defensibility," there had been—and would be—
no large-scale riot for years.[27] It is impossible to imagine a late-century mayor
wrestling with mobs as did Quincy in the twenties and Theodore Lyman in the
thirties. All of the city had been brought under more or less effective patrol,
and the voters were demanding that the streets be cleared not only of arsonists
but of drunks, peddlers, and truants. Traffic problems were settled not by
teamsters with their fists but by officers with whistles. The responsibility for
individual safety had been decisively shifted to these agents of the law; uniformed men with revolvers were stationed not only in potentially dangerous
areas but in the quiet confines of the public library.[28] And the end result,
reflected in many arrests for minor breaches of conduct, was a degree of
"order" which would have astonished and perhaps dismayed an earlier and
rougher generation.

The progressive heightening of standards of propriety, and with it the increasing reliance on official law enforcement, were processes which, while
most sharply visible in Boston, were common to the whole society. Traditionally, criminologists have interpreted the zigs and zags of recorded criminal
statistics in terms of individual events or situations—war, for example, or depression. But the change in social behavior reflected in the two dominant
curves of criminality in Massachusetts is so long term and so widespread as to
suggest a connection with the most fundamental of contemporary social processes, that of industrial urbanization itself. The nature of that connection has
never been studied in detail, but it may at least be outlined.

Massachusetts in 1835 had a population of some 660,940, 81 percent rural,
overwhelmingly preindustrial and native born.[29] Its citizens were used to considerable personal freedom. Whether teamsters, farmers, or artisans, they were
all accustomed to setting their own schedules, and the nature of their work
made them physically independent of each other. None of the more common
occupations provided any built-in checks against various kinds of personal excess. Niether fits of violence nor bouts of drunkenness disrupted any vital patterns. Individual problems, sins or even crimes, were not generally cause for
wider social concern.

Under these circumstances, while scarcely a frontier, the Commonwealth
could afford a fairly high degree of lawlessness. No city in the state boasted
a professional police, and the machinery of justice was not equipped to handle
many cases. Many of the more common forms of violence or crime were

simply not reported to the agents of law, as those affected either shrugged off their injuries or struck back directly.

But the impact of the twin movements to the city and to the factory, both just gathering force in 1835, had a progressive effect on personal behavior throughout the 19th century and into the 20th. The factory demanded regularity of behavior, a life governed by obedience to the rhythms of clock and calendar, the demands of foreman and supervisor. In the city or town, the needs of living in closely packed neighborhoods inhibited many actions previously unobjectionable. Both blue- and white-colar employees in larger establishments were mutually dependent on their fellows; as one man's work fit into another's, so one man's business was no longer his own.

The results of the new organization of life and work were apparent by 1900, when some 76 percent of the 2,805,346 inhabitants of Massachusetts were classified as urbanites.[30] Much violent or irregular behavior which had been tolerable in a casual, independent society was no longer acceptable in the more formalized, cooperative atmosphere of the later period. The private, direct response to criminal injury was no longer necessary or approved. All cities and most towns had acquired police forces, constantly expanding to meet greater expectations. Throughout the state, the victims of violence and theft were conditioned to seek official help. The move to the cities had, in short, produced a more tractable, more socialized, more "civilized" generation than its predecessors.[31]

The trend in the direction of higher standards and a lower level of violence may be measured from the early 19th century through much of the 20th. But what is true in the long run is not necessarily evident in the short. While the process or urbanization has helped to raise standards of personal behavior, it may not do so by itself. And there is some indication in the history of 19th-century Massachusetts that under unfavorable conditions migration to the cities may at some times have increased the incidence of violently unsocial behavior. This may well be true, at least, of the long generation between 1835 and 1860.

The existing statistics, alone, are no sure guide to what was actually happening during these crucial early decades. The Boston arrest figures were not kept until 1849. For the state as a whole, much of the remaining evidence remains ambiguous. As explained above, the two main indices, the rate of grand jury indictments and of imprisonments for felony, point stubbornly in opposite directions. But there is good reason to suspect that the period from the mid-1830's to the Civil War illustrates at least a partial, and important, exception to the general developments previously sketched.

From the war on to the end of the century and beyond, the industrial development of Massachusetts, however painful for those involved, was at least proceeding at a pace and along lines already laid out. The era just before was the one which witnessed the turbulence of transition. No similar timespan in fact encompassed a more rapid increase in the urban population. Between 1835 and 1860, while the total population was growing from 660,940 to 1,231,066, the proportion of city dwellers leaped from 19 to 44 percent of the total.[32] At the same time, too, the major railroad lines were laid in patterns still existing. As steam began to replace waterpower as the major source of industrial energy, the factories, earlier confined to rural sites near waterfalls, began to move into the cities.

Social dislocation, meanwhile, accompanied economic. All through the
period, and especially during and after the "hungry forties," heavy Irish immigration exacerbated all of the problems of city living. By 1855, some
68,100 of the 168,031 residents of Boston were natives of Ireland.[33] Up-
rooted from a rural setting, wholly without skills, the newcomers experienced
the kind of culture shock, prejudice, and alienation which would plague other
waves of migrants later. Crowded into stinking hovels, some of them underground, their miserable conditions of living strained all of the city's institutions of charity and police. Smallpox, once virtually eliminated, became again
a problem, cholera struck hard, and the death rate about the middle of the
century climbed to the highest point in the city's recorded history.[34]

In terms of its effect on behavior, all of these rapid and wrenching changes
promoted the worst aspects of living in the city without benefit of its com-
pensations. It must be stressed that economic developments were not fully
able to keep pace with migration. Between 1837 and 1845, it has been estimated, the amount of large-scale or factory employment did not increase at all[35]
And in the 15 years following, while the total of factory employees grew to
something like 25,000 or 30,000, the number of outright paupers in the metropolitan area was increasing at an even faster rate, to reach a peak of nearly
13,000 in 1860.[36] Without the discipline imposed by regular employment,
this first large-scale flow of migrants into the city was a kind of mutual disaster.
The raw arrivals from the countryside, Yankees as well as Irish, had not yet
learned to weave warily through crowds, with their arms held in close. Often
radically insecure, in neighborhoods still unstable, they sought release in drink.
But to drink with strangers requires different rules, and more restraints, than
drinking in more familiar situations. In this era of swinging elbows, bewilderment, and desperate unemployment, it is hard to find evidence that the level
of violence was declining.

Indeed it is easy to find the opposite. During this whole period Massachusetts was wracked by political instability, aggravated by one unpopular war
and the overhanging threat of another one.[37] The 1850's, in particular, witnessed a resurgence of mob violence as Know-Nothings and Irishmen, opponents
and defenders of slavery, all found occasions to take to the streets.[38] These
clashes, superimposed on and partly resulting from the already unhealthy
social condition of Boston, were deeply disturbing to the inhabitants. If the
real incidence of criminal behavior was not actually rising at this time, then
surely it was not falling at the rate apparent in the generations following the
Civil War.

All evidence points to the long-term drop in criminal activity as normative,
and associated with urbanization. But the process was not complete without
the accompaniment of rapid industrial development also. It was this which
provided the means of absorbing raw migrants, of fitting them into a "system"
which socialized and accommodated them into more cooperative habits of life.
Without this other process, migration to the city alone, simply by multiplying
human contacts, may very well multiply the incidence of criminally violent
interaction among inhabitants unsuited to its demands.

Because of its clear connection with ethnic prejudice, and its dangerous
political and social implications, the violent state of Boston during the 1850's
was the source of considerable public concern. But the relation between concern about violence and violence itself is not always so uncomplicated. Both

in the 19th and the 20th centuries, the attitudes of newspapers, scholars, and
the public generally have been various and volatile, the product often of special
interests or misinformation. This makes such attitudes difficult to measure.
But they are nevertheless crucially important to the study of criminal disorder.

In the long run and in the short, popular concern has a direct effect on the
shape of criminal statistics. As it was changing public standards which accounted for the rising total of arrests during the 19th century, so police departments still concentrate on those offenses of greatest current interest.
Moreover, it is not simply the actual level of criminal activity, but the balance
between this and social attitudes, which determines how much violence is a
"problem" at any given time.

While public "attitudes" are slippery concepts to compare, it does seem
that in the sense above the state of Massachusetts, and the United States in
general, had a criminal problem less worrisome in the 19th century than in
the 1960's. The citizens of the Commonwealth, still close to their rural antecedents, were indeed afraid of cities, which one legislative committee called
"the common sewers of the state."[39] And one major source of this fear was
the "poverty, vice, and crime" commonly associated with Boston, in particular.[40]
But hostile critics were more interested in the first two than in the last, and
reformers endlessly debated the causal relation between them. The charge
that the city had lost control of its "dangerous classes" was used in several attempts to limit self-government in Boston, but mob action was the only form
of violence which generally figured in these complaints, and "crime" was used
typically as a synonym for "vice."[41] It is significant that the laws concerning
drink, especially, were subject to constant revision, but except for a reduction
in the number of cases involving the death penalty, the general criminal code
was not.[42] Legislative action or inaction mirrored public concern in this case.
As the sons and daughters of Massachusetts migrated to the metropolis, the
image conjured by the fearful was the rake or tempter, not the robber or rapist.

Nevertheless, however overshadowed by other issues, there were periodic
outbursts of concern about violence or other crime. Often these occurred in
response to some new development, or threat, for which the public or authorities were unprepared. In fact, the history of these threats, and the responses
to them, comrpises much of the history of criminal law enforcement.[43]

Thus the multiplication of banks and bank notes, through the 1820's, provided golden opportunities for counterfeiters. The nature of the problem, in
this case, required a network of private bankers' agents to cooperate, across
state and even national boundaries, with the appropriate public authorities.
Anti-Catholic rioting, in the 1830's, was a principal spur to the development of
professional police. During the 1870's, the growing sophistication of professional criminals, dramatized by a spectacular series of bank robberies, led to
an overhaul of existing detective methods in many American cities. During
the same period, bands of healthy native vagrants, fugitives from the new industrial age, were a subject of great concern to the readers of sensational newspapers, who feared the violent potential in these "wild-eyed" strangers. The
response in this case was harsher police action, and a tightening of the rules
governing charity and soup kitchens.

These concerns were at any rate real, and had often lasting effects, although
they had little to do with the overall crime rate. Another and more frequent
kind of scare resulted not from some genuinely new problem but from sudden
attention focused on an old one. Lincoln Steffens, as a cub reporter in New

York, learned how easy it was to manufacture a "crime wave," with techniques still familiar.[44] Thus a particularly brutal murder or a series of muggings could touch off a wave of arrests "on suspicion."[45] Often it was simply an investigation or expose of some endemic form of crime which generated a sudden excitement, during which the public was assured that Boston was facing a threat of unprecedented proportions.

But it is impossible, from these brief scares, to get any clear sense of direction. While the definition of the tolerable was altering with time, it was altering slowly and imperceptibly. And there is no evidence that, as the century progressed, the gap between the level of order expected and the level actually obtaining was changing in any constant direction. It is true that the police often felt that they were faced with problems of unprecedented magnitude, and chiefs decades apart warned that the level of juvenile delinquency, and the general breakdown of authority, threatened the very basis of society.[46] Other observers too, perhaps beguiled by the image of a more peaceful golden age in the past, sometimes asserted that crime was growing faster than the population. But this tendency to fear was balanced throughout the century by pride in growth and progress. And the many apocalyptic statements may be countered with an equal number of others, more optimistic. Thus even in the troubled year of 1859, the State's attorney general could declare that "at no time in the history of Massachusetts have life, liberty, and property been more secure than at present."[47]

In short, while it is possible now to discover a long-term drop in the level of violence, contemporaries were simply not aware of this. The degree of public concern has never been, nor is it now, an accurate index of the degree of criminal activity. Indeed the reverse is often true. And it is doubly ironic that a drop in the actual incidence of disorder has been accompanied by—and contributed to—a heightened sensitivity to disorder. Such sensitivity, by leading to a more demanding standard of conduct, has been essential to the functioning of an interdependent urban society. But unless the process is recognized and understood, it may have unsettling effects. There are times when for various reasons the level of violence overbalances current expectations. In such situations the social pressure to maintain and extend high standards, and to enforce them universally, may result in frustration. The frustration may translate into fear. And this fear, in turn, may focus on the very urban process which helped to create those standards, on the growth of cities itself.

References

1.   See *The Challenge of Crime in a Free Society: A Report by The President's Commission on Law Enforcement and The Administration of Justice* (Washington, 1967), p. 29.

2.   Four studies are especially germane: Harold A. Phelps, "Frequency of Crime and Punishment," *Journal of the American Institute of Criminal Law and Criminology*, vol. XIX, No. 2 (Aug. 1926), pp. 165-180, which covers Rhode Island between 1897 and 1927; Sam Bass Warner, *Crime and Criminal Statistics in Boston* (Boston, 1934), "Crime as a Function of Anomie," *Journal of Criminal Law, Criminology, and Police Science* (June 1966), covering Buffalo from 1854 to 1956; and Theodore Ferdinand, "The Criminal Patterns of Boston Since 1849," *The American Journal of Sociology* (July 1967), pp. 84-99, which runs to 1951. These all differ in purpose and sophistication, and none is directly concerned with the long-term decline, which helps to make their results the more striking.

3.   A survey of many of the official and criminal records of Boston and Massachusetts
        is contained in Roger Lane, *Policing the City: Boston, 1822-1885* (Cambridge,
        Mass.: Harvard University Press, 1967), pp. 225-229 and 239-241.

4.   See the works by Ferdinand, Warner, and Lane, in footnotes 2 and 3, above. There
        is no attempt, in these or in this paper, to measure the extent of statutory or
        white-collar crime.

5.   Thorstein Sellin and Marvin E. Wolfgang, *The Measurement of Delinquency* (New
        York, 1964), p. 31.

6.   Ferdinand, "Criminal Patterns of Boston," p. 87. Together with roughly similar
        results in Powell's study of Buffalo, these figures suggest that the main conclu-
        sions of the present paper, which is largely confined to the 19th century, may be
        projected up to the founding of the Uniform Crime Reports and beyond.

7.   Ferdinand, "Criminal Patterns of Boston," p. 99.

8.   Statewide arrest figures were not compiled until very late in the 19th century,
        and comparing those for different cities involves many of the same problems as
        plague students of the Uniform Crime Reports.

9.   In this paper except where specifically noted, no distinction is made between
        violent crimes—against the person—and other serious offenses. Such terms as
        "crime" or "disorder" are used to cover both.

10.   For references in this table, see Roger Lane "Crime and Criminal Statistics in
        Nineteenth Century Massachusetts," *Journal of Social History* (December 1968),
        footnote 8.

11.   For references, see *ibid.*, footnote 8.

12.   For references, see *ibid.*, footnote 10. 1840 is the first year for which these figures
        are available.

13.   For references, see *ibid.*, footnote 11. The year 1841 is the first for which these
        figures are available.

14.   Compare *The Challenge of Crime*, p. 235, and Lane, *Policing the City, passim,*
        especially pp. 112-113.

15.   For testimony of both reformers and conservatives, see especially Massachusetts
        House Document No. 415, *Reports on the Subject of a License Law . . . Together
        With a Stenographic Report of the Testimony* (Boston, 1867), *passim.*

16.   Alice Felt Tyler, *Freedom's Ferment: Phases of American Social History to 1860*
        (Minneapolis, 1944), ch. 13, especially p. 311.

17.   Lane, *Policing the City*, pp. 41 and 71.

18.   *Ibid.*, p. 211.

19.   Unfortunately, neither the federal nor the state census permits an accurate state-
        wide count of policemen during the 19th century.

20.   Lane, *Policing the City*, pp. 230-232. The trend has continued. Modern police,
        despite the introduction of patrol cars and call wagons, make fewer arrests, in
        general, than did their predecessors, especially when the whole class of minor auto
        violations is eliminated.

21.   Quoted in *ibid.*, p. 25. For the other information in this paragraph see ch. 2
        passim.

22.   *Ibid.*, p. 204.

23.   *Ibid.*, pp. 29-35.

24.   *Ibid.*, pp. 104-105.

25.   *Ibid.*, p. 224.

26.   These are figures for the average sentences to the state penitentiary. The range
        of offenses listed remained about the same through the century. For references,
        see Lane, "Crime and Criminal Statistics," footnote 14.

27.   *Annual Report of the Commissioners of Police of the City of Boston for . . . 1885*
        (Boston, 1885) pp. 28-30.

28.   Lane, *Policing the City*, p. 173.

29.   Population figures are from *The Census of Massachusetts . . . 1905* (Boston, 1909),
        vol. 1, p. xxxi. The urban definition is based on a population of 8,000.

30.   *Ibid.*

31.   It should be noted that after the 1880's, when Boston already had nearly 2 police-
        men per 1,000 inhabitants, which is close to the present nationwide average for
        major cities, it was the smaller places only where the arrest rate continued to
        climb dramatically. Boston, because of its very small geographical area, was ahead

of most American cities in this respect. It was still possible in other places to raise the arrest figures by extending patrol and demanding higher standards in previously neglected areas, such as outlying slums. This process, and the reduction of the "dark figure" which results from better policing in general, may account for many apparent "rises" in crime rates which occur right up to the present.

32. See footnote 29.
33. Oscar Handlin, *Boston's Immigrants: A Study in Acculturation* (rev. ed., Cambridge, 1959), p. 244.
34. *Ibid.*, pp. 114-116.
35. Ibid., *p. 74.*
36. *Ibid.*, p. 74 and 256.
37. For political conditions in Massachusetts, see William Gleason Bean, "Party Transformation in Massachusetts, 1848-1860, with Special Reference to the Antecedents of Republicanism" (unpublished Ph.D. dissertation, Harvard University archives, 1922), *passim.*
38. Lane, *Policing the City,* pp. 72-74, 90-91, and 94-95.
39. *Ibid.,* p. 132.
40. First used by Josiah Quincy in his "remarks on some of the Provisions of the Massachusetts Affecting Poverty, Vice, and Crime" (Cambridge, 1822), these last four words became a stock phrase among the Commonwealth's reformers.
41. Lane, *Policing the City,* especially pp. 122-125, 128-134, 142-156, and 213-219.
42. *Ibid., passim.* For the criminal code, summed up in revisions compiled in 1835, 1859, 1881, and 1900, see p. 239.
43. For references in the following paragraph, see *ibid.,* pp. 55-56, 29-35, 142-156, 157-160, and 193-195.
44. Lincoln Steffens, *Autobiography* (New York, 1931), pp. 285-291.
45. In 1865, inspired by a fear of returning veterans much like that following World War II, the police made some 2,532 such arrests. See Lane, *Policing the City,* p. 149.
46. See, e.g., *ibid.,* pp. 68, 137, and 34.
47. *Ibid.,* p. 117.

Chapter 13

A CONTEMPORARY HISTORY
OF AMERICAN CRIME*

By Fred P. Graham

The land is full of bloody crime and the city is full of violence. —Ezekiel VII: 23

On a rainy night last June a "frost notice"—a word-of-mouth warning system used by the U.S. Marines to inform personnel of emergency situations—went out to all Marines in and around the Washington, D.C., area. It concerned the fashionable Georgetown section of residential Washington, a stately neighborhood of tree-lined streets and expensive townhouses where such citizens as Allen Dulles, Averell Harriman, Dean Acheson, and Abe Fortas have their homes.

"It would be inadvisable to frequent the Georgetown area currently," the frost notice warned the Marines, "and in general exercise caution and restraint in Washington." The reason for the warning was that in the early hours of that morning, June 5, two young Marine lieutenants had stopped in Georgetown for coffee in an all-night hamburger shop, had exchanged remarks with a trio of black militants who had come from California for the Poor Peoples' Campaign, and had been shot dead. Only 3 nights earlier an 18-year-old high school senior had been shot to death after a bumping incident with a stranger outside a pharmacy two blocks away. In the 6 weeks before that, the area had been plagued by a series of vicious muggings.

The spectacle of Marines being warned away from Washington's most prestigious neighborhood (all the crimes were within shouting distance of the familiar townhouse from which John F. Kennedy had announced his Cabinet appointments in 1960) was only one of a number of bizarre incidents that seemed to show that violence had become more prevalent and threatening than before. Bus drivers in Washington and Baltimore had gone on strike in protest against being required to carry change, because a number had been beaten and one had been killed by robbers. An all-night grocery chain in Cleveland had issued free food vouchers to policemen so that their comings and goings would frighten away potential robbers. Pistol practice had dis-

*© Fred P. Graham, 1969.

Fred Graham is an attorney and legal correspondent for the *New York Times.* Copyright 1969 by Fred P. Graham, from his book on crime and the Supreme Court entitled *The Self-Inflicted Wound,* to be published by The Macmillan Co.

placed ladies' bridge clubs as the center of social activity in some suburban communities. A book by a former Ice Follies performer on judo and self-defense for ladies was selling briskly, along with such titles as "How To Avoid Burglary, Housebreaking, and Other Crimes," and "How To Defend Yourself, Your Family, and Your Home."

Small wonder that in the summer of 1968 the Harris poll found 81 percent of the people believing that law and order had broken down, and that all of the presidential candidates were promising to do something about it.

"Crime is rising nine times faster than the population" was a stock punchline of Richard M. Nixon's all-purpose campaign speech. Vice President Humphrey noted that the annual number of homicides was lower than it was in 1930, but he, too, campaigned from the assumption that the crime rate is getting out of hand. George Wallace never failed to warn his listeners that they might get hit on the head on the way home by a thug who would probably be out of jail before they got out of the hospital.

With most Americans from the President down believing that crime has risen to emergency proportions, there has emerged a puzzling paradox: many of those who have given the subject the most study have, until recently, concluded that it is not so.

Attorney General Ramsey Clark became the whipping boy of the 1968 political campaign because he had expressed the belief in an unguarded moment that "there is no wave of crime in this country." In 1968 Robert M. Cipes, a lawyer and consultant to the President's Commission on Crime in the District of Columbia, published a book, "The Crime War," which proceeded from the thesis that "in fact there is no crime wave," but rather that "current statistics simply reflect the fact that we are digging into the reservoir of unreported crimes." Intellectuals who were not specialists in the field also tended to accept this view. Dr. Karl Menninger, founder of the famed Menninger Clinic of psychiatry, concluded after writing a book on crime and punishment that—

> No crime statistics are dependable; most crime is not reported. Most violent crime takes place in the home. Most nonviolent crime takes place in department stores. My own belief is that there is less violence today than there was 100 years ago, but that we have a much better press and communications to report it.

The President's Commission on Law Enforcement and Administration of Justice, reporting in 1967, could not say after an 18-month study if the crime rate is higher than it has been before, or if Americans have become more criminal than their counterparts in earlier times.

At the center of this controversy had been the ever-rising crime index of the Federal Bureau of Investigation. This index, which has been widely accepted by politicians, policemen, and editorial writers as the official barometer of crime, has also been described by Harvard crime expert Lloyd E. Ohlin as "almost worthless—but it is the only thing there is." Thornstein Sellin, the dean of American criminal statisticians, has been quoted in *Life* magazine as saying that the United States "has the worst crime statistics of any major country in the Western world." The *New York Times* quoted Sophia M. Robinson of the Columbia School of Social Work as saying that "the FBI's figures are not worth the paper they are printed on." Other experts were quoted to the same effect in the press.

Until the last few years, it was fashionable for criminologists to debunk the crime index in this vein when periodic flaps over the FBI's figures erupted and the news media solicited the academicians' views. However, their quoted statements were decidedly more critical than the articles that these same experts were writing for their fellow professionals. Whether they were being quoted out of context (as some claimed) or whether they were victims of betrayed innocence by reporters who did not bother to cushion the professors' true opinions in qualifying padding, the outcome was that the academicians' criticisms of the FBI's statistics were overstated in the mass media. The result was that while the general public tended erroneously to accept the crime index as gospel, the sophisticated readers who delved far enough into news articles to find the scholars' comments were usually persuaded that the statistical proof of rapidly increasing crime was almost certainly wrong. Most of the academic experts did not intend to go that far—but the most respected ones agreed, at least until 1967 or 1968, that the FBI had not proved its case.

This division of opinion was most pronounced with regard to violent crimes. The President's Crime Commission stressed repeatedly that while thefts and other property crimes were rising rapidly, the increase in the type of violent crime that most people fear was lagging far behind. All of this doubt and division cast an aura of unreality about the political dialogue over such suggested reforms as Nixon's demand for changes in the Supreme Court's confessions decisions, Humphrey's call for a tenfold increase in law enforcement spending, and Wallace's suggestion that Federal judges' lifetime tenures be ended.

So long as some of the most thoughtful crime specialists in the country questioned whether violent crime was rising at an unusual or unexpected rate, there was every reason to hold back on any institutional changes, and especially such drastic ones. But since the President's Crime Commission issued its report in February 1967, events have occurred which have convinced most of the previously skeptical experts that violent crime is rising dangerously, and that the increase can be expected to continue for a decade, at least. The exact nature and extent of this rise is still blurred. But that it is occurring—that the dark prophecy of the crime statisticians and the politicians is coming true—is no longer disputed by the experts.

This has come about in a curious way. In the early 1960's, the academicians could see that a crime scare was being launched on the basis of questionable conclusions drawn from unreliable statistics. Many of them committed themselves publicly then to the proposition that the statistical "crime rise" was overblown. The Crime Commission hinted as much, although it stopped short of laying the blame at the doorstep of J. Edgar Hoover and the FBI, where most of it belonged. Yet after the Commission issued its report in early 1967, crime reports from around the country and special studies in key urban areas have satisfied the most serious doubts of the academic skeptics. In effect, these data have confirmed the conclusions about rising violence that Mr. Hoover had been drawing all along—unjustifiably, the experts thought—from the earlier data.

Despite the circumstances, the justification of J. Edgar Hoover and his crime statistics is certain to have a profound impact on the future of the law-and-order controversy, and possibly of the Supreme Court. The controversy over the mathematics of crime will continue over the meaning of the statistics and the manipulations and distortions to which they are subjected, but the frame of reference has shifted in a dramatic way. Crime—violent crime—is increasing rapidly, and few criminologists will now deny it.

There were three good reasons why, prior to release of the 1967 statistics, thoughtful crime experts bridled at the assumption that violent crime was in a dangerous spiral. First, history shows that there has been a rhythm to criminal violence in the United States, and that its rate has probably been higher at times in the past than it is now. Second, the crime scare had been generated by crime statistics that were so questionable that some critics considered them unworthy of belief, and by distortions and exaggerations of those statistics. Finally, even those statistics did not show an alarming rise in violent crime until 1967.

Attempting to put the recent spurt of lawlessness in perspective, the Crime Commission said:

> There has always been too much crime. Virtually every generation since the founding of the Nation and before has felt itself threatened by the spectre of rising crime and violence.
>
> A hundred years ago contemporary accounts of San Francisco told of extensive areas where "no decent man was in safety to walk the street after dark; while at all hours, both night and day, his property was jeopardized by incendiarism and burglary." Teenage gangs gave rise to the word "hoodlum"; while in one central New York City area, near Broadway, the police entered "only in pairs, and never unarmed." A noted chronicler of the period declared that "municipal law is a failure . . . we must soon fall back on the law of self preservation." "Alarming" increases in robbery and violent crimes were reported throughout the country prior to the Revolution. And in 1910 one author declared that "crime, especially its more violent forms, and among the young is increasing steadily and is threatening to bankrupt the Nation."
>
> Crime and violence in the past took many forms. During the great railway strike of 1877 hundreds were killed across the country and almost 2 miles of railroad cars and buildings were burned in Pittsburgh in clashes between strikers and company police and the militia. It was nearly a half century later, after pitched battles in the steel industry in the late thirties, that the Nation's long history of labor violence subsided. The looting and takeover of New York for 3 days by mobs in the 1863 draft riots rivaled the violence of Watts, while racial disturbances in Atlanta in 1907, in Chicago, Washington, and East St. Louis in 1919, Detroit in 1943 and New York in 1900, 1935, and 1943 marred big city life in the first half of the 20th century. Lynchings took the lives of more than 4,500 persons throughout the country between 1882 and 1930. And the violence of Al Capone and Jesse James was so striking that they have left their marks permanently on our understanding of the eras in which they lived.

No comprehensive crime figures were collected prior to 1933, but studies of individual cities have been made, and they show that crime characteristically has its ups and downs, rather than a steady growth along with the population. James Q. Wilson, a crime expert at Harvard, has said that the early studies "agree that during the period immediately after the Civil War the rate of vio-

lent crime in the big cities was higher than at any other time in our history."
Almost all of the available data also indicate that the crime rate rose rapidly
during the post-World War I period and the economic boom of the twenties,
and that it nosedived within a year or so after the bust in 1929. Although no
national figures were collated prior to 1933, figures were available for many
cities for 1930-32, and they all show that the downward trend had begun
from a crime rise that peaked before 1930. Studies in Boston, Chicago, New
York, and other individual cities have shown that the rates were higher in the
World War I years and the twenties than they were in the forties, and a detailed analysis of crime in Buffalo, N.Y., showed that crime peaked in the
1870's and at the end of World War I, then dipped in the 1940's.

These studies differ in the timing of the crime peaks, but they all show the
steep downswing in crime in the forties. The only available national crime
statistics that predate 1933, homicide figures collected by the Department of
Health, Education, and Welfare, confirm this slump in the forties. (See Fig.
13-1.) Although the FBI's figures cannot indicate the height of the peak prior
to 1933, they suggest the same pattern as shown by graphs drawn by the

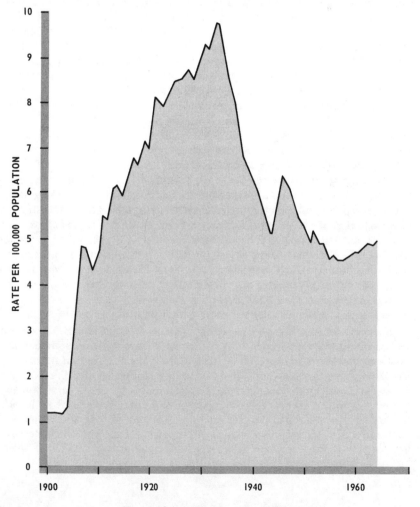

Figure 13-1.—Homicide rates, 1900-64.

Crime Commission from FBI data, and bear out the impression that crime rates, like women's skirts, go up in periods of prosperity. (See Fig. 13-2.) However, when the FBI publishes its own crime charts, it always slices off the downward years, showing only the upward side, which seems to bear out its claim of "record highs" in crime, even in mild years. One reason for this is that the FBI's statistical system was overhauled in 1958, and the Bureau doesn't consider the pre- and post-1958 figures to be entirely fungible. Yet as a result of slicing off the earlier years, the FBI gets this skyrocket effect. (See Fig. 13-3.)

The crime index has given "law and order" an important element in common with the other political issues that have stirred the emotions of the modern electorate—the proposition that things are bad and are likely to get worse can be demonstrated by statistics. Figures on paper were not always a *sine qua non* of scare politics. The prosecutions of the Mormons were not supported by statistical evidence that polygamy was deleterious; there were no figures to support the Red scare that led to the Palmer raids in 1919, and nobody thought it necessary to show on paper that the Japanese-Americans were a threat before the Nisei were rounded up after Pearl Harbor. But since World War II, Americans have not easily been persuaded that evil threatens unless the threat could be reduced to figures on paper. One of the pioneers of statistical politics, Senator Joseph McCarthy, demonstrated that this requirement need not cramp a statesman's style. For so long as the figures are sufficiently obscured that they cannot be absolutely refuted ("I have here in my hand a list of 205 . . . members of the Communist Party . . ."), they usually satisfy the public desire for quantum proof. That this was not some political witchcraft peculiar to Senator McCarthy was later demonstrated by John F. Kennedy during his missile-gap stage and still later by Lyndon B. Johnson, who discovered an alarmingly large category of the "poor" and then substantially reduced its size, all by statistics.

According to behavioral scientists, the reason why statistics are so willingly swallowed as adequate food for thought on public issues is that society has a gift for accepting and then turning into emotional symbols those statistical indicators that confirm and reinforce existing conceptions. People believe those statistics that tell them what they already believed. This, according to sociologist Albert D. Biderman, is the key to the great prestige of crime statistics in the United States. "The crime index," Professor Biderman says, "shares with many indicators the property of owing much of its credibility and popularity to its being consistent with beliefs formed by everyday experience . . . . [It] serves as a short-hand certifier of beliefs, rather than as a shaper of them."

This once became so galling to Attorney General Nicholas deB. Katzenbach that he is said to have seized a sheet of crime statistics one day, pounded his desk and growled: "It's bad enough to lose the war on crime, but to lose it five times a year is too much!" The offending paper was one of the most predictable of Government documents—the latest report by the Federal Bureau of Investigation on crime. These compilations of crime statistics from local police departments, released to the public in the form of four quarterly reports and a fifth annual recapitulation, are known as Uniform Crime Reports. For the past decade they have been truly uniform in at least one sense—they have invariably declared that crime is rising at a terrifying rate.

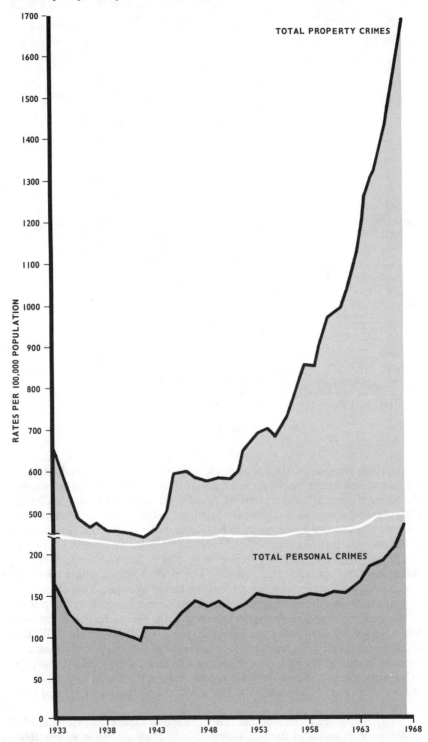

Figure 13-2.—Index crime trends, 1933-67.

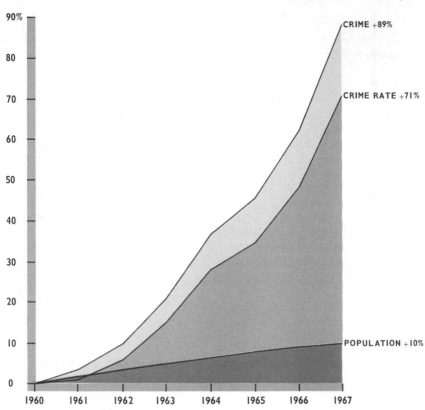

Figure 13-3.—Crime and population, 1960-67.

By 1966, the year of Mr. Katzenbach's outburst, the periodic crime increase announcement had become a familiar Hoover's Comet that burst upon the national scene at regular intervals, always followed by a trail of indignant editorials and congressional speeches deploring rising crime. In 1968—a typical year—the reports produced these headlines in the *New York Times:* "Major Crimes up 16 percent in '67," "First-quarter Rate of Crime in U.S. Rise 16%," and "Crime Rise of 19% Reported by FBI." After a decade of this steady drumbeat of crime rises, many, if not most, Americans have become conditioned to feel that as a function of the law of averages, their chances of escaping rape, murder, or mugging much longer must be about to run out.

As the federal official primarily responsible for contending with the problem of crime, Mr. Katzenbach had good reason to be irked, for the FBI's stewardship of the nation's crime statistics has resulted in a hysteria that seems more beneficial to the FBI as a crime-fighting public agency than to the public's enlightenment. Three elements appear to have combined to puff the crime picture out of shape, and the FBI could at least have ameliorated two of them.

First, the figures themselves are easily the most suspect statistics published under the imprimatur of the U.S. Government. They are highly susceptible to reporting vagaries, do not allow for built-in increases due to shifting age ratios in the population, and do not clearly separate crimes against property from more serious offenses against people.

These flaws are built into the system and the FBI is not necessarily responsible for them, but in its zest for bearing bad news the Bureau has compounded the mischief that is inherent in the system. The FBI, with its flair for publicity, has managed five times a year to wring the maximum amount of public terror out of a statistical system that was conceived (by the International Association of Chiefs of Police) as a technique for keeping lawmen informed of the trends of their trade. It has consistently emphasized the alarming implications of the statistics (even in good years, such as 1959 and 1961, when crime declined in relation to the population), and has not adequately pointed out their inadequacies.

Finally, the FBI's statistical image of a rising national crime rate has been translated into a personal threat in the minds of many Americans through the instant shared experience of television coverage of a few spectacular crimes and riots. The Crime Commission found that this has created a pervasive "fear of strangers." It noted the interaction between crime statistics and vivid exposure of a few events:

> Many circumstances now conspire to call greater attention to crime as a national, rather than a purely local, problem. Concern with crime is more typically an urban than a rural phenomena and the rural population of the country is declining. At one time, for a majority of the population, reports of crime waves related only to those remote and not quite moral people who inhabited cities.
>
> Now, also, more people are informed by nationally oriented communications media and receive crime reports from a much wider territorial base. In recent years news of the violent and fearful mass killing of eight nurses in a Chicago apartment, five patrons of a beauty shop in Mesa, Arizona, and 13 passersby on the University of Texas campus in Austin received detailed coverage throughout the country. The fear of the people of Boston in 1966 of the brutal attacks of the "Boston Strangler" must have been sympathetically shared and understood in many homes across the land. Some part of the public fear of crime today is undoubtedly due to the fact that the reports of violent crime we receive daily are drawn from a larger pool of crime-incident reports than ever before. But perhaps most important has been the steady stream of reports of rising crime rates in both large and small communities across the Nation. From all this has emerged a sense of crisis in regard to the safety of both persons and property.

The political effects of this have already been profound. During the 1968 Presidential campaign a reporter for the *New York Times* polled the citizens of Webster City, Iowa, which calls itself "Main Street, U.S.A." He found the overriding issue to be "crime in the streets," with particular concern about riots and unruly demonstrations. But when the interviewer inquired about crime in "Main Street, U.S.A.," the complaints were that youngsters were drinking beer, driving fast, and breaking an occasional window. Pressed further, the city fathers complained that trucks hauling turkey feathers through town were unlawfully failing to cover their cargoes to keep from littering Main Street. Another reporter, who found the citizenry of Garnett, Kansas, up in arms over crime, discovered that there hadn't been a rape there for 12 years, nor a murder for 21, and that the only person in jail was a 17-year-old hotrodder.

To understand how this exaggerated image of "crime" gained currency, long before the academic experts agreed that violence was climbing, it is necessary to comprehend the mechanics of the Uniform Crime Reports. Local police departments voluntarily report to the FBI the volume of crimes known to the police, offenses cleared by arrest, persons held for prosecution, and persons released or found guilty of offenses. Of the 29 different crimes reported, the FBI uses only 7 in its crime index. The "index" crimes, chosen because they are serious and are thought to be bellwethers of criminal activity, are murder, forcible rape, robbery (muggings, armed robbery, and theft by threat of force), aggravated assault (assault with intent to kill or seriously injure), burglary (breaking and entering to steal), larceny of $50 or more and auto theft. From this the FBI publishes the famous crime index, which is simply the rate of these offenses per 100,000 people.

The Uniform Crime Reports are naturally suspect because the FBI's crime index reflects only *reported* crime. There is known to be so much crime that is either not reported to the police, or not reported by them to the FBI, that only slight changes in reporting habits could have a yo-yo effect on the crime index. The Crime Commission learned from house-to-house surveys that the volume of unreported crime is far greater than anyone had imagined—double, triple, and even 10 times the volume of offenses that are actually reported, depending on whether the crime involved is the type that shames the victim or whether it is the kind the police are thought likely to solve.

Because there is so much unreported crime, it is theoretically possible to have a "crime wave" on the index charts, when in fact nothing but reporting habits have changed. Thus a crime scare could result from victim sophistication—a realization that only reported thefts can become valid income tax deductions or insurance claims, or a new willingness by nonwhites to report crimes to the police.

The same crime "rise" can occur when the police become more diligent in reporting crime. For years the police of Chicago reported many times more robberies than the city of New York, which has more than twice as many people (in one year, Chicago reported eight times as many robberies). Finally, in 1949, the FBI stopped including New York's statistics because it did not believe them. New York has since been reinstated, but periodically its police have slipped back into their old ways of neglecting to report painful facts.

There seem to be two principal reasons for this tendency by the police to "fudge" on crime reports. One is that much of the crime occurs in Negro neighborhoods, between Negroes, and there has sometimes been an easygoing tolerance of it by the police. It was neither investigated nor reported as carefully as crime was elsewhere. The other reason is that increasing crime is political trouble for city administrations, and they like to give the impression that it is under control. Ambitious police officials realize that their superiors want crime kept down, with the result that complaints sometimes get "lost." The Crime Commission found a secret "file 13" in one city containing a catalog of complaints that were not officially reported, and a single precinct in Philadelphia once had 5,000 more crime reports on file than it had officially recorded.

Some experts suspect that both motives for underreporting are losing their validity, and that a good portion of the crime bulge in certain cities is due to the new official willingness to tell all about crime. In recent years more Negro policemen have been hired and more attention given to ghetto crime. This concern has probably dissipated the feeling that Negro complaints are not worth reporting. Also, with the Supreme Court and not the police being widely blamed for the increase in crime, some resentful policemen are said to be reporting crime with a vengeance. The late Police Chief William Parker of Los Angeles once startled a visiting Federal official by his candid discussion of the huge chart on his wall depicting the rise of crime. Each crime peak was topped with the title of a Supreme Court decision in favor of defendants' rights. Chief Parker explained that the police had seen, years before the Court issued its landmark rulings, that a crime boom was coming despite their best efforts—and that they had been lucky to have the Supreme Court to serve as a lightning rod for the criticism. He said that this was partially responsible for his decision to begin making speeches and writing articles about the connection between crime in the streets and judicial decisions.

Jerome Daunt, the chief of the FBI's crime statistics operation, concedes that some of the index crimes are subject to wide reporting fluctuations, but he points out that some are not. Mr. Daunt, a lean, serious man who learned his crime statistics on the job as an FBI agent, makes the point that certain crimes by their nature are almost always reported: bank robberies, because none is too insignificant to report; assault by gun, because the law requires physicians to file reports; murder, because there is a body to be explained.

Bank robberies have increased even faster than the general index, with a rise of 248 percent from 1960 to 1967. Assault by gun rose 84 percent in the 5 years from 1962 to 1967. Much has been made of the fact that criminal homicide has actually declined by 70 percent since 1933, but Mr. Daunt has an explanation for this: "Police response, ambulance response, and improved medical techniques," he says. "It's like the decline in the relative number of war wounded who die—because they get better, quicker treatment."

"Trends—it is the trends in crime statistics that count," declares Mr. Daunt, "and we have been right on the trends." The FBI has indeed been right on the trends (except that its gloomy projections of future crime levels have invariably fallen short of reality) and this has been due in some part to its painstaking efforts to eliminate error—especially by checking for reporting failures whenever reports began to run suspiciously counter to expectations. But part of this success must also be attributed to the melancholy fact that in dealing with crime, if one predicts disaster long enough, events will finally bear him out.

The most valid complaint against the FBI is not that its figures have been soft, but that the Bureau has not presented them honestly to the public. When the FBI first began to sound the alarm about rising crime a decade ago, the overall increase was small and the violent crime rate was actually frequently in decline. In 1961, for instance, the crime rates for violent offenses decreased across the board. Murder, forcible rape, robbery, and aggravated assault all declined. Yet the overall crime index rate rose by 3 percent because of a modest increase in property crimes. J. Edgar Hoover darkly announced that "major crimes committed in the United States in 1961 have again reached an all-time high," adding that during the year there were "four serious crimes per minute." The reason for the rise was that then, as now, about 9 out of 10 offenses included in the crime index do not involve violence, so that even a modest rise in property offenses can lift the entire crime index. Currently, murders, rapes, and assaults make up only 8 percent of the crimes reported in the index.

If robberies are included as "violent crimes" (about one-fourth of them result in injuries to the victims), it is still true that more than four-fifths of the index crimes are nonviolent thefts of property—burglary, larceny of $50 or more, and car theft. Since the crime rates for these offenses were, until recently, consistently higher than the rates for violent crimes, they inflated the overall crime index and gave the impression that violent crime was rising faster than it actually was. This has led to the charge that the FBI's crime index is really a gage of "joyriding" by youngsters in other peoples' cars. In any year the number of auto thefts in the crime index will far outnumber all of the violent crimes taken together, and because 9 out of 10 stolen cars are recovered and returned to their owners, the fearsome "crime rate" is far less a reflection of the pain of victims of rape and assault than the temporary aggravation of those who left their keys in their cars.

Another complaint about the FBI's crime-reporting system is its tendency to tempt exaggeration, oversimplification, and even manipulation of the crime increase. By taking the population increase (1½ percent per year) over a given stretch of years and dividing it into the percentage of crime increase, it can be said that crime is growing many times faster than the population. For instance, if the population increased by approximately 10 percent over a 7-year period, but the number of reported index offenses grew by 88 percent, it could be said that "crime outpaced the population growth by almost nine to one"—J. Edgar Hoover's latest assessment of the recent crime rise. Once announced, this slightly exaggerated calculation from the highly suspect crime index can be cited as government proof that "crime is growing nine times faster than the population." And when the public recalls that only 1 year earlier Mr. Hoover used the multiple of 7 to describe the increase, and that 2 years before that he used the figure 5, it is given an avalanche impression of "crime"—the threat of attack by strangers—that is puffed out of any relation to the actual threat that any individual will become a victim of violent crime.

An even more warped impression is given by the "crime clocks" that the FBI publishes each year. This baffling presentation, year after year, of the shrinking average interval between the commission of various offenses across the country, seems to have no purpose other than sheer terror. Because the population is growing, the interval between crimes would necessarily narrow each year, even if the crime rate was not increasing. Thus the hands of the FBI's "crime clocks" invariably show fewer minutes between crimes than for the previous year. The "crime clock" device lends itself to shocking conclusions that mean nothing, as a published interpretation of the 1966 figures show: "An American woman is raped every 12 minutes. A house in the United States is burglarized every 27 seconds. Someone is robbed every 4½ minutes in this nation."

By reducing crime to these terms, the "fear of strangers" syndrome is justified in a way that is not borne out by the risks of everyday life. Statistically, the risk of attack by strangers is one of the least likely hazards that the average person encounters. The risk of death from willful homicide in any given year is about 1 in 20,000, and almost three out of four murders are committed by family members or friends. The result is that a person's likelihood of being killed in a car crash is almost 15 times the chances that he will be murdered by a stranger. His risk in any given year of being attacked by a stranger and hurt badly enough to require any degree of hospitalization is about 1 in 4,500—and this is an average possibility: If he lives away from high-crime areas his risk is much lower. As Ramsey Clark used to put it, the average individual's chance of being a victim of a crime of violence is once in 400 years, and Clark always added that if one wished to improve his odds he could avoid his relatives and associates—since they are statistically the most likely to do him harm.

What this shows is that extremely subjective conclusions can be drawn from the basic crime data in this country and that the FBI has consistently presented it in a way that tends to make little old ladies stay indoors and strong men look over their shoulders. As one observer pointed out, rather than publishing the fact that some unfortunate individual is murdered every 48 minutes, the FBI could have told the country that the average citizen's chances of becoming a murder victim on any given day are about 1 in 2 million, and that then he might well be willing to brave those odds without hedging on personal freedom of movement or the country's traditional scheme of personal rights.

As slippery as these figures can be in the hands of crime experts, politicians can turn them to quicksilver. During the 1968 Presidential campaign, Richard Nixon observed that crime had increased 88 percent under the Democratic administration. Attorney General Clark went on television with the reply that crime had risen 98 percent during the Eisenhower period. Aghast, the Republican Task Force on Crime fired back with this statement:

> . . . crime in the 8 Eisenhower years between 1953 and 1960 did not increase by 98 percent. That charge is simply inaccurate.
>
> Crime reported in 1960, the last year of the Eisenhower administration, was 63 percent greater than in 1952, the last year of the Truman administration.
>
> This, of course, covers 8 years. If the experience of 1967 holds true this year, the 8-year Kennedy-Johnson record will show a whopping 118 percent increase for the comparable period, or almost double the rate under a Republican administration. Parenthetically, if only a 7-year frame of reference is used, they fare even worse. During the first 7 years of the Eisenhower administration the crime increase was 43 percent, less than half of the 88 percent recorded during the 7 years thus far under Kennedy and Johnson.

Vice President Humphrey said he deplored this crime numbers game—and added that if he were inclined to play it he could point out that the eight States with the highest crime rates all had Republican Governors.

Because the FBI's crime index was so frequently abused, because its figures were suspect, because even those figures showed the crimes of violence lagging far behind, and possibly because they were liberals indulging in wishful thinking, the academicians refused throughout most of the sixties to admit that a serious criminal-violence problem had been proved.

The first break in the familiar statistical pattern came when the 1967 crime reports from across the country were tabulated by the FBI. The usual pattern

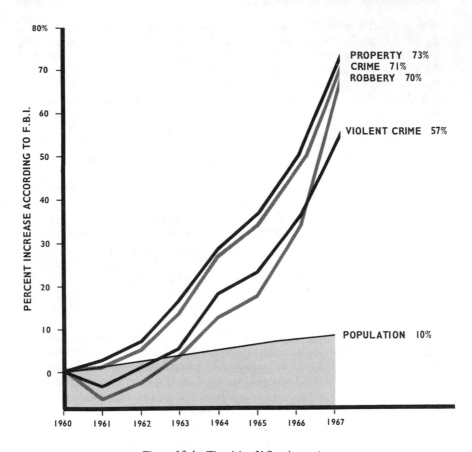

Figure 13-4. —The rising U.S. crime rate.

of relatively low violent-crime rates and high property offenses was shattered by a 16-percent overall increase, composed of a 16-percent rise in violent crimes and a 17-percent increase in property offenses.

But most startling to crime experts was the 28-percent jump in the crime of robbery, which many criminologists consider the bellwether offense in the crime index. Since robbery always involves a threat of force, if not its use, it gives an indication of the public's proclivity toward violence. And since the offender and the victim are usually strangers, the family-quarrel element does not distort the picture. For that reason, criminologists were shocked to see robbery suddenly increasing as rapidly as the property crimes (Fig. 13-4). Preliminary figures for the first 6 months in 1968 confirmed the trend: robbery increased another 29 percent over the high 1967 level.

Meanwhile, new studies showed what Professor Ohlin termed "a pronounced increase in the readiness in people to resort to armed attack." In Philadelphia, where the volume of robberies fluctuated up and down after 1960, the rate of persons injured in robberies began to rise in 1962 and climbed steadily. "Perhaps it is because the robbers tend to be younger, and the young are more likely to use violence," concluded criminologist Marvin E.

Wolfgang; "but there has been a considerable increase in the level of violence in robberies."

Ronald H. Beattie, chief of California's Bureau of Criminal Statistics, who had declared as late as 1966 that the available crime statistics "indicate no substantial increase in aggressive crimes during recent years," took another look in 1968 and said that violent crime was growing even faster than crimes against property. Most experts now believe that this rapid surge in crime, with its new heavy component of crimes of violence, will continue and perhaps will accelerate, at least for the next 10 years. The reason is that the types of people who, as one observer put it, are "untamed in the ways of society," and are thus inclined to commit crimes, are increasing in proportion to the population as a whole.

By far the most crime prone of this "untamed" class are young men. More 15-year-olds are arrested for serious crimes than any other group. Yet thanks to the postwar baby boom, there are proportionally more of them around to commit crimes than ever before, and their numbers are growing. Each year since 1961 an additional 1 million youths have reached the age of 15 than did the year before, and already almost one-half of the population is under 25. According to crime experts, almost half of the total increase in arrests in the first half of the 1960's was simply because there were more younger people around.

Another complicating factor is urbanization. Study after study shows that the violent crime rate of Negroes who have moved from the South into the large urban cities is far higher than the national crime rate for Negroes. The same is true, but with less emphasis, for cities as a whole; crime rates invariably rise in proportion to the proximity to an urban center. Concomitant with the anonymity of urban life—where everybody is a stranger to everyone else and the fear of detection and shame of arrest are diminished—a familiar pattern of bold, casual criminality has developed.

There are other indices, all of them pointing upward. Statistics show that communities with large transient populations experience high crime rates, and demographers predict increasing population mobility in the coming years. High crime and narcotics addiction accompany each other, and the narcotics arrests (although heavily weighted with marihuana cases) almost doubled in 1967 over 1966. Some scientists believe that overcrowding alone can cause antisocial behavior, and the decrease in living space is obvious. It is sad but not surprising that Professor Wilson concludes, "We shall be fortunate if we can even slow the rate of increase in crime; we shall be impossibly blessed if we can actually reduce the level of crime."

Chapter 14

SOUTHERN VIOLENCE*

By Sheldon Hackney

Violence has always been a facet of human experience and a problem for human society. For those interested in determining the causes of violence, and perhaps constructing cures, nothing could be more important than the fact that different societies and different eras produce widely varying rates of violence. Unfortunately for the investigator, even moderately reliable data are available only for the recent past and only for relatively modernized countries. This limits the possibility of cross-national comparisons. For this reason, regional variations within modernized nations become an extremely important source for the comparative analysis of the ecology of violence. The most fruitful area within the United States for such a study is the South, a region with a pattern of violence that stands in striking contrast to that of the nation at large and about which there is a well-developed scholarly literature.

A tendency toward violence has been one of the character traits most frequently attributed to Southerners.[1] In various guises, the image of the violent South confronts the historian at every turn: dueling gentlemen and masters whipping slaves, flatboatmen indulging in a rough-and-tumble fight, lynching mobs, country folk at a bear baiting or a gander pulling, romantic adventurers on Caribbean filibusters, brutal police, panic-stricken communities harshly suppressing real and imagined slave revolts, robed night riders engaged in systematic terrorism, unknown assassins, church burners, and other less physical expressions of a South whose mode of action is frequently extreme.[2] The image is so pervasive that it compels the attention of anyone interested in understanding the South.

H. C. Brearley was among the first to assemble the quantitative data to support the description of the South as "that part of the United States lying below the Smith and Wesson line."[3] He pointed out, for example, that during the five years from 1920 to 1924 the rate of homicide per 100,000 population for the Southern states was a little more than two-and-one-half times greater than for the remainder of the United States. Using data from the *Uniform Crime Reports* concerning the 1930's, Stuart Lottier confirmed and elaborated Brearley's findings in 1938. He found for this period also that homicide was concentrated in the Southeastern states. Of the 11 ex-Confederate states,

*This chapter is copyrighted by the American Historical Association, 1969; reprinted by permission of the copyright owner.

Sheldon Hackney is assistant professor of history at Princeton University. This essay is a revised version of his article, "Southern Violence," *American Historical Review,* Vol. LXXIV (February, 1969), pp. 906-925. It is reprinted here by permission of the *American Historical Review.*

Louisiana showed the lowest homicide rate, but it was 74 percent greater than
the national average, and no non-Southern state had a higher rate. Interestingly, while murder and assault were oriented to the Southeastern states, robbery rates were highest in the Central and Western states.[4] These findings
were replicated in 1954 using data on crime for the years 1946 through 1952.[5]
The pattern of high rates of serious crimes against persons and relatively lower
rates of crimes against property for the South is consequently quite stable.

At the time that Brearley was setting forth the evidence for Southern leadership in physical aggression against people, another statistical study primarily of
American suicide rates revealed that the South was the area whose people had
the least propensity to destroy themselves.[6] Austin Porterfield in 1949,
using mortality tables from *Vital Statistics*, brought the murder and the suicide
indices together and showed that there was a general inverse relationship between the two rates among the states, and that Southern states ranked highest
in homicide and lowest in suicide.[7] In 1940, the national average rate of
suicide per 100,000 population was 14.4 and of homicide was 6.2, but the
old and cosmopolitan city of New Orleans had a suicide rate of 11.1 and a
homicide rate of 15.5. Even though some Southern cities exceed some non-
Southern cities in suicide rates, the New Orleans pattern of more homicides
than suicides is typical of the South but not of the nation. Porterfield comments that "suicide in every non-Southern city exceeds homicide by ratios
ranging from 1.19 to 18.60, while suicide rates exceed homicide rates in only
8 of the 43 Southern and Southwestern cities, 5 of those being in the
Southwest."[8]

Violence in the South has three dimensions. Relative to the North, there
are high rates of homicide and assault, moderate rates of crime against
property, and low rates of suicide. The relationship between homicide and
suicide rates in a given group is best expressed by a suicide-homicide ratio

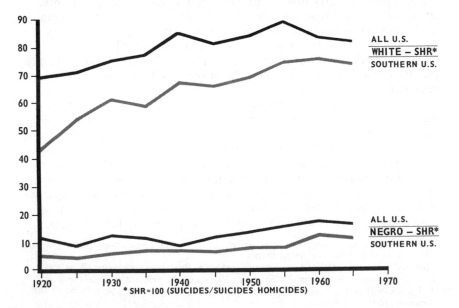

Figure 14-1.—Suicide-homicide ratios.

(SHR = 100 (suicides/suicides + homicides)). The closer the SHR approaches 100, the greater is the proportion of the total number of homicides and suicides accounted for by suicide. The European pattern, shared by white Northerners but not by Negroes or white Southerners, is for suicides to far outnumber homicides so that the SHR is in excess of 80. The ratios in table 14-1, displayed graphically in figure 14-1, measure the difference between Southerners and other Americans with regard to violence.

Table 14-1.—Suicide-homicide ratios for four categories of Americans, 1915-64[a]

Year	U.S. white SHR	Southern white SHR	U.S. Negro SHR	Southern Negro SHR
1915	77.4	[b]62.9	23.7	[b]11.3
1920	69.3	[b]43.4	11.2	[b]05.6
1925	70.9	[b]53.5	09.2	[b]05.0
1930	75.0	[b]61.1	11.9	[b]06.0
1935	76.2	59.9	11.4	06.3
1940	83.3	68.5	09.6	06.5
1945	80.3	66.4	11.1	06.8
1950	82.4	69.8	12.4	09.3
1955	88.3	73.1	15.6	09.7
1960	82.0	74.4	17.0	12.2
1964	81.1	73.2	16.7	11.1

[a]Suicide-homicide ratio = 100 (suicides/suicides + homicides). As the ratio approaches 100, it registers the increasing preference for suicide rather than murder among the members of a given group. The ratios were computed from figures taken from: Forrest E. Linder and Robert D. Grove, *Vital Statistics Rates in the United States, 1900-1940* (Washington, 1943), and U.S. Department of Health, Education, and Welfare, *Vital Statistics of the United States*, for the appropriate year.

[b]In 1915, only Virginia was represented in the SHR for Southern whites and Negroes. In 1920, all of the ex-Confederate states were included in the figures except Alabama, Arkansas, Georgia, and Texas. Arkansas, Georgia, and Texas were still not reporting in 1925, but by 1930 only Texas was excluded. From 1935 on, all Southern states are included.

Because the statistics for "the United States" include the statistics for the Southern states, the differences between Southern and non-Southern suicide-murder ratios are understated. Even so, the differences are significant. In the North and the South, but more so in the South, Negroes commit murder much more often than they commit suicide. Among white Americans, Southerners show a relatively greater preference than do non-Southerners for murder rather than suicide. The latter pattern is evident in figure 14-2, which plots white SHR's by state. The Southern and Southwestern states tend to cluster in the upper left part of the graph, signifying high homicide but relatively low suicide rates.

High murder and low suicide rates constitute a distinctly Southern pattern of violence, one that must rank with the caste system and ahead of mint juleps in importance as a key to the meaning of being Southern. Why this should be so is a question that has puzzled investigators for a long time, and their answers have been various. When one loyal Southerner was asked by a probing Yankee why the murder rate in the South was so high, he replied that he reckoned there were just more folks in the South that needed killing.

Few apologies surpass this one in purity, but there is a more popular one that tries to explain the high homicide rates in the Southern states by the

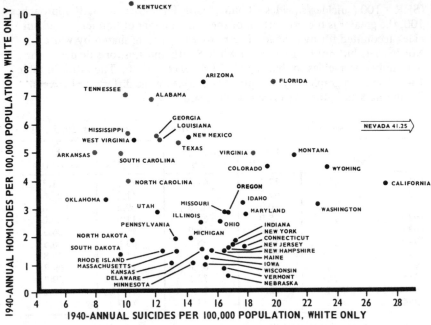

Figure 14-2.—Regional homogeneity in homicide-suicide ratios.

extremely high rates of violence among Negroes who constitute a large part
of the population. As table 14-1 indicates, however, Southern whites considered by themselves vary from the national norm in the same direction as
Negroes, though to a much lesser extent. In addition, Porterfield points out
that for the 12 Southern states with the heaviest Negro population, the
coefficient of correlation between serious crimes and the percentage of Negroes
in the population is –0.44. There is actually a tendency for states to rank
lower in serious crimes as the percentage of Negroes in the population
increases.[9]

A more sophisticated theory is that Southern white society contains a
larger proportion of lower status occupations so that the same factors that
cause lower status groups in the North to become more violent than the rest
of society have a proportionately greater effect on the South. The difference
in rates would then be accounted for by the numerical bulge in the high risk
group, and only the stratification of society would be peculiarly Southern.
Unfortunately for this theory, Southern cities, in which whites show the
distinctive pattern of Southern violence, actually have greater percentages of
the white population in higher status jobs than do Northern cities.[10] It is not
the class structure that causes the Southern skew in the statistics.

In the same way, the agricultural nature of Southern life might account for
the pattern of Southern violence. The fact that the peculiar configuration
exists in Southern cities as well as in the countryside could possibly be accounted for by the large migration into the city of people who learned their
ways of living and dying in the country. Table 14-2 shows that both homicide
and suicide rates are lower for rural districts than for urban areas in the
United States. This results in an SHR for the white population of rural dis-

Table 14-2.—Homicide and suicide rates by race and by size of population group,
United States, 1940

	U.S.	Cities 100,000 and Up	Cities 10 to 100,000	Cities 2,500-10,000	Rural
Suicide (all ages, both sexes):					
All races	14.4	16.8	15.6	15.1	12.0
White	15.5	17.8	16.4	16.0	13.3
Nonwhite	4.6	7.2	5.8	4.5	3.0
Homicide (all ages, both sexes):					
All races	6.2	7.1	5.7	7.3	5.7
White	3.1	3.2	2.5	3.7	3.3
Nonwhite	33.3	43.3	43.0	51.9	23.1

Source: Forrest E. Linder and Robert D. Grove, *Vital Statistics Rates in the United States, 1900-1940* (Washington: Government Printing Office, 1943). Table 24, pp. 534-553.

tricts considered by themselves of 80.1, as compared with an SHR of 83.7 for the white population of the nation as a whole. The SHR of 68.8 in 1940 for Southern whites, both urban and rural, is significantly lower than the national ratios and indicates that Southern whites were much more given to acting out their aggressions than the white population of either the cities or the countryside in the rest of the nation.

Another way of testing the notion that the rurality of the South may be the root of its strange configuration of violence is summarized in table 14-3, a comparison of the SHR's of the 11 ex-Confederate states with those of the 11 most rural non-Southern states. The non-Southern states, mostly Western, are closer in time to frontier days and are currently much more subject to instability caused by inmigration than are the Southern states, but otherwise the two sets of states are similar enough for purposes of comparison. The percentage of population living in the urban areas of the Southern states ranged from 13.4 percent to 36.7 percent with the mean falling at 26.1 percent, while in the 11 non-Southern states the degree of urbanization ranged from 13.6 percent to 36.7 percent, with the mean at 31.2 percent. In order not to distort the comparison more than necessary, Nevada, with an extraordinary suicide rate of 41.3 per 100,000 population, is omitted from the comparison. At the same time, Virginia and Florida, with very non-Southern SHR's, are retained in the Southern sample. The results still show a significant difference between the suicide-murder ratio of the Southern states and that of the most rural non-Southern states. The strange bent of Southern violence cannot be accounted for by the rural nature of Southern society.

Poverty is also a logical factor to suspect as the underlying cause of the South's pattern of violence. Howard Odum computed that the Southeast in 1930 had 20.9 percent of the nation's population but only 11.9 percent of the nation's wealth.[11] Whether or not the region was poor before it was violent is an undetermined matter. Even more to the point, poverty alone cannot explain high homicide rates. The decline of homicides during business depressions in the United States underlines this argument, as does the fact that crime rates among second-generation immigrants are much higher than among first-generation immigrants despite the fact of increased material welfare.[12]

Table 14-3.—Suicide and homicide rates and suicide-homicide ratios for Southern states and 11 most rural non-Southern states, 1940

Population group	Suicide-homicide ratio
Southern nonwhite	6.7
National nonwhite.	12.2
Southern white	68.8
Non-Southern, white rural (11 states).	79.0
National white rural.	80.1
National white	83.7

Southern states	White		Rural non-Southern states	White	
	Suicide rate	Homicide rate		Suicide rate	Homicide rate
Alabama	11.7	6.9	Arizona	15.2	7.5
Arkansas	8.0	5.1	Idaho	17.7	3.3
Florida	19.8	7.5	Iowa.	15.2	1.3
Georgia	12.1	5.6	Kansas	13.0	1.1
Louisiana	12.4	5.5	Montana	21.1	4.8
Mississippi	10.1	5.7	Nebraska	16.8	.7
North Carolina . . .	10.4	4.0	New Mexico	14.2	5.7
South Carolina . . .	9.7	5.0	North Dakota . . .	9.7	1.4
Tennessee	10.0	7.1	South Dakota . . .	10.5	1.8
Texas	13.6	5.3	Vermont	16.7	.8
Virginia	18.4	5.0	Wyoming	23.5	4.5
Average	12.4	5.6	Average	15.8	4.2

Source: Forrest E. Linder and Robert D. Grove, *Vital Statistics Rates in the United States, 1900-1940* (Washington: Government Printing Office, 1943), Table 20. All rates per 100,000 population.

One study has found no significant correlation between crime rates and the proportion of the population on relief by county in Minnesota, whereas there was a strong correlation between crime rates and the degree of urbanization. Like the rural poor in Minnesota, the Japanese of Seattle were poor but honest and nonviolent.[13]

Nevertheless, though the data are extremely questionable, there is a significant positive correlation between the SHR for the 56 world polities for which information is readily available and almost every measure of modernization that can be quantified.[14] It is difficult to determine whether it is underdevelopment or the process of change that accounts for this, for scholars have noted that the process of modernization generates conflict and violence of various sorts.[15] For developing as well as for industrialized nations, education is the most powerful predictor of a country's SHR, but indices of industrial and urban activity, along with reflections of the society's general welfare, are also significantly correlated with the SHR. This is true for the 56 world polities considered together as well as for the European nations considered as a group and for the non-European countries taken together. That Southerners over the past half century have been growing more similar to non-Southern Americans in their tastes in violence as the gap between the nation and the South in economic development has slowly narrowed also argues that there may be no increment of violence in the South that is not "explained" by the relative slowness of the region's development.

Multiple regression analysis offers a technique for testing the possibility that variations in the key indices of modernization operating in an additive fashion might account for the South's particularity in rates of violence. Six independent variables measuring the four factors of wealth, education, urbanization, and age are included in this analysis. Except where indicated below, their values are taken from the *United States Census* for 1940. Urbanization is stated as the percentage of the population living within towns of 2,500 or more; education is measured by the median number of school years completed by persons 25 years old and older; "income" is the state's per capita personal income in dollars for 1940; unemployment is expressed as the percentage of the working force out of work; "wealth" is the state's per capita income in dollars in 1950; and age is the median age of the population. The values of each variable except "income" are recorded by race. "South" is a dummy variable included in the analysis in order to see if any of the unexplained residue of the dependent variable is associated with the fact of its occurring either inside of or outside of the South. All of the ex-Confederate states were assigned the value of one, while all non-Southern states were recorded as zero. The dependent variables that require "explaining" are the suicide rate, the homicide rate, the sum of the suicide rate and homicide rate, and the suicide-homicide ratio. Even though these rates are taken from the most reliable source, *Vital Statistics for the United States*, there may well be large errors between the published rates and the true rates. Some violent deaths are never recorded, and many are improperly classified, but there is no reason to suspect that there has been a long-term, systematic bias in the collection and recording of the statistics for the Southern states. For the purposes of the crude comparison between South and non-South, the *Vital Statistics* are acceptable.

The results of the analysis are summarized in table 14-4. The coefficient of correlation between each of the independent variables and the dependent variable is found in the column labeled "simple." The percentage of the variation in the dependent variable that is associated with, and thus "explained" by, the variation in the independent variable is found by squaring the coefficient of correlation. For example, education is the best single predictor of the white suicide rate. The simple coefficient of correlation of 0.62 between education and suicide in table 14-4 indicates that approximately 30 percent of the variation in the white suicide rate among the 48 states in 1940 is associated with variations in the educational level of the populations. The fact that the correlation is positive means that the suicide rate tends to rise from one state to the next as the educational level rises. Conversely, the negative coefficients of correlation between each of the independent variables, except region, and the white homicide rate indicates that the homicide rate tends to decline as the indices of development rise.

The effect on the dependent variable of all of the independent variables considered together is measured by the coefficient of multiple correlation, R. Thus 72 percent of the white suicide rate and 52 percent of the white homicide rate are explained by the seven independent variables operating in an additive fashion. The coefficient of partial correlation expresses the relationship of each independent variable with the unexplained portion of the de-

Table 14-4.—Multiple regression analysis—violence, development, and sectionalism in the United States, 1940

Dependent variable by state	R² variation explained	Urbanization		Education		Income		Unemployment		Wealth		Age		South	
		Simple	Partial	Simple	Partial	Simple	Partial	Simple	Partial	Simple	Partial	Simple	Partial	Simple	Partial
White suicide rate	*0.72	.25	*-0.64	*0.62	0.52	*0.56	0.14	0.22	0.33	*0.53	0.35	*0.55	*0.59	-0.31	*0.42
White homicide rate . . .	*.52	*-.45	-.24	-.17	.09	-.42	.23	-.13	.26	-.42	-.12	*-.58	.24	*.54	.49
White homicide-suicide rate	*.57	.07	*-.59	.52	*.44	.36	.20	.15	.35	-.34	.22	-.30	*.41	-.09	*.50
White homicide-suicide ratio.	*.72	*.53	-.02	*.40	.11	*.63	-.24	.25	-.18	*.62	.29	*.76	.49	*-.68	*-.53
Nonwhite suicide rate. .	.30	.08	-.13	.30	.25	*.47	.26	.15	-.09	.34	-.00	.13	-.04	-.34	.08
Nonwhite homicide rate	.25	-.07	-.28	-.19	-.25	-.11	.18	-.17	.21	-.09	-.04	.04	*.40	.28	*.37
Nonwhite homicide-suicide rate	.22	-.02	-.30	-.03	-.12	.13	.27	-.08	.15	.09	-.04	.10	.35	.09	*.37
Nonwhite suicide-homicide rate.	.35	.27	.36	.36	.31	*.43	.18	.30	-.11	.36	-.10	.12	-.40	-.36	-.09

*The chances that a random ordering of the data would produce a relationship this strong are less than 1 in 100.

pendent variable after the independent variables acting collectively have done all the explaining possible. The coefficient of partial correlation for the dummy variable, South, is the most important yield of the multiple regression analysis.

Even though the seven independent variables acting together explain 72 percent of the variation of the white SHR among the 48 states in 1940, 28 percent ($r = -0.53$) of the remaining portion of the variation of the white SHR is associated with the South. This means that the white SHR is lower in the South than can be accounted for by the lower indices of urbanization, education, wealth, and age. Similarly, there is a significant portion of the variation from state to state in the white homicide rate, and in the white suicide rate, that is unexplained by variations in measures of development but that is explained by Southernness.

If the deviation of the South from the national norms for violence cannot be attributed to backwardness, or at least not to the static measures of underdevelopment, there are other possible explanations that should be considered. The concept of anomie, developed by Emil Durkheim in his study, *Suicide,* in 1898, is frequently mentioned as an explanation of both homicide and suicide. Anomie has meant slightly different but not contradictory things to different investigators. It is most generally understood to be a social condition in which there is a deterioration of belief in the existing set of rules of behavior, or in which accepted rules are mutually contradictory, or when prescribed goals are not accessible through legitimate means, or when cognition and socialization have been obstructed by personality traits that cluster about low ego strength.[16] In its manifestation in the individual, in the form of anomy, it is a feeling of normlessness and estrangement from other people. An anomic person feels lost, drifting without clearly defined rules and expectations, isolated, powerless, and frustrated. In this state, there is a strong strain toward deviant behavior in various forms. The problem is that both homicide and suicide are thought to be related to it, and the theory does not predict what sorts of people or what groups will favor one form of behavior rather than another.

To look at Southern violence as the product of anomie in any case would involve a great paradox. The most popular explanation of the high rates of American violence as compared to Europe places the blame on the rapid urbanization, secularization, and industrialization of the United States and on the social characteristics associated with this remarkable growth: geographic and status mobility, an emphasis upon contractual relationships and upon social norms rather than upon personal relationships, competitive striving, and a cultural pluralism that involves a high level of dissonance among the values that everyone tries to put into practice.[17] The South has traditionally served as the counterpoint to the American way of life for the reason that it seemed to differ from the North in these very aspects.[18] Southerners have a greater sense of history than Northerners, a greater attachment to place, and more deferential social customs. By all reports, Southerners place more emphasis on personal relations and on ascribed statuses than do Northerners. Not only do Southerners prize political and social cohesion, but by most measures the South is much more homogeneous than the non-South.[19] Yet, though the South differs from the North on so

many of the factors that supposedly contribute to anomie and thus to violence, the South is the nation's most violent region.

There is one body of theory that would seem to predict higher rates of
violence precisely because of the South's homogeneity. Reformulating the
observations of Georg Simmel and Bronislaw Malinowski, Lewis Coser writes
that "we may say that a conflict is more passionate and more radical when it
arises out of close relationships." "The closer the relationship," so the
reasoning goes, "the greater the effective investment, the greater also the
tendency to suppress rather than express hostile feelings. . . . In such cases
feelings of hostility tend to accumulate and hence intensify." Such a theory
fits the empirical observation that individuals who express hostility retain
fewer and less violent feelings of antagonism toward the source of their
irritation.[20] But Coser himself states that, though conflicts within close
relationships are likely to be intense when they occur, "this does not necessarily point to the likelihood of more *frequent* conflict in closer relationships
than in less close ones." There are situations in which accumulated hostilities
do not eventuate in conflict behavior and may even serve to solidify the
relationship.[21]

The frustration-aggression hypothesis involves similar perplexities.[22] For
example, one of the alternative ways of adapting to frustration is to turn the
frustration inward upon the self. In extreme cases this can result in suicide.[23]
A psychoanalyst has concluded after an extensive study that a major portion
of Sweden's very high suicide rate is caused by the frustrations arising from a
highly competitive, success-oriented society.[24] The general rise in suicide
rates in the United States during economic downturns argues that the same
mechanism is at work among some segments of the population. Consequently,
nothing in the frustration-aggression hypothesis predicts the direction the
aggression will take.

There are currently two theories that attempt to explain the generally inverse relationship between homicide and suicide as reactions to frustration.
The first, developed by Andrew F. Henry and James F. Short, Jr.,[25] is based
on the assumption that both homicide and suicide are the result of frustration-
aggression and builds upon Porterfield's initial suggestion that the strength of
the relational system might have something to do with an individual's choice
of either homicide or suicide.[26] Henry and Short adduce data on the relationship of homicide and suicide rates to the business cycle and to certain
statistically distinct groups. They reason that overt aggression against others
"varies directly with the strength of external restraint over the behavior of the
adult—external restraint which is a function of strength of the relational system and position in the status hierarchy."[27]

Martin Gold has pointed out, however, that contrary to the assumption of
Henry and Short, upper status people are likely to be more restrained by the
expectations of others than are lower status people. Even more damaging is
Gold's demonstration that the Henry and Short hypothesis does not correctly
predict the greater preference of women for suicide rather than homicide,[28]
nor does it correctly predict the fact that suicide rates are lower among the
middle classes than at either extreme of the social scale.

The second theory, fashioned by Martin Gold, attempts to relate differences in child rearing practices to preferences for hostility or guilt as an
accommodation to frustration. Specifically, Gold shows that there is a posi-

tive correlation between the incidence of physical punishment commonly used in the child-rearing practices of certain groups and the rate of homicide for that group. His conclusion is that physical disciplining of children leads to aggression against others rather than against the self.[27] To confound the theory, restrictive child-rearing practices in Europe evidently do not lead to the physical violence that such practices among the lower classes in America are supposed to produce. There is also considerable doubt that there is a significant class differential in the degree of physical punishment used to discipline children.[30] William and Joan McCord found in their study of juveniles that there was no strong relationship between disciplining methods and criminality except when a child is rejected by his parents or when his parents provide him with a deviant role model. Harsh discipline does less damage than neglect.[31] That there is some causal relationship between the socialization of aggression and a group's SHR is reason enough to suppose that it will provide a fruitful line of research, but before it can be a useful ingredient of an explanation of Southern violence, anthropologists and historians need to know much more about regional differences in child-rearing techniques.

Whether or not the cause can be located in child-rearing practices, several bodies of evidence point to the conclusion that Southern violence is a cultural pattern that exists separate from current influences. For instance, several commentators have suggested that the habit of carrying guns in the South made murder a much more frequent outcome of altercations among Southerners than among Northerners. This argument is buttressed by a 1968 survey, reported in table 14-5, which showed that 52 percent of Southern white families owned guns, as opposed to only 27 percent of the white families of the non-South. It may be, however, that this differential in gun ownership is the result of a violent turn of mind rather than the cause of violence. This is the implication of the fact that when the House of Representatives in 1968 passed a weak gun-control bill to restrict the mail-order sale of rifles, shotguns, and ammunition by the overwhelming vote of 304-118, representatives of the 11 ex-Confederate states nonetheless voted 73-19 against the bill.[32] It should be noted too that some Southern states have relatively strict firearms laws without dramatically affecting their homicide rates.[33] Furthermore, the assault rate is extremely high in the South, indicating that Southerners react with physical hostility even without guns.

A glance at table 14-4 reveals that for Negroes either the data are grossly skewed or there is little relationship between violence and the selected indices

Table 14-5.—*Percent of families owning firearms*

	Yes	No	Not sure
Total white	34	65	1
South	52	45	3
Non-South	27	72	1
Total nonwhite	24	70	6
South	34	61	5
Non-South	15	78	7

Source: Survey of national statistical sample by Opinion Research, Inc., for a Columbia Broadcasting System program Sept. 2, 1968.

of social welfare. There is the barest hint that, controlling for the selected factors, there is some explanatory value in sectionalism, a conclusion that has independent verification. Thomas F. Pettigrew and an associate found that the major correlate of the rate of Negro homicide in the North was the proportion of Negroes in a given area who had been born and raised in the South and that this was in addition to the effect of migration itself. It had long been known that homicide was much less frequent among Northern then among Southern Negroes, but this finding suggests that violence in the South is a style of life that is handed down from father to son along with the old hunting rifle and the family Bible.[34]

The great contribution to the discussion of Southern violence made by Wilbur J. Cash in his book, *The Mind of the South*, was precisely this, that Southern violence is part of a style of life that can be explained only historically.[35] According to Cash's own poetic and impressionistic rendering, violence grew up on the Southern frontier as naturally as it grows up on any frontier. Violence was an integral part of the romantic, hedonistic, hell-of-a-fellow personality created by the absence of external restraint that is characteristic of a frontier. The cult of honor, with its insistence on the private settlement of disputes, was one form taken by the radical individualism of the South, but there were other influences at work. The plantation, the most highly organized institution on the Southern frontier, reinforced the tendency toward violence that had been initiated by the absence of organization. This was so, Cash argues, for two reasons. In the first place, whites on the plantation exercised unrestrained dominance over blacks. In the second place, whites were generally raised by blacks and consequently were deeply influenced by the romantic and hedonistic Negro personality. Cash does not explicitly say what forces produced this Negro personality, but the implication is that Negro personality is fixed by the laws of genetics. But if the more likely position is taken that Negro and white personalities are shaped by environment and experience, then the reader is left with yet another Cashian paradox: violence in the white personality stems at the same time from the effect of being unrestrained and from imitating the Negro personality which was formed out of a situation of dependency and subordination.

It may be that the mediating variable that brings together the various inconsistencies in Cash's explanation of how violence came to be established in the late ante-bellum period as part of the Southern personality is the absence of law. Not disorganization nor individualism, not dominance nor submission, not lack of restraint—none of these forces played as important a role as the absence of institutions of law enforcement in forcing Southerners to resort to the private settlement of disputes. Cash makes this explicit in his treatment of Reconstruction, the second frontier.

During Reconstruction, according to Cash, Southern whites resorted to individual and collective violence because the courts were dominated by carpetbaggers and scalawags. Though this is logical, it is not consistent with Cash's earlier argument that the growth of law had been inhibited on the ante-bellum frontier by the desire of Southerners to provide their own justice. Apparently the direction of causation in the relationship between law and violence changes in accordance with the needs of Cash's interpretation.

Just as the first and second Southern frontiers simultaneously promoted social solidarity and individualism, the third Southern frontier, Progress, changed the South in the direction of the American norm of Babbittry while at the same time accommodating continuity in the basic traits of the Southern mind. A further paradox is involved in the impact of progress on the pattern of violence. Because violence originally arose from individualism, Cash says, the growth of towns should have brought a decrease in rates of violence. This decrease did not materialize because progress also brought poverty and poverty destroys individualism. Cash in effect argues that individualism produced violence in the ante-bellum period and the loss of individualism produced violence in the 20th century.

Though Cash failed to produce a coherent theory of Southern violence, he did focus on two factors that are obvious possibilities as the chief motive forces of Southern violence: the frontier experience and the presence of the Negro. The American frontier did spawn violence, but it seems improbable that the frontier could have much to do with the fact that in the 20th-century Southern states on the Eastern seaboard have much higher rates of violence than the nation at large. There is also considerable difficulty with the notion that the presence of large numbers of Negroes accounts for the great propensity of whites for violence. There is, in fact, very little interracial homicide,[36] and there is no reason to question John Dollard's hypothesis that Negroes murder and assault each other with such appalling frequency because of their daily frustrations in dealing with white men. Because aggressions against whites would call forth extreme negative sanctions, frustrated Negroes display their aggressive feelings to other Negroes.[37] If this is the case, it is difficult to see how high rates of violence among the dominant white group would also be attributed to the white-Negro relationship, especially when the presence of Negroes in the North is not accompanied by a proportionate rate of violence among the whites. It is also interesting that whites in South Africa who also experienced frontier conditions and a subordinate nonwhite population have a homicide-suicide ratio almost identical to the ratio for the American North but quite different from that of the Southern whites.

Subservience, rather than dominance, may be the condition that underlies a pattern of low SHR's. Franz Fanon, in his controversial book, *The Wretched of the Earth*, suggests that the oppressed status of a colonial people produced a pattern of aggressiveness directed against fellow colonials and a need to achieve manhood through violence. That task of revolutionaries is to mobilize the aggressive drives, provide them a sustaining ideology, and direct them against the oppressors.[38] The South's defeat in the Civil War and its position as an economic dependency of the industrial Northeast qualifies it for consideration as a violent colonial region. In addition to the difficulty of separating the effects of subserviency from the effects of sheer underdevelopment, the problem with this line of reasoning is that the heroic myths created about the "Lost Cause" and the relatively early return of home rule after the Civil War may have mitigated the trauma of defeat and social dislocation. It would be difficult to maintain that the South's historical experience as a region is the equivalent of the sort of cultural conflict that leads to the loss of self-esteem, disrupts the processes of socialization, and initiates the cycle of self-crippling behavior within the subordinate group.[39] Furthermore, American Indians have responded to their experience of defeat and repression with higher rates of suicide and other intrapunitive behavior rather than with aggression against others. Similarly, while industrialization was transforming

and disrupting its established folk culture, Harlan County, Ky., had the highest
homicide rates in the country, but a study of community growth in New
England finds suicide and depressive disorders highly correlated with the
disruptive impact of geographic mobility.[40]

Though the social sciences offer no clearly authenticated hypothesis that
predicts the relationship in different populations between homicide and
suicide rates,[41] there are some potentially illuminating investigations currently in progress. Assuming that depressed mental patients are people who
have turned anger inward through the mechanism of introjection and guilt
when under chronic stress, while paranoid patients are those who have turned
anger outward through the mechanism of denial and projection, one study has
found an interesting association between the pattern of intrafamily communication and the direction taken by mental pathology when it occurred. Depressed patients in this study came from families in which the children were
forced to try by themselves to attain the desired forms of behavior through
positive, "ought" channels. Children in the families of paranoid patients
were forced into acceptable modes of behavior by negative "ought not"
procedures.

"In families of *depressed* patients the child comes to view his environment
as non-threatening to him physically. It is something to be manipulated by
him in order to bring about the desired effects that will win approval. There
is directionality here, and it is *from* the child *toward* his environment. On
the other hand, in families of *paranoid* patients the child comes to view his
environment as having potentially harmful properties that he cannot control
and that must be avoided in some way. Here the directionality is *from* the
environment *toward* the child."[42]

The hypothesis is that a manipulative attitude toward the environment
will be associated with intrapunitive behavior and that a passive attitude
toward the environment, with the absence of the internalization of a feeling
of responsibility for the self, will be correlated with a greater use of projection in ego-defense.

There are firm indications that cultural patterning as well as child-rearing
techniques will affect the perception of the environment and the orientation
of the personality on the paranoia-depression continuum. In Burma, a
hierarchical and age-graded society, the social and physical environment is
typically perceived as potentially harmful, and Burma has one of the highest
homicide rates in the world.[43] There is also the possibility of a connection
between the high rates of violence among Afro-Americans and the recent
diagnosis that the Negro psyche has been rendered paranoic by the hostile
American environment.[44]

Testing the hypothesis that a paranoidal perception of the environment is
the root cause of the pattern of violence in the white South is a problem for
future scholarship. The most immediately useful technique would be an
opinion survey of attitudes toward violence, perceptions of the environment,
feelings of personal efficacy, and other measures of alienation. There may be
regional differentials in these categories as well as class, age, and sexual differentials. A rigorous comparison of rates of violence in perhaps a Kentucky
county and an Ohio county at comparable stages of settlement is also a
promising approach. The records of the county court, the reports of the
state attorney general, and newspaper surveys might produce useful data on

individual as well as collective violence. Some effort must be made to determine when the South became violent. The timing may reveal much about the relationship of slavery to violence. The possible effects of Scotch-Irish immigration, population density, temperature, and religious fundamentalism should be investigated with quantitative methods. Even though the SHR's of Australia and Canada fit the European mold, some insight may derive from pursuing such comparative cases in a detailed manner. There is much that can be done.

Meanwhile, in the search for a valid explanation of Southern violence the most fruitful avenue will probably be one that seeks to identify and trace the development of a Southern world view that defines the social, political, and physical environment as hostile and casts the white Southerner in the role of the passive victim of malevolent forces. When scholars locate the values that make up this world view and the process by which it was created and is transmitted, the history of the South will undoubtedly prove to have played a major role. The un-American experiences of guilt, defeat, and poverty will be major constituents of the relevant version of that history,[45] but perhaps they will not loom so large as the sense of grievance that is at the heart of the Southern identity.

The South was created by the need to protect a peculiar institution from threats originating outside the region. Consequently, the Southern identity has been linked from the first to a siege mentality. Though Southerners have many other identities, they are likely to be most conscious of being Southerners when they are defending their region against attack from outside forces: abolitionists, the Union Army, carpetbaggers, Wall Street and Pittsburgh, civil-rights agitators, the Federal Government, feminism, socialism, trade unionism, Darwinism, communism, atheism, daylight saving time, and other byproducts of modernity. This has made for an extreme sensitivity to criticism from outsiders and a tendency to excuse local faults as the products of forces beyond human control or beyond local control. If the South was poor, it was because the Yankees stole all the family silver and devastated the region in other ways after the Civil War. If industrialization seemed inordinately slow in the South, it was because of a conspiracy of Northern capitalists to maintain the South as an economic colony. Added to this experience with perceived threats has been the fact that almost every significant change in the life of the South has been initiated by external powers. This is even true of industrialization. Though there was a fervent native movement to sponsor industrialization, absentee ownership has been characteristic. Furthermore, the real qualitative change in the Southern pattern of low value-added industry came as a result of World War II and the activities of the Federal Government.

Being Southern, then, inevitably involves a feeling of persecution at times and a sense of being a passive, insignificant object of alien or impersonal forces. Such a historical experience has fostered a world view that supports the denial of responsibility and locates threats to the region outside the region and threats to the person outside the self. From the Southern past arises the symbiosis of profuse hospitality toward strangers and the paradox that the Southern heritage is at the same time one of grace and violence.

References

1. For example, see Charles O. Lerche, Jr., *The Uncertain South: Its Changing Patterns of Politics in Foreign Policy* (Chicago, 1964), pp. 48-49. Representative comments can be found in: John Richard Alden, *The South in the Revolution, 1763-1789* (Baton Rouge, 1957), pp. 34-35, and 41; Clement Eaton, *A History of the Old South* (2d ed., New York, 1966), pp. 260, 395, 404, 407, and 415; John Hope Franklin, *The Militant South, 1800-1861* (Cambridge, Mass., 1956); David Bertelson, *The Lazy South* (New York, 1967), pp. 101-113, and 241; and H. V. Redfield, *Homicide, North and South: Being a Comparative View of Crime Against the Person in Several Parts of the United States* (Philadelphia, 1880).
2. A stimulating essay on this theme is Frank Vandiver, "The Southerner as Extremist," in Frank Vandiver, ed., *The Idea of the South* (Chicago, 1964), pp. 43-56. A lighter treatment of the same subject is Erskine Caldwell, "The Deep South's Other Venerable Tradition," *New York Times Magazine* (July 11, 1965).
3. "The Pattern of Violence," in W. T. Couch, ed., *Culture in the South* (Chapel Hill, 1934), pp. 678-692; and *Homicide in the United States* (Chapel Hill, 1932).
4. Stuart Lottier, "Distribution of Criminal Offenses in Sectional Regions," *Journal of Criminal Law and Criminology*, vol. XXIX (Sept.-Oct. 1938), pp. 329-344.
5. Lyle Shannon, "The Spatial Distribution of Criminal Offenses by States," *Journal of Criminal Law and Criminology*, vol. XLV (Sept.-Oct. 1954), pp. 264-273.
6. Louis I. Dublin and Bessie Bunzel, *To Be or Not To Be: A Study of Suicide* (New York, 1933), pp. 80 and 413.
7. Austin Porterfield, "Indices of Suicide and Homicide by States and Cities: Some Southern-Non-Southern Contrasts with Implications for Research," *American Sociological Review*, vol. XIV (Aug. 1949), pp. 481-490.
8. *Ibid.*, p. 485.
9. Austin Porterfield, "A Decade of Serious Crimes in the United States," *American Sociological Review*, vol. XIII (Feb. 1948), pp. 44-54. See also James E. McKeown, "Poverty, Race, and Crime," *Journal of Criminal Law and Criminology*, vol. XXXIX (Nov.-Dec. 1948), pp. 480-483.
10. Norval D. Glenn, "Occupational Benefits to Whites From the Subordination of Negroes," *American Sociological Review*, vol. XXVIII (June 1963), pp. 443-448. See particularly table 1.
11. *Southern Regions of the United States* (Chapel Hill, 1936), p. 208.
12. Edwin H. Sutherland and Donald R. Cressey, *Principles of Criminology* (6th ed., New York, 1960), pp. 92 and 146-149.
13. Van B. Shaw, "The Relationship Between Crime Rates and Certain Population Characteristics in Minnesota Counties," *Journal of Criminal Law and Criminology*, vol. XL (May-June 1949), pp. 43-49.
14. Simple intercorrelations were run between the indices of homicide and suicide and measures of social and economic activity using data from: Bruce M. Russett *et al.*, eds., *World Handbook of Political and Social Indicators* (New Haven, 1964); and Statistical Office of the United Nations Department of Economic and Social Affairs, *Demographic Yearbook, 1963* (New York, 1964), table 25, pp. 592-611.
15. Richard S. Weinert, "Violence in Pre-Modern Societies: Rural Columbia," *The American Political Science Review*, vol. LX (June 1966), pp. 340-347; Harry Eckstein, ed., *Internal War* (New York, 1964); E. J. Hobsbawm, *Primitive Rebels* (New York, 1959). An important synthesis and statement of theory is Ted Gurr, "Psychological Factors in Civil Violence," *World Politics*, vol. XX (Jan. 1968), pp. 245-278.
16. Herbert McCloskey and John H. Schaar, "Psychological Dimensions of Anomy," *American Sociological Review*, vol. XXX (Feb. 1965), pp. 14-40.
17. David Abrahamsen, *The Psychology of Crime* (New York, 1960), pp. 18-21 and 177-183. These relationships are greatly illuminated by the discussion in David M. Potter, *People of Plenty: Economic Abundance and the American Character* (Chicago, 1954).

18. William H. Taylor, *Cavalier and Yankee: The Old South and American National Character* (Garden City. N.Y., 1963); C. Vann Woodward, "A Southern Critique for the Gilded Age," *The Burden of Southern History* (Baton Rouge, 1960), pp. 109-140.

19. Jack P. Gibbs and Walter T. Martin, *Status Integration and Suicide: A Sociological Study* (Eugene, Ore., 1964), particularly table 6, p. 54.

20. Lewis A. Coser, *The Functions of Social Conflict* (New York, 1956), pp. 57, 62, and 71; Albert Pepitone and George Reichling, "Group Cohesiveness and Expression of Hostility," in Neil J. Smelser and William T. Smelser, *Personality and Social Systems* (New York, 1963), pp. 117-124.

21. Coser, *The Functions of Social Conflict,* p. 72.

22. John Dollard, Neil E. Miller, Leonard W. Doob, O. H. Mowrer, and Robert R. Sears, *Frustration and Aggression* (New Haven, 1939); Leonard Berkowitz, *Aggression: A Social Pyschological Analysis* (New York, 1962); Aubrey J. Yates, *Frustration and Conflict* (New York, 1962).

23. Karl Menninger, *Man Against Himself* (New York, 1938), p. 23. The assumption that homicide and suicide are simply aggressions manifested in different directions is the basis of the concept of the suicide-homicide ratio.

24. Herbert Hendin, *Suicide and Scandinavia: A Psychoanalytic Study of Culture and Character* (Garden City, N.Y., 1965), ch. 5.

25. *Suicide and Homicide: Some Economic, Sociological, and Psychological Aspects of Aggression* (Glencoe, Ill., 1954).

26. Porterfield, "Indices of Suicide and Homicide by States and Cities," p. 488.

27. Henry and Short, *Suicide and Homicide,* p. 119.

28. Martin Gold, "Suicide, Homicide, and the Socialization of Aggression," *The American Journal of Sociology,* vol. LXIII (May 1958), pp. 651-661. Gold originated the SHR, which he called the suicide murder ratio.

29. *Ibid.*

30. Melvin L. Kohn, "Social Class and the Exercise of Parental Authority," in Smelser and Smelser, *Personality and Social Systems,* pp. 297-314; Martha Sturm White, "Social Class, Child Rearing Practices, and Child Behavior," *ibid.,* pp. 286-296; Bernard C. Rosen and Roy D'Andrade, "The Psychosocial Origins of Achievement Motivation," *Sociometry,* vol. XXII (1959), pp. 185-215, cited in Marshall B. Clinard, ed., *Anomic and Deviant Behavior: A Discussion and Critique* (New York, 1964), pp. 260-261. Bernard Berelson and Gary A. Steiner, *Human Behavior: An Inventory of Scientific Findings* (New York, 1964), pp. 479-481.

31. William McCord and Joan McCord, *Origins of Crime: A New Evaluation of the Cambridge-Somerville Youth Study* (New York, 1959), pp. 172 and 198.

32. *New York Times,* July 25, 1968.

33. Carl Bakal, *The Right to Bear Arms* (New York, 1966), pp. 346-353.

34. Thomas F. Pettigrew and Rosalind Barclay Spier, "The Ecological Structure of Negro Homicide," *The American Journal of Sociology,* vol. LXVII (May 1962), pp. 621-629.

35. Wilbur J. Cash, *The Mind of the South* (New York, 1940, Vintage edition, 1960), pp. 32-34, 44-52, 76, 115-123, 161, 220, 424.

36. Marvin E. Wolfgang, *Patterns in Criminal Homicide* (Philadelphia, 1958), pp. 222-236.

37. John Dollard, *Caste and Class in a Southern Town* (3d ed., Garden City, N.Y., 1949), ch. 13.

38. Franz Fanon, *The Wretched of the Earth* (New York, 1963).

39. Thomas Stone, Dorthea C. Leighton, and Alexander H. Leighton, "Poverty and the Individual," in Leo Fishman, ed., *Poverty and Affluence* (New Haven, 1966), pp. 72-96.

40. Paul Frederick Cressey, "Social Disorganization and Reorganization in Harlan County, Kentucky," *American Sociological Review.* vol. XIV (June 1949), pp. 389-394; Henry Wechsler, "Community Growth, Depressive Disorders, and Suicide," *The American Journal of Sociology,* vol. LXVII (July 1961), pp. 9-16.

41. Jack O. Douglas, *The Social Meanings of Suicide* (Princeton, 1967), pp. 3-160.

42. Hazel M. Hitson and Daniel H. Funkenstein, "Family Patterns and Paranoidal
     Personality Structure in Boston and Burma," *The International Journal of
     Social Psychiatry,* vol. V (Winter 1959).
43. *Ibid.*
44. William H. Grier and Price M. Cobbs, *Black Rage* (New York, 1968).
45. C. Vann Woodward, "The Search for Southern Identity," *The Burden of Southern
     History,* pp. 3-26.

PART VI

INTERNATIONAL CONFLICT AND INTERNAL STRIFE

Psychoanalysts no sooner popularized the concept of displacement than some scholars made an analytic leap of faith to propose that wars represented a displacement of aggressions within the community onto foreign enemies. Conflict theorists, relying more on reason than faith, suggested that in the face of external conflict, members of a community were likely to join ranks and minimize their differences. Some factually oriented sociologists and political scientists pointed out that unsuccessful wars had frequently led to revolutionary movements: for example, in Russia in 1918, in Bavaria the next year, and Italy several years after that. Opponents of the war in Vietnam have suggested that the increase in domestic turmoil in recent years is the work of those who take their cues from the international actions of the government.

Some cautions, but no definitive answers, for grand theorizing about connections between external and internal conflicts are suggested by the examination of the historical and contemporary experience of the United States in the following two chapters. Robin Brooks points out that some of the wars the United States has fought have been accompanied by direct internal protest, others not. When specifically antiwar protest has occurred, its immediate sources have been the belief that a particular war was unjust, and resentment against its contingent requirements of conscription and material support. Opposition on both grounds was especially widespread during the Civil War, in both the North and the South; during World War I; and during the Vietnam war. In the latter two wars the protesters seldom resorted to violence on their own

initiative. They were however frequent targets of
retaliatory violence by groups of outraged citizens
and by the police and military. Despite the historical continuity of American antiwar protest, and
especially of the patterns of severe governmental
response, Brooks concludes that the contemporary
anti-Vietnam protest is of such an unprecedented
magnitude and reflects such a broad constituency
that historical guidelines have little to tell us.

Raymond Tanter examines systematically the
relations between the Vietnam involvement and the
incidence of various forms of domestic turmoil.
His evidence supports the obvious connection:
that periods of escalation were accompanied by a
high incidence of antiwar protest. Less obviously,
opposition has not increased consistently with the
absolute level or duration of the war. Brooks'
paper provides an important qualification to the
last point: although the incidence of war protest
may not have increased as the war has dragged on,
the most militant protestors have come increasingly to challenge the legitimacy of the political
system that conducts the war and to assert their
willingness to use violence to oppose it.

The evidence for an association between the Vietnam war and the supposed breakdown of norms
that has led to domestic turmoil other than antiwar protest is inconclusive, in Professor Tanter's
judgment. Crimes, strikes, and urban riots have
seasonal fluctuations that are more striking than
any correspondence with events in Vietnam. Urban
riots were most numerous in the years of escalation,
but it is at best a hypothesis that the phenomena
are related.

Chapter 15

DOMESTIC VIOLENCE AND AMERICA'S WARS: AN HISTORICAL INTERPRETATION

By Robin Brooks*

INTRODUCTION

This essay analyzes the domestic protest and violence that erupted in response to American involvement in the nine major wars carried on by the United States since 1775: the Revolution, the War of 1812, the Mexican War, the Civil War, the Spanish-American War, World Wars I and II, the Korean war, and the current war in Vietnam. The focus is further limited to include only those conflicts with a clearly antiwar component—e.g., the New York City Draft Riots of 1863—while excluding the racial violence of World Wars I and II and the ghetto rebellions of the last 4 years. Violence initiated by opponents of the war or by those who support it—whether civilians, police, or military—is examined, but not technically nonviolent events like the legal repression of draft resisters or the relocation of Japanese-Americans in 1942. Further, a distinction is made between violence that in effect represents support for the other side in internecine conflicts like the Civil War or the American Revolution, and violence arising from opposition to war beyond America's borders or to the means by which it is carried on. The inquiry seeks to understand why there have been so few antiwar riots in the American past, despite much opposition to American wars, and to draw some conclusions about similarities and differences between antiwar violence during the present conflict, and that in our past.

HISTORICAL RETROSPECT

Opposition to the Revolution

The American Revolutionary era is replete with violence involving mobs and unofficial bodies of men. Before the actual outbreak of the Revolution,

*Robin Brooks is associate professor of history at San Jose State College, where he specializes in the American Revolution and the Early National period. His publications include "Alexander Hamilton, Melancton Smith, and the Ratification of the New York Constitution," *William and Mary Quarterly*, 3d series, vol. XXIV (Oct. 1967).

numerous violent outbreaks occurred: the Boston Massacre, the Gaspé
incident, the Regulator movement, tenant riots in Westchester County, N.Y.,
and the mobbing of Stamp Act collectors, to cite just a few. During the war
itself, bloody conflicts between Tories and Whigs occurred frequently in New
York, the Carolinas, and along the frontier. But these seemed to have involved
less opposition to the war itself than a taking of sides in a civil war. None of
them, I believe, fits the criteria of an antiwar riot.

The so-called "Fort Wilson" riot, in Philadelphia, October 4-6, 1779, is
somewhat more difficult to categorize. The origins of the Fort Wilson riot
might be described as a popular movement to punish some opponents of war,
but it quickly moved beyond that limitation. After the British evacuated
Philadelphia, early in 1779, popular resentment against suspected Tories
mounted. The suspects included some Quakers, at once conscientious opponents of war, but also British sympathizers and wealthy merchants. When
the Pennsylvania government's appointed committee did not seem to be
acting effectively, the popular militia moved to take the law into its own
hands. Its committee, composed of one man from each company, moved
swiftly against Tories—and also against "engrossers, monopolizers, and those
who sympathized with them, as well as certain lawyers who had appeared as
counsel for the accused at the Tory trials."[1] Placards appeared, denouncing
several prominent leaders of the Revolution, among them Declaration of
Independence signers Robert Morris (speculating in flour) and James Wilson
(lawyer for the Tories).

The militia committee and its sympathizers, after attempting in vain to find
leaders among prominent radicals like painter Charles Wilson Peale, set out to
punish the evildoers. After arresting several suspects, including a number of
Quakers, they headed toward the home of James Wilson. Wilson's friends,
among them some of the most prominent Philadelphia Whigs, had armed and
barricaded themselves in his house. The mob approached, and one of its
leaders, a ship's joiner, disclaimed any intention of attacking Wilson, he explained that they supported the constitution of Philadelphia, but that "the
laboring part of the city had become desperate from the high price of the
necessaries of life."[2] The procession marched on and had mostly passed
Wilson's house when a member of the garrison, a Captain Campbell, opened a
window and waved a pistol at the crowd. Who fired first is not known, but
in the exchange of shots Campbell was mortally wounded. A battle ensued
with casualties on both sides, quelled only when the Philadelphia Light-Horse
Cavalry, led by Gen. Joseph Reed, the state's chief executive, charged upon
and dispersed the mob.

Twenty-seven of its number were jailed, while Wilson and his fellow defenders left town. Many returned—Wilson prudently accepted his friends'
counsel to stay away—to organize plans for dealing with the militia, whose
officers had proposed violent measures to free their friends. This action was
forestalled when the militiamen were set free on bail, and General Reed
managed to conciliate both sides. Ultimately no one was prosecuted, as the
Assembly declared an Act of Amnesty for all implicated persons. In summa-
tion, the riot was only peripherally connected with opposition to war, and
more clearly a case of class or economic conflict.[3]

In Dutchess County, N.Y., during July 1776, and again in Columbia County
in August 1777, farmers took up arms against Revolutionary authorities, and

were suppressed after some fighting. But is it not possible to discern from the fragmentary surviving records whether they acted out of opposition to the war per se, which fell harshly upon them in requisitioning goods and supplies and in sometimes requiring military service as a proof of loyalty, or whether their actions were simply an expression of economic grievances or of loyalty to His Majesty George III.[4] Nor can we find clear-cut evidence of civilian riots against the British authorities occupying New York and other cities. On balance, it appears there was very little antiwar violence of kind that might usefully be compared to that of our own time.

The War of 1812 and the Mexican War

The War of 1812, in contrast, is neatly organized for the purposes of our study. It furnished one major and one minor riot, plus a fine scholarly explanation of the sources of social cleavage of the day.

The Baltimore Federalist newspaper, the *Federal Republican*, published a harsh critique of President Madison and the Republican Party for the declaration of war against Britain, just a few days after the event. A loyal mob promptly destroyed the editor's house and his press, forcing him to flee to the District of Columbia. But other Baltimore Federalists, taking a principled stand for freedom of the press and their right to express their antiwar opinions, arranged to have another issue of the paper (published in Washington) circulated in Baltimore and carrying a Baltimore address on the masthead. They shut themselves up in the house they named, armed, and prepared to defend their rights. On July 27, 1812, the mob attacked the twenty defenders. After a sharp battle, in which some of the attackers were killed or wounded, the mob brought up cannon. The mayor's intervention, with cavalry, halted the action. He then persuaded the Federalists to go to jail to await trial. Inexplicably, the troops protecting the jail were called off—other members of the city militia had refused to serve—thereby exposing the prisoners to renewed attack. The mob—led by two butchers— broke into the jail, took out the prisoners, and beat them savagely. Eight were beaten into insensibility and tossed into a heap in front of the jail, from where the mob refused to allow them to be removed until noon the next day. General Lingan, a hero of the Revolution, was beaten to death. Gen. Henry Lee, former Governor of Virginia, colleague of Washington, and father of Robert E. Lee, nearly suffered the same fate; almost 2 months later he could neither talk nor eat solid food. Other Federalists were manhandled and tortured for hours before finally escaping or being released. No punishment was visited upon the mob.[5]

In direct response to this event, New Englanders opposed to the war took revenge on one of their own. On August 3, 1812, Massachusetts Congressman Charles Turner, who had voted for war, returned to his home in Plymouth. In addition to being a Republican Congressman, he was also Chief Justice of Sessions for Plymouth County. This made no difference to his antiwar Federalist neighbors, who seized him on the main street and kicked him through the town.[6]

Neither Henry Adams, in his great history of the period, nor the histories of any of the major towns record any other mob action during the War of 1812. But Roger N. Brown, in *The Republic in Peril: 1812,* offers an explanation of the bitter cleavage in politics. He contends that Federalists and Republicans were deeply divided, each certain that the other side had the worst motives—for going to war or for opposing it—in mind, and that each side was prepared to go to almost any lengths to frustrate its enemies: "Republican and Federalist views of party opposites are largely false . . . wild parodies of the truth." Such views stem from "personal inexperience with political parties that encouraged men to identify opponents with their fears." What experience they had, "derived as it was from history and the factional contests of the colonial period, instinctively presumed prolonged opposition to rest on selfish, even traitorous motives. . . . Eighteenth-century political thought extolled the blessings of the harmonious commonwealth and condemned sustained organized party activity" for ignoring the common good in pursuit of power.[7]

Given such sharp polarization as Brown describes, why do we find such little violence during the War of 1812? One explanation might lie in the comparatively high degree of consensus within each section; e.g., Baltimore was overwhelmingly Federalist, so that no opposition dared raise its head after the riots. But such an explanation does not explain why violence did not flare up in the marginal areas. Perhaps a more useful explanation might run counter to Brown's, to suggest that many people did not care much about the war one way or the other, while the open, legitimate, and effective channels of expression—the press and the political system—afforded adequate outlets for the concerned minorities.

At least this is the explanation offered by Charles G. Sellers for the lack of antiwar riots during the Mexican War.[8] (There may have been some such incidents, but a sampling of the press and periodicals, diaries, town histories, and other secondary accounts does not reveal any of which I am aware.) The Mexican War also elicited sectional cleavage, very similar to that of 1812, with New England largely opposed and the South and West largely in favor. But because political opinion could easily be translated into effective protest and political movements, Sellers suggests, there would be little cause for riots on the part of those opposed to the war. Since the actual fighting from the outbreak of the war until the capture of Mexico City lasted less than 18 months and produced an uninterrupted string of U.S. victories, we might speculate that antiwar protests would be less than desperate while prowar groups could afford to be tolerant of misguided scrupulousness.

The Civil War

The Civil War, of course, is quite another matter. Replete with all sorts of violence arising from opposition to the war, both North and South, it confronts the historian with the need to make fine distinctions about the purposes of the participants. Only a few days after the firing on Fort Sumter had initiated the conflict, some 10,000 Confederate sympathizers in Baltimore, carrying the Stars and Bars at their head, attacked approximately 2,000 Union troops from Massachusetts and Pennsylvania who were passing through "mobtown" en route to Washington, D.C. The soldiers opened fire to protect themselves, but it took the resolute action of the Baltimore police to enable them to escape the fury of the mob. At least 12 citizens and 4 soldiers died in the affray. Yet this conflict belongs properly to the history of the Civil

War itself, rather than to the category of antiwar violence.[9] Subsequently French S. Evans, who had been a well-known newspaper editor before the war, fled Baltimore to escape an irate mob prepared to punish him for the expression of pro-Union sentiments.[10]

Similarly, many actions of Unionists in the South might properly fall within the category of pro-Northern demonstration rather than that of antiwar protest. Georgia Lee Tatum's *Disloyalty in the Confederacy* tells us that in almost every State of the Confederacy, conscription roused bitter opposition among the poor whites. The German areas of Texas, the mountains of Appalachia and the Ozarks, and the swamps of Florida all became centers for deserters and the disaffected from which guerrilla warfare emanated and into which Confederate recruiting officers and provost marshals could venture only with the escort of the Army. Let us consider three events which might be considered as reflecting in some measure antiwar violence.

Western North Carolina was originally a source of loyalty to the Confederacy. But when the conscription law omitted owners of 20 or more slaves from its purview, disaffection flared up. W. W. Holden, editor of the Raleigh *Standard*, became the leader of the antiwar movement in the state, writing editorials that came perilously close to treason in the eyes of many. On September 9, 1863, a detachment of Georgia troops en route through Raleigh attacked the office of the *Standard*. The next day a Unionist mob attacked and destroyed the Raleigh *State Journal*, the pro-Confederate paper in town. Although Governor Vance maintained a neutral attitude during this period of strife, Holden ran against him as a peace candidate for Governor in 1864. Those voting for Holden in some areas where pro-Confederate sentiment still ran strong found themselves subjected to what one of the state's historians euphemistically called "violent unpopularity."[11]

German settlers around Austin, Texas, generally opposed the Confederate cause. Draftees at Industry, Texas (in Austin County), in December 1862, attacked a Confederate officer and drove him away, after which they organized armed bodies to defend themselves, threatening to destroy those of their fellow Germans who were loyal to the Confederacy.[12] At the same time, citizens of Randolph County, in northern Alabama, defied the Conscription Act. Led by their very active Peace Society, an armed mob raided the county jail forcibly to free arrested deserters.[13]

Opposition to conscription proved to be the major source of mob violence in the North, too. German immigrants in Port Washington, Wisconsin, attacked a draft commissioner, destroyed draft machinery, and sacked the homes of prominent Republicans until dispersed by troops. This story could be repeated in almost every midwestern state. One enrolling officer was killed in Indiana, another in Wisconsin. An Irish mob in Chicago manhandled a U.S. marshal.[14]

But the most notorious case of all was the great New York City Draft Riot, of July 13-17, 1863, one which dwarfs by comparison all contemporary racial or antiwar violence. Estimates of the size of the mobs, which fought police, militia, and federal troops, run as high as 50,000. Its most recent chronicler suggests total deaths were as many as 1,300 and damage above $5 million, while acknowledging that these must remain imprecise estimates. Official records list 18 persons killed by the rioters, 11 of them Negroes; but more than 70 persons, most of them Negro, were reported missing, and many of them were never accounted for. Nor is there agreement about the general causes of the riot. The Conscription Act, of course, provided the occasion, as it went into operation only 2 days before the eruption of the riots. But the vicious persecution of blacks by the mobs, largely made up of poor Irish immigrants, indicates that the identification of the Civil War with the cause of Emancipation was a major factor, compounded by competition for jobs and status at the bottom of the urban pecking order. Class animosity entered into the equation, too, because the $300-exemption clause made the war into "a rich man's war but a poor man's fight."[15]

New York City was not the only center of antidraft rioting in the East. Irish miners in the anthracite coalfields of Pennsylvania rioted; so did Connecticut draftees.[16] But the draft was not the only source of antiwar violence during the Civil War; the organized peace movement in the North also led to violence.

Clement Vallandigham, Ohio Peace Democratic Congressman, proved the main focus of antiwar agitation in the North. On May 1, 1863, Union troops arrested Vallandigham in his hometown of Dayton for a speech denouncing the war. A mob of his sympathizers burned down the proadministration paper, the Dayton *Journal* (and when the fire got out of hand, a good bit more of the town). Federal troops were called in to quell the rioting, and did so after killing one member of the mob. In Indianapolis that same month, a pro-Vallandigham rally was broken up by armed soldiers with considerable violence erupting, none of it fatal.[17]

Many antiwar demonstrations and rallies suffered a similar fate. As early as August 16, 1961, veterans (of 3 months' service) broke up a peace meeting in Saybrook, Connecticut. At Stepney, in the same state, loyalist from Bridgeport led by P. T. Barnum and sewing-machine heir Elias Howe, Jr., attacked a meeting and tore down its peace flag. Returning to Bridgeport, despite the pleas of Barnum and Howe, the mob, now swelled to over 8,000, destroyed the Copperhead Bridgeport *Farmer*.[18] Other Copperhead papers like the Columbus [Ohio] *Crisis*, the Dubuque [Iowa] *Herald*, and the Chicago *Times* suffered from attacks by soldiers and civilians. But in both Connecticut and in the Midwest, federal crackdowns on the peace movement—involving violation of due process for those arrested by suspension of habeas corpus and arbitrary incarceration without trial—succeeded in destroying organized peace activity in the North.[19] David Donald has ascribed the greater ability of the North than the South to suppress opposition to an excess of democracy in the Confederacy; I suspect that the victories of Grant and Sherman in 1863 and 1864 also played a large part, insofar as "nothing succeeds like success."[20]

The Spanish-American War

The Spanish-American War—John Hay's "splendid little war"—was effectively over in 3 months. It had been enormously popular to begin with, and cost only 379 battle casualties (although more than 5,000 Americans died from disease and food poisoning), so it should be no surprise to discover that there was no antiwar violence. Curiously, there was considerable opposition in high places to the war's imperial fruits—the annexation of Puerto Rico, the Philippines, etc. Mark Twain, Andrew Carnegie, William James, House Speaker Thomas Reed, and E. L. Godkin, editor of the *Nation,* were all active in the Anti-Imperialist movement. But none of these men could have—and none showed the slightest interest in—organized popular antiwar violence, and none was forthcoming from any other source.[21]

World War I

Opponents of War, 1917-1918, by H. C. Peterson and Gilbert C. Fite, provides an outstanding treatment of antiwar violence during World War I. The persistence and scale of violence, as well as the social base of opposition to this war, make it the nearest thing to a parallel with the present situation. But it differs sharply with the present in that almost every case of violence occurred when patriotic mobs attacked opponents of war. From the long and appalling list of incidents compiled by Peterson and Fite, I could find only the following two in which the initiative for violence appeared to originate with the antiwar movement.

An anticonscription meeting of 2,000 persons in New York City on June 15, 1917, almost led to a riot. Word that soldiers and sailors had surrounded the hall and intended to question members of the audience as they came out caused a near panic. According to the New York *Times* report, the servicemen who tried to block the doors were hit by flying wedges of the audience, and cursed by more than 10,000 more onlookers outside the hall.[22]

More serious was the "Green Corn Rebellion" of eastern Oklahoma. Before the outbreak of war, poor tenants and sharecroppers had formed the Working Class Union, a syndicalist organization associated with the Industrial Workers of the World. In August 1917, several hundred of these farmers assembled, intending to march on Washington, take over the Government, and stop the war. They expected to be joined by many thousands more who objected to the war and the draft across the country. While waiting for other WCU members to rally to them, they subsisted on unripe green corn. They had cut some telegraph wires and attempted without success to destroy railroad bridges, when they were attacked and dispersed by patriotic posses. Some 450 antiwar farmers were arrested; many were released but minor offenders were sentenced to incarceration from 60 days to 2 years, and the leaders drew 3- to 10-year sentences.[23]

In all the other cases Peterson and Fite record, violence was initiated by patriots. In Boston, in July 1917, 8,000 Socialists and other radicals staged an antiwar parade. Sailors and soldiers, attacking in regular formations upon command by an officer, broke up the parade; the paraders were beaten and the Socialist Party headquarters raided. None of the approximately 10,000 persons involved in the attack was arrested; 10 of those attacked were.[24] In Collinsville, Illinois, a young man of German birth, registered as an enemy alien and professing Socialist leanings—but with no record of having opposed the war overtly—was lynched by a drunken mob. When its leaders were indicted, their attorneys called their act a "patriotic murder," and the local jury acquitted them after 25 minutes' deliberation.[25]

At Rutgers University, in the only case of a campus riot I have found prior to the present conflict, fellow students demanded that Samuel Chovenson, an antiwar Socialist, speak at their Liberty Loan rally. When he refused, they stripped him, covered him with molasses and feathers, and paraded him through New Brunswick.26 Berkeley, California, also had its riot, although it was not primarily a campus affair: a mob attacked religious pacifists, burned down their tabernacle (a tent), and dunked them in their baptismal tank—whereupon the authorities arrested the pacifists and jailed them.27

A major source of opposition to World War I was the People's Council of America for Peace and Democracy. Its meetings were broken up in Philadelphia, Wilmington, and Chicago. When pacifist minister Herbert Bigelow, a Socialist, attempted to speak under the Council's auspices in Newport, Kentucky, a mob seized, bound and gagged him, drove him 20 miles into a forest and lashed him repeatedly with a blacksnake whip on his bare back. The assistant Attorney General of the United States commented that no statement against the attackers would be considered unless it was by a "responsible citizen," while the dean of the University of Minnesota Law School, denouncing the People's Council, said that "wartime was no time to quibble about constitutional rights and guarantees."28 When Irish opponents of the war paraded carrying a red flag in Butte, Montana, on June 6, 1917—the day after the draft law went into effect—patriotic citizens, reinforced by the police and by the state militia with fixed bayonets, dispersed the demonstration. Twenty arrests were made, all of demonstrators.29 Elsewhere, sailors and soldiers broke up a Philadelphia anticonscription meeting.30

The Industrial Workers of the World, advocates of direct action and sabotage in the interest of revolutionary syndicalism, pose a special problem of interpretation. They had been the most militant and violent opponents of the American capitalist system, especially in the West, before the war. As revolutionaries, they were hardly pacifists, but they sharply opposed the war as a war for big business. In this circumstance patriotism became the cover under which the enemies of the IWW could destroy it. Mass jailings, beatings, and deportations of "Wobblies" took place in Arizona, Montana, and other states. In Butte, patriotic vigilantes seized IWW organizer Frank Little, dragged him through the streets tied behind their automobile until his kneecaps were scraped off, then hanged him to a railroad trestle. The New York *Times* commented, on August 1, 1917, that the lynching was "deplorable and detestable," but noted that "IWW agitators are in effect and perhaps in fact, agents of Germany. The Federal government should make short work of these treasonable conspirators against the United States."31

For the *Times*, then and subsequently, the only alternative to lynching was federal suppression and dissent against the war. The *Christian Science Monitor* agreed. It editorialized on May 4, 1918: "The most regrettable thing about the whole matter is that, owing to the failure of the state and federal courts to deal adequately with the problem, private citizens are left, in self-protection, to take the law into their own hand." Governor Lowden of Illinois, U.S. Attorney General Gregory, and other members of the Cabinet, and many Senators and Congressmen agreed. The upshot was the Sedition Act, a sweeping amendment to the Espionage Act, aimed to muzzle all except "friendly" criticism of the Government, the armed forces, the Constitution, the flag, and the war. Its signature into law by President Wilson on May 16, 1918, led to some 1,500 arrests, effectively superseding mob action against opponents of war as it effectively wiped out all expression of dissent.32

Peterson and Fite provide an appropriate conclusion: they note that "a strong minority bitterly resented the war and conscription," but (as

Attorney General Gregory said) "their propaganda was almost immediately suppressed and destroyed."[33]

World War II

World War II was totally unlike World War I. Norman Thomas, veteran Socialist and pacifist leader, reported in 1943:

> Now it is true that there has been almost no interference by legal authorities or by mobs with public meetings. There has been . . . no parallel to the wholesale arrests under the Espionage Act. . . . In every previous war in which we have engaged there has been organized opposition of various strength. Last time, despite rigorous suppression, opposition was persistent and by no means confined to enemy sympathizers. Opposition to active participation in this war, strong before Pearl Harbor, completely dissolved after the surprise attack by Japan and the Japanese and German declarations of war against the United States. . . .

Roger Baldwin, director of the American Civil Liberties Union (itself formed to protect pacifists in their expression of antiwar opinions during World War I), agreed fully with Thomas. He noted that firm, effective Government action had "tended to allay fear and to create the conviction that any movements obstructive of the war are well in hand."[34] As a result, he found, "we experience no hysteria, no war-inspired mob violence, no organization of virtuous patriots seeking out seditious opinion, and no hostility to persons of German or Italian origin." He did note the hostility to persons of Japanese origin, but commented that "while painfully in evidence, [it] is largely confined to the Pacific Coast and smaller communities in the West."[35]

Attorney General Earl Warren of California, testifying before a congressional hearing concerned with the forcible removal of these same Japanese-Americans, warned that "my own belief concerning vigilantism is that the people do not engage in vigilante activities so long as they believe that their Government through its agencies is taking care of their most serious problem." Only if they believe that that is not happening do they "start taking the law into their own hands." Mr. Warren, in asking for this racist action—Japanese removal—was also making an important point about our treatment of serious dissent in wartime: either the Government suppresses it legally, or the people will suppress it violently. Despite the long, uncertain course of World War II, its origins guaranteed that there would be such little dissent that the people could tolerate what the Government did not suppress.[36]

The Korean War

The Korean war appears as an excellent example of consensus through crackdown. Like the War of 1812, the Korean war generated one brief flash of opposition. On August 2, 1950, New York City opponents of the war, mostly leftists, held a rally despite refusal by the police to grant them a permit. The rally drew a few thousand people, but they were quickly dispersed by a heavy police force. The New York *Times* reporter noted that "some of the demonstrators who refused orders to disperse were badly beaten by the police. Some were charged by mounted police who rode onto crowded sidewalks. On the whole, however, the police used restraint."37 There were two other newsworthy incidents, both comparatively minor: Four workers in the Linden, New Jersey, plant of General Motors attempted to hand out antiwar leaflets at the plant. Their fellow employees beat them and threw them out of the plant, GM refused to rehire them, and the United Auto Workers expelled them from the union.38 In San Francisco, a meeting of Harry Bridges' Longshoremen's Union erupted into a riot when Bridges tried to substitute a peace resolution for one supporting the actions of the United States in Korea. (A Senate committee reported that it was seeking ways to jail Bridges, and his deportation hearing followed almost immediately.)39 Unlike other conflicts, the Korean war began during a period of greater peacetime repression than the country had ever known; as a result the Government itself, with committees of the House and Senate playing a role equal to or greater than that of the administrative branch, played an enormous role in quashing dissent, leaving very little room for the efforts of would-be vigilantes.40

The War in Vietnam

And so we come down to the present. Violence in the early stages of the war in Vietnam resembled the model of the Korean war and most American wars, in that peaceful demonstrators were attacked by citizens or by the police. In October 1965, demonstrators in Berkeley, California, declared their intention to close down the Oakland Army Terminal by massive, nonviolent action. They were easily turned aside, without violence, by the massed Oakland police on the borders of that city. Violence erupted when members of the Hell's Angels motorcycle gang attacked seated demonstrators, but this was quickly quelled by the same Oakland police. Subsequently, nonviolent pickets were attacked repeatedly while picketing the Port Chicago, California, naval facility, and draft-card burners in Boston were beaten by a Boston mob. As late as April 1967, antiwar demonstrations took the form of peaceful protest marches (with no violence in San Francisco, and very little in New York), but there was a reversion to type during the summer of 1967, when pickets protesting the appearance of President Johnson at the Century-Plaza Hotel in Los Angeles were badly beaten by police. The demonstrators were overwhelmingly a nonviolent group, although they did include a few activists who provoked the police onslaught by jeers and intemperate language.41

But the events of "Stop-the-Draft Week"—October 16-22, 1967—appear to be something of a watershed. In California, radical student leaders announced that they would close the Oakland Selective Service Induction Center "by any means necessary." But tactical divisions reflecting opposing principles within the anti-Vietnam movement led to a division of labor. On Monday, October 6, members and sympathizers of "the Resistance" sat in nonviolently and were arrested nonviolently. On Tuesday, several thousand students and other radicals attempted physically to seal off the induction center, and were violently dispersed by the Oakland police. Few were arrested, but many were beaten or gassed in response to their token resistance (those who resisted nonviolently, and newsmen, seemed to bear the brunt of the police onslaught). Wednesday saw a return to nonviolence, and when Thursday passed almost without any demonstration, it appeared that the protestors faced an inglorious defeat. But inexplicably, Friday became a day of new, escalated tactics by the militants. Instead of trying to stand up to the police, some 15,000 activists dispersed all over the neighborhood in the vicinity of the induction center. They dragged parked cars into intersections and over-turned them there or deflated their tires; they blocked traffic with potted plants and trash cans; and by fleeing and regrouping they easily avoided the superior power of the police. These mobile tactics succeeded in sharply reducing physical violence against the demonstrators.

If "the capture of intersections" delayed the work of the induction center scarcely an hour or two, the demonstrators regarded their actions as a moral victory. Beyond their ingenious tactical innovations, the militants had also embarked on a new stage in opposition to the war: no longer was the leader-ship of the movement in the hands of the nonviolent opponents of war, but rather the initiative lay with the activists who, in words at least, claimed the right to self-defense and even to take the offensive against the enemy— although in fact they were singularly unsuccessful in effectively opposing police violence with violence of their own.

The crowning event of Stop-the-Draft Week was "The Siege of the Penta-gon," on Saturday and Sunday, October 21-22. Here again, a classically non-violent demonstration, numbering 50,000-100,000, had to share the stage with demonstrators who proclaimed their intention to use force, though the advocates of violence were in much smaller proportion to the rest than at Oakland. Most of the action during the day was nonviolent, but in the small hours of the night, soldiers and federal marshals beat many of the young demonstrators severely.[42]

Taken together, the Oakland and Pentagon riots indicate a change in focus on the part of radical opponents of the war. Until then most opponents of the war had tacitly accepted the legitimacy of American institutions by sub-mitting voluntarily to the penalties for civil disobedience; now, however, many of the dedicated radical opponents of the war had denied legitimacy to the institutions as well as to the war, thus expressing their rejection of the notion that justice is to be found at the heart of the American system.[43]

This new tendency dominated the events of the next months, as the scene of violence shifted to the campus. Beginning with a riot which developed when police broke up a demonstration against Dow Chemical Co. at San Jose State College, in November 1967, violent confrontations between students and police occurred repeatedly, with recruitment by Dow Chemical, the CIA, and the Armed Forces triggering the action. Among the sharper struggles were those at the Universities of Wisconsin and Iowa, Cornell, Long Beach State College, and San Francisco State College, culminating in the Columbia riots of May 1968. Two points may be noted:

(1) The student protesters verbally expressed their determination to stop Dow et al. by any means necessary, thereby inviting the violence.

(2) In almost all cases the students committed violence against property, whereas the police beat up the (ineffectually) resisting students.[44] Certainly this new pattern obtained in the two major riots of 1968: the Columbia riots of May, where radical students, acting in cooperation with blacks, seized buildings and were violently dispossessed, and in the Chicago convention

riots of August 1968. The last are particularly instructive as examples of the new pattern.

A handful of militant activists uttering vocal threats to "destroy the system" succeeded in provoking massive police attacks against an irresolute mass of young people who shared the militants' description of the illegitimacy of "the system," but were not seriously prepared to move beyond rhetorical dedication to revolutionary goals. Whether this state of affairs will long obtain is open to question, but at present there appears to be an enormous gap between the perception by tens of thousands of radical students that both the war and the "the system" are illegitimate, and their readiness—however stridently proclaimed—to act in accordance with that perception. Their inability to act is not so much a matter of attitude as it is a matter of their lack of effective power. But this in turn rests on the present unwillingness of other millions of American college students (who agree with the radicals about the wrongness of the war, as shown by their support of Eugene McCarthy and other peace candidates) to act outside "the system" (and their support of McCarthy, who insisted he was trying to give them an alternative within it, shows this point, too).[45]

The present equilibrium is quite unstable. It is highly unlikely that large numbers of students can be persuaded to accept the legitimacy of the present war. Therefore, continuation of the status quo in Vietnam is likely to have the effect of persuading them to accept the radicals' proclaimed identity between the war and "the system." In such a case, violent repression like that which took place at Chicago will only increase their acceptance of the legitimacy of violent resistance—though the facts of power in America may limit such actions to one or another form of guerrilla tactics like those of Oakland's Friday, October 30, 1967, riots. On the other hand, rapid termination of the war in Vietnam—by negotiated peace and withdrawal—would serve effectively to isolate the radicals by apparently undermining the major premise of their argument that war and imperialism are necessary concomitants of "the system."

CONCLUSION

Violent conflict arising from opposition to the Vietnam war has followed a course quite different from that in earlier wars, the only possible exception being antiwar violence in the Confederacy. For the crucial fact seems to be that antiwar rioting shows no signs of diminishing. In attempting to explain this fact, the study of the past is of some help, if only to point up contrasts. Other wars have been unpopular, at least in some sections—the War of 1812, the Mexican War, and the Spanish-American War—without evoking significant violence. But each of these was relatively short. Furthermore, in each there were effective channels for opposition short of violent protest; today opponents can demonstrate peacefully, but such demonstrations seem to make little inroads upon an unresponsive political structure (the failure of the peace candidacies of McCarthy and Kennedy, which had promised to open such channels, will undoubtedly heighten the sense of frustration which is one component of violent protest). Unresolved minority tensions, like those of the Civil War, undoubtedly heighten the intensity of domestic conflict. Apart from the War of 1812 and the Korean war (and of course the Confederacy),

American arms have won decisive victories, and both of these conflicts came to a halt much more rapidly than the present conflict. Other wars have had prestigious people in opposition, or have been opposed by dedicated and well-organized radicals, or by a large part of a social group (workers in World War I), or by significant ethnic or sectional minorities—the Vietnam conflict has all of these in tandem.

But there is much that is without historical parallel. In no previous American war have youth and students been significantly in opposition; previously they were a major source of patriotic sentiments. And with the single exception of the losing effort of the Confederate South, in no previous war have its opponents been able to see their case gaining increasing popular support. Nor is there any example of such wisespread opposition to an American war coming from the academic and literary community.

For a conclusion we might look to St. Thomas Aquinas. He defined a just war as one meeting three qualifications: the ruler must be legitimate; the cause must be just; and the means employed must be proportionate to the ends in view. Apart from civil wars, there has seldom been any question about the legitimacy of American Government. Every American war has produced a few opponents who thought the cause unjust, but (perhaps duration is of significance in this equation) these have been relegated to one section or ethnic group without greatly changing the attitudes of large patriotic majorities—again the civil wars are an important exception. Proportionality of means to ends first became a question at the beginning of the century, when Mark Twain and other intellectuals denounced the torture of prisoners in the Philippines. But atrocity stories only heightened American patriotism during World War I, World War II, and the Korean war, because Americans or neutrals were the victims of enemy barbarities. Violent opposition to the Vietnam war seems to have begun with the question of proportionality—the questions of napalm, defoliation, saturation bombing, etc.—and to have escalated to the point where a large minority of the American people question the justice of this war, and some begin to question the very legitimacy of "the system" that, in the minds of radical opponents of the war, has produced these effects.

History teaches, when it does, by analogy. That is, we look for similarities in the causal sequences of events which produce like effects. So Americans facing mounting civil disorder and riots during a period of war, arising out of opposition to that war, seek to understand this phenomenon by searching through our past wartime experience. Unfortunately, the past does not have much to tell us; we will have to make our own history along uncharted and frightening ways.

References

1. J. Thomas Scharf and Thomas Westcott, *History of Philadelphia 1609-1884* (3 vols., *Philadelphia: L. H. Everts & Co., 1884*) I, p. 401.
2. *Ibid.*
3. *Ibid.*, pp. 401-403. A few weeks later a mob of sailors, complaining of low pay, rioted in Philadelphia, *ibid.*, p. 403. Jesse Lemisch, "Jack Tar in the Streets: Merchant Seamen in Revolutionary America," *William & Mary Quarterly*, 3d ser., vol. XXV (July 1968), pp. 371-407, lists many sailors' riots, but the only one

which was an antiwar riot during wartime was a 3 day anti-impressment riot in Boston, Nov. 17, 1747, during King George's War (p. 391).

4. *Journal of the Provincial Congress* . . . (2 vols., Albany: T. Weed, 1842), vol. II, pp. 309-311: *Minutes of the Committee . . . for Detecting Conspiracies* . . . (2 vols., New York: New York Historical Society 1924-25), II, pp. 442-443. In the 1776 action the revolutionary authorities described the rioters as Tories. See also Richard M. Brown, "Historical Patterns of Violence in America," elsewhere in this volume.

5. J. Thomas Scharf, *History of Maryland From the Earliest Times to the Present Day* (3 vols., Hatboro, Pa.: Tradition Press, 1967; reprint of 1879 ed.), vol. III, pp. 3-25. See also Henry Adams, *History of the United States during the First Administration of James Madison* (New York: C. Scribner's Sons. 1890), vol. II. pp. 405-408 (vol. VI of Adams' great *History* of the period 1800-17), says the "well-organized" mob consisted mainly of "low Irish and Germans."

6. Adams, *History,* vol. II, p. 400.

7. Brown, *The Republic in Peril: 1812* (New York: Columbia University Press, 1964). pp. 181-183.

8. Sellers, personal conversation, Sept. 30, 1968. Professor Sellers is presently completing his study of the Polk administration.

9. Scharf, *History of Maryland,* vol. II, pp. 403-413.

10. Charles L. Wagandt, *The Mighty Revolution: Negro Emancipation in Maryland, 1862-1864* (Baltimore: Johns Hopkins Press, 1964), p. 28.

11. Georgia Lee Tatum, *Disloyalty in the Confederacy* (Chapel Hill: The University of North Carolina Press, 1934), pp. 115, 122, 132-133, citing H. G. De Roulhac Hamilton.

12. *Ibid.,* p. 46.

13. *Ibid.,* p. 58.

14. Frank L Klement, *The Copperheads in the Middle West* (Chicago: University of Chicago Press, 1960), pp. 26-27, 78-80. See also Ella Lonn, *Desertion During the Civil War* (Gloucester, Mass.: Peter Smith, 1966, reprint of 1928 ed.(, p. 204; and George Fort Milton, *Abraham Lincoln and the Fifth Column* (New York: Collier Books, 1962; paperback reprint of 1942 edition), pp. 72-73, 116.

15. James McCague, *The Second Rebellion: the Story of the New York City Draft Riots of 1863* (New York: Dial Press, 1968), pp. 177-179 and *passim.*

16. Milton, *Lincoln and the Fifth Column,* pp. 109-111; John Niven, *Connecticut for the Union: the Role of the State in the Civil War* (New Haven: Yale University Press, 1965), p. 90.

17. Klement, *Copperheads,* pp. 92, 98. Klement argues that the peace movement was in no way related to any organized pro-Southern scheme; Northern Republican soldier-politicians foisted that canard on the public and on history.

18. Niven, *Connecticut,* pp, 300-302.

19. Klement, *Copperheads,* pp. 88, 320; Niven, *Connecticut,* p. 302.

20. David Donald, "Died for Democracy," in Donald, ed., *Why the North Won the Civil War* (New York: Collier Seeks, paperback 1965; reprint of 1960 ed.), pp. 97-90.

21. Robert L. Beisner, *Twelve Against Empire: the Anti-Imperialists, 1898-1900* (New York: McCraw-Hill, 1968), 10-12 and *passim.* I have not discovered any antiwar riots arising from opposition to the longer and more severe war of "pacification" of the Philippines, 1899-1902.

22. Peterson and Fite, *Opponents of War, 1917-1918* (Madison, Wis.: University of Winconsin Press, 1957), pp. 30-31.

23. *Ibid.,* pp. 40-41.

24. *Ibid.,* pp. 45-46. James Weinstein, *The Decline of Socialism in America, 1912-1925* (New York: Monthy Review Press, 1967), pp. 139-141, list other cases of mob violence against Socialists.

25. Peterson and Fite, *Opponents of War,* pp. 202-204. The Washington *Post* commented: "In spite of excesses such as lynching, it is a healthful and wholesome awakening. . . ."

26. *Ibid.,* p. 199.

27. *Ibid.,* pp. 197-198.

28. *Ibid.*, pp. 74-79; Weinstein, *Decline of Socialism,* p. 145, identifies Bigelow as a Socialist.
29. Peterson and Fite, *Opponents of War,* p. 28.
30. *Ibid.,* p. 32.
31. *Ibid.,* pp. 48-60.
32. *Ibid.,* pp. 211-230.
33. *Ibid.,* pp. 41-42.
34. Richard Polenberg, ed., *Americans At War: the Home Front, 1941-1945* (Englewood Cliffs, N.J.: Prentice-Hall, 1968), pp. 94-95, citing Thomas' article in *Common Sense,* vol. XII (May 1943), pp. 156-159.
35. Polenberg, *Americans At War,* pp. 92-94, citing Baldwin, "Freedom in Wartime," *Report of the American Civil Liberties Union* (June 1943), pp. 3-6.
36. Polenberg, *Americans At War,* p. 102, citing Warren's testimony before the House of Representatives, *National Defense Migration Hearings* (Washington, 1942), vol. XXIX, pp. 11010-11019.
37. New York *Times,* Aug. 3, 1950, p. I. There is no secondary account of this period that treats this issue.
38. *Ibid.,* Aug. 1, 1950, p. 13; Sept. 15, 1950, p. 18.
39. *Ibid.,* July 12, 1950, p. 16; July 13, 1950, p. 22.
40. Two incidents will help to illustrate the temper of the times. Four men and one woman drew 6-month and 1-year jail sentences for having painted the words "Peace" and "No H-Bomb" on a Brooklyn park entrance—before the outbreak of the Korean war. The judge accused them of stabbing our men fighting in Korea in the back. (New York *Times,* Aug. 2, 1950, p. 6). The Social Science Research Council accepted a $100,000 grant from the Markle Foundation to devise a test for detecting traitors (New York *Times,* Nov. 19, 1951, p. 25).
41. The riots growing out of our involvement in Vietnam are so much a part of our time (and more fully cataloged in other studies) that I have not documented them separately. The *New York Times Index* is the best guide. I have also used clippings from the San Francisco *Chronicle.* Radical and underground papers like the *Guardian* (formerly the *National Guardian*), the Berkeley *Barb,* the *Mid-Peninsula Observer,* and the Los Angeles *Free-Press,* as well as journals like *Ramparts* and *Liberation,* give the demonstrators' view of events—some of which I observed at firsthand.
42. Norman Mailer, *The Armies of the Night* (New York: New American Library, 1968), Irving L. Horowitz, "The Struggle Is the Message: An Analysis of Tactics, Trends, and Tensions in the Antiwar Movement" (unpublished MS, 1968), p. 42, notes that "the level of violence is greatest on the West Coast and in the Berkeley-Oakland-San Francisco area."
43. *Ibid.,* p. 10, Horowitz says: "The anti-war movement can be considered as an ideology in search of a tactic." I think Horowitz exaggerates the role of ideology in the antiwar movement, while underestimating its nihilism, personified by some of the culture heroes of the New Left: Bob Dylan, the Doors, Arthur Brown, and Rolling Stones—note the Stones' recent hit. "Street-Fighting Man."
44. Compare Horowitz, p. 43.
45. *Ibid.,* pp. 35-36. By "the system," antiwar radicals denote the interrelated complex of political, economic, social and cultural institutions of the United States and the ideology which supports them. (Daniel Walker) *Rights in Conflict* (New York: New American Library, 1968).

Chapter 16

INTERNATIONAL WAR
AND DOMESTIC TURMOIL:
SOME CONTEMPORARY EVIDENCE

By Raymond Tanter*

Consider a typical issue of a U.S. newspaper; it may carry news on such events as the Vietnam war, demonstrations on university campuses, urban riots, labor strikes, and violent crime. Is the United States on the offensive abroad and on the retreat in the face of the young, the black, the poor, and the criminal at home?[1]

The media carries the message of the violent ones. "Draft Beer, Not Boys," "Hell no, we won't go," and "Burn, Baby, Burn!" echo in the streets and are faithfully recorded by the press. But coexisting with these expressions of dissent, and similarly recorded, are shouts like "Commie-Fink" and demands for "Law and Order" to get rid of "Crime in the Streets."

Most Americans assume, from the militant protests and backlashes by the "forgotten Americans," that turmoil of various kinds is on the increase at home as well as abroad. What are the connections between the intensity of the Vietnam war and the level of turmoil in America? Do they rise and fall together over time? What does the theoretical literature suggest regarding international war and domestic turmoil in general?

THEORY AND PRIOR ANALYSIS

Scholars such as Georg Simmel and Lewis Coser have theorized about conflict within and between groups in general:

(1) The unity of a group is frequently lost when it does not have an opponent.[2]

(2) Hostilities help maintain group boundaries and are frequently consciously cultivated to guarantee existing conditions.[3]

(3) If a group with a basic consensus regarding its preservation engages in outside conflict, internal cohesion is likely to increase.[4]

---

*Raymond Tanter is associate professor of political science at the University of Michigan and author of many articles on internal and foreign conflict. In 1967, he was the Deputy Director for Behavioral Sciences of the Advanced Research Projects Agency, Department of Defense.

(4) Groups may look for enemies to help maintain and/or increase internal cohesion.[5]

(5) Exaggeration of the danger of an enemy serves to maintain group structure when it is threatened by internal dissension.[6]

These propositions from Simmel and Coser suggest that international war may offer alternatives to domestic turmoil; they do *not* seem to anticipate a situation in which international war may provoke domestic turmoil. Proposition (3) above is a partial exception in its suggestion that a basic consensus is an intervening variable; that is, if a group without a basic consensus regarding its preservation engages in outside conflict, internal turmoil may follow. Simmel and Coser, however, do not deal directly with international war.

A growing number of students of international politics do focus on the relations between foreign and domestic conflict behavior. Quincy Wright is one of them, and seems to agree with Simmel and Coser when he suggests:

> By creating and perpetuating in the community both a fear of invasion and a hope of expansion, obedience to a ruler may be guaranteed.[7]
>
> Rulers have forestalled internal sedition by starting external wars.[8]
>
> In the later stages of the Napoleonic Wars, Napoleon began to appreciate the value of war as an instrument of internal solidarity.[9]

In addition to Wright, Richard Rosecrance asserts that over time there is a tendency for international instability to be associated with the domestic insecurity of elites.[10] Moreover, Ernst Haas and Allen Whiting suggest an explanation of this relationship. They contend that the elites become fearful of losing their domestic positions during periods of rapid industrialization and widespread social change; they then try to displace the attention of the disaffected population onto some outside target. The authors suggest, however, that this form of self-preservation rarely leads to war.[11]

Rosecrance's finding of a correlation between international instability and domestic insecurity of elites contrasts with evidence reported by Samuel Huntington, who concludes that a decrease in the frequency of interstate conflict is likely to lead to an increase in the level of domestic violence.[12] Both Rosecrance and Huntington, however, have the international system as their unit of analysis rather than the individual nation.

A study using the nation as a unit of analysis identified a small negative relationship between internal subversion and foreign conflict behavior among 77 nations during 1955-57. That is, nations with high levels of subversion tend to avoid issuing threats to other nations and have relatively few antiforeign demonstrations.[13] Rudolph Rummel also found a consistently positive, though low, relationship between measures of turmoil (riots, demonstrations) and such foreign conflict variables as threats, accusations, protests, and antiforeign demonstrations in a country.[14] In a replication of the Rummel study for later years, the author of this paper also found a small positive relationship between indicators of turmoil and measures of diplomatic conflict activity. For example, the number of riots and the frequency of troop movements within a country were positively associated ($r = 0.40$) among 82 nations during 1958-60. In general, though, both the Rummel and the author's studies showed only slight positive relationships between foreign and domestic conflict behavior, which increased with a timelag between the two.[15]

A longitudinal study by Pitirim Sorokin inspired the Rummel-Tanter cross-national efforts. He visually examined data for a number of nations across 14 centuries, A.D. 525 to 1925, and found a small positive association between unsuccessful external wars and later internal disturbances. Sorokin concludes, however, that international war and domestic disturbances are independent of one another.[16]

In summary, the theorists generally agree that there should be an inverse relationship between internal and external conflict behavior. Some cross-national studies find a negative relationship between subversion and foreign conflict behavior and a positive relationship between turmoil and diplomatic conflict. Moreover, a longitudinal study concludes that unsuccessful wars tend to be followed by revolutionary disturbances. This type of longitudinal study has implications for the present study of the Vietnam war and turmoil in the United States. If Sorokin's findings are generalized to the United States, one would expect that the longer the Vietnam war lasts without apparent success, the greater would be the level of domestic turmoil. Now let us turn to Vietnam and American turmoil.

THE VIETNAM WAR AND U.S. TURMOIL

In March 1965 the United States made an extensive commitment of forces to South Vietnam. One indicator of escalation is the rate of change in U.S. troop strength in Vietnam. Although U.S. casualties increased from 1965 to 1968 at approximately the same rate, the increases were of different magnitudes. For this reason, and because disorder seems most likely to have fluctuated with the troop buildup, the troop strength data are used as the indicator of escalation.[17]

Indicators of domestic turmoil fall into two categories. Most important for this paper is the Movement in both its antiwar and civil-rights phases. A secondary set is labor and criminal activity. Most of the subsequent discussion focuses on a comparison of the Movement with the war. Primary turmoil indicators are the frequencies, rates of change, and populations participating in antiwar protests; levels of urban riots; and participation in civil-rights demonstrations. Secondary indicators are the number of labor strikes and levels of violent crime.[18]

The tentative hypotheses are as follows:

(1) As U.S. troop commitments to Vietnam increase, domestic turmoil increases.

(2) The longer the period of time in which the United States is engaged in Vietnam, the higher the frequency of domestic turmoil, or, alternatively, the fewer the total incidents of domestic turmoil, but the more intensive are individual incidents.

Table 16-1 lists annual totals of U.S. force levels in Vietnam and domestic turmoil indicators. The secondary measures of labor and criminal activity are important because of their coverage of a long period, which enables a comparison of their trends before and during U.S. involvement in Vietnam. For example, strikes for 1961-68 and violent crime for 1961-67 show trends in those incidents before, as well as during, the Vietnam war. The percentage increase in strikes from 1964 to 1965 is 7.6 percent; for 1965 to 1966 it is 11.9 percent; and for 1966 to 1967 it is 2 percent. Comparable increases for violent crimes

Table 16-1—Annual totals of indicators of U.S. domestic turmoil and Vietnam troop commitments, January 1961-July 1968

	1961	1962	1963	1964	1965	1966	1967	1968
Indicator of troop commitment:								
U.S. DOD strength in Vietnam (000)[a]			15	23	184	385	486	537
Indicators of domestic turmoil:								
Antiwar protests[b]					57	53	58	17
Participants in antiwar protests (000)[c]					222	137	385	329
Urban riots/clashes[d]				16	23	53	82	65
Participants in civil rights demonstrations (000)[e]					117	51	37	42
Labor strikes (00)[f,g]	34	36	34	37	39	44	45	26
Violent crime (000)	1,926	2,048	2,259	2,604	2,780	3,243	3,802	h

See footnotes 17 and 18 for all data sources.

(a) Data recorded from Jan. 1, 1963, to July 31, 1968. Figures are for the end of the calendar years. Department of Defense (DOD) includes all U.S. forces assigned to Vietnam.

(b) Data recorded from Jan. 1965 to Sept. 1, 1968.

(c) Data recorded from Jan. 1965 to Sept. 1, 1968.

(d) Data recorded from Jan. 1964 to May 31, 1968.

(e) Data recorded from Jan. 1965 to May 31, 1968.

(f) Data for 1967 are preliminary.

(g) Data recorded to June 30, 1968; data for 1968 are preliminary.

(h) Data unavailable at this writing. The first quarter of 1968 shows a 17-per-cent increase over the same period of 1967.

are 6 percent, 11 percent, and 16 percent. While the incidence of crimes is increasing, the aggregate changes are not very dramatic. The talk about crime rates in the context of a bipartisan law-and-order political campaign in 1968 implied that even sharper increases had occurred.

A second set of observations about the turmoil indicators is that they all are seasonal within years, and they appear to be unrelated to Vietnam commitments. Figures 16-1 to 16-7 chart the indicators for the war and for turmoil over time. Figure 16-1 is the plot of the cumulative total of U.S. Department of Defense (DOD) forces in South Vietnam. Figure 16-2 juxtaposes the antiwar protests and the urban riot indicators. Figure 16-3 shows the rate of change in the frequency of antiwar protests. Figure 16-4 is the number of participants in antiwar protests, figure 16-5 the number of participants in civil-rights demonstrations. Figures 16-6 and 16-7 are the frequencies of labor strikes and violent crimes, respectively.

Note that the curve for the war (16-1) looks much different from the other curves. Specifically, the seasonal fluctuations of the domestic turmoil indicators contrast sharply with the smooth increase and then decrease of the rate of U.S. buildup in Vietnam. Let us examine specific indicators. A glance at figure 16-2 illustrates that the frequency of antiwar protests exhibits a seasonal fluctuation with the academic year. This probably reflects the fact that many of the participants are associated with the academic community, and may react more strongly to the requirements of the academic year than to the international conflict they oppose.

Consider the trends in the data over specific periods of time, rather than their monthly fluctuations. A relationship between antiwar protests and international conflict emerges. The heavy line in figure 16-3 is the slope or line of "best fit"[19] for the incidence of the antiwar protests for January 1965 to November 1965; it indicates the rate of change over time in the number of protests. This is the period during which the United States made its first large increase in troops, and this line is approximately the same as the line of best fit for increasing troop strength. But the absolute number of antiwar protests declines after November 1965. It appears, then, that antiwar protests were a response to a *change* in U.S. forces, rather than a response to their actual magnitude. The mean frequency of antiwar protests decreases from 4.56 per month during the entire escalation phase (approximately January 1965-January 1967) to 3.55 per month during the leveling-off phase (about February 1967-July 1968). (No significance tests are applied to these data.)

Jeffery Milstein and William Mitchell[20] observe a similar relationship between U.S. bombing and the rate of North Vietnamese infiltration.

> . . . U.S. bombing of North Vietnam may physically decrease infiltration, but escalation of the bombing is matched by North Vietnamese escalation of troop commitments. Thus, the North Vietnamese appear to be reacting to proportional changes in U.S. bombing rather than to actual levels . . . . In fact, escalation of the bombing produces subsequent counterescalation, as predicted by the Richardson hypothesis. Once a high level of bombing is attained, however, Communist troop commitments are subsequently at a lower level.

Escalation of troop strength is one thing. What about the effect of the war's length on the magnitude of protests? Looking at the number of participants

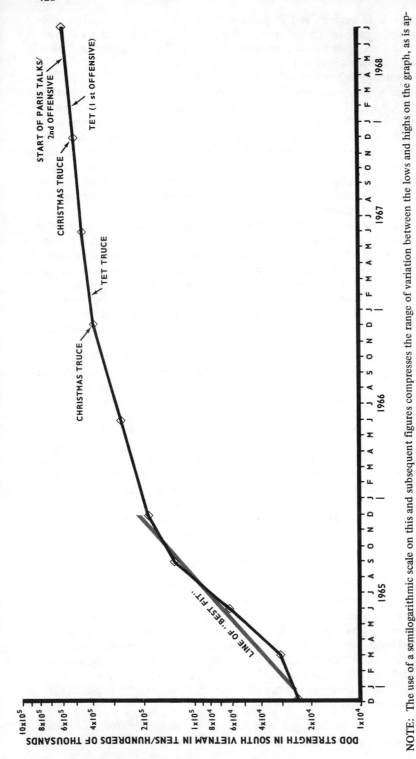

Figure 16-1. – Department of Defense strength in South Vietnam.

NOTE: The use of a semilogarithmic scale on this and subsequent figures compresses the range of variation between the lows and highs on the graph, as is apparent from an examination of the numbers on the vertical axis.

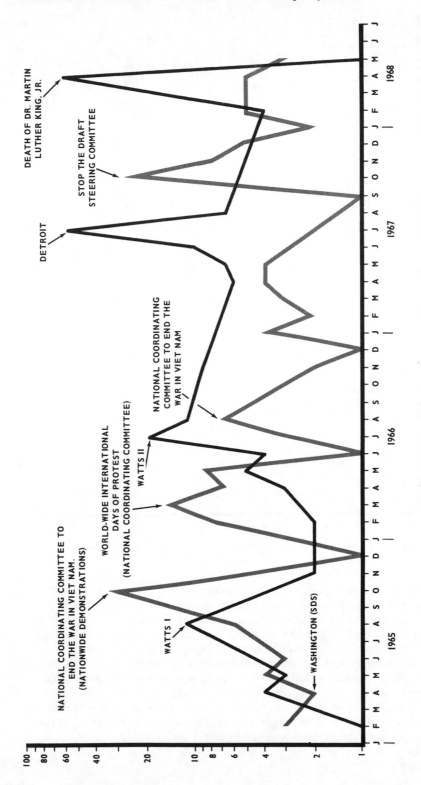

Figure 16-2.—Number of antiwar protests and urban riots.

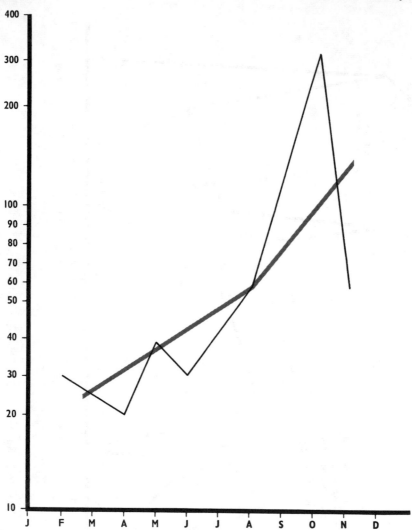

Figure 16-3. – Antiwar protests: levels and rate of change (United States, 1965).

in antiwar protests (figure 16-4) over this same period of time, we find a different tendency. The rate of change (slope omitted) of the number of protest participants during the initial Vietnam escalation period appears negatively related to the slope of Vietnam escalation. That is, the higher the rate of change in Vietnam escalation, the lower the rate of change in protest participation. In addition, the mean number of protest participants increases from about 14,400 per month during the escalation phase to approximately 38,700 per month during the leveling-off phase. Though fewer demonstrations were held, more people attended them, which may be due to the aggregation of groups into larger units. The number of people participating in antiwar protests thus may be a response to the level of commitment, the duration of U.S. involvement, or both.

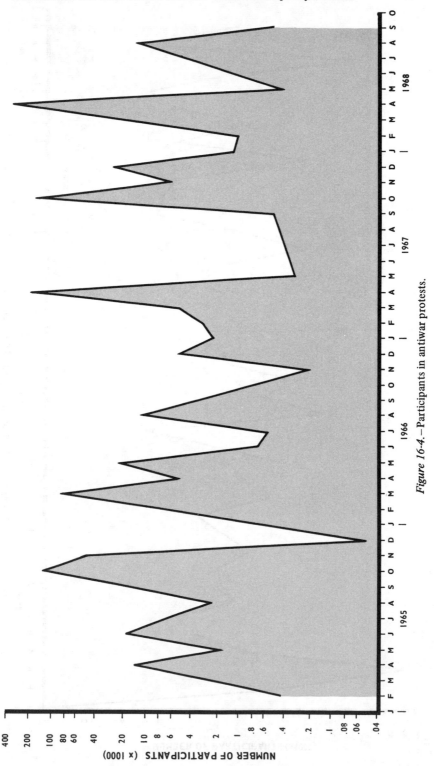

Figure 16-4. – Participants in antiwar protests.

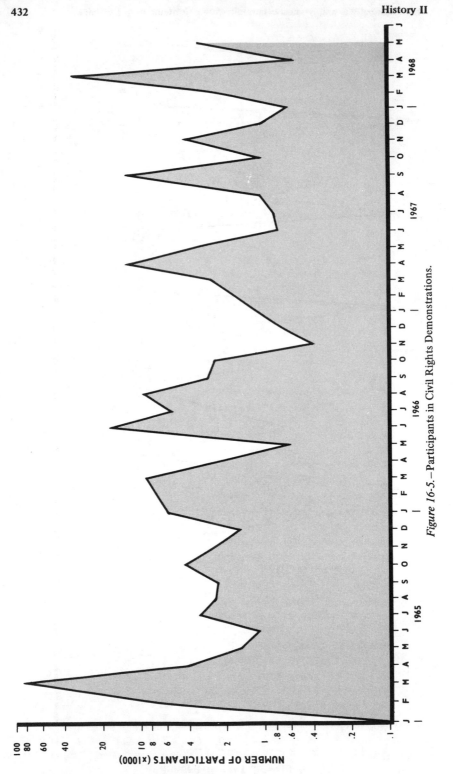

Figure 16-5. – Participants in Civil Rights Demonstrations.

Now to the second indicator of domestic turmoil: urban riots, whose frequencies are plotted in figure 16-2. There are annual cycles with monthly fluctuations that are proportionately constant throughout the entire period under discussion, independent of either U.S. force levels, escalation, or length of the war. For 1965 through 1967, the riots peak in July, giving credence to the "long hot summer" proposition of common currency. A different trend characterizes 1968. The peak month in 1968 is April—a response to the assassination of Dr. Martin Luther King, Jr. What if the frequency of riots had followed the pattern of past summers? Then, the additional "King riots" should have resulted in a marked increase in the total number of riots in 1968 over 1965-67. Although precise data are unavailable here, impressionistic observation suggests that the long hot summer of 1968 never materialized. The total number of riots in 1968 may be only slightly higher than those of previous years.

Some observers consider urban riots as a tactical change of civil-rights activity from nonviolent protest to a new militancy. The author does not have here data on the number of civil-rights demonstrations to compare with numbers of urban riots. Data are available, however, on the number of people participating in civil-rights demonstrations. Note in figure 16-5 that there appears to be a seasonal cycle much like that of labor strikes. High participation in civil-rights demonstrations seems to be a spring and early-summer phenomenon, with peak activity from March until June. For 1967, however, there is more activity during the fall than the spring. Refer back to table 16-1 and consider the sharp drop in participation in civil-rights demonstrations from 1965 to 1966. Less than half as many persons participated in 1966 as in 1965. Participation dipped even lower in 1967, but increased dramatically in 1968. Although the data cover only the first 5 months in 1968, more people participated in civil-rights demonstrations here than in all of 1967.

Now what about civil rights in relation to Vietnam? Let us divide the civil-rights participation into two phases coincident with the escalation and leveling off of U.S. troop strength in Vietnam. The period up to January 1967 can be considered a time of escalation, the period after that month a leveling-off phase. During the escalation period there is an average of about 6,700 participants in civil-rights demonstrations monthly, contrasting to the mean of perhaps 5,000 per month in the leveling-off phase, a decrease of 26 percent. The levels of participation may be related to the escalation but not to the absolute level of troop strength, similar to our interpretation of the evidence concerning Vietnam escalation and the antiwar protests.

We observed that the level of antiwar protests decreases slightly from an average of about four to three per month from the escalation to levelling off in Vietnam. The average number of people protesting the war, however, increases from approximately 14,400 to 38,700 per month. One interpretation of the slight decrease in the average number of war protests is that the groups began to merge into larger, more sophisticated combinations. But does this account for the increase in protesters? Assuming that the universe of white activists is fairly constant, from where do the extra protesters come? Perhaps some shifted away from civil-rights activity as integration gave way to Black Power as a dominant theme. The ex-rights activists became available for the war protests in a kind of "Movement Migration." A slight radicalization of the black bourgeoisie, moreover, might account for the increased number of par-

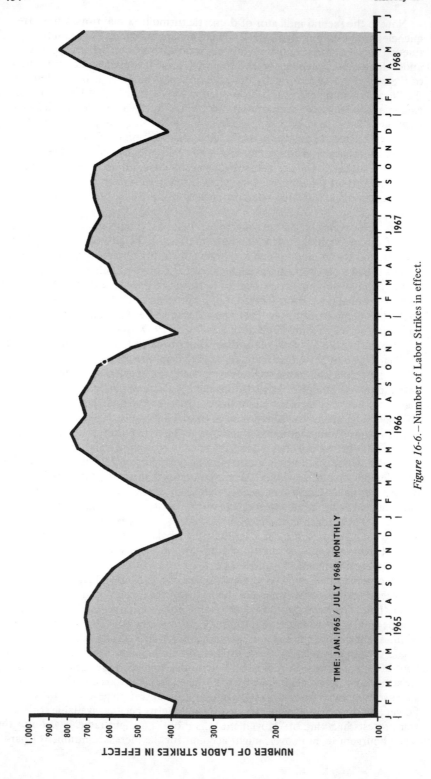

Figure 16-6.—Number of Labor Strikes in effect.

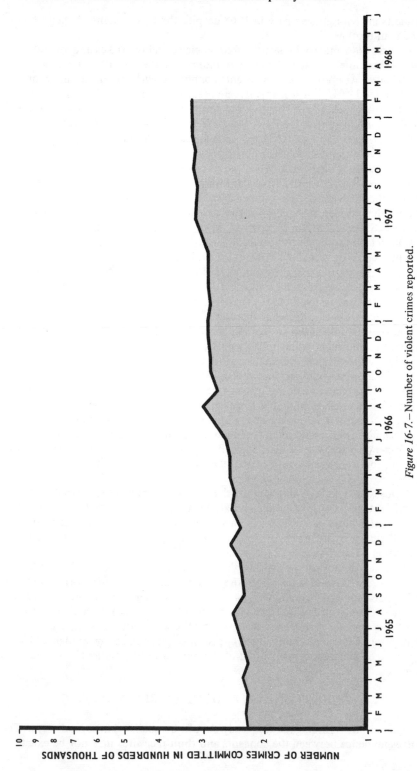

Figure 16-7.– Number of violent crimes reported.

ticipants in civil-rights activity in 1968 despite the loss of some of their "blue-eyed soul brothers."

Figures 16-6 and 16-7 chart the frequencies of labor strikes and violent crimes over time. As with the primary indicators, there is definite annual periodicity. At no point do any events connected with either escalation or absolute level of U.S. forces in Vietnam seem to compare with the fairly stable annual strike cycles. The shape of the curve appears determined by the dates on which union contracts expire. Like the frequency of violent crimes, labor strikes maintain approximately the same annual cycle throughout the period of U.S. involvement in Vietnam, though in fact the absolute number of strikes increases slightly over time. When the number of participants involved in labor strikes is plotted, the curve is similar though not as smooth as the curve for the number of strikes. The number of participants increases slightly over time, as does the number of strikes, but the same annual cycle repeats itself regardless of U.S. force levels in Vietnam in any particular year. (The plot of participation in labor strikes is not presented here.)

The frequency of violent crimes also exhibits annual periodicity. The monthly fluctuations for the entire period under consideration remain proportionately constant irrespective of both the rate of escalation and the absolute level of U.S. forces in Vietnam. Though the pattern of monthly fluctuations is the same, each year brings an increase in the number of crimes committed and also in the rate at which the number is increasing. This may suggest that as the war continues, it facilitates a state of "normlessness" in which traditional strictures against criminal acts lose their effectiveness. From 1961 to 1963 the absolute number of crimes as well as the annual rate of increase rose. There is, however, a decrease in the percentage increase between 1964 and 1965. Initial escalation of U.S. forces in Vietnam did not appear to strengthen the rate of increase in crimes, nor even maintain it. This might be because the escalation of forces required an increase in the draft call and therefore removed a number of possible offenders from the population without yet resupplying it with a proportionate amount of Vietnam veterans to keep the population stable.

Figures 16-1 to 16-7 thus suggest that the Vietnam war escalation and the length of U.S. participation are unrelated generally to the secondary domestic turmoil indicators—numbers of labor strikes and violent crimes. The initial rate of change in antiwar protests, however, may be a function of the Vietnam escalation. The change in demonstrations declines, moreover, with a decrease in the escalation of the war, although the U.S. forces number more than half a million. A somewhat similar pattern seems to characterize urban riots and civil-rights participation. The number of participants in antiwar protests fluctuates annually enough to say that any increase would probably not be a response to any "atmosphere of violence" sustained by the length of the war. The fact that more poeple participate in fewer activities perhaps can be explained by a dynamic of social movements, that of the merger of "Movement" organizations.

QUALIFICATIONS AND POLICY RELEVANCE

The tentative findings of this study should be qualified in several ways. The correspondence between the concepts and their measures may not be exact.

For example, the indicators of the war and turmoil levels may not be adequate to the task. Justifications for using these indicators include their high correlation with other measures and their prior use in earlier systematic studies. U.S. casualties might have been used as an indicator of escalation rather than forces sent to Vietnam, but because these two variables are closely correlated, they can be used interchangeably. The indicators used for turmoil are justified by the results of a series of systematic studies. There is considerable evidence regarding the defining characteristics of turmoil. Factor analysis, a data-reduction method, yields a "turmoil" factor across several studies, consisting of demonstrations, riots, and general strikes. Although these studies are cross-national, the longitudinal results are not likely to differ substantially because different cross sections yield a similar turmoil factor.[21]

Another basis for qualifying the tentative findings is the reliability of the data. The accuracy required of data depends upon a study's purposes. Because this study focuses on the extent to which escalation and the length of the war relate to indicators of turmoil over time, a fairly high degree of error can be tolerated: the relative magnitude of each series is more important than their absolute levels. A more serious problem arises if there is a systematic bias introduced as a consequence of changing definitions and/or means of acquiring information, which may be the case with the violent crime statistics. Even here, however, error would have to be extremely large each month, and in the same direction, for the author to have accepted the violent crime data as having confirmed his initial hypotheses.

A third basis of qualification is the level of aggregation of data. For example, as regards crime information, it may be necessary to separate urban versus rural violent crimes and to plot urban crimes separately. An assumption of this study, however, is that this need not be done because most violent crime does in fact occur in urban areas.

The following statement of policy relevance of the tentative findings is suggestive rather than definitive. The initial escalation of the Vietnam war may be a primary cause of breakdown in social order. Rates of increase in several important indicators of domestic turmoil are related to the escalation of the war. Based on past patterns, a policy of further escalation abroad by the new administration in Washington may result in an increase in the turmoil at home. Furthermore, correctives to turmoil should take into account the relative decline in the rates of increase in turmoil that parallel the slowdown in the Vietnam buildup.

References

1.   Acknowledgments are made to Patricia Kwik for assistance in data acquisition, analysis, and interpretation; to Ted Robert Gurr, Irving L. Horowitz, Bryan T. Downs, and Stephen W. Burks for the use of their data; and to the National Science Foundation for a grant to the Comparative International Processes project.
2.   Georg Simmel, *Conflict and the Web of Intergroup Affiliations* (Glencoe, Ill.: The Free Press, 1955), p. 97.
3.   *Ibid.,* p. 97.
4.   Lewis A. Coser, *The Functions of Social Conflict* (Glencoe, Ill.: The Free Press, 1957), pp. 92-93.
5.   *Ibid.,* p. 104.

6.   *Ibid.,* p. 106.
7.   Quincy Wright, *A Study of War, II* (Chicago: University of Chicago Press, 1942), p. 1016.
8.   Wright, *I,* p. 140.
9.   Wright, *II,* p. 725.
10. Richard N. Rosecrance, *Action and Reaction in World Politics* (Boston: Little, Brown, 1963), p. 304.
11. Ernst R. Haas and A. S. Whiting, *Dynamics of International Relations* (New York: McGraw-Hill, 1956), pp. 61-62.
12. Samuel P. Huntington, "Patterns of Violence in World Politics," in S. P. Huntington (ed.), *Changing Patterns of Military Politics* (New York: The Free Press, 1962), pp. 40-41.
13. Rudolph J. Rummel, "Testing Some Possible Predictors of Conflict Behavior Within and Between Nations" in *Peace Research Society (International) Papers,* III, 1964, p. 17.
14. Raymond Tanter, "Dimensions of Conflict Behavior Within and Between Nations, 1958-1960," *Journal of Conflict Resolution,* X (March 1966), pp. 41-64, 46.
15. Tanter, pp. 61-62.
16. Pitirim Sorokin, *Social and Cultural Dynamics, III* (New York: American Book Co., 1937), pp. 487, 492.
17. Department of Defense Strength: 1965-1966, from John Voevodsky, *Quantitative Behavior of Warring Nations,* Mar. 27, 1968, mimeo; 1967-1968, Department of Defense, Unclassified Statistics on Vietnam, table 6. Department of Defense strength is the total number of U.S. military (Army, Navy, USMC, USAF, USCG) personnel in South Vietnam. All data are for the end of the period.
18. Data sources:
        (a) Antiwar protests: Computed from a list of all protests with a stated anti-war purpose in Irving L. Horowitz, Washington University, "The Struggle Is the Message: Tactics, Trends, and Tensions in the Anti-War Movement." Position paper prepared for the National Commission on the Causes and Prevention of Violence. Third draft: Sept. 23, 1968, mimeo.
        (b) Urban riots: Bryan T. Downs with Stephan W. Burks, "The Black Protest Movement and Urban Violence," paper read at the annual meeting of the American Political Science Association, Washington, D.C., Sept. 1968, mimeo.
        (c) Labor strikes: Computed from Department of Labor "Table E-1. Work Stoppages Resulting From Labor-Management Disputes," *Monthly Labor Review,* September 1968.
        (d) Violent crime: Computed from Federal Bureau of Investigation, U.S. Department of Justice, *Crime in the United States—Uniform Crime Reports* (1961-68).
        (e) Civil-rights demonstrations: Ted Robert Gurr, "Civil Rights and School Integration Demonstrations," June 1963 to May 1968, unpublished list.
19. Briefly, the line of "best fit" is drawn through the mean of the observations so as to minimize the sum of the distances from any point to the line.
20. Jeffrey Milstein and William Mitchell, "The Dynamics of the Vietnam Conflict: A Quantitative Analysis and Predictive Computer Simulation," paper prepared for delivery to the Peace Research Society (International) Conference to study the Vietnamese war, June 3-4, 1968, Cambridge, Mass.
21. Raymond Tanter, "Dimensions of Conflict Behavior Within Nations, 1955-60: Turmoil and Internal War," *Peace Research Society (International) Papers,* III (1965), p. 174.

PART VII

COMPARATIVE PATTERNS OF STRIFE AND VIOLENCE

A historian who contributed to this volume remarked, before editorial consultation, that it was difficult, perhaps impossible, to judge the relative levels of violence among nations. The chapters of this and the next part demonstrate that some instructive comparisons can be made. One kind of comparison, exemplified in the following two chapters, abstracts some general qualities or quantities from many occurences of group violence in order to make general statements about all such cases. Such comparisons have two purposes: to describe, and to explain.

Such descriptions and explanations can provide answers, partial ones at least, to some worrisome questions Americans pose to one another. Is the United States truly a "violent society" by comparison with other nations? The first of the following studies by Ted Robert Gurr, shows collective protest and violence in the United States in the mid-1960's to be greater, in relative terms, than in most of the European democracies but much less than in many other of the 114 nations studied. Moreover, civil strife in the United States shares the general characteristics of strife in other modern, democratic, and Western nations, but is strikingly dissimilar from strife in other groups of nations. Even the ethnic character of much American protest and group violence is paralleled by the experience of other Western nations. The unsatisfied demands of ethnic, regional, and other communal minorities are chronic sources of turmoil in many other Western nations, and relatively more common in Western nations than in most non-Western nations. Most of the results of this comparative study are reported here for the first time.

Is there some unique seed of evil at the heart of the American social order that nonetheless makes the tumult of recent years inexplicable in general terms? Both of these studies measure some general "causes" of strife and violence and determine their importance by comparing them statistically with measures of the extent of violence. Neither of them suggests that American violence is incomprehensible. Rather the evidence is that the same kinds of things have gone wrong in the United States that have gone wrong in many other nations, Western and non-Western, with predictable kinds of consequences. Americans may be unique in their wealth and uncommon in their immigrant heritage, but they are scarcely uncommon in their ability to mismanage their social affairs.

For example, Ivo and Rosalind Feierabend and Betty Nesvold inquire into the general connections between social change and political violence. Almost every desirable facet of our material and social lives are the products of massive and ongoing socioeconomic change. But anguish and violence as well as progress have been among the consequences of change in Western and non-Western societies—violence by those whose stable circumstances of life were disrupted, violence by those whose hopes for personal achievement were disenchanted. The authors identify patterns of change that are usually peaceful, other that are likely to generate the systemic frustrations that dispose men to violent political action. They then examine some types of change in 84 nations over a 30-year period and ask how they are related to violence in those nations, and to many of the nations' other characteristics. Political violence is least in traditional and modern societies, greatest in societies in the process of more or less rapid social change that we call "modernization." The evidence is that the more rapid are economic, social, and political change, the greater is political unrest—but with significant qualifications and exceptions. Among modernizing societies, for example, political instability is highest where education is rapidly expanding but economies are stagnant. The relations between change and disorder are complex, but their complexity is comprehensible and open to empirical examination. So far as the United States is concerned, it has the socioeconomic and political characteristics associated with civil peace in most other nations. But some specific groups are caught up in cycles of social change that resemble those of transitional societies both in their nature and in their violent consequences.

Does the United States have a potential for revolution commensurate with the fantasies of a few militants and the nightmares of some defenders of "law and order?" Quantitative assessment of some general causes of strife in the study by Professor Gurr demonstrates that the United States now has the general conditions associated with turmoil in other nations: intense, persisting discontents among some groups and a tumultuous history that provides justification enough for violent collective protest and violent defense. The comparisons also indicate that the nation has many of the social and political conditions that make revolutionary explosions of discontent unlikely in other countries. Yet all these conditions are subject to change. The direction and nature of their change will determine the future extent and forms of violence in America. But one principle seems evident from the comparative statistical evidence: whatever the historical, political, or social character of a nation, its citizens are likely to resort repeatedly to public protest and violence so long as they have severe and persisting grievances.

Chapter 17

A COMPARATIVE STUDY
OF CIVIL STRIFE[1]

By Ted Robert Gurr*

Group protest and violence is episodic in the history of most organized political communities and chronic in many. No country in the modern world has been free of it for as much as a generation. Sorokin analyzed the histories of 11 European states and empires over a 25-century span and found that they averaged only four peaceful years for each year in which major outbreaks of civil strife were in progress.[2] A comparison of average levels of disturbance, from the 6th to the 19th century, indicates that the most violent century, the 13th, had only twice the level of violence of the 18th, the most peaceful century.[3] Between 1900 and 1965, Calvert estimates that 367 revolutions occurred, defining revolution as forcible intervention to replace governments or change their processes. Of these, 135 occurred between 1946 and 1965, an average of 6.75 a year compared with an average of 5.56 a year for the entire 65-year period.[4] The Feierabends found that between 1948 and 1961, collective antigovernmental action occurred in all but one of 82 independent countries.[5] Between 1961 and 1967, some form of civil strife is reported to have occurred in 114 of the world's 121 larger nations and colonies.[6]

Relatively few occurrences of strife are "revolutionary." Most are manifestations of opposition to particular policies of governments or of hostilities between competing groups. Moreover, certain kinds and levels of civil strife are more likely to occur in some kinds of nations, and under some kinds of socioeconomic conditions, than under others. The kinds of systematic evidence mentioned above have been used not only to determine differences in the types and extent of civil strife among nations but to test various explanations of its causes. This paper summarizes some results of a comprehensive study of civil strife in 114 nations and colonies during the years from 1961 through 1965. This information is used in the first two sections, below, to make descriptive comparisons between characteristics of civil strife in the United States and other nations, and finally to estimate the relative importance of different causes of strife.

*The author is assistant professor of politics and faculty associate of the Center of International Studies at Princeton University. His publications include *Why Men Rebel* (Princeton University Press, forthcoming); *The Conditions of Civil Violence: First Tests of a Causal Model,* with Charles Ruttenberg (Princeton: Center of International Studies, 1957); *American Welfare,* with Alfred de Grazia (New York University Press, 1961); and a number of articles.

LEVELS AND TYPES OF CIVIL STRIFE AMONG
CONTEMPORARY NATIONS

In this study, "civil strife" means all collective nongovernmental attacks on persons or property that occur within a political system, but not individual crimes. We included symbolic attacks on political persons or policies such as political demonstrations and political strikes. Their inclusion does not reflect a normative judgment about their desirability or their legality; demonstrative protests are legal under some conditions in some countries, illegal in many others. Whatever their legal status, they are essentially similar to violent forms of protest: they are collective manifestations of substantial discontent that typically occur outside institutional frameworks for action. The violence used by regimes to maintain social control is not included as an aspect of civil strife because we are concerned with the extent to which ordinary citizens, not officials, resort to force. Regime coercion and violence can be both a cause of and a response to civil strife, and for the purposes of this study is analyzed in those terms, not as an integral part of strife.

Three general kinds of civil strife were distinguished in the study, in addition to more specific kinds:

> *Turmoil.*—Relatively spontaneous, unorganized strife with substantial popular participation, including political demonstrations and strikes, riots, political and ethnic clashes, and local rebellions.
> *Conspiracy.*—Highly organized strife with limited participation, including organized political assassinations, small-scale terrorism, small-scale guerrilla wars, coups d'état, mutinies, and antigovernment plots.
> *Internal war.*—Highly organized strife with widespread popular participation, accompanied by extensive violence and including large-scale terrorism and guerrilla wars; civil wars; "private" wars among ethnic, political, and religious groups; and large-scale revolts.

Information was collected on all such events reported in general news sources for 114 nations and colonies from 1961 through 1965. More than 1,000 events were identified, counting waves of demonstrations, riots, or terrorism over related issues as single "events." For each reported event or group of related events, we recorded such information as the kinds of socioeconomic groups involved, the approximate number of people who took part, their apparent motives or grievances, whom or what they attacked, how long they persisted, the severity of governmental response, and the costs of the action in terms of damage, casualties, and arrests.

Two kinds of comparisons of this information are reported here. The first, discussed in the following section, is based on summary measures of the magnitude of civil strife for each country. The "magnitude" of strife is a combined measure that takes into account its duration, pervasiveness, and a relative intensity. Additional data were collected for the United States, to update and increase the accuracy of some of the comparisons. Statistical comparisons in which the United States is shown separately are based on relatively precise American data for the 5-year period from June 1, 1963, through May 31, 1968, related to the 1961-65 data for other countries. Specific procedures used in collecting and summarizing the American and foreign data are described in appendix I, and the actual scores for 114 countries listed.

The second kind of comparison, discussed in the second section below, takes into account differences among groups of countries in the socioeconomic classes of people that typically initiate civil strife, their motives, their targets, and relative levels of violence. For this set of comparisons the countries of the world are divided into groups according to their economic, political, and regional characteristics. Appendix II describes the basis for each grouping and lists the groups in which each country was included.

Characteristics of American and Foreign Civil Strife

More than 2 million Americans resorted to demonstrations, riots, or terrorism to express their political demands and private antagonisms during the 5 years that ended in May 1968. No more than a fifth of them took part in activities prescribed by law, but their actions reportedly resulted in more than 9,000 casualties, including some 200 deaths, and more than 70,000 arrests. As table 17-1 shows, civil-rights demonstrations mobilized about 1.1 million Americans, antiwar demonstrations about 680,000, and ghetto riots an estimated 200,000. Riots were responsible for most of the consequent human suffering, including 191 deaths, all but a few of them Negroes. Almost all other deaths, an estimated 23, resulted from white terrorism against blacks and civil-rights workers. There is no direct way of determining whether these 5 years were the most tumultuous in American history. Some suggestive comparisons can be made with other nations in the contemporary era, however. Tables 17-2, 17-3, and 17-4 provide comparisons of some of the quantifiable information on strife in the United States against the characteristics of strife in other nations in the years 1961 through 1965.

The United States in the mid-1960's experienced relatively more civil strife than the majority of nations in the world, but far less than some. Compared with all other nations, it ranks 24th in total magnitude of strife. When the measures that make up the "magnitude" scores are examined, the United States ranks 27th among nations in the pervasiveness of strife; about 11 out of 1,000 Americans took part in strife, compared with an average of 7 per 1,000 in all other countries. The relative intensity of strife in the United States has been considerably lower, its proportional casualties ranking 53d among 114 nations; its duration very high, ranking 6th among all nations. Most civil strife in the United States was turmoil, in magnitude of which the country ranks 6th among nations. The magnitude of conspiracy, which in the United States took the form of interracial terrorism, ranks 38th among all nations.

The most meaningful standard of comparison is provided by the 17 other democratic nations of Western Europe and the British Commonwealth—the nations against which Americans typically judge their cultural, political, and economic progress. In magnitudes of all strife, and of turmoil, the United States ranks first among these nations, though only slightly ahead of France, Italy, and Belgium; Italy alone had a greater degree of conspiracy in this period. These overall rankings are made more meaningful when the component measures are examined. Strife was more pervasive in six of the European nations than in the United States and more intense in two. Only in the relative duration of strife does the United States markedly surpass all other Western nations.

Table 17-1.—Characteristics of major types of civil strife in the United States, June 1963-May 1968[a]

Type of event	Number of events identified[b]	Estimated number of participants[c]	Reported number of casualties[d]	Reported arrests[e]	Total magnitude of events[f]
Civil rights demonstrations[g]	369	1,117,600	389	15,379	7.53
Antiwar demonstrations[h]	104	680,000	400	3,258	5.62
Student protests on campus issues[i]	91	102,035	122	1,914	4.02
Antischool integration demonstrations[j]	24	34,720	0	164	1.66
Segregationist clashes and counter-demonstrations[k]	54	31,200	163	643	3.24
Negro riots and disturbances[l]	239	(200,000)	8,133	49,607	8.30
White terrorism against Negroes and rights workers[m]	213	(2,000)	112	97	2.48
All turmoil[a]	. . . . . .	2,174,655	9,285	. . . . . .	13.40
All conspiracy[a]	. . . . . .	2,040	122	. . . . . .	3.00
All strife[a]	. . . . . .	2,176,695	9,407	. . . . . .	13.64

[a]The data in this table include many estimates; all are imprecise. A number of less extensive forms of strife are not specifically shown, among them interracial clashes not involving civil-rights activities; terrorism within the Black Muslim movement; organized black terrorism against whites (negligible in this period); the local rebellion of Mexican-Americans in New Mexico in June 1967; and labor violence. Data on these events are included in the summary measures of magnitudes of strife.

bAs reported in news sources, with the inclusions and exclusions listed in footnotes (g) to (m). Demonstrations and riots that last for more than 1 day are counted as one. Simultaneous demonstrations in several neighborhoods or cities are counted separately.

cDespite the apparent precision of some of the figures, the component figures for many events are rough estimates and in some instances "guess-estimates" assigned by coders. Figures in parentheses are especially tentative.

dIncluding deaths and injuries. Riots reportedly resulted in the deaths of 191 persons; white terrorism in the deaths of 23. Injury reports are of questionable reliability, since there are no standard reporting practices for them. Minor injuries usually are unreported.

ePeople reported in news sources to have been detained. No totals are shown because of incomplete data on arrests for types of strife not separately listed.

fThe magnitude scores are not additive. Scores should be expanded to their fifth power to determine the actual average of their component Pervasiveness, Intensity, and Duration scores. Procedures by which magnitude scores are derived are described in app. I.

gAs reported in the New York Times Index, including civil rights and school integration demonstrations. Excluded are events involving less than 100 people, boycotts, and demonstrations that become riots or clashes with segregationists. Also see (i), below.

hBased on data reported by Irving Louis Horowitz, "The Struggle Is the Message," paper prepared for the Task Force on Group Protest and Violence, National Commission on the Causes and Prevention of Violence, Sept. 1968, tables 1, 2, and 3. The Horowitz data were revised to maintain comparability with other data by elimination of events involving less than 100 people and by exclusion of indoor rallies and protest meetings. Also see (i), below.

iStudent demonstrations on issues other than civil rights and peace, as reported in the New York Times Index. Student civil-rights protests are included under civil-rights demonstrations; student antiwar protests are included under antiwar demonstrations.

jDemonstrations opposing busing, integration, and local control of schools by Negroes, as reported in the New York Times Index. Excluded are demonstrations involving less than 100 people; and boycotts, strikes, and walkouts.

kDemonstrations by white segregationists opposing civil-rights demonstrations and collective public attacks by segregationists on rights demonstrators, as reported in the New York Times Index. Excluded are events in which less than 100 white demonstrators or attackers were involved.

l"Hostile outbursts" initiated by blacks, as reported by Bryan T. Downes with Stephen W. Burke, "The Black Protest Movement and Urban Violence," paper read at the annual meeting of the American Political Science Association, Washington, D.C., Sept. 1968, pp. 12-15.

mSmall-scale, clandestine acts of terror and violence, including bombings, arson, shootings, beatings, and major cross-burning incidents, as reported in the New York Times Index. Ordinarily no estimates of the number of participants are available.

Table 17-2.—Some general characteristics of strife in the United States, 1963-68,
compared with strife in other nations, 1961-65

	United States[a]	Average for 17 democratic European nations[b]	Average for 113 politics[c]
Proportion of population that participated (pervasiveness)	1,116 per 100,000	676 per 100,000	683 per 100,000
Pervasiveness rank of the United States compared with	. . . .	7	27
Casualties from strife as proportion of population (intensity)	477 per 10,000,000	121 per 10,000,000	20,100 per 10,000,000
Intensity rank of the United States compared with	. . . .	3	53
Duration rank of the United States compared with[d] . . .	. . . .	1	6
Rank of total magnitude of strife in the United States compared with	. . . .	1	24
Rank of magnitude of turmoil in the United States compared with	. . . .	1	6
Rank of magnitude of conspiracy in the United States compared with	. . . .	2	38

[a]The population estimate used for weighting participation and casualties from strife in the United States is 195 million. Information for the United States is more detailed than for other countries; as a consequence the U.S. data is somewhat inflated by comparison with the non-U.S. data.

[b]Nations used in this comparison are Australia, Austria, Belgium, Canada, Denmark, Finland, France, Greece, Ireland, Italy, Netherlands, New Zealand, Norway, Sweden, Switzerland, United Kingdom, and West Germany.

[c]All polities included in the study except the United States.

[d]Duration is the total number of days of all strife events in a country, not weighted by population, hence no comparative proportional measures are shown.

Specific comparative information on characteristics of strife in 20 Western and non-Western nations is shown in table 17-3. It is apparent from these data, as it is from the listing of magnitude-of-strife scores in appendix II, that some countries in all regions of the world, at all levels of economic development, have had less domestic conflict than the United States. With few exceptions, the countries more strife torn than the United States have experienced internal wars, like Venezuela, Algeria, and Indonesia.

Table 17-3. — Characteristics and magnitude of civil strife in selected nations, 1961-65, compared with the United States, 1963-68

Nation	Pervasiveness (participants per 100,000)[a]	Duration (sum of all events)[b]	Intensity (casualties per 100,000)[c]	Total magnitude of strife[d]
Selected European and Latin nations:				
Sweden	0	0	0	0.0
U.S.S.R.	10	3 months	.5	3.6
Canada	40	5 months	.5	4.9
Mexico	150	1 week	2	4.7
United Kingdom ·	80	1 year	.5	5.4
Japan	300	2 months	1.0	5.9
Brazil	1,100	4 months	.5	7.4
Belgium	6,700	1 month	6	10.5
France	2,200	2 years	4	12.1
United States . . .	1,100	5 years	5	13.8
Venezuela	1,300	5 years +	120	20.3
Other nations:				
Jamaica	20	1 day	0	1.5
U.A.R. (Egypt) . .	70	1 month	.5	3.9
Malaya	650	1 day	.5	4.5
Pakistan	200	3 months	1.5	6.3
Ghana	550	1 month	8	7.9
South Africa . . .	600	2 years	3	10.0
Ecuador	1,100	3 months	12	10.1
India	1,600	4 years	1	11.0
Rhodesia	150	2 years	50	16.4
Algeria	900	4 years	150	19.5
Indonesia	1,300	5 years	[e]4,000	33.7

[a]Total estimated participants in all strife events identified, weighted by population. All figures shown here are rounded to reflect their relative imprecision.

[b]Sum of the duration of all events identified, rounded to reflect the imprecision of the data.

[c]Sum of estimated deaths and injuries in all events identified, weighted by population, rounded to reflect the imprecision of the data.

[d]See footnote (f), table 17-1, and app. I.

[e]This figure is probably grossly inflated because it includes an unrealistic estimate of injuries associated with the massacre of several hundred thousand Indonesian Communists. (See app. I.)

Generally, civil strife in the United States has been somewhat more pervasive and of much longer total duration than strife in the majority of nations, but of average intensity. The relative human cost of strife has been much less than in countries wracked by internal wars, and less than that of several Western democratic nations. On the basis of this evidence, America has been in recent years a more tumultuous nation than any other Western nation, but not a more violent one. It has had frequent and widespread turmoil, most of it peaceful and legal, but relatively little of the intense, organized violence that accompanies widespread conspiratorial and revolutionary movements.

Differences in Magnitudes of Strife Among World Regions

The forms and magnitudes of civil strife vary greatly among types of nations, as is shown in table 17-4.[7] The most developed nations have considerably less turmoil and conspiracy than others, and almost never undergo internal wars. The most strife-torn countries are the "developing nations," not the least developed. Differences are equally great among nations grouped by type of political system. The most peaceful nations are the "polyarchic," those which approximate Western democratic forms and processes of government. The centrist countries, those which have autocratic one-party or no-party governments, are only slightly more prone to violence. Strife is likely to be far more pervasive and violent in countries ruled by small, modernizing elites and

Table 17-4.–Average magnitudes of civil strife, 1961-65, by type of nation[a]

	Magnitude of turmoil	Magnitude of conspiracy	Magnitude of internal war	Total magnitude of strife
Average for 114 nations	5.2	3.0	3.3	9.1
United States, 1963-68	13.4	3.0	.0	13.6
Nations grouped according to level of economic development:[b]				
High (37)[c]	3.8	1.8	.7	5.5
Medium (39)	6.5	3.8	4.3	11.6
Low (38)	5.1	3.4	4.0	9.9
Nations grouped according to type of political system:				
Polyarchic (38)[c] . .	4.9	1.8	1.0	6.5
Centrist (28)	4.2	2.9	2.1	7.2
Elitist (32)	5.4	3.5	6.8	12.4
Personalist (16) . . .	6.5	4.9	3.9	11.4
Nations grouped according to geocultural region:				
European (27)[c] . . .	3.6	1.2	.2	4.6
Latin (24)	5.6	4.0	2.9	9.6
Islamic (21)	5.4	3.2	3.7	9.7
Asian (17)	5.2	2.4	5.7	10.7
African (25)	6.1	4.2	5.1	11.7
Nations grouped according to racial homogeneity[d]				
Multiracial societies (39)	6.0	3.5	4.3	10.7
Other societies (81).	4.8	2.8	2.9	8.4

[a]See footnote (f), table 17-1, and app. I. Total magnitude of strife scores for each country are shown in app. II.

[b]The bases on which countries are grouped are indicated in app. II.

[c]Including data on the United States for 1961-65.

[d]For this comparison, "multiracial" societies are those whose population in the early 1960's included 5 percent or more of at least two of the following "racial" groups: Orientals, Amerindians, East Indians, Polynesians, Europeans, Negroes, Semites. The category includes all Latin American countries except Haiti, Argentina, Uruguay, and Paraguay; white-ruled Southern African countries and territories; Ethiopia, Sudan, Chad, and Niger; Algeria and Saudi Arabia; Malaya, Singapore, Cambodia, and Thailand; Israel, United States, Puerto Rico, and New Zealand.

in nations characterized by unstable, "strong-man" rule. It is noteworthy, though, that turmoil is very nearly as great among the democratic nations as it is among all nations; the establishment and survival of democracy are associated with the minimization of conspiracy and internal war, but not of the kinds of demonstrative and riotous protest that have characterized the United States in the past decade.

The countries of Eastern and Western Europe, combined with Israel and the English-settled countries outside of Europe, have had the lowest relative levels of all forms of strife, when compared either with other geocultural regions or the economic and political groupings. When strife does occur in these nations, it is highly likely to take the form of turmoil, internal war almost never. Asian and African nations have the highest levels of internal war and total strife, Latin and Islamic nations somewhat less. Conspiratorial movements are substantially more common in Latin America and tropical Africa than elsewhere.

The final set of comparisons groups nations according to their "racial" homogeneity. Multiracial societies tend to have greater levels of strife of all kinds, not merely turmoil, but the differences are moderate, not great. It is by no means certain that ethnic conflicts are responsible even for these differences. Countries with ethnic diversity also are more likely than others to have regional and political diversities, which also tend to generate internal conflicts.

None of these comparisons necessarily implies a causal connection between economic development, type of political system, or geocultural region and levels of civil strife. It could be argued, for example, that polyarchic nations can maintain democratic processes and institutions because of a lack of intensely violent internal conflict, and that intense conflicts within the elite give rise to "personalistic" patterns of government rather than vice versa. However, the results of the groupings do make it possible to anticipate the kinds and levels of strife specific kinds of countries are likely to experience. Such statements do not apply inevitably to specific cases, of course. Examination of the American data provides a striking illustration. The prospects for domestic peace are greatest for a nation that is highly developed, democratic, and European by geographical location or settlement. The United States meets all three criteria, yet has higher levels of turmoil and total strife than the average for any group of nations. The prospects for domestic violence are greatest for Asian and African nations that have low or medium levels of development and elitist or personalist political systems. Cambodia, the Ivory Coast, and Malagasy meet these criteria, yet have had lower levels of strife than any of the averages shown in table 17-4. General differences in economic development, political forms, and cultural heritage affect levels of civil strife; they do not determine them in any absolute sense.

ACTORS, OBJECTIVES, AND HUMAN COSTS

The measurable aspects of magnitudes of civil strife are not the only nor necessarily the primary determinants of strife's impact on political systems. Nor are they the only characteristics of collective protest open to systematic cross-national comparison. The socioeconomic classes and organizations that participate in strife are as important in evaluating its causes and effects as the number of people who take part. Their motives, and the men and institutions against which they act, are likely to be as consequential for the survival of their societies and governments as the intensity of action itself. Some of the evidence on differences among nations in these characteristics of strife is summarized below, and the American experience interpreted by reference to it.

Group Participation in Civil Strife

People of almost all walks of life have taken part in civil strife in the United States in the past decade. Civil rights and peace demonstrations have included tens of thousands of workers, students, and professional people. Ghetto rioters have included relatively large proportions of unskilled workers, but also many of the unemployed, skilled workers, and a few members of the black bourgeoisie.[8] "Backlash" protest and violence have mobilized both working- and middle-class whites. Only public employees have participated relatively little, aside from the tacit support some police have given to white vigilante groups and the violent responses of police and soldiers to some riots and some demonstrations.

Comparative evidence suggests that cross-class participation in strife is not exceptional; it is the norm, in European nations even more than others. Table 17-5 summarizes some of the evidence. An examination of turmoil events in all nations shows that working-class people take part in about three-quarters of them. However, the middle groups of society participate almost as often, in 60 percent of cases. Students are the middle group most often involved, but members of the business and professional classes also are present in substantial numbers in at least a fifth of all events. Even the nominal members of the political establishment, the "regime classes," occasionally take to the streets. A noteworthy difference emerges when group participation in all countries is compared with group participation in the European nations: in these countries, including the United States, middle classes are just as likely to participate in turmoil as are the working classes, and the regime classes are twice as likely to do so as they are in the world at large. It also should be noted that turmoil throughout the world usually—in three cases out of four—involves members of only one general class, whereas in European nations two or more classes participate in nearly half the events. These comparisons do not take into account the relative or absolute numbers of people from different classes involved in turmoil. They do strongly suggest, however, that turmoil in the contemporary world is not solely or primarily a lower-class phenomenon but a cross-class form of protest that is likely to mobilize discontented people whatever their social status.

Class participation in conspiratorical activity presents a distinctly different picture when all cases are examined. The conspiracy—terrorism, bombing, revolutionary plotting—is usually the work of middle and regime classes, not the lower classes. In the European nations, however, the pattern of participation is similar to that of turmoil: the working classes are more likely to participate than the middle classes, the middle classes more likely to do so than regime classes. The comparison is somewhat questionable, since participants could be identified in only 13 European cases, compared with 233 in the world at large.

Table 17-5.—Specific socioeconomic classes that participated in civil strife, 1961-65, by type of strife

| Type of socioeconomic class | Percentages of events in which specified classes are reported to have participated[a] | | | | |
| | Turmoil | | Conspiracy | | Internal war all nations[b,c] |
	All nations[b]	European nations[c]	All nations[b]	European nations[c]	
Working classes:					
Peasants, farmers . . .	18	17	4	n.d.	93
Urban workers, unemployed	40	41	5	n.d.	36
Any working-class groups[d]	73	67	25	62	100
Middle classes:					
Students	45	54	5	0	27
Petite bourgeoisie . . .	8	11	7	10	24
Professionals	11	12	18	20	33
Any middle-class groups[d]	61	70	41	46	63
Regime classes:					
Military, police	1	2	50	23	31
Civil servants	3	5	7	0	23
Political elite	3	7	32	8	31
Any regime groups . .	7	13	70	23	48
Percentage of events in which 2 or more of the 3 general classes participated. . .	39	47	30	30	76

n.d. = no data (computations not made).

[a]Percentages for specific classes are based on events for which specific information on participation is reported. Percentages for the 3 general types of classes are based on events for which either specific or general information is reported. A class is said to have participated if it apparently made up more than a tenth of the rank and file or more than a third of the leadership of an event.

[b]Data for events in 114 nations and colonies.

[c]Data for events in 27 Eastern and Western European nations plus developed English-speaking countries elsewhere, including the United States. Only two internal wars occurred in these countries, too few to justify inclusion of separate group-participation data.

[d]These percentages include a large number of events for which general but not specific class participation is known, hence they are not directly comparable with the percentages shown for specific class participation.

Patterns of class participation in internal war are intermediate between those of conspiracy and turmoil. The lower classes took part in all the 54 internal wars for which we have information, as would be expected by the definition of such events. The leaders and cadres of internal wars are more likely to include members of the middle classes than regime classes: very often both are involved.

Random crowds seldom initiate civil strife. We also can examine differences and similarities among nations in the kinds of organizations that provide the cohesion that is necessary for collective action. Group cohesion may be

provided by communal organization, or simply by people's awareness that
they belong to the same ethnic, religious, or territorial community. Group
contexts for action may also be provided by economic organizations, such as
trade unions and cooperatives; by legal political organizations, such as political parties and issue-oriented groups like antiwar organizations; by clandestine

Table 17-6.—Group contexts for civil strife, 1961-65, by type of nation

| Type of nation | Percentages of strife events known to have been initiated by groups of the specified types[a] | | | | | |
	Communal groups[b]	Economic groups[c]	Political groups[d]	Governmental groups[e]	Clandestine groups[f]	Other groups[g]
All nations (114)	20	7	42	10	15	6
Nations grouped according to level of economic development:						
High (37)	22	9	45	5	14	5
Medium (39)	17	7	47	9	13	6
Low (38)	23	5	27	16	21	7
Nations grouped according to type of political system:						
Polyarchic (38). . . .	19	8	50	5	13	5
Centrist (28)	28	5	34	4	21	8
Elitist (32)	26	5	38	13	12	5
Personalist (16) . . .	4	12	45	18	17	4
Nations grouped according to geocultural region:						
European (27)	34	9	40	1	14	3
Latin (24).	2	12	55	13	12	6
Islamic (21	18	7	34	11	20	10
Asian (17)	19	3	47	11	16	4
African (25)	32	5	33	11	14	5

[a]Based on data for approximately 1,020 strife events of all types. Of these events, 113
were clashes between nongovernmental groups, for example, between two political or
communal groups; only the group that initiated each clash is counted. Groups of several general types participated in some other strife events; only the largest group was
coded in such cases.

[b]Percentages of events in which initiators acted as members of territorial, religious, ethnic, or linguistic groups, whether or not formally organized.

[c]Percentages of events in which initiators acted primarily as members of organizations of
workers, the unemployed, craftsmen, traders, or employers.

[d]Percentages of events in which initiators acted as members of open political organizations, including political parties, politically oriented interest groups, and crowds at political meetings.

[e]Percentages of events in which initiators acted as members of the executive, administrative, or legislative structure, including military and police units, and the official party in
one-party states.

[f]Percentages of events in which initiators acted as members of prescribed political or
nonpolitical groups.

[g]Percentages of events in which initiators acted either as members of unstructured
crowds or apolitical student groups.

groups like guerrilla and terrorist movements; and by the governmental hierarchy itself, including the civil service and military establishment. The type of group context for civil strife was identified in more than a thousand of the civil-strife events and series of events in 1961-65; table 17-6 summarizes some of the data.

Several general patterns can be noted. Among nations generally, political groups most often mobilize people for strife, in 42 percent of cases, compared with communal groups in 20 percent of events and clandestine groups in 15 percent. Strife in the more developed and democratic nations is more often organized by legal political groups than in other nations and is less often carried out by clandestine groups. The implications are that strife is a recurrent facet of the political process and that the effect of economic development and political democratization is to channel it into the political process rather than to insulate politics from violence. At the same time the intensity and seriousness of violence in politics tends to decline. The most developed nations also experience substantially less strife within the governmental hierarchy than do other nations; that is, fewer plots, mutinies, and attempted coups by dissatisfied members of the political establishment. Such strife is also very infrequent in both democratic and centrist (authoritarian) nations, though presumably for different reasons. There also is a tendency for strife by economic organizations to increase as development increases.

Another significant contrast is provided by the relative frequency with which communal groups initiate strife. They are more often involved in strife in the most and least developed nations than in developing countries, and most often so in European and tropical African nations—in a third of events in both groups. Their relative preponderance in Africa is a manifestation of the unresolved tribal and ethnic cleavages that afflict that continent. In the European nations they seem to be residual group hostilities, ones that have persisted beyond the resolution of fundamental political and economic group conflicts. It is highly likely that increases in economic well-being and popular political participation for majority groups in European nations exacerbate the hostilities of regional and ethnic minorities that do not have what they regard as a fair share of those benefits. The United States, of course, manifests the problem to a striking degree; the evidence here suggests that it is also common in other Western nations.

Apparent Objectives of Civil Strife

With few exceptions, the demands or apparent objectives of participants in civil strife in the United States have been limited ones. Civil-rights demonstrators have asked for integration and remedial governmental action on Negro problems; they have not agitated for class or racial warfare. Peace marchers vehemently oppose American foreign policy and some of the men who conduct it; none of them have attempted to overthrow the political system. Black militants talk of revolutionary warfare; such sentiments are rarely voiced by those who participate in ghetto riots. By the testimony of most of their words and actions, they have been retaliating against the accumulated burden of specific grievances: inconsistent and coercive police control, economic privation, and social degradation. The United States has experienced chronic conspiratorial violence in the past decade, but it has been almost entirely defensive. Southern Klansmen and Northern vigilante groups have not opposed the existing socioeconomic or political system so much as they have tried to protect their conception of it and their position in it from Negroes, Jews, criminals, Communists, and a host of other perceived enemies. There are vociferous advocates of guerrilla, class, and racial warfare in the United States, and some of them have begun to take the lead in some antigovernment demonstrations and university rebellions. Nonetheless their objectives seem shared by few of their fellow participants. Their actions are comparable to those of rioters and demonstrators the world over, not those of guerrillas or revolutionary conspirators.

The comparative evidence summarized in tables 17-7 and 17-8 suggests that the dominant objectives of Americans who participate in strife more closely resemble the objectives of those in the European nations than elsewhere. Several characteristics of the worldwide patterns of demands or objectives of strife should be pointed out. In 93 percent of the events we examined, some kinds of political objectives were apparent. These political demands are twice as common as social ones, and social more than twice as common as economic ones. This does not necessarily imply that economic and social grievances are less important than political ones. It does suggest that when economic and social grievances are expressed, they are voiced in political terms.

Another general characteristic is that the objectives of turmoil are typically more limited than those of conspiracy and internal war. The objectives usually expressed in turmoil are opposition to particular governmental policies and actors, and the promotion of a group's particular social interests. Conspirators by contrast more often want to seize political power than attain any other specific objective. Internal wars usually manifest a variety of unlimited objectives, almost always including the seizure of regional or national power, often on behalf of a particular class or communal group. Internal wars also are more likely to reflect explicit economic objectives than are turmoil or conspiracy.

The objectives of particular kinds of strife in European nations differ somewhat from those of all nations. Turmoil in European nations is somewhat more likely to be based on opposition to or demands for specific governmental actions than turmoil elsewhere, and considerably more likely to include explicit social objectives. Ideological issues and promotion of the interest of a particular community, for example, are relatively common issues of conflict in European nations. Explicit demands for "social goods" such as removal of social barriers to mobility, rights of equal treatment, free association, and more and better education are much more common in European nations than elsewhere. The objectives of conspiratorial activity in European nations are sharply different from conspiratorial objectives elsewhere; they are relatively limited and resemble the objectives of European turmoil. European conspirators seldom want to seize political power, but are much more likely to oppose particular political policies and actors. They also are quite likely—in 59 percent of the 27 instances—to have explicit social objectives, usually ideological or communal ones.

When all types of strife are combined and their objectives compared, in table 17-8, some of these relationships become more sharply apparent. The seizure of political power is rarely an objective of strife among highly developed, democratic, or European nations. When nations are grouped according to their level of economic development, it is apparent that the lower the level

Table 17-7.—Objectives manifested in civil strife, 1961–65

Type of motive	Percentages of events in which specified objectives were expressed or apparent from actions[a]				
	Turmoil		Conspiracy		Internal war, all nations
	All nations	European nations	All nations	European nations	
Political objectives:					
Retaliation	4	3	2	7	4
Seize political power	1	0	37	4	25
Increase political participation .	2	1	0	0	2
Oppose competing political group	6	4	2	11	0
Promote or oppose a specific governmental policy	23	33	7	21	0
Promote or oppose a political actor	8	4	13	14	0
Oppose a foreign nation's policies or actors	20	13	3	11	0
Several or diffuse political objectives	26	26	32	33	67
Any political objectives	90	85	98	100	98
Economic objectives:					
Retaliation	1	0	0	0	0
Seize economic goods	2	1	3	0	9
Change economic distribution patterns	7	10	4	0	7
Several or diffuse economic objectives	8	11	1	0	19
Any economic objectives.	18	22	8	0	36
Social objectives:					
Retaliation	5	7	3	7	5
Promote or oppose belief systems.	11	17	10	15	5
Promote or oppose an ethnic, linguistic, religious, or regional community	15	23	7	33	30
Increase social goods	1	19	2	4	2
Several or diffuse social objectives	11	6	9	0	43
Any social objectives	43	71	32	59	87
Number of events.	653	136	294	27	55

[a]Objectives are those attributed to participants in news sources or apparent from the nature of the event. For example, peace demonstrations in the United States and Spanish student riots against governmental bans on student organization would be coded "promote or oppose a specific governmental policy"; a civil-rights demonstration would be coded both "promote or oppose a specific policy" and "promote or oppose a community"; a French general strike against a government wage freeze would be coded both "promote or oppose a specific policy" and "change economic distribution patterns"; white attacks on civil-rights demonstrators would be coded "retaliation" under "Social Objectives"; and so forth. Coding categories are defined in Gurr with Ruttenberg, app. A. Only primary objectives were coded, but in many cases, especially in internal war, participants had several major objectives of each general type. For example, an antiwar demonstration at a speech of a U.S. Cabinet member would be coded "several political objectives" because it reflects opposition both to the individual and a policy he supports. Percentages shown for each subheading do not necessarily add to the total because of rounding errors.

Table 17-8.—*Some types of objectives manifest in civil strife, 1961-65, by type of nation*

Type of nation	Percentages of events in which specified types of objectives were expressed or apparent from action[a]						
	Seize political power	Increase participation or oppose competitors	Promote/ oppose policies or actors	Promote oppose community	Any political objectives	Any economic objectives	Any social objectives
All nations (114)	13	6	26	13	93	16	43
Nations grouped according to level of economic development:							
High (37)	6	6	56	13	92	16	46
Medium (39)	12	5	40	10	92	15	36
Low (38).	22	6	27	17	94	18	49
Nations grouped according to type of political system:							
Polyarchic (38) . . .	6	6	49	14	91	16	47
Centrist (28).	8	5	38	10	91	10	51
Elitist (32).	17	8	33	18	93	20	45
Personalist (16) . . .	22	2	44	5	98	16	20
Nations grouped according to geocultural region:							
European (27). . . .	1	7	49	25	87	18	69
Latin (24)	22	4	55	0	96	15	4
Islamic (21)	10	3	34	13	96	13	66
Asian (17)	6	1	47	13	95	17	52
African (25).	22	12	23	18	86	17	40

[a]Categories of objectives are combinations of categories shown in table 17-7. "Increase participation or oppose competitors" combines "increase political participation" and "oppose competing political group." "Promote/oppose policies or actors" combines "promote or oppose a specific governmental policy," "promote or oppose a political actor," and "oppose foreign nation's policies or actors."

of development, the more common are attempts to seize power. The higher the level of development, however, the more likely does strife represent opposition to specific policies and individuals. Demands for increased political participation, a common student grievance in the United States and elsewhere, for example, are relatively uncommon and do not vary greatly among nations according to levels of economic development; they do tend to be more common in African and European states than in others.

There are substantial differences among groups of nations in social objectives for civil strife. They are substantially more common in European and Islamic nations than in others, and very infrequent in Latin American nations. This does not necessarily mean that Latin Americans lack social grievances, only that they seldom are voiced in specific demands in strife. It should be pointed out that, by contrast, the groups of nations do not differ substantially in the relative frequency of political or economic objectives for civil strife. Political objectives predominate, being salient in at least 86 percent of the events in each set of nations. Economic objectives are relatively uncommon, characterizing between 10 and 20 percent of events in each group.

One specific category of social objectives, promotion of or opposition to interests of specific communities, is separately shown in table 17-8 because it includes the explicit demands of American civil-rights demonstrators, the implicit demands of ghetto rioters, and the sometimes violent resistance of white Americans to those demands. This kind of social objective is more common in civil strife in the European nations than any other, being specifically identifiable in a quarter of all occurrences of strife. Country-by-country examination of the evidence suggests that the relative frequency of such motives in the European nations is only partly the result of the inclusion of the United States in this group. More important, it indicates that incomplete assimilation of minority groups into national life is one of the pervasive unresolved problems of the Western nations. Examples are the conflicts between French- and English-speaking Canadians, the Flemish and the Waloons of Belgium, Coloureds and whites in England, Catholics and Protestants in Northern Ireland, Arabs and Jews within Israel. Other manifestations are the chronic and sometimes violent separatist activities of German-speaking Italians, Basques and Catalonians in Spain, Welsh nationalists, Bretons in France, Ukrainians in the Soviet Union, and the people of the Swiss Jura. Such conflicts tend to be low keyed; if they are not resolved, however, they can flare up repeatedly in intense strife, as they have in the United States, Belgium, and Spain.

The Targets of Civil Strife

Even the members of a rampaging mob are selective in the targets they attack. They, along with demonstrators, conspirators, and rebels, focus their actions on the objects and people that symbolize their grievances. Table 17-9 shows that there is little difference among the primary targets of turmoil when the European nations are compared with all nations. Property is attacked in about 4 cases out of 10, private property slightly more often than public. Political actors are by far the most common objects of verbal and physical attack. Demonstrations are typically directed against the political figures who are held responsible for grievances by their sins of commission or omission; riots usually include attacks on several kinds of political actors, including both officials and the police. A fifth of turmoil events are focused on foreign political actors, usually representatives of governments with unpopular foreign policies. The United States has been the target of many such demonstrations and riots throughout the world; Americans also have taken to the streets to oppose actions of the governments of the Soviet Union, Cuba, and other countries. Nonpolitical actors—usually members of ethnic groups—are attacked in about a fourth of turmoil events, somewhat more often in the European nations than in others.

The objects of conspiratorial attacks do vary substantially between European and other nations. The European conspirator is much more likely to vent his anger on property, less likely to attack public figures. The statistical differences reflect the fact that European conspirators more often resort to symbolic and indirect political opposition—for example, bombing public buildings and police barracks—than to direct attacks on the lives and governments of political leaders. Conspiratorial attacks on members of ethnic or

Table 17-9.—Primary targets of civil strife, 1961–65, by type of strife

Type of target	Percentages of events in which specified primary targets are identifiable[a]				
	Turmoil		Conspiracy		Internal war, all nations[b,c]
	All nations[b]	European nations[c]	All nations[b]	European nations[c]	
Property targets:					
Public.	15	18	26	36	76
Private	18	22	17	36	69
Foreign.	17	14	7	7	24
Any property	37	39	36	64	82
Political actors:					
Public figures	28	27	56	39	2
Military and police	16	14	9	4	13
Private political groups . . .	8	4	2	7	2
Several of the above	16'	23	16	18	76
Foreign public figures and military personnel. . . .	20	21	4	11	25
Any political actors	83	83	85	75	93
Nonpolitical actors:					
Communal groups.	14	22	3	4	36
Economic actors.	4	2	–	–	–
Several groups, and random victims	3	6	7	4	44
Any nonpolitical actors (including others)	21	31	11	11	80
Number of events	666	136	315	28	55

[a]The primary targets are the places or people on which violence, threats, or demands are focused. For example, the Watts riot of 1965 was coded as directed against private and public property, the police, and several types of nonpolitical actors (both white store-keepers and random white victims). Peace marches were coded as directed against public figures, since they constituted demands made on political leaders. Percentages do not necessarily add to subtotals because the subcategories shown here are not all mutually exclusive or exhaustive.
[b]See footnote (b), table 17-5.
[c]See footnote (c), table 17-5.

other nonpolitical actors are rare. The reemerging American phenomenon of terroristic attacks by white vigilantes on Negroes and their white supporters, and the new phenomenon of black-militant attacks on whites, have relatively few parallels among either Western or non-Western nations. Such group hostilities elsewhere usually inspire riots, not terrorism.

Internal wars by their very nature involve attacks on many targets: property, public and private; politicians; national and foreign soldiers and police; and nonpolitical opponents and victims of all sorts. Turmoil is more likely than internal war to be focused on a few objects and individuals, while conspiracy is likely to be even more narrowly focused.

The Human Costs of Civil Strife

Americans have been shocked by the occurrence of nearly 200 deaths in ghetto riots, by political assassinations, and by several dozen killings by black and white terrorists in recent years. By comparison with most nations, however, the proportional loss of American lives in civil strife has been low. Table 17-10 summarizes comparative information on the human costs of strife. An estimated 750,000 people lost their lives in civil violence between 1961 and 1965, the great majority of them victims of internal wars. Although almost all types of civil strife in the United States resulted in casualties, the relative loss of life has been comparable to that of other developed nations and of other European nations. Both turmoil and conspiracy lead to relatively few deaths in the highly developed nations, in democratic countries, and in the European and Latin American nations. The loss of life tends to be greatest in

Table 17-10.—The human costs of civil strife, 1961–65, compared with the United States, 1963–68

Type of nation	Percentages of events with casualties[a]		Average number of deaths per event[b]			Deaths per million popula-tion[c]
	Tur-moil	Conspir-acy	Tur-moil	Conspir-acy	Internal war	
All nations (114)	59	42	18.1	17.2	13,900	238
United States, 1963–68[d]	–	–	–	–	–	1.1
Nations grouped according to level of economic development:						
High (37)[e]	56	38	3.5	9.2	160	1.7
Medium (32).	59	45	28.4	22.1	12,000	264
Low (38)	69	39	17.2	18.9	18,500	841
Nations grouped according to type of political system:						
Polyarchic (33)[e]	61	33	8.8	8.3	3,600	12
Centrist (28).	54	52	38.9	23.1	2,200	19
Elitist (32)	58	44	16.2	20.6	20,000	1,604
Personalist (16)	62	40	12.0	17.5	4,300	223
Nations grouped according to geocultural region:						
European (37).	61	25	11.5	0.4	220	2.4
Latin (24)	63	44	5.9	16.2	2,900	76
Islamic (21)	53	45	19.2	23.5	6,500	222
Asian (17)	45	42	42.6	25.7	35,000	357
African (25)	64	43	18.5	17.5	4,900	539

[a]Percentage of events of each type in which any deaths or injuries were reported among initiators, their opponents, or victims. Executions of initiators are included. All internal wars result in casualties, hence no separate percentages are shown. Also see (d), below.

[b]Based on totals of all reported deaths. Only rough and questionably reliable estimates of deaths are available for most internal wars. The averages are rounded to reflect this imprecision. Also see (d), below.

[c]Total reported deaths for the countries in each group divided by the total population of the countries in that group.

[d]Percentages and deaths per event for the United States, 1963–68, are not reported because the data are not comparable. Many turmoil events counted in the 1961–65 period are waves of related outbreaks, each wave counted as one "event." Strife events in the United States, 1963–68, were recorded on an occurrence-by-occurrence basis without attempting to categorize them in waves.

turmoil and conspiracy events in the developing nations, centrist nations, and Asian countries.

By far the most striking differences among groups of nations are in deaths per million population. The rate in the least-developed nations, 841 per million, is 500 times the 1.7 rate in the most developed nations. The rates in the democratic and centralized countries, 12 and 19 per million, respectively, are about one one-hundredth of the 1,604 rate in the new nations that are characterized by elitist leadership and relatively weak and unstable political institutions. When nations are grouped according to geocultural region, civil-strife death rates appear to vary with the regions' relative levels of economic development. The rate is substantially the lowest in the European nations, 2.4 per million; some 30 times greater in Latin America, which is considerably less developed; and 150 to 200 times greater in the underdeveloped Asian and African states.

It is not justifiable to conclude from these figures that increasing economic development leads directly to decreasing deaths from civil violence. It is a truism that people discontented with their poverty are more likely to rebel than people whose economic desires are satisfied, but even these descriptive data suggest that their political environment has a major influence on the consequences of rebellion. Democratic and centrist countries are likely to have both the coercive capacity to restrain strife with minimal loss of life and the institutional structures that can provide alternatives to and solutions for violence. The least-developed countries that have relied on elitist or personalistic leadership, however, confront two interrelated and almost insoluble problems. Their economies produce too little to satisfy the economic aspirations of many of their citizens. Their leaders, for lack of will, ability, or resources, are often unable to establish strong and pervasive means of coercive and institutional control. When civil strife does occur in these countries, the regimes are usually strong enough to resist it but lack the capacity either to suppress it or to remedy its causes. The consequence is likely to be an escalating spiral of inconsistent and ineffective repression and increasing popular resistance, culminating in the peace of the charnel house that is statistically manifested in the death rates shown in table 17-10.

COMPARATIVE EVIDENCE ON THE CAUSES OF CIVIL STRIFE

Some Psychological Preconditions of Civil Strife

The popular and sociological cliché is that "frustration" or "discontent" or "relative deprivation" is the root cause of rebellion. Cliché or not, the basic relationship is as fundamental to understanding civil strife as the law of gravity is to atmospheric physics: relative deprivation, the phrase used in this research, is a necessary precondition for civil strife of any kind. The greater the deprivation an individual perceives relative to his expectations, the greater his discontent; the more widespread and intense is discontent among members of a society, the more likely and severe is civil strife. Relative deprivation is not whatever the outside observer thinks people ought to be dissatisfied with. It is a state of mind that I have defined as a discrepancy between people's expectations about the goods and conditions of life to which they are justifiably entitled, on the one hand, and, on the other, their value capabilities—the degree to which they think they can attain those goods and conditions.

This is not a complicated way of making the simplistic and probably inaccurate statement that people are deprived and therefore angry if they have less than what they want. Two characteristics of value perceptions are more important than this "want-get ratio": people become most intensely discontented when they cannot get what they think they deserve, not just what they want in an ideal sense; and when they feel they are making inadequate progress toward their goals, not whether they have actually attained them or not.

Underlying the relative deprivation approach to civil strife is the frustration-aggression mechanism, apparently a fundamental part of our psychobiological makeup. When we feel thwarted in an attempt to get something we want, we are likely to become angry, and when we become angry the most satisfying inherent response is to strike out at the source of frustration. Relative deprivation is, in effect, a perception of thwarting circumstances. How angry men become in response to the perception of deprivation is determined partly by the relative importance to them of the expectations to which they are striving; the number of alternatives they have yet to try; and the degree of the discrepancy itself. If angry men believe that collective protest or violence are legitimate responses to anger, and if they think that protest or violence will help alleviate their discontent, the impetus to civil strife is strengthened. If they believe that strife is unjustified and unlikely to succeed, they are more likely to contain their anger or to divert it into other activities.

In brief, the basic psychological factors in the genesis of civil strife are the intensity and extent of deprivation-induced discontent in a group, and people's attitudes about the justifiability and utility of collective protest and of collective violence in response to discontent.[9] To evaluate the relative importance of these psychological variables as causes of civil strife, we devised indirect measures of deprivation and justificatory attitudes about strife for a large number of national populations, and related them statistically to measures of the magnitude of civil strife. Some of the procedures and results are summarized here.

Relative Deprivation as a Cause of Civil Strife

The first step toward assessing deprivation-induced discontent among nations was to identify general patterns of social conditions that cause it. Four patterns of conditions likely to cause discontent are shown in figures 17-1 through 17-4. In the first (fig. 17-1), group deprivation results when expectations increase without an accompanying increase in the potential for their satisfaction. The pattern has been called the "revolution of rising expectations." To test its importance, we assumed that expectations should be increasing most rapidly in countries in which education has been expanding most rapidly, and that expectations should be highest in countries with the highest educational levels. To take account of differences in capabilities, we hypothesized that discontent would be greatest in countries in which educational levels were expanding more rapidly than the economy.

Measures of educational levels, and of educational levels and changes relative to economic levels and changes, were constructed for 119 nations and

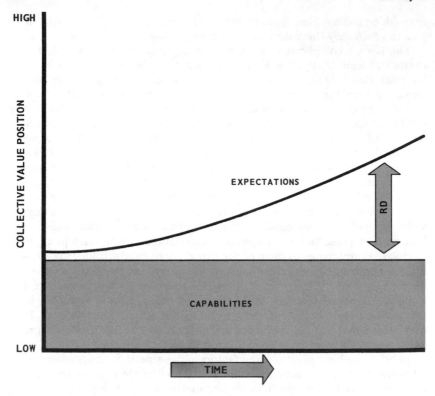

Figure 17-1.–Aspirational deprivation.

Note

"Relative deprivation (RD)" is men's perception of discrepancy between their value expectations and their value capabilities.

"Collective value position" is the average level or amount of goods and conditions of life that members of a collectivity have or expect to attain.

"Value expectations" are the average value positions justifiably sought by members of a collectivity.

"Value capabilities" are the average value positions members of a collectivity perceive themselves capable of attaining or maintaining.

correlated with measures of magnitude of civil strife for 1961–63. As predicted, we found that the countries with the most rapidly expanding educational systems experienced the greatest strife, but the correlation for all nations was relatively weak, +0.16. When education was related to economic conditions, however, the results contradicted the assumptions and hypotheses. For example, we found that strife was high in countries with high economic growth but stable or declining education, and lower in countries with relatively little growth but expanding education. We also found that, in the developing nations, the greater the relative increase in higher and technical education compared to the level of development, the less likely was turmoil and the lower the magnitude of strife. These and other findings all point to one

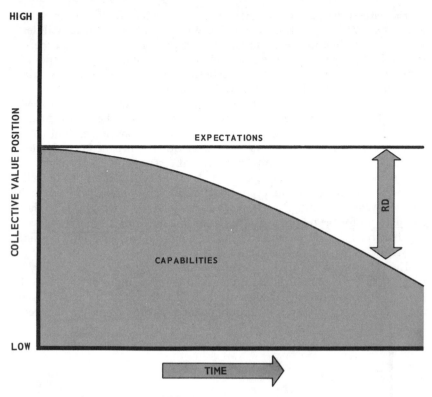

Figure 17-2.—Decremental deprivation.

general conclusion: In both developed and developing societies, but not in
the least developed, *the expansion of educational opportunities is less likely
to raise expectations to an unsatisfiably high level than it is to provide ambitious men with an increased sense of capacity to attain their expectations.*[10]
There almost certainly are circumstances in which exposure to new and better
ways of life increases men's expectations beyond the possibility of attainment
and to the point of violent reaction; expanding education appears to meliorate
rather than reinforce them.

The pattern of deprivation-inducing conditions in figure 17-2 is one of declining capabilities in the presence of stable expectations. Such "decremental
deprivation" is experienced, for example, by people deprived of long-held
political liberties; by groups with stable incomes who are hurt by increased
taxes or inflation; and by middle-class groups threatened with displacement
by the upward mobility of groups below them on the socioeconomic ladder.
The pattern tends to lead to defensive protest and violence, sometimes of a
revolutionary sort. The American Revolution was preceded by British attempts to increase political and economic control over the colonies; the Civil
War by Northern attempts to restrict slavery; the first Ku Klux Klan by
Northern subjugation and Negro mobility after the Civil War; current vigilante
activity in Northern cities by declining law and order and expansion of Negro
neighborhoods.

The pattern that seems most often associated with revolutionary movements is shown in figure 17-3: a period of substantial increase in capabilities
or satisfactions followed by a substantial relative decline. Prolonged experience of increasing well-being generates intense expectations about continued
increases; if changing circumstances make those expectations seem unsatisfi-
able, the likely consequence is intense discontent.[11]

For the purpose of estimating the extent and importance for strife of these
two kinds of deprivation, we developed many measures of short-term deterioration in political and economic conditions among nations in the 1950's and
early 1960's. The assumption was that any short-term decline in economic
conditions, and any governmental policies that restricted political activity or
reduced people's socioeconomic status, increased deprivation. Both the relative degree of decline and the proportion of a national population likely to be
affected were estimated. (No attempt was made to distinguish between the
two patterns for the purpose of cross-national comparison.) We hypothesized
that the greater the degree and scope of all such relative declines in a nation,
the greater its magnitude of strife.

The pattern in figure 17-4 represents persisting deprivation. In the very
long run, men's expectations about the goods and conditions of life to which
they are entitled are likely to adjust to what they are capable of attaining. In
the medium run, however, some groups may persistently demand and expect

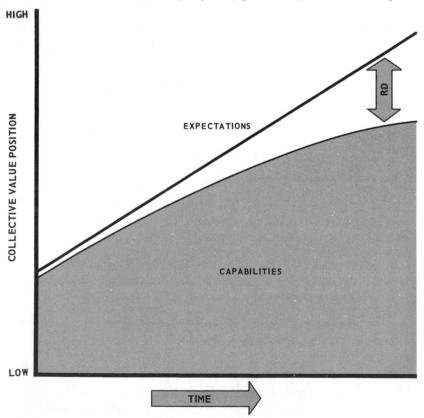

Figure 17-3.—Progressive deprivation.

such conditions as greater economic opportunity, political autonomy, or freedom of religious expression that their societies will not or cannot provide.
Six kinds of persisting deprivation were measured, again taking into account
both their relative severity and the proportion of people in each nation who
were affected by them: economic and political discrimination, political sepa-
ratism, dependence on foreign economies, lack of educational opportunity,
and religious divisions. A combined measure was devised to facilitate simple
comparisons with magnitudes of civil strife.[12]

Some results of the correlation analysis are summarized in table 17-11.
With few exceptions, both short-term and persisting deprivation are significant
causes of the various forms of civil strife among groups of nations. Among
highly developed nations, for example, differences in short-term deprivation
explain $(0.57)^2$ or 32.5 percent of differences in total magnitude of strife;
and differences in persisting deprivation account for $(0.32)^2$ or 10 percent of
differences in strife. Two qualifications reinforce the significance of these
findings. One is that the relationships are relatively strong, despite the fact
that deprivation was measured only partially and indirectly, often on the basis
of suspect data. The fact that the correlations between deprivation and strife
in the least-developed countries are somewhat weaker than in the developed
countries, for example, may reflect the unreliability of economic and other
data for these countries. A second qualification is that, generally, deprivation

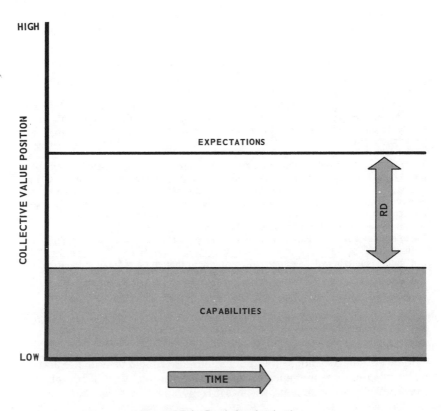

Figure 17-4.—Persisting deprivation.

Table 17-11.—Correlations between deprivation and magnitudes of civil strife
1961–65, by type of nation

Type of nation	Correlations[a] between short-term deprivation and magnitudes of—			Correlations[a] between persisting deprivation and magnitudes of—		
	Tur-moil	Conspir-acy	Total strife[b]	Tur-moil	Conspir-acy	Total strife[b]
All nations (114)[c]	32	45	47	27	30	35
Nations grouped according to level of economic development:						
High (37)[c]	50	38	57	30	28	34
Medium (39).	29	55	58	28	46	29
Low (38)	*04	41	23	*19	*07	31
Nations grouped according to type of political system:						
Polyarchic (38)[c]	28	49	46	48	29	46
Centrist (27)[d]	47	63	55	37	*31	52
Elitist (32)	*15	49	58	33	*14	37
Personalist (16)	58	*05	*21	*10	52	*35
Nations grouped according to geo-cultural region:[e]						
Anglo-Nordic (10)[c]	73	82	80	65	83	80
Western Europe (11)	*16	*08	*30	59	*–31	*41
Eastern Europe (8)	78	*–05	79	*37	*–47	*–05
Latin (24).	43	*28	51	59	43	42
Islamic (21)	37	37	*22	*–06	*26	47
Asian (17)	*25	53	56	*30	*15	*28
African (23)	*15	50	55	*15	*11	*22

[a]The figures shown are product-moment correlation coefficients multiplied by 100. A perfect positive relationship is 100; a perfect negative relationship, –100. The differences among nations in magnitudes of strife that are statistically "explained" by variations in deprivation can be determined by squaring each correlation coefficient. For example, among all nations, variations in extent of short-term deprivation explain $(0.47)^2$ or 22 percent of differences in total magnitude of strife. Asterisked (*) coefficients are statistically significant at less than the 0.10 level.

[b]Total magnitude of civil strife, including internal war. The groups of nations vary so greatly in frequencies of internal war—some groups having none, 1, or 2, others 20 or more—that comparisons of correlations with magnitudes of internal war among groups of nations are misleading. Among all nations the correlations of short-term and persisting deprivation with magnitude of internal war are, respectively, 0.34 and 0.24.

[c]Including data on the United States for 1961–65.

[d]Excluding the colony of Papua-New Guinea, which was included in this group in preceding tables.

[e]The nations are grouped somewhat differently here than in preceding tables. (See app. II.)

is an apparent cause of all major forms of strife, and of most forms in most groups of countries. This general similarity of results strongly supports the underlying theoretical argument.

Some differences among groups of nations also should be noted. Short-term deprivation is more important as a cause of turmoil than of conspiracy in the most developed nations, whereas it is more important as a cause of conspiracy in the less-developed nations. This difference also is apparent among the geocultural regions: short-term deprivation leads to conspiracy in the least-developed, Asian and African nations; and to turmoil in the more-developed, European and Latin nations. We pointed out above that conspiracy is usually organized by the upper and middle classes. The inference is that in less-developed countries, deprivation of the kinds indexed in this study is more strongly felt by these groups than by the working classes. The deprivations that give rise to turmoil in the less-developed countries may be those caused by the social dislocations of socioeconomic development itself, which are not well represented in these measures.

An unusual pattern is apparent when the "Anglo-Nordic" and the other two groups of European nations are compared. The correlations between deprivation and strife in the Nordic and English-speaking countries are far higher than in any other group of nations. Differences in deprivation account for almost all their differences in strife. The findings reflect partly the close connection between the degree and extent of discriminatory deprivation in countries like South Africa, Rhodesia, and the United States and high levels of ethnic strife in them, and the relative lack of discrimination and negligible strife in the Nordic countries, Australia, and New Zealand. To the same point, we found in an earlier study of the causes of civil violence in 1961–63 that the proportional size of groups subject to discrimination, however intense, correlated 0.30 with magnitude of strife in 119 nations.

In the other Western European nations, persisting deprivation is more closely related to turmoil than short-term depriviation. This is consistent with the findings, discussed above, that persisting deprivation is a source of chronic disorder throughout the Western community, not only in the United States. On the other hand, the lack of relationship between short-term deprivation and magnitudes of strife has two possible explanations. One is that the immediate causes of strife in Europe are of a specific and idiosyncratic kind not represented in general measures of deprivation. Another is that much European strife is a manifestation of tactical political motives more than of intense discontent. One observation supports the second interpretation: the fact that the political demonstration, riot, and strike are established tactics of both leftwing and rightwing groups in the three European countries with highest magnitudes of strife—Italy, France, and Greece. Both explanations probably apply, and are relevant to other countries as well: the resolution of a nation's most critical problems may lead to heightened awareness of other problems, and in some circumstances to the institutionalization of turmoil as a response to them.

In the Eastern European nations, deprivation is rather closely related to turmoil, the only consequential form of strife that occurred in the Communist countries in the 1961–65 period. This may seem surprising, given the common assumption that collective expressions of opinion are so carefully controlled by the Communist regimes that demonstrative protest occurs only at times and places when control is deliberately or accidentally loosened. Other analyses show, however, that turmoil is substantially lower in these nations than in other European nations. Totalitarian control seems to minimize absolute levels of strife, but in spite of it intense discontents are likely to be given some public expression even in the short run.

Legitimacy and Tradition of Strife as Causes of Civil Strife

It is all but impossible, without opinion survey evidence, to ascertain men's attitudes about the justifiability and utility of collective protest and violence. Historical and survey evidence suggests that Americans as a whole are more favorably disposed to violence as a solution to problems than many other national groups.[13] For purposes of cross-national comparison, we used two indirect measures to represent these attitudes. A measure of the legitimacy of the political system was devised, on the theoretical assumption that people are less likely to attack their political leaders, or to engage in violence against others, if they have a high positive regard for the political system. Highest legitimacy scores were given to nations whose political system was developed solely by indigenous leaders, rather than borrowed or imposed from abroad, and which had endured for the longest time without substantial structural change.

The second measure is of levels of collective violence in the period from 1946 to 1959. The assumption is that the greater strife has been in a country's past, the more likely some of its citizens are to regard it as justifiable, and the more likely some of them would have found it partially successful in the past, and hence regard it as potentially useful in the future. A history of civil strife should thus facilitate future strife, a relationship that is historically documented in detail for the United States in other contributions to this volume.

The correlations between the measures of legitimacy and past levels of strife are shown in table 17-12. Among nations generally, and among most groups of nations, the legitimacy of the political system does inhibit magnitudes of violence, and historical levels of strife do facilitate future strife. But these conditions are not as important, for all nations, as are differences in levels of deprivation, as a comparison with table 17-11 indicates. Comparison of groups of nations suggests why: there are striking differences among them in the efficacy of legitimacy in reducing strife, and in the facilitating effects of past strife on future events.

Legitimacy most strongly inhibits civil strife in the developing nations; in the democratic and the personalist nations; in the non-Communist Western nations; and in Latin, Islamic, and Asian nations. It has relatively weak effects in the most- and least-developed nations; the nations governed by modernizing elites; and in African and Communist nations. In centrist (authoritarian) regimes it tends to inhibit conspiracy but has no effect on turmoil. Historical levels of strife very strongly facilitate subsequent strife in the most-developed, democratic, and Western European nations. Their effects are inconsequential or negative in the developing, personalist, and Eastern European nations.

Many special interpretations could be made of these results. Only some general ones are suggested here. Legitimacy presumably has little inhibiting effect on strife in the new, least-developed nations and in the authoritarian nations because their regimes generally have low legitimacy. Only high degrees of loyalty to leaders and institutions are likely to inhibit strife under conditions of intense deprivation. We know that the dislocations associated with nation-building and socioeconomic development generate intense conflict within nations. The regimes of developing nations, including a number of Latin and Islamic nations, have high apparent legitimacy; Chile, Costa Rica,

Table 17-12.—Legitimacy of the political system and historical sanctions for strife
as determinants of magnitudes of civil strife, 1961–65, by type of nation

Type of nation	Correlations[a] between legitimacy and magnitudes of—			Correlations[a] between historical levels of strife and magnitudes of—		
	Tur-moil	Conspir-acy	Total strife[b]	Tur-moil	Conspir-acy	Total strife[b]
All nations (114)[c]	-30	-29	-38	29	23	29
Nations grouped according to level of economic development:						
High (37)[c]	*-10	*-23	*-20	57	48	65
Medium (39).	-44	-34	-52	*-23	*18	*01
Low (38)	*-24	*-11	*-23	38	*14	37
Nations grouped according to type of political system:						
Polyarchic (38)[c]	-46	*-18	-45	51	61	64
Centrist (27)[d]	*10	-32	*-08	*11	*-04	*-07
Elitist (32)	-36	*-05	*-26	29	*13	53
Personalist (16)	-66	-43	-58	*16	*09	*-28
Nations grouped according to geo-cultural regions:[e]						
Anglo-Nordic (10)[c]	*-45	-72	-61	59	*34	57
Western Europe (11)	-50	*-25	-57	77	57	87
Eastern Europe (8)	*-27	61	*-29	*49	*-49	*07
Latin (24)	-40	*-16	-39	*27	55	37
Islamic (21)	-46	49	-37	46	*09	*29
Asian (17)	*-33	*-19	-63	*-07	56	*39
African (23)	*-25	*-08	*-24	47	36	43

[a]See footnote (a), table 17-11. Asterisked (*) coefficients are statistically significant at less than the 0.10 level.
[b]See footnote (b), table 17-11. In all nations the correlations of legitimacy and historical levels of strife with magnitudes of internal war are, respectively, –0.26 and +0.15.
[c]Including data on the United States for 1961–65.
[d]See footnote (d), table 17-11.
[e]See footnote (e), table 17-11.

Morocco, and Iran are examples. The efficacy of legitimacy in minimizing strife in these kinds of countries is manifest in the relatively high correlations for these groups of countries in table 17-12.

The close connection between past and future strife in the developed, democratic, and Western nations supports the conclusion of the preceding section that a number of these nations are, in effect, inherently tumultuous. This is partly the result of persisting deprivations, and also of the existence of historical traditions that sanction protest and violence as justifiable responses to a variety of grievances and conflicts. The lack of connection between past and future strife in the developing nations almost certainly reflects the current tensions of socioeconomic change, tensions that in most of them became severe only in recent years, when the pace of change increased.

Social Control and Facilitation as Determinants of Magnitudes of Civil Strife

The extent and intensity of relative deprivation, and justificatory attitudes about protest and violence, are psychological determinants of the potential

for civil strife. Whether or not men act on their dispositions to collective action depends partly on some structural characteristics of their societies. Three
general kinds of societal characteristics were examined in the cross-national
study: the nature of coercive control; the strength of political and economic
institutions; and the availability of physical, organizational, and material support for dissidents.

Coercive control.—Conventional wisdom and studies of riots and revolutions all emphasize the importance of actual or threatened coercion in minimizing the occurrence and extent of strife. If men are sufficiently afraid of
the consequences, the argument goes, they will not riot. Comparative studies
of civil strife, and psychological theory, both suggest that the relationship is
not so simple: some kinds of coercion are more likely to increase than to
deter strife. Several cross-national studies show that strife tends to be greatest
in countries that have medium-sized military and security forces, lowest in
those with either small or very large forces.[14] Another study suggests that
political instability is greatest in countries that exercise intermediate degrees

*Table 17-13.—Coercive control, institutionalization, and facilitation as determinants
of the total magnitude of civil strife, 1961-65, by type of nation*

Type of nation	Correlations[a] between total magnitude of civil strife and—			
	Coercive control		Strength of insti- tutions	Facilita- tion
	Relative size of forces	Size weighted by loyalty		
All nations (114)[b]	*–13	–51	–34	66
Nations grouped according to level of economic development:				
High (37)[b]	*–12	–53	–29	59
Medium (39)	*–15	–49	*–02	58
Low (38)	*14	–31	–32	67
Nations grouped according to type of political system:				
Polyarchic (38)[b]	n.d.	–55	–36	65
Centrist (27)[c]	–37	–44	*–26	57
Elitist (32)	*25	–44	–35	76
Personalist (16)	*27	*–29	52	*27
Nations grouped according to geo-cultural region:				
Anglo-Nordic (10)[b]	*–39	–68	–75	*–44
Western Europe (11)	74	*–18	*–14	58
Eastern Europe (8)	*03	*17	*23	*–12
Latin (24)	*–08	–56	*–03	*33
Islamic (21)	*05	–61	*–29	71
Asian (17)	*–08	–74	*15	80
African (23)	*15	*–19	–45	82

n.d.=no data (computations not made).
[a]See footnote (a), table 17-11. Asterisked (*) coefficients are statistically significant at
  less than the 0.10 level.
[b]Including data on the United States for 1961-65.
[c]See footnote (d), table 17-11.

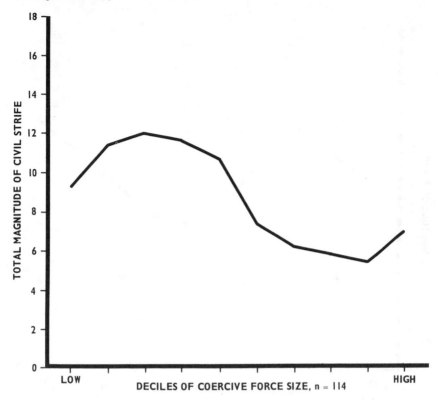

Figure 17-5.—Coercive force, size, and magnitudes of civil strife, 1961-65.

of political control, lowest in those that are either highly democratic or totalitarian.[15] The proposed explanation for these findings is that medium levels of coercive threat and control are more likely to increase men's anger and will to resist than to restrain them from strife. The consistency with which coercion is used is probably even more important than the degree of control. Coercion is "consistent" to the extent that all the "guilty" are subject to sanctions in proportion to the seriousness of their action, and the "innocent" not sanctioned. The literature of civil strife provides many examples of cases in which random or terroristic coercion by troops or police intensified violence, transforming peaceful demonstrations into riots, riots and conspiracies into revolutionary movements.[16]

Two measures of coercive control were used in the cross-national study. One indexed the size of military and internal security forces relative to the adult population. The second weighted the relative size of such forces according to their loyalty to the regime, on the assumption that the greater their historical and contemporary loyalty, the more likely they would be to make consistent use of force and the less likely they would be to use illegal force against the regime.[17] Some correlational results are shown in the first two columns of table 17-13. As expected, the size of forces is weakly and inconsistently related to magnitudes of strife. The strongest relationship is found in the Western European nations, in which the larger are coercive forces, the

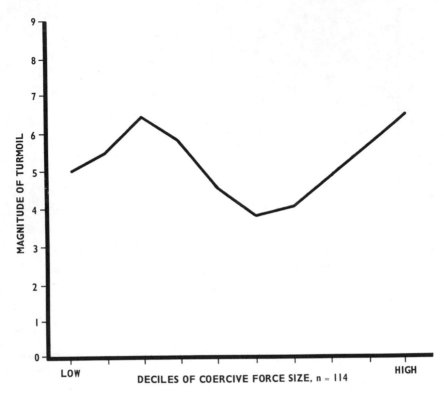

Figure 17-6.—Coercive force, size, and magnitudes of turmoil, 1961-65.

greater is strife. Positive relationships of this sort also are apparent in the elitist and personalist nations, and in the least-developed nations. But when the
loyalty of the military establishment, and the implied consistency of coercion,
are taken into account, a definite inhibitory effect on strife is apparent in
most nations. When coercive forces are both large and loyal, the magnitude of
strife tends to be low, with the apparent exceptions of Africa and Eastern and
Western Europe.

   Evidence regarding the inconclusive effects of reliance on large military
and police establishments alone to maintain domestic order is shown in figures 17-5 through 17-8. Figure 17-5 relates coercive force size to total magnitude of civil strife for all nations. It is evident that total strife is likely to be
highest in countries with low-to-medium-sized coercive forces, but not those
with very small forces. Moreover, at the very highest levels of coercive force
size there is a slight tendency for magnitudes of strife to increase. Such an
S-shaped curve is considerably more pronounced in the comparison of coercive force size with magnitudes of turmoil; turmoil peaks at both moderate
and very high force levels.

   Two other factors should be considered in interpreting these results. It is
likely that countries with protracted political violence expand their coercive
forces to counteract it. It also is plausible that armies in countries facing
foreign threats cause less dissatisfaction—by their presence or actions—than

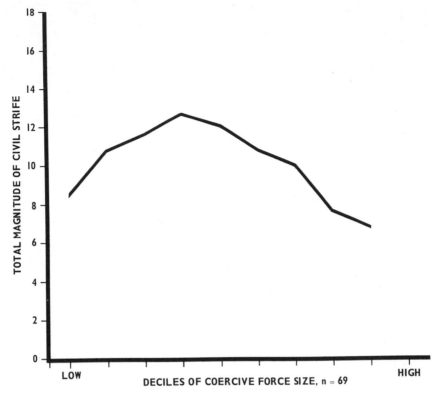

Figure 17-7.—Coercive force, size, and magnitudes of civil strife, 1961-65,
69 low-conflict politics.

armies in states not significantly involved in international conflict. Countries
with one or both of these characteristics were removed and the relationship
plotted for the remaining 69 countries, with the results shown in figure 17-7;
the curvilinear relationship is again clearly evident.

The graph in figure 17-8 shows the relationships between coercive force
loyalty and, respectively, total strife and turmoil. The relationships are essentially linear, though in neither instance does the level of strife approach zero
when size and loyalty approach their maximum. For turmoil in particular,
the results at the outer end of the "loyalty" scale are inconclusive.

Figure 17-9 plots measures of coercive force size against total magnitude of
strife in the 21 states of the Western community, including the United States.
In these nations there is a strong positive relationship between size and magnitude of strife: the larger are armies and police, the greater is internal conflict.
The only countries that deviate markedly from the pattern are Rhodesia,
whose political and military circumstances are substantially different from the
other countries shown, and Finland. The relationship is even more clear when
turmoil alone is plotted against force size, as it is in figure 17-10.

The correspondence of force size and levels of strife does not necessarily
imply a simple causal connection between the two. The military establishment is relatively large in most Western countries because of cold-war tensions,

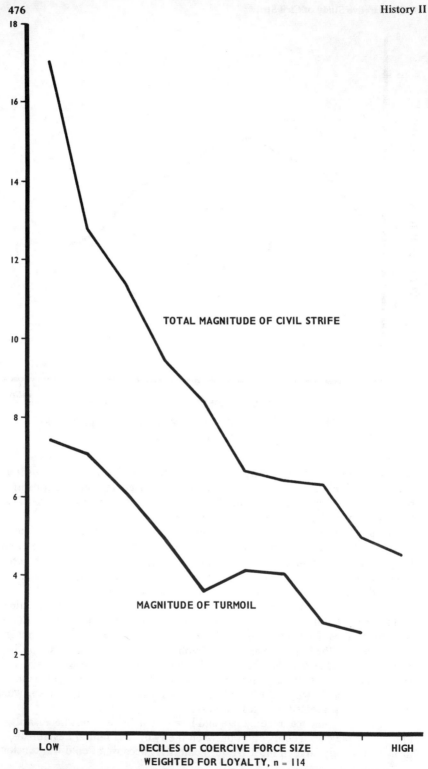

TOTAL MAGNITUDE OF CIVIL STRIFE

MAGNITUDE OF TURMOIL

LOW   DECILES OF COERCIVE FORCE SIZE   HIGH
                    WEIGHTED FOR LOYALTY, n = 114

Figure 17-8.—Coercive force, size, weighted for loyalty and magnitudes
of civil strife, 1961-65.

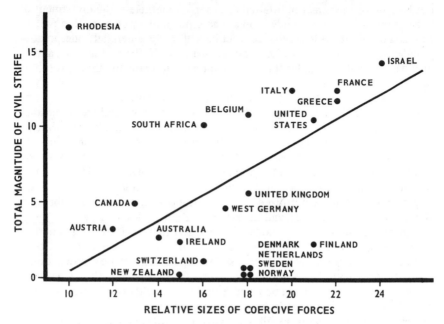

Figure 17-9.—Coercive force, size, and magnitudes of civil strife
in the Western community, 1961-65.

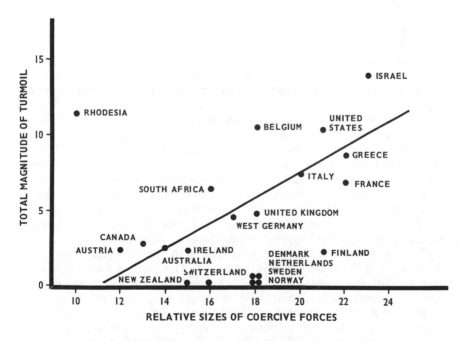

Figure 17-10.—Coercive force, size, and magnitudes of turmoil
in the Western community, 1961-65.

not because of the threat of internal disorder. Nonetheless, the investment of large portions of national budgets in armaments; military conscription policies; and involvement in foreign conflict have directly generated widespread popular opposition in the United States and France in the past decade, and may have provided a similar though less dramatic impetus to public protest in other Western nations.

Strength of institutions.—If social institutions beyond the family and community level are broad in scope, command large resources, and are stable and persisting, the disruptive effects of discontent ought to be minimized. Such institutions are likely to provide additional, peaceful means for the attainment of expectations, and also may provide discontented men with routinized and typically nonviolent means for expressing their grievances. The measure of institutional strength used in this study took into account the proportion of gross national product utilized by the central government; the number and stability of political parties; and the relative size of trades unions.

The results summarized in table 17-13 suggest that institutional strength tends to minimize strife in some groups of countries but not in others. Strong institutions have this effect in the most-developed, democratic nations, especially the Anglo-Nordic countries. They also are associated with low levels of strife in the least-developed countries, especially the elitist and African states. They have little effect on strife in the developing or Latin American nations, however, and in the nations with personalistic political systems, strong institutions apparently facilitate strife. The probable cause of these discrepancies is that the efficacy of strong nongovernmental institutions in minimizing strife depends on their political orientations. If the leaders of political parties and trade unions are strongly opposed to political leaders and their policies, they are likely to direct their organizations into demonstrative and sometimes violent oppositional activity. In Latin America and in some continental European nations, for example, such activity by political parties of the left and right and by unions is quite common. The establishment or reinforcement of strong and stable organizations thus does not necessarily minimize the potential for civil strife; the determining factors are likely to be the discontents and loyalties of the members of those organizations.

Facilitation.—A great many social and environmental conditions may facilitate the outbreak and persistence of strife. It is easier to organize collective action in organizations of likeminded individuals. Ideologies may provide the discontented with the belief that violent responses to depriving circumstances are justified. Jungle or mountain fastnesses can provide secure base areas for rebels. Three kinds of facilitation were measured in this study: the size and status of Communist parties (except in countries in which they were in power); the extent of isolated terrain; and the degree of foreign refuge, training, and supplies provided to rebels during the 1961–65 period.[18]

The last of these characteristics was expected to be an especially strong determinant of the magnitude of internal wars. This partly accounts for the high correlations shown in table 17-13 between facilitation and magnitudes of strife; the correlations are highest in the elitist, Islamic, Asian, and African nations, those in which internal wars have been most common. The high correlations between facilitation and strife in the polyarchic (democratic) and Western European nations reflects primarily the oppositional activities of Communist parties in them, only secondarily foreign support for rebels. Generally, extremist political activity by both left and right in the Western nations in the 1960's has led to turmoil of limited objectives, not to the guerrilla or revolutionary activities that attract and require material foreign support. One noteworthy finding was that facilitation, as measured in this study, has a statistically insignificant association with magnitudes of strife in Latin American countries. Despite dramatic cases of Communist instigation of revolutionary movements in Latin America, Communist activity and support apparently had little systematic effect on levels of Latin American strife in the early and mid-1960's.

Levels of Explanation of Civil Strife

Most of the causal variables used in this study have the predicted effects on levels of civil strife. To determine their combined explanatory power, the seven major variables discussed above were used in multiple correlation analyses, with the summary results shown in table 17-14. On the average, nearly three-quarters of the differences among nations in levels of civil strife are explained, in a statistical sense, by the conditions measured. The Latin nations are the only ones for which the level of explanation seems low. It is low, however, only by comparison with the other results. All the measures used in the study are relatively imprecise and indirect. Differences within nations, and their unique historical and contemporary characteristics, all play significant and largely unspecified parts in the genesis of civil strife. Given these limitations on this kind of study, the levels of explanation shown in table 17-14 are surprisingly high. These "explanations" are only statistical. Nonetheless they are persuasive evidence for the essential accuracy of most of the underlying theoretical arguments that dictated the measures to be used, and also suggest that the variables used represent many if not all the consequential, general causes of civil strife.

Some forms of strife in some groups of nations are less well explained than others. Turmoil, for example, is best accounted for when nations are grouped on the basis of geocultural similarity, poorly explained when they are grouped by level of economic development. A general interpretation is that the causes of turmoil are more closely linked with cultural differences than with stages of economic development or with type of political system. In other words, the cultural heritage of a nation may tell us more about the conditions to which discontented men are sensitive than information about its economic or political system. Conspiracy is poorly explained in the least-developed nations, and also in the elitist and African nations, most of which are among the least developed. Conspiracy in many of these nations may reflect the largely dispassionate tactics of men seeking political power in situations in which there is little else worth seeking. Discontented they may be, for lack of power, but their discontents are not easily determined by the procedures used in this study, and the likelihood of their expression is probably influenced strongly by many unique rather than a few common circumstances. The minimal explanation provided for internal wars in Latin America, and the relatively weak accounting for all Latin strife, suggests that Latin American strife has causes distinctively different from those of other groups of nations. The common observation that strife in Latin America is "institutionalized" is one approach to the explanation of the difference.

Table 17-14.—*Explained variation* (R^2) *in magnitudes of civil strife, 1961–65,*
using all causal variables, by type of nation[a]

Type of nation	Percentages of variation explained in magnitudes of—			
	Turmoil	Conspiracy	Internal war	Total strife
All nations (114)[b]	28	39	47	64
Nations grouped according to level of economic development:				
High (37)[b].	49	41	45	66
Medium (39)	30	58	62	71
Low (38).	45	22	57	82
Nations grouped according to type of political system:				
Polyarchic (38)[b]	45	63	41	64
Centrist (27)[c]	60	67	50	81
Elitist (32).	43	32	71	74
Personalist (16)	70	63	65	71
Nations grouped according to geo-cultural region:[d]				
Western community (21)[b;d]. . . .	66	57	74	74
Latin (24)	62	45	22	49
Islamic (21)	60	73	65	67
Asian (17)	36	61	79	87
African (23).	64	42	76	81
Average variation explained among groups[e].	53	52	59	72

[a]Results of multiple correlation analysis using the 7 major explanatory variables discussed previously: short-term and persisting deprivation, legitimacy, historical levels of strife, coercive force size weighted by loyalty, institutionalization, and facilitation. The figures shown as percentages are multiple correlation coefficients squared (R^2), which represent the variation in magnitudes of strife in each group of nations that is statistically explained by the measures taken together. The R^2 statistic is always less than the sum of the separate, squared correlation coefficients because the casual variables themselves are intercorrelated. The correlation matrix for all polities is reported in Gurr, "A Causal Model of Civil Strife."
[b]Including data on the United States for 1961–65.
[c]See footnote (d), table 17-11.
[d]Multiple correlation coefficients are distorted in the direction of perfect "explanation" when the number of variables used approaches the number of cases (countries). To minimize this effect the Eastern European group (8 nations) is excluded from this table and the Anglo-Nordic and Western Europe groups are combined.
[e]The average of the percentages for the 12 groups of nations.

One other pattern in the results worth noting is that the magnitudes of the specific forms of strife are less well explained than total magnitudes of strife in almost all groups of nations. There are partial, technical explanations for this. The most likely substantive explanation is that, despite its widely different manifestations and consequences, all civil strife has fundamentally similar causes, and that distinctions among its general or specific forms are somewhat arbitrary. Our general interpretation, which is largely supported by the results of this study, is that strife is predicated on intense discontents. The precise nature of those discontents, the forms in which they are expressed, their objects, and their immediate consequences are mediated by specific historical and social circumstances. But there seems to be an inescapable social dynamic to collective discontent. Societies in which there are intense and widespread discontents have a potential for disruptive internal conflict that sooner or later will find expression, whatever is done to control or divert it, short only of alleviating its causes.

A COMPARATIVE INTERPRETATION OF CIVIL STRIFE IN THE UNITED STATES

The United States unquestionably has experienced strife of greater intensity and pervasiveness in recent years than all but a very few other Western democracies. It is equally certain that violence in America has been less extensive and less disruptive than violence in a substantial number of non-Western nations. Americans have not experienced any strife whose scale or threat to the political order approaches the internal wars of countries like Venezuela, Colombia, the Sudan, or Iraq, much less the grim, nationwide bloodletting of the Congo, Indonesia, South Vietnam, or Yemen. Americans also have had little experience of the chronic revolutionary conspiracy and terrorism that characterizes countries like Algeria, Syria, Guatemala, or any of a dozen other nations. But this is merely to say that conditions in the United States could be worse. They provide little comfort when the tumult of the United States is contrasted with the relative domestic tranquillity of developed democratic nations like Sweden, Great Britain, and Canada, or with the comparable tranquillity of nations as diverse as the Soviet Union, Yugoslavia, Turkey, Malagasy, and Malaya.

Probably the most important general conclusion suggested by the descriptive evidence of the first part of this paper is that civil strife in the United States is different in degree but not in kind from strife in other Western nations. Turmoil is by far the most common form of strife in the United States and in the nations against which we compare ourselves in political, cultural, and economic terms. The antigovernment demonstration and riot, the violent clash of political or ethnic groups, and the student protest are pervasive forms of protest and conflict in modern democracies. Other nations have them in good measure also, but they also are much more likely to have serious conspiratorial and revolutionary movements. Such activities have been no more common in the United States than in other Western nations, despite the lip-service given them. A comparative study of revolutionary movements would suggest that few of the advocates of "revolution" in the United States or most other Western countries have the dedication or skills to organize and sustain an effective revolutionary movement.

There also are distinct similarities between the classes and groups of people who participate in strife in the United States and those who participate in other European countries. Strife in the European countries is a cross-class phenomenon: it is quite likely to mobilize members of both the working and the middle classes, but rarely dissatisfied members of the political establishment. Strife also is likely to occur within or on the periphery of the normal political process in the Western nations, rather than being organized by clandestine revolutionary movements or cells of plotters embedded in the political and military hierarchy. All evidence suggests that some overt strife is an inevitable accompaniment of social existence. If so, it is certainly preferable—

from the viewpoint of maintaining a semblance of social order—that it take the form of open political protest, even violent protest, rather than concerted, violent attempts to seize political power.

Similarities between the United States and other Western countries are also apparent in the comparative information on the human costs of strife. Civil strife in the United States has been chronic and pervasive, and has resulted in many bloodied heads, but the consequent loss of life has been proportionally no greater than in most European nations and substantially less than in many democratic nations.

One obvious and distinctive characteristic of civil strife in the United States is the extent to which it is a manifestion of ethnic hostilities. We repeatedly found evidence of parallel problems in other developed, European, and democratic nations. The unsatisfied demands of regional, ethnic, and linguistic groups for greater rights and socioeconomic benefits are more common sources of civil conflict in Western nations than in almost any other group of countries. This is apparent from the relative frequency with which such communal groups initiate strife in Western countries; the frequency with which communal objectives are expressed in strife; and the frequency with which strife includes attacks by members of communal groups on one another. The partial or discriminatory distribution of rights and benefits to minority groups, and the lack of national tolerance for their desires for establishing their own satisfying ways of life, appears to be a pervasive unresolved problem among modern nations. It is a problem that has persisted in many Western countries long beyond the solution of fundamental questions about the nature of the state, the terms of political power and who should hold it, and economic development. Such problems are also found in less-developed and non-Western countries, where they often lead to intense and protracted civil wars or to massive communal rioting. Their manifestations in Western nations are usually less severe. It is nonetheless ironic that nations that have been missionaries of technology and political organization to the rest of the world, nations that claim to provide more satisfying lives for the majority of their citizens than any others in human history, have thus far been unwilling or unable to provide satisfactory conditions of life for all their citizens.

The comparative evidence on the causes of civil strife takes account of three levels of causation. The fundamental cause of civil strife is deprivation-induced discontent: the greater the discrepancy between what men believe they deserve and what they think they are capable of attaining, the greater their discontent. The more intense and widespread discontents are in a society, the more intense and widespread strife is likely to be. The specific nature of discontents and the patterns of social conditions that create and intensify them vary widely within and among societies. Nevertheless it is possible to identify and measure some of the general economic, political, and social conditions that are associated with short-term and persisting deprivation. Findings summarized above show that differences in the extent and degrees of deprivation among nations are responsible for a substantial part of their differences in magnitudes of strife. Among the Anglo-Nordic nations, including the United States, differences in persisting deprivation—especially the deprivation associated with discrimination—are very closely related to strife: two-thirds the variation in magnitudes of strife among them is explainable by differences in the degree and extent of persisting deprivation.

People's attitudes about the legitimacy of their political system and the justifiability of civil strife represent a second level of causation: such attitudes significantly influence the extent to which intense discontents are expressed in collective action. Evidence of this study demonstrates that the greater the apparent legitimacy of political regimes, the lower are all forms of strife in almost all groups of nations. The relationship is especially strong among the Anglo-Nordic countries. People's historical experience of strife is a significant determinant of justificatory attitudes about future strife. Among the developed, Western, and the democratic nations, those with the highest historical levels of civil violence are quite likely to have high levels of contemporary strife. The United States is no exception to the rule: along with countries like France and Italy, it has had a tumultuous past and a tumultous present.

The third level of causation comprises the structural characteristics of nations and their governments that facilitate or minimize violent responses to discontent. One of the more striking findings of this study is that the size of military and police establishments has no consistent effects on strife. For nations generally, strife tends to be highest when coercive forces are of moderate or very large size proportional to population, lowest when they are either small or relatively large. The dubious value of large military and police establishments for minimizing civil strife is especially evident in the 21 nations of the Western community: among them, the larger the military and police establishment, the greater the magnitudes of strife. Other evidence suggests that the consistency with which coercion is employed is more important in minimizing strife than the size of the forces that employ it.

Another social characteristic associated with low levels of strife is the existence of strong and pervasive political and economic institutions. The Anglo-Nordic nations with large trade unions, stable political party systems, and large governmental sectors are more free of strife than those that lack these characteristics. The United States has the second of these three characteristics; compared with other Anglo-Nordic nations, however, unionization and the governmental sector are relatively small.[19] Facilitating social conditions, like the existence of extremist political organizations and the provision of external support for rebels, are important conditions of high magnitudes of violence in most types of nations but not in the Anglo-Nordic nations.

When measures of the three kinds of causal conditions of civil strife are all taken into account, most of the differences among nations in magnitudes of strife are accounted for. In the 21 nations of the Western community, 74 percent of the differences are statistically explained, for other groups of nations an average of 72 percent. One question that remains to be answered is, Which are the most important and immediate causes of strife? A series of causal analyses, reported elsewhere, was made in an attempt to answer this question.[20] When total strife in all nations was examined, we found that the immediate causes are, in declining order of importance, facilitation, persisting deprivation, short-term deprivation, and legitimacy. When magnitudes of turmoil in all nations were analyzed, only three conditions were directly related to current strife: persisting deprivation, historical levels of strife, and legitimacy. When the nations of the Western community were examined as a separate group, the results were similar: the immediate determinants of magnitudes of strife are historical levels of strife, long-term deprivation, facilitation, and legitimacy, in that order of importance.

These results do not indicate that conditions such as institutionalization and coercive capacities are irrelevant to strife, but that they are indirect causes. If institutionalization is high, coercive potential is likely to be high; if both are high, facilitation is likely to be low, and strife as a consequence is also likely to be low. The effects of short-term deprivation on magnitude of turmoil also are largely controlled by the immediate causes: if past strife and facilitation are low and coercive potential high, short-term deprivation is not likely to lead directly to turmoil. On the other hand, if past strife and facilitation are high and coercive potential low, the relationship of short-term deprivation to strife is magnified.

These findings have some general implications for explaining and resolving civil disorder in the United States. The United States has several of the conditions that in other nations lead directly to civil strife. Persisting deprivation characterizes the lot of most black Americans, whatever lipservice and legal remedies have been given to equality. Repeatedly we found evidence that comparable deprivation is a chronic and all but inevitable source of strife among other nations. If the general relationship holds for the United States, then the country is likely to be afflicted by recurrent racial turmoil as long as ethnic discrimination persists. The United States also has a history of turmoil, which increases the likelihood that all Americans, white and black, will respond to discontent with demonstrative and sometimes violent behavior. Traditions of violence are unalterable in the short run; the discontents whose disruptive effects are magnified by such traditions are susceptible to change.

The United States also has certain characteristics that in other countries tend to minimize the most destructive manifestations of discontent. Most Americans have a high regard for the legitimacy of their political system, however much they may object to some of its policies. If that legitimacy is maintained and reinforced, discontent is unlikely to lead to conspiratorial and revolutionary movements. On the other hand, if policies of government anger enough people badly enough, legitimacy is likely to be undermined. American political and economic institutions are also relatively strong by comparison with most countries of the world, if not by comparison with some Anglo-Nordic nations. Coercive potential also is high: the military and police are numerous and unlikely to support civil violence. Facilitative conditions are low: extremist political organizations have been few and small, and material foreign support for civil strife was and is nonexistent. Such generalizations nonetheless conceal major internal variations. Americans in many cities and regions have been underorganized and underserved by local governments. Police tactics have in many cases been inconsistent and repressive, intensifying rather than minimizing discontent. These conditions can be corrected by strengthening local organizations and improving the quality and training of police. Such policies may reduce levels of violence; if the experience of other nations is a guide, only the resolution of the underlying discontents that give rise to strife will eliminate it.

In conclusion, the United States has many of the conditions that in other nations lead to high levels of turmoil, but it also has the conditions that minimize the more intense and disruptive forms of civil strife. Both kinds of conditions are subject at least to limited change. If governmental legitimacy and military loyalties are seriously undermined and popular discontents persist and intensify, revolutionary movements are a distinct possibility. They occur in other countries under just such circumstances. If legitimacy, institutional capabilities, and the consistency of techniques of social control are increased and intense discontents alleviated, turmoil is likely to subside. A society in which intense discontents are manifest in riotous outbreaks and demonstrative public protest can count itself fortunate that they are not expressed in concerted revolutionary action. The members of that society at least have warning and time to ward off the more destructive manifestations of discontent, if they can and will treat its causes rather than its symptoms.

References

1. The research reported in this paper was supported in part by the Center for Research in Social Systems (formerly SORO) of the American University, and by the Advanced Research Projects Agency for the Department of Defense. This support implies neither sponsor approval of this article and its conclusions nor the author's approval of the policies of the U.S. Government toward civil strife. The assistance of Charles Ruttenberg and Diana Russell in research design, data collection, and analysis is gratefully acknowledged. Robert Van den Helm replicated and corrected the correlational analyses. Mary Fosler, Joel Prager, and Lois Wasserspring assisted in data collection. Research was conducted at the Center of International Studies, Princeton University.

2. *Social and Cultural Dynamics, Vol. III: Fluctuation of Social Relationships, War, and Revolution* (New York: American, 1937), p. 504.

3. *Ibid.*, pp. 383-506.

4. Peter A. R. Calvert, "Revolution: The Politics of Violence," *Political Studies*, vol. XV (No. 1, 1967), p. 1.

5. See Ivo K. and Rosalind L. Feierabend, "Aggressive Behaviors Within Polities, 1948-1962: A Cross-National Study," *Journal of Conflict Resolution*, vol. X (Sept. 1966), pp. 249-271; and Betty A. Nesvold, "A Scalogram Analysis of Political Violence," *Comparative Political Studies*, vol. II (July 1969).

6. Data for 1961-63 for 119 polities are reported in Ted Gurr with Charles Ruttenberg, *The Conditions of Civil Violence: First Tests of a Causal Model* (Princeton: Center of International Studies, Princeton University, Research Monograph No. 28, 1967). Data for 1961-65 for 114 polities are summarized in appendices to the present paper.

7. Note that the magnitude scores greatly understate the actual differences among and within nations, as explained in app. I. Scores should be expanded to their fifth power to determine the actual average of their component Pervasiveness, Intensity, and Duration scores.

8. For studies of ghetto riot participation, see *Report of the National Advisory Commission on Civil Disorders* (New York: Bantam Books, 1968), pp. 127-135; Governer's Select Commission on Civil Disorder, State of New Jersey, *Report for Action* (Trenton: Stateof New Jersey, 1968), pp. 129-131; Nathan E. Cohen, "The Los Angeles Riot Study," in Shalom Edleman, ed., *Violence in the Streets* (Chicago: Quadrangle, 1968), pp. 333-346; and Robert M. Fogelson and Robert B. Hill, "Who Riots? A Study of Participation in the 1967 Riots," *Supplemental Studies for the National Advisory Commission on Civil Disorders* (Washington, D.C.: National Advisory Commission on Civil Disorders, 1968), pp. 217-248.

9. The theoretical argument is made systematically and empirically documented in Ted Robert Gurr, *Why Men Rebel* (Princeton: Princeton University Press, in press), chs. 2, 3, 6, and 7. The relevance of frustration-aggression theory to civil strife is proposed in Gurr, "Psychological Factors in Civil Strife," *World Politics*, vol. XX (Jan. 1968), pp. 245-278.

10. The analyses are reported in Gurr with Ruttenberg, *The Conditions of Civil Violence*, pp. 71-76. But also see the paper by the Feierabends and Nesvold, elsewhere in this volume, which reports contradictory findings.

11.   This pattern was first proposed by James C. Davies, "Toward a Theory of Revo-
       lution," *American Sociological Review,* vol. XXVII (1962), pp. 5-19. He provides
       evidence that the pattern preceded the Russian Revolution, Dorr's rebellion in
       Rhode Island in 1842, and the Egyptian revolution of 1952. Also see his paper
       elsewhere in this volume.
12.   Evidence for the deprivation measures were obtained from a variety of news,
       historical, and statistical sources. Procedures and sources are described in Gurr,
       "A Causal Model of Civil Strife: A Comparative Analysis Using New Indices,"
       American Political Science Review, vol. LXII (Dec. 1968).
13.   Some suggestive survey evidence to this point is summarized in Gurr, *Why Men
       Rebel,* ch. 6. The historical evidence is amply provided by other papers in this
       volume.
14.   See Douglas Bwy, "Political Instability in Latin America: The Cross-Cultural
       Test of a Causal Model," *Latin American Research Review,* vol. III (Spring 1968),
       pp. 17-66 and Gurr with Ruttenberg, *The Conditions of Civil Violence,* pp. 81-85.
15.   Jennifer G. Walton, "Correlates of Coerciveness and Permissiveness of National
       Political Systems: A Cross-National Study," M.A. thesis, San Diego State College,
       June 1965.
16.   Some of this evidence is reviewed in Gurr, *Why Men Rebel,* ch. 8. Also see the
       comparative study of governmental uses of coercion in Cuba and Venezuela by
       Gude, elsewhere in this volume.
17.   Procedures used to construct these measures are described in Gurr, "A Causal
       Model of Civil Strife." The basic data for size of forces are military personnel
       per 10,000 adults and internal security forces per 10,000 adults, which were re-
       scaled, weighted equally, and combined; the maximum possible score for a
       country is 30, the minimum 3. The U.S. score is 22. The "loyalty" scores used
       to weight these estimates take into account the length of time since the last
       forceful intervention of the military or police against the regime, and the fre-
       quency with which they resorted to illicit force in the 1961-65 period.
18.   The facilitation measures are described in Gurr, "A Causal Model of Civil Strife."
       A better measure of organizational support for civil strife would take account of
       the size and status of all extremist political organizations; comparative data were
       available only for Communist parties.
19.   Country data supporting this judgment are reported in Gurr, *New Error-
       Compensated Measures for Comparing Nations: Some Correlates of Civil Vio-
       lence,* Research Monograph No. 25 (Princeton: Center of International Studies,
       Princeton University, 1966).
20.   See the causal model analyses in Gurr, "A Causal Model of Civil Strife," and
       Gurr, "Urban Disorder: Perspectives from the Comparative Study of Civil
       Strife," in Louis H. Masotti and Don R. Bowen, eds, *Riots and Rebellion: Civil
       Violence in the Urban Community* (Beverly Hills: Sage Publications, 1968), pp.
       51-67.

PROCEDURES USED IN COLLECTING AND SUMMARIZING CIVIL STRIFE DATA

Civil strife is defined as all collective, nongovernmental attacks on persons or property that occur within the boundaries of an autonomous or colonial political unit. By "nongovernmental" is meant acts by subjects and citizens who are not employees or agents of the regime, as well as acts of such employees or agents contrary to role norms, such as mutinies and military coups d'etat. Operationally the definition is qualified by the inclusion of symbolic attacks on political persons or policies, e.g., political demonstrations, and by the exclusion of turmoil events in which less than 100 persons take part.

To obtain systematic data on civil-strife events, a set of coding sheets and a coding manual were devised for recording a variety of information about any strife event. The coding sheets and coding manual are published in Ted Gurr with Charles Ruttenberg, *Cross-National Studies of Civil Violence* (Washington, D.C.: Center for Research in Social Systems, The American University, 1969, in press), app. A.

A large number of sources were scanned and coded to get as full as possible a record of the strife events that occurred in 114 polities in the 1961-65 period. Three sources were systematically searched: the *New York Times*; *Newsyear* (the annual volumes of *Facts on File*); and *Africa Digest*. This information was supplemented from a variety of other sources, among them *The Annual Register of World Events; Africa Diary: Weekly Record of Events in Africa; Hispanic-American Report*; and country and case studies. Some 1,090 strife events were thus identified, coded, and the data punched on IBM cards. Many small-scale strife events, and some larger ones, probably were unreported in these sources and hence are not included. Moreover, much reported and estimated data are inaccurate in varying degrees. However, neither random nor systematic error seem great enough to affect substantially the analyses or conclusions reported here.

It was not always possible or desirable to record full information on each single event identified. When a number of related events occurred in a country over a single issue, like the series of antiwar demonstrations in the United States, they were summarized in a single record and tabulated as a single "event."

Data often were not available from the sources. For characteristics like class participation, motives, targets, and arrests, estimates were made on the basis of indirect evidence when possible, otherwise coded "no basis for judging." Data estimation procedures were used when numbers of initiators and numbers of casualties were not reported precisely. Methods used to estimate number of initiators serve as examples. The coding sheet contained two "number of initiators" scales. The first was a modified geometric progression of two, used to record proximate estimates of initiators; its first interval was 1 to 40, its highest 55,001 to 110,000. For purposes of summing such estimates to obtain total number of initiators, the midpoint of each interval was used. The second scale was used for recording rough estimates, sometimes coder estimates, of number of initiators, ranging from "less than 100" (set equal to 40 for purposes of computing totals) to "10,001 to 100,000" (set equal to 40,000). Data for events for which no estimate could be made were supplied by calculating and inserting means for the appropriate subcategory of event. For example, riots with no data on initiators were assumed to have the average number of initiators of all riots for which estimates were available.

Casualties were coded similarly to number of initiators, the principal missing-data component being estimates of injuries. The ratio of injuries to deaths was calculated for all events of each subcategory (e.g., all riots, all nonpolitical clashes) for which both data were available, and was used to estimate injuries for all such events for which "deaths" estimates but not injuries estimates were given. The general ratio for all well-reported strife was 12 injuries for each death.

"Duration" of strife events was almost always determinable from sources. It was coded on a geometric progression whose first two intervals were "one-half day or less" and "one-half to one day," and whose upper intervals were 4 to 9 months, 9 to 15 months, etc. No event was assigned a duration of more then 5 years, though some began before and/or persisted after the 1961-65 period.

To estimate relative magnitudes of civil strife, three kinds of summary measures were calculated from this data:

> *Pervasiveness:* The extent of participation in civil strife in a polity, operationally defined as the sum of the estimated number of participants in all acts of strife as a proportion of total population, expressed as participants per 100,000 population.

> *Intensity:* The human cost of strife, indexed here by the total estimated casualties, dead and injured, in all strife events in a polity as a proportion of total population, expressed as casualties per 10 million population.

> *Duration:* The persistence of strife, indexed here by the sum of the spans of time of all strife events in each polity, whatever the relative scale of events, expressed as total days of strife.

Pervasiveness, Intensity, and Duration scores were calculated separately for each of three major forms of strife in each country: turmoil, conspiracy, and internal war. They also were calculated for all strife taken together for each polity. All these scores were converted into logarithms using a log $(X+1)$ transformation. To obtain combined magnitude scores for turmoil, conspiracy, internal war, and total strife (TMCS), the three component logged scores for each form were added; divided by 8 to obtain their eighth root; and the antilog used as each country's magnitude score. Country TMCS scores and ranks are shown in table 17-15, below. *It should be emphasized that these combination procedures result in scores that are not additive. To compare magnitudes of strife between countries with TMCS scores of 3.0 and 10.0, for example, the scores should be expanded to their fifth power (3.0^5 and 10.0^5) to determine the actual average of their respective Pervasiveness, Intensity, and Duration scores.* The component scores are highly skewed, which makes this transformation necessary for a variety of statistical tests used in the study.

Additional data on the types, number of events, and characteristics of civil strife in the United States were collected for the period June 1, 1963, through May 31, 1968, using the sources and guidelines specified in the foot-notes to table 17-15. Estimates of number of participants, casualties, and duration were obtained on an event-by-event basis to increase the precision of the magnitude scores. Classes of participants, motives, targets, and coercive response were not separately coded. The magnitude-of-strife scores for the United States in the comparisons in the first section of this paper are based on this information. Comparisons of groups, motives, and targets of action in the first section are based on the summary of 1961-65 data for the United States, as are the correlational results in the second section.

Appendix Table 17-15. – List of polities, total magnitude of strife (TMCS) scores, 1961-65, and groupings

Polity	TMCS		Bases for grouping[a]		
	Score	Rank	Economic development	Political system	Geocultural region
Congo-Kinshasa[b] ..	48.7	1	Medium	Elitist	African
Indonesia[b]	33.7	2	Medium	Elitist	Asian
South Vietnam....	32.8	3	Low	Elitist	Asian
Rwanda[b]	28.2	4	Low	Elitist	African
Yemen	23.6	5	Low	Elitist	Islamic
Angola	22.1	6	Low	Centrist	African
Dominican Republic	21.9	7	Medium	Personalist	Latin
Iraq	20.5	8	Medium	Personalist	Islamic
Venezuela........	20.3	9	High	Polyarchic	Latin
Sudan..........	20.2	10	Low	Elitist	Islamic
Algeria	19.5	11	Medium	Centrist	Islamic
Syria...........	17.8	12	Low	Personalist	Islamic
Colombia	16.9	13	Medium	Polyarchic	Latin
Rhodesia	16.4	14	Medium	Centrist	African/European
Uganda.........	15.6	15	Low	Elitist	African
Zambia.........	15.5	16	Medium	Elitist	African
Bolivia	15.2	17	Medium	Polyarchic	Latin
Cuba...........	15.2	18	Medium	Centrist	Latin
Kenya..........	15.0	19	Medium	Elitist	African
Guatemala	14.5	20	Medium	Personalist	Latin
Israel[b]	14.0	21	High	Polyarchic	European
Burma	13.9	22	Medium	Elitist	Asian
Nigeria	13.8	23	Low	Elitist	African
Argentina........	13.2	24	High	Personalist	Latin
Ethiopia.........	13.2	25	Low	Centrist	African
Camerouns.......	13.1	26	Low	Elitist	African
Italy...........	12.3	27	High	Polyarchic	European
Peru...........	12.3	28	Medium	Personalist	Latin

Appendix Table 17-15.—List of polities, total magnitude of strife (TMCS) scores, 1961-65, and groupings—(Continued)

Polity	TMCS		Bases for grouping[a]		
	Score	Rank	Economic development	Political system	Geocultural region
France	12.1	29	High	Polyarchic	European
Tunisia	11.8	30	Medium	Elitist	Islamic
Greece	11.6	31	Medium	Polyarchic	European
Malawi[b]	11.6	32	Low	Elitist	African
Singapore	11.5	33	Medium	Polyarchic	Asian
Papua-New Guinea	11.3	34	Low	Centrist	Asian
India	11.0	35	Medium	Polyarchic	Asian
Burundi	10.9	36	Low	Elitist	African
Belgium	10.5	37	High	Polyarchic	European
Nepal	10.3	38	Low	Centrist	Asian
Thailand	10.3	39	Medium	Personalist	Asian
South Korea	10.2	40	Medium	Personalist	Asian
United States[c]	10.2	41	High	Polyarchic	European
Ecuador	10.1	42	Medium	Personalist	Latin
South Africa	10.0	43	High	Centrist	African/European
Mozambique	9.8	44	Low	Centrist	African
Guinea	9.5	45	Low	Elitist	Islamic
Panama	9.5	46	Medium	Personalist	Latin
Nicaragua	9.4	47	Medium	Personalist	Latin
Portugal	9.3	48	Medium	Centrist	Latin
Iran	8.4	49	Medium	Centrist	Islamic
Honduras	8.3	50	Low	Personalist	Latin
Mali	8.3	51	Low	Elitist	Islamic
Philippines	8.3	52	High	Polyarchic	Asian
Ceylon	8.2	53	Low	Polyarchic	Asian
Jordan	8.1	54	Medium	Centrist	Islamic
Ghana	7.9	55	Medium	Elitist	African
Somalia	7.9	56	Low	Elitist	Islamic
Haiti	7.8	57	Low	Personalist	Latin
Dahomey	7.7	58	Low	Elitist	African
Brazil	7.4	59	Medium	Polyarchic	Latin
Chad	7.2	60	Low	Elitist	African
Morocco	6.7	61	Medium	Polyarchic	Islamic
Liberia	6.6	62	Low	Centrist	African
Sierra Leone	6.5	63	Low	Elitist	African
Libya	6.3	64	Low	Polyarchic	Islamic
Pakistan	6.3	65	Low	Elitist	Islamic
Tanganyika	6.2	66	Low	Elitist	African
Uruguay	6.2	67	High	Polyarchic	Latin
Japan	5.9	68	High	Polyarchic	Asian
Lebanon	5.8	69	Medium	Personalist	Islamic
Niger	5.8	70	Low	Elitist	Asian
China	5.7	71	Medium	Centrist	Asian
East Germany	5.5	72	High	Centrist	European
El Salvador	5.4	73	Medium	Personalist	Latin
United Kingdom	5.4	74	High	Polyarchic	European
Czechoslovakia	5.3	75	High	Centrist	European
Spain	5.2	76	High	Centrist	Latin
Senegal	5.1	77	Low	Elitist	Islamic
Paraguay	5.0	78	Medium	Personalist	Latin
Turkey	5.0	79	Medium	Polyarchic	Islamic
Canada	4.9	80	High	Polyarchic	European
Chile	4.9	81	High	Polyarchic	Latin
Mexico	4.7	82	High	Polyarchic	Latin

Appendix Table 17-15.—List of polities, total magnitude of strife (TMCS) scores, 1961-65, and groupings—(Continued)

Polity	TMCS		Bases for grouping[a]		
	Score	Rank	Economic development	Political system	Geocultural region
West Germany	4.6	83	High	Polyarchic	European
Malaya	4.5	84	Medium	Polyarchic	Asian
Togo............	4.1	85	Low	Elitist	African
Bulgaria	3.9	86	High	Centrist	European
U.A.R.	3.9	87	Medium	Centrist	Islamic
Cambodia........	3.8	88	Low	Elitist	Asian
U.S.S.R..........	3.6	89	High	Centrist	European
Poland	3.3	90	High	Centrist	European
Yugoslavia	3.3	91	High	Centrist	European
Austria..........	3.1	92	High	Polyarchic	European
Puerto Rico	2.9	93	High	Polyarchic	Latin
Hungary	2.8	94	High	Centrist	European
Costa Rica	2.7	95	Medium	Polyarchic	Latin
Australia	2.6	96	High	Polyarchic	European
Ireland	2.3	97	High	Polyarchic	European
Finland..........	2.1	98	High	Polyarchic	European
Afghanistan	2.0	99	Low	Centrist	Islamic
Ivory Coast	1.8	100	Low	Elitist	African
Jamaica	1.5	101	Medium	Polyarchic	Latin
C.A.R.	1.3	102	Low	Elitist	African
Switzerland	1.2	103	High	Polyarchic	European
Saudi Arabia......	1.1	104	Low	Centrist	Islamic
China-Taiwan	.0	105	High	Centrist	Asian
Denmark	.0	106	High	Polyarchic	European
Hong Kong.......	.0	107	Medium	Centrist	Asian
Malagasy.........	.0	108	Low	Elitist	African
Netherlands	.0	109	High	Polyarchic	European
New Zealand	.0	110	High	Polyarchic	European
Norway	.0	111	High	Polyarchic	European
Romania	.0	112	High	Centrist	European
Sweden	.0	113	High	Polyarchic	European
Volta	.0	114	Low	Elitist	African

a. Economic development level was assessed on the basis of conditions in the late 1950s and early 1960s, the type of political system on the basis of conditions in the early 1960s. Some polities would be reassigned on the basis of conditions in them in the late 1960s.

b. These scores are believed to be unrealistically high because of data estimation procedures used.

c. The United States is ranked on the basis of 1961-65 civil-strife data. On the basis of June 1963-May 1968 data, it ranks 24th, with a TMCS score of 13.6

PROCEDURES USED IN SELECTING AND GROUPING COUNTRIES FOR CROSS-NATIONAL COMPARISON

The universe of analysis includes all distinct national and colonial political entities that had a population of 1 million or more in 1962, excluding four countries for which data were judged unreliable (Albania, Mongolia, North Korea, and North Vietnam) and one (Laos) on grounds that it was a state in name only during the period in question. The remaining 114 polities include more than 98 percent of the world's population.

The 114 countries were grouped in several different ways to permit comparison of the effects of different levels of economic development, types of political system, and geocultural region on characteristics of strife. The bases of the groupings are as follows:

ECONOMIC DEVELOPMENT

Mary Megee, "Problems of Regionalizing and Measurement," *Peace Research Society: Papers,* vol. IV (1965), pp. 7-35, identified several factors underlying various measures of economic development for 153 nations and territories. The two major factors found were "industrial development" and "social overhead (infrastructure) and government expenditures." Countries were plotted according to their scores on these two dimensions into four quadrants: those low on both factors (very underdeveloped); those low on one of the factors (developing); and those high on both. A similar set of "regions" (groupings) also identified by Megee included one very underdeveloped set of nations, three sets of developing nations, a number of developed nations, and several dozen "isolate cases." We used the latter set of grouping, with certain modifications: Megee's "very underdeveloped" constitutes our "low economic development" group; her three groups of developing nations were combined into our "medium" group; and the developed nations constitute our "high" group. Megee's "isolate" polities were assigned to one of these three groupings on the basis of their quadrant locations. Six nations that fall just inside the "developed" quadrant we reclassified in the "medium" group: Cuba, Jamaica, Portugal, Greece, Turkey, and Indonesia. China-Taiwan was reclassified to the "high" group because of its very high industrialization score. Some apparent errors in her classifications also were corrected on the basis of her own and other data. Finally, a few polities not included by Megee were assigned to our categories on judgmental grounds. The economic groups of the 114 polities are shown in table 17-15.

TYPE OF POLITICAL SYSTEM

The background conditions for civil strife were expected to vary markedly
from one type of political system to another, suggesting that polities be
grouped on the basis of their political characteristics. The grouping used is
based on the results of a Q-factor analysis of 68 specifically political variables
for 115 nations, by Arthur S. Banks and Phillip M. Gregg, "Grouping Political
Systems: Q-Factor Analysis of *A Cross-Polity Survey," American Behavioral
Scientist,* vol. IX (Nov. 1965), pp. 3-6. The component variables are measures
of such conditions as the degree or nature of ideological orientation, interest
articulation, power distribution, role of the military, colonial tutelage (if any),
and many others.

The factor analysis distinguished five classes of nations, each characterized
by rather distinct patterns of political behavior and rule. We have used the
authors' labels for them: *polyarchic,* nations that approximate Western democratic political structures and processes; *centrist,* Communist and other non-
Latin American authoritarian regimes; *elitist,* recently independent, predominantly African states with relatively small, modernizing elites: *personalist,*
predominantly Latin regimes characterized by unstable personalistic political
leadership; and *traditional,* four nations such as Yemen. We reclassified polities
from the traditional class to the larger group they most closely resembled.
We also judgmentally assigned polities included in our 114 but excluded by
Banks and Gregg to the remaining four groups. The political groups are shown
in table 17-15.

GEOCULTURAL REGIONS

Assignment of nations to geocultural region was made on judgmental
grounds, with some guidance from a factor analytic study by Bruce M. Russett,
"International Regions and International Integration: Homogeneous Regions,"
Yale University, Department of Political Science, 1965 (mimeo). The groups
were distinguished as follows:

Latin (24):   All Latin American and Caribbean nations, plus Puerto Rico,
    Spain and Portugal.
Islamic (21): Countries whose populations are 50 percent or more Muslim,
    including the North African and Middle Eastern nations, Lebanon, and
    Saharan and sub-Saharan African countries of Guinea, Mali, Niger, Senegal,
    Somalia, and Sudan.
African (23): Non-Islamic African states and colonies. In the analyses of
    the first two sections of this paper, South Africa and Rhodesia were added
    to this group; in the correlation analyses in the third section, they are in-
    cluded in the Anglo-Nordic group, below.
Asian (17):   Non-Islamic nations and colonies of mainland Asia and its
    periphery, including Papua-New Guinea but excluding Australia and New
    Zealand.
European (27): The countries of Eastern and Western Europe (except Spain
    and Portugal), plus the United States, the English-settled states of the
    British Commonwealth, and Israel. For the correlational analyses, these
    countries were divided into three more homogenous groups:

Anglo-Nordic (10): The three Nordic nations, Great Britain, the United States, and the English-settled states of the British Commonwealth, to which were added South Africa and Rhodesia.

Western Europe (11): Other non-Communist European states, plus Israel.

Eastern Europe (8): The European Communist nations.

Specific country designations are shown in table 17-15.

Chapter 18

SOCIAL CHANGE AND POLITICAL VIOLENCE: CROSS-NATIONAL PATTERNS

By Ivo K. Feierabend, Rosalind L. Feierabend, and Betty A. Nesvold*

This study examines selected aspects of social change and their effect upon political violence and the internal political stability of nations.[1] The inquiry is predominantly empirical rather than speculative in nature. It is also extensive in scope, scrutinizing 84 nations in an attempt to discern broad global patterns of both change and violence.

In general, the study compares nations for their relative levels of political stability or instability, modernization, and rates of socioeconomic change. By means of these comparisons, the study approaches the question: In what ways are social change and development related to political violence within the sample of 84 nations at mid-20th century?

This broadly comparative, cross-national approach has its shortcomings. Important depth and detail are lost in the panoramic overview that would be more thoroughly preserved in intensive exploration of a single country. On the other hand, the advantage of the broader method lies in its scope. The examination of many cases can reveal patterns that may go unnoticed, or that may be obscured, in the unique circumstances of a specific case.[2]

THEORETICAL CONSIDERATIONS

The notion of social change is complex. It refers to movement through time of a variety of ecological, socioeconomic, political, structural, cultural, and ideational aspects and conditions of social existence. The problem is not only to clarify those aspects of social reality that are changing but also to specify the nature of the change. Is the social universe changing slowly or

---

*Ivo Feierabend is professor of political science; his wife Rosalind, associate professor of psychology at San Diego State College. Dr. Nesvold is assistant professor of political science at the College. The Feierabends have written a number of articles and papers based on their comparative studies of political instability, including "Aggressive Behaviors Within Polities, 1948-1962: A Cross-National Study," *Journal of Conflict Resolution*, vol. X (Sept. 1966), pp. 249-271. Their work received the American Association for the Advancement of Science's 1966 Socio-Psychological Prize for research in the behavioral sciences. Dr. Nesvold is the author of "A Scalogram Analysis of Political Violence," *Comparative Political Studies*, vol. II (July 1969).

swiftly; is change continuous or discontinuous, or perhaps accelerating in some aspects and lagging in others? Elusive notions such as progress, growth, decline, and decay all entail some particularized view of change. Assumptions as to the direction of change are implicit in the concept of development, which suggests that change proceeds from one stage to another, or perhaps through several developmental phases. Withdrawal from one stage and movement toward another is referred to as "transition." The entire notion of change is sometimes identified with such periods of transition.[3]

Social Change and Violence

The assumption of a relationship between change and violence is based on arguments that are intuitively persuasive. Change, especially extensive, rapid, and abrupt change, is an unsettling and bewildering human experience. It is likely to create strain in the psyche of the individual and crisis in the social order. Old ways, familiar environments, deep-seated habits, and social roles become obsolescent, while a new way of life and a new routine are not yet clearly established. Social change is perhaps analogous to the experience of the individual who moves suddenly from one community to another. He lives in a new dwelling, interacts with a new set of individuals, faces new and strange situations that require an inordinate amount of difficult adjustment.

To project this example to a broader social base, one might argue that massive change that moves people physically into new environments, exposes their minds to new ideas, and casts them in new and unfamiliar roles is very likely to create collective bewilderment. This bewilderment may find its expression in turmoil and social violence. However, there are other, conflicting theoretical speculations that are equally persuasive. These suggest that change has beneficial and pacifying social consequences. If social change is perceived as bringing gratification, if it fulfills aspirations, there is no reason to expect social crisis in its wake. On the contrary, obstructing such change, or slowing its pace, should result in social discontent registered in protest movements and violence.[4]

Given these contradictory insights, the idea of change alone is not sufficient to explain the occurrence of violent political behavior. It is only when change brings with it social circumstances that breed discontent and strain, that it may be assumed to be responsible for social turmoil. Other modes of change will not so qualify. On the contrary, they may have a stabilizing effect on the political order. The blanket assertion that change breeds violence is too simplistic.

Our theoretical assumption linking change to violence begins with the notion that political turmoil is the consequence of social discontent. This commonsense assumption is predicated on a motivational rather than a structural orientation. And it reaffirms the often-repeated insight that political protest and revolution begin in the minds of men. Nevertheless, structural and processual variables are intimately a part of the wider view, since men's experience of change in the ecological, social, or political universe may create the revolutionary state of mind. In other words, although our assumptions are based on psychological, motivational factors, we are nevertheless interested in analyzing change in environmental, structural circumstances of political systems. What is required is some refinement of the idea of discontent and strain. Also needed is an effort to identify those modes of change and development that can be presumed to lead to the discontent that is the necessary precondition of political instability and violence.

Change, Systemic Frustration, and Aggression

While the concept of aggression has received extensive elaboration within psychology, the frustration-aggression hypothesis seems the most useful for our purposes.[5] In its most basic and fundamental formulation, this hypothesis maintains that aggression (as well as some other specified behaviors) is the result of frustration. Frustration itself is defined as the thwarting or interference with the attainment of goals, aspirations, or expectations. On the basis of frustration-aggression theory, it is postulated that frustration induced by the social system creates the social strain and discontent that in turn are the indispensable preconditions of violence. The commonsense assertion that revolutionary behavior has its root in discontent, and the more technical postulate that frustration precedes aggression, are parallel statements indicating a common insight.

The concept of frustration is often thought more appropriate to individual than to social circumstances. We believe, however, that the notion of *systemic frustration* makes the concept applicable to the analysis of aggregate, violent political behavior within social systems.[6] We define systemic frustration in reference to three criteria: (1) As frustration interfering with the attainment and maintenance of social goals, aspirations, and values; (2) as frustration simultaneously experienced by members of social aggregates and hence also complex social systems; and (3) as frustration or strain that is produced within the structures and processes of social systems. Systemic frustration is thus frustration that is experienced simultaneously and collectively within societies.

Guided by this definition, we may adopt two basic propositions from the frustration-aggression hypothesis and restate them with reference to social systems: (1) Violent political behavior is instigated by systemic frustration; and (2) systemic frustration may stem, among other circumstances of the social system, from specific characteristics of social change.

Four general hypotheses further qualify the notion of systemic frustration: (1) Systemic frustration at any given time is a function of the discrepancy between present social aspirations and expectations, on the one hand, and social achievements, on the other. (2) In addition, present estimates or expectations of future frustrations (or satisfactions) are also responsible for level of present frustration (or satisfaction). (3) Uncertainties in social expectations in themselves increase the sense of systemic frustration. (4) Conflicting aspirations and conflicting expectations provide yet another source of systemic frustration.

The first hypothesis focuses on the discrepancy between aspirations, expectations, and attainments within the present situation. This discrepancy is a result of the interplay between these factors in the present, and level of frustration is postulated to be a function of the number of aspirations involved, their level of valuation, their frequency of occurrence within various population strata, their expected level of attainment, and the degree of certainty with which these expectations are held. Similar criteria apply to the

notion of social attainment. It should also be pointed out that it is perceived
rather than actual social attainment that is important.

The distinction between aspirations and expectations needs clarification.
In simplest definition, aspirations are the goals that people wish to attain.
Also included in the definition are presently valued possessions that people
desire to maintain. Expectations, on the other hand, include only the portion
of aspirations which we expect to achieve. Strictly speaking, expectations refer always to the future. Yet expectations are disappointed (or fulfilled) in
the context of the present. And this is the measure of systemic frustration as
formulated in the first hypothesis.

The expectation of future frustration or satisfaction may also intensify or
counteract present predicaments. The second hypothesis recognizes this possibility, hence uses the term "expectation" in a somewhat different sense. It
does not refer to expectations regarding the present situation, but present expectations of future occurrences. The third hypothesis singles out uncertainty as yet another source of frustration. Uncertainty is a special quality of
expectations. Ambiguity as to whether the future will bring disaster or salva-
tion should be considered a distressful experience, adding to the present sense
of frustration. Only in the case of disaster is certainty likely to be judged as
more frustrating than uncertainty. Finally, the fourth hypothesis sees conflict as a systematically frustrating circumstance. Conflict is considered a specific case of frustration in which an individual's alternative motives, aspirations, and expectations work at cross-purposes, blocking one another.[7] The
notions of intensity, scope, and distribution of aspirations are as relevant in
this context as in the previous one.

Patterns of Social Change and Discontent

These theoretical propositions refine the general notion of systemic frustration and social discontent, but the important question still remains: What
modes of change and development may we assume to lead toward systemic
frustration? Let us point to a few studies in the recent literature of political
violence, in order to identify objective social situations that are presumed to
create a sense of systemic frustration.

Davies, in his analysis of several revolutions, concludes that, contrary to
Marxian expectations, revolutions do not occur during periods of prolonged
abject or worsening situations of social deprivation.[8] Neither does the evidence sustain the insight of de Tocqueville and others, that revolutions are
perpetrated during periods of relative prosperity and improvement. Instead,
Davies postulates a J-curve of socioeconomic development, whereby revolution occurs in social systems in which social well-being has been continually
raised for an extended period of time, followed by an abrupt and sharp setback. His explanation is in accord with our notion of discontent and systemic
frustration. We may suggest that certainty of social expectations was reinforced during the period of continued socioeconomic development. The
sharp reversal in social fortunes creates an intolerable discrepancy between
achievement and expectation. It is also possible that the unexpected reversal
in attainment creates an alarmist expectation of continued severe decreases in
levels of achievement. Such a fear for the future, possibly an exaggerated
fear, motivates present actions as much as do actual present conditions.

Figure 18-1 graphically portrays Davies' hypothesis of the J-curve pattern of change. Furthermore it takes into account not only the sense of frustration that is created by disappointed expectations in the present, but also depicts estimates of the future. If men still anticipate future gratifications (depicted by line A in fig. 18-1), political violence is less likely to occur in the present. If, on the other hand, they anticipate intensified frustration (depicted by line B), the likelihood of violence is strengthened. In the latter case, the sense of frustration resulting from disappointed expectations in the present is intensified by the gap between present level of achievement and an even more pessimistic estimate of the future.

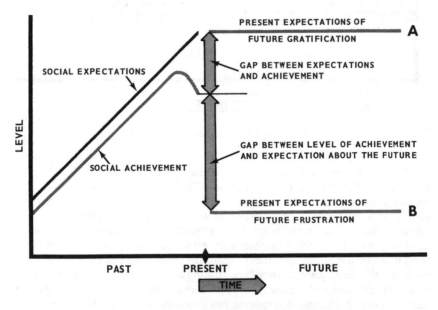

Figure 18-1. — J-curve change model—deterioration pattern.

Another type of J-curve may be equally productive of social discontent. A sudden and unexpected improvement in social circumstances may give rise to hopes of better things to come. If actual improvement is not sufficiently high to meet the newly aroused expectations, an intolerable gap between expectation and attainment will ensue, constituting systemic frustration. Again the argument is based on a contrast effect, one that gives impetus to expectations. The novelty of gratification following a long history of deprivation may give the aspect of reality to long-suppressed aspirations. It is exaggerated hope for the future, in this case, which inevitably breeds disappointment.[9]

Figure 18-2 illustrates this situation. As shown, the social achievement line intersects the line of expectations at time t_1, or shortly after achievement exceeds expectations. Hence this is the point of social satisfaction. Yet at t_2, where achievement does not keep pace with soaring, newly awakened expectations, a gap occurs comparable to that in Davies' J-curve model. Expectations regarding the future in this model also may either detract or add to the present sense of systemic frustration.

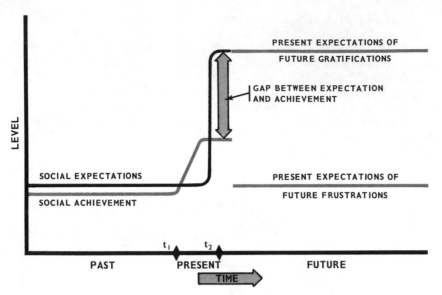

Figure 18-2. – J-curve change model–improvement pattern.

These models of social change indicate the dynamics of motivational factors stipulated in the first two hypotheses. There are also social circumstances that can be judged as unlikely to stimulate social discontent. Examples in the social process are situations in which objective achievement remains constant, no matter what that level may be, or situations in which acceleration or deceleration of change are either consistent or slight. Situations in which a minimal, gradual, or constant amount of change is experienced are the least likely to introduce striking discrepancies between present social expectations and present levels of achievement. Also, by avoiding contrast effects in achievement, expectations about the future are held fairly realistically in line with attainments. These social situations are represented in figure 18-3.

With reference to Figure 18-3C, it should be noted that even deteriorating social circumstances may not in themselves be stimulants to violent behavior, provided the deterioration is gradual and constant. On the other hand, very rapid social deterioration should have the consequences postulated in the J-curve of Davies: a discrepancy between expectations and achievements is created by rapid decline in social attainments. It is also conceivable that a rapidly improving situation could follow the pattern of the J-curve in figure 18-2.

This impact of rapid and consistent change is illustrated in figures 18-4 and 18-5. The model in figure 18-4 assumes that a rapidly deteriorating level of attainment creates not only an increasing gap between presently disappointed expectations and achievement but also that the speed of deterioration is almost certain to create a very pessimistic outlook for the future. In the case illustrated in figure 18-5, which may seem less persuasive as a model for the outburst of civil violence, the rise in social achievement is outstripped by an even steeper curve of rising expectations. Another point to be made regard-

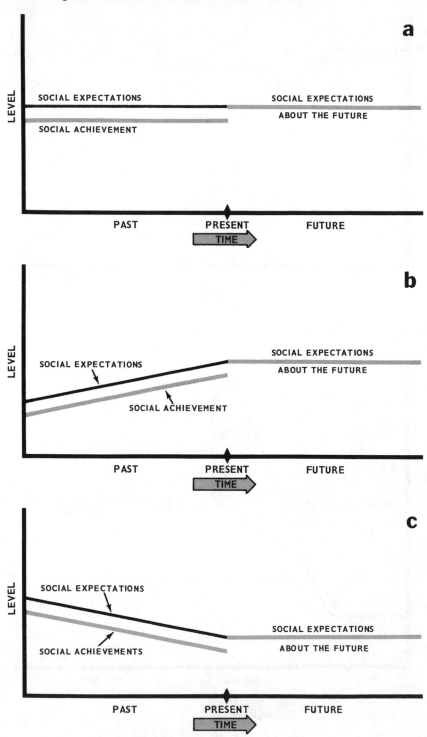

Figure 18-3.—Minimal changes model.

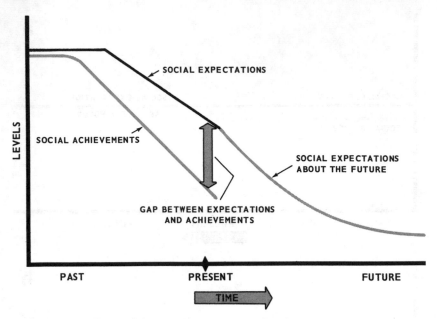

Figure 18-4.—Rapid-change model—deterioration pattern.

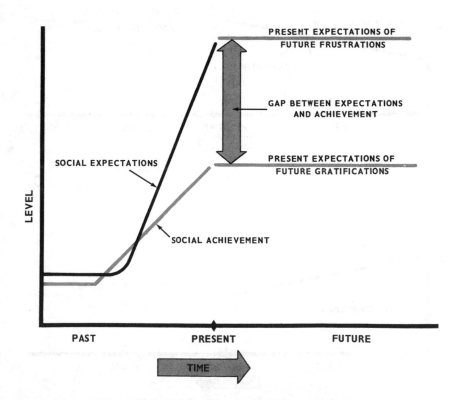

Figure 18-5.—Rapid-change model—improvement pattern.

ing the rapid-change model is that, if social achievement were growing as a power function rather than as a straight line, the gap between expectations and achievement could be eliminated.

The dynamics of the systemic frustration situations sketched in the figures reflect the sudden onset of improvement or deterioration, as well as rapid rates of growth or decline. The point to be stressed is that levels of social expectation depend very much on past performance of the social system. Men who experience a constant history of either frustration or satisfaction will develop learned expectations consistent with their experience. Abrupt change in objective circumstance, especially a reversal of direction but also, at least at the outset, a very rapid rise or decline, will have a sharp and sometimes unrealistic impact on expectations. The consequent lack of alignment between expectations and attainments creates the intolerable discrepancy which is postulated as the motivational antecedent to political violence.

Unrealistic expectations regarding the future may also be pinned to a major change in circumstance that is clearly certain to occur at a particular point in time. The irreality of such expectations is that a variety of other changes are also anticipated concomitant with the single, clearly stated event.

There are situations in the present century in which exaggerated expectations regarding some future event are likely to bring an immediate sense of sharp systemic frustration. Speaking of the trauma of independence in West Africa, Victor LeVine points out that the advent of independence is often counted upon to provide a panacea for all the social ills besetting a country.[10] When independence does occur, however, it falls far short of providing a perfect solution to all problems. This experience proves a shattering frustration if, in fact, such high expectations were held (fig. 18-6). It is indisputable that the extent of revolutionary behavior in Africa increased sharply after independence was granted. It was the expectation of momentous change that proved illusory.

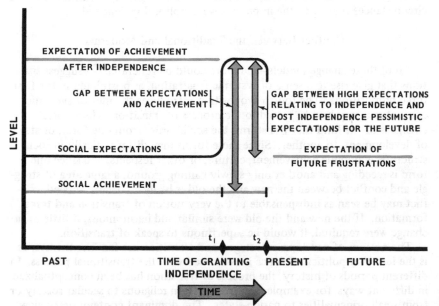

Figure 18-6.—Disappointed expectations tied to future events.

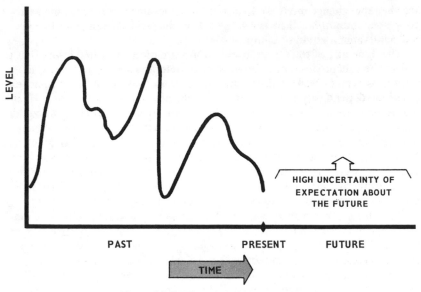

Figure 18-7. – Fluctuation change model.

In figure 18-7, flux in social and economic performance or policy is postulated as creating social discontent and political violence. Flux is likely to
create ambiguity and uncertainty of expectations, as suggested in the third
hypothesis. Discontinuous economic growth, that is, alternating periods of
relative prosperity and economic slump in short succession, or conflicting policies simultaneously pursued or sequently administered, as well as other inconsistencies within the domain of social change, exemplify another set of
circumstances that ripen the impulse toward political violence.[11]

Conflict Between the Traditional and Modern

All of these change models—and more could be generated[12]—suggest situations that give rise to a sense of systemic frustration, as postulated in the first
three propositions. The fourth proposition introduces the idea of systemic
conflict and may best be traced to the process of transition. Here, social
change is of the kind that transforms the social order from one form, or stage
of development, to another. Since these forms may differ radically in social
structure, economic achievement, culture, or other respects, and since one
form is receding and another only slowly gaining ground, a large area of struggle and conflict between the new and the old is likely to occur. Indeed, conflict may be seen as indispensable to the very notion of transition and transformation. If the new and the old were similar and harmonious, if little or no
change were required, it would be superfluous to speak of transition.
The notions of development, stages, and transition are familiar themes, as
is the idea that political violence is associated with the transitional process. In
different periods of history, the process of transition has been conceptualized
in different ways; for example, as a change from religious to secular society or
from small principalities to nation-states. The dominant contemporary view

stresses the process of modernization, which is seen as engulfing the less-developed nations of today's world. In this view, nations may be classified into three groups: modern societies, traditional societies, and modernizing societies. The latter are passing through the transitional stage from traditional society to modernity. Generally, this period of transition is regarded as one that entails an inordinate amount of strain, tension, and crisis.[13]

On the evidence, members of transitional societies aspire to the benefits of modernity, yet modern goals may be blocked by the values inherent in traditional society.[14] Any modicum of modernity introduced into traditional society will conflict with its traditions. The farther the process of transition progresses, the more likely and the more intense the conflicts between modern and established patterns. The situation may be depicted as a massive conflict, reflected in myriad individual psyches of different strata of the population and infecting different domains of the social process. It may lead to intergroup conflict between more traditional and more modern strata with conflicting social roles, structures, and expectations.

Figure 18-8 attempts to schematize the pattern. If we assume that many traditional patterns are in fact incompatible with modernity, then the midpoint of the transitional process is the point of highest intensity of conflict and hence the point of highest systemic frustration. The stage of transition is also the one most likely to be characterized by a high incidence of violent activity. It is at this midpoint that the accomplishments of modernity equal those of tradition, and the drive toward modernity is offset by the contradictory and equal attraction of traditional ways. This should be the stage of the most intense struggle between the traditional and the modern. Figure 18-8 symbolizes this systemic conflict situation with two intersecting arrows representing traditional and modern drives. The closer the transitional process to the stage of modernity (tradition), the stronger the modern (traditional) drive, and the weaker the traditional (modern) drive. (This strengthening and weakening of drives is depicted by the varying width of the two arrows.) The forces determining the strength and weakness of the two drives are specified

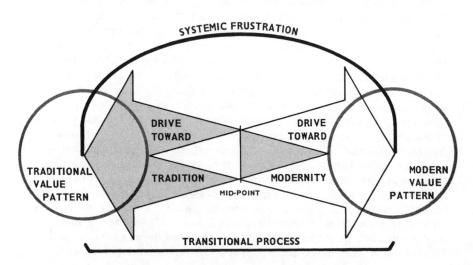

Figure 18-8.—Systemic—conflict model of transition.

by the psychological hypothesis that postulates a strengthening of drive with proximity to the goal.[15] Hence the closer the transitional country to either modernity or tradition, the less the systemic conflict. As a country approaches either end of the transition continuum, the attraction toward the closest value pattern overcomes the drive in the opposite direction.

The Processes of Modernization

It can be argued that all of the conditions conducive to systemic frustration are produced by the modernization process, in addition to the occurrence of systemic conflict. Modernization, especially since World War II, affects an uneven array of nations at different levels of development. The less-developed nations, even those very close to the image of traditional society, are exposed to the modern ways of the more advanced nations. This exposure alone may create new aspirations and expectations and leave them unmatched by social achievements.

Modernity itself denotes a very specific mode of culture and social organization. It includes the aspiration and capacity in a society to produce and consume a wide range and quantity of goods and services. It includes high development in science, technology, and education, and high attainment in scores of specialized skills. It includes, moreover, a secular culture, new structures of social organization and more specialized and differentiated participation, new sets of aspirations, attitudes, and ideologies. Modern affluent nations with their complex economic, political, and social systems serve best as models of modernity to nations emerging from traditional society.

The adoption of modern goals, although an integral aspect of modernity, is hardly synonymous with their attainment. The arousal of an underdeveloped society to awareness of complex modern patterns of behavior and organization brings with it a desire to emulate and achieve the same high level of satisfaction. But there is an inevitable lag between aspiration and achievement. The more a country is exposed to modernity and the lower its level of development, the greater the discrepancy between achievement and social aspirations. It is postulated that the peak discrepancy between systemic goals and their satisfaction, and hence maximum systemic frustration, is likely to occur during the transitional phase. Highly modern and truly traditional nations should experience less systemic frustration—in the modern nations, because of their ability to provide a high level of attainment commensurate with modern aspirations; in the traditional nations, unexposed to modernity, because modern aspirations are still lacking. Figure 18-9 depicts the increasing and decreasing gap between modern aspirations and modern achievements.

A similar logic is applicable not only to social aspirations but also to social expectations. Furthermore, there may also be a feedback effect stemming from modern social attainment. It could be argued that the satisfaction of modern wants and aspirations reinforces the expectation of further satisfaction. As modern aspirations are formed through the process of exposure to modernity, if even a few aspirations are satisfied, these few satisfactions may create the drive and expectation for more, thus adding to the sense of systemic frustration. If so, it could be assumed that the faster the rate of modern achievement, the greater the feedback effect and the more thorough the "revolution of rising expectations." It is in this sense that rapid rates of

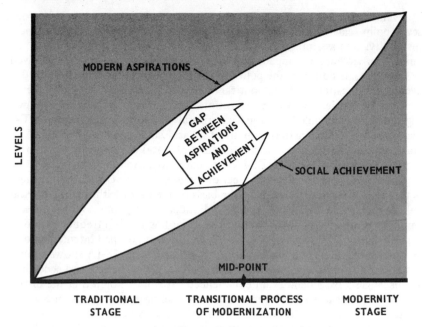

LEVELS

MODERN ASPIRATIONS

GAP BETWEEN ASPIRATIONS AND ACHIEVEMENT

SOCIAL ACHIEVEMENT

MID-POINT

TRADITIONAL
STAGE

TRANSITIONAL PROCESS
OF MODERNIZATION

MODERNITY
STAGE

Figure 18-9.—Model of uneven growth of modern aspirations and
achievement during transition.

change, as opposed to gradual change toward modernity, could lead to more
rather than less frustration, the situation postulated in the model in figure
18-5. At the same time, rapid achievement could reduce the gap between aspirations and attainment and hence reduce the sense of frustration. Rapid
rate of change in the establishment of modernity in this estimation then could
have contradictory effects.

The aura of uncertainty also hangs over the entire process of social change,
a consequence of its conflicts and confusions. There is ambivalence of attitudes to old ways now on the wane, as well as toward the modern future. Ambiguity epitomizes the transitional process, and ambiguity is postulated to increase frustration.

MEASUREMENT OF POLITICAL INSTABILITY

The complexity of the theoretical propositions elaborated in the previous
section make them difficult to test precisely through the use of cross-national
aggregate data. We may, however, assess empirically the relationship between
levels or stages of development and political violence, as well as between violence and some selected measures of rate of socioeconomic change.[16]

To do so, the first task is to measure the level of political violence or political instability in a large sample of nations of the world. The study includes
84 nations which are examined for an 18-year period, 1948-65. Every reported event relevant to political instability that occurred in these countries
during the time period is recorded to form a cross-national data bank of political instability events. (See the appendix for a detailed description of the
data.)

Events are scaled in terms of an intensity weighting that assigns values on a seven-point scale. The scale ranges from 0, extreme stability, to 6, extreme instability. In assigning scale values to events, the criteria used are the amount of violence accompanying the event, the number of persons involved in the event, its duration, the political significance of persons involved in the event, and an estimate of the political repercussions of the event upon the society as a whole. Typical scale positions assigned to events are the following: regularly scheduled election, 0; dismissal or resignation of cabinet official, 1; peaceful demonstration or arrest, 2; assassination (except of chief of state) or sabotage, 3; assassination (of chief of state) or terrorism, 4; coup d'etat or guerrilla warfare, 5; civil war or mass execution, 6.

Countries are profiled in a number of different ways. One basic technique is to assign countries to groups on the basis of the event with the highest scale value experienced during the time period under investigation. Within these intensity groupings, countries are ranked according to both frequency and intensity scores. The types of profiles yielded by this grouped intensity and frequency technique are illustrated in table 18-1. Table 18-1A shows country instability profiles for the entire 18-year period, 1948-65, grouped according to the single most violent event experienced. It will be noted that the distribution is highly skewed, with most countries falling at scale position 5 and quite a few at scale position 6. This profiling tells us that, within this relatively long time period, a large number of countries experienced a high level of instability, although perhaps only temporarily. It also shows that there is a smaller number of countries that did not experience a single severely unstable event in the entire 18 years. If instability scores are averaged for three six-year subperiods within the 18 years, as in table 18-1B, a more normal distribution is obtained. In this profiling, countries that have experienced severe internal turmoil, but only briefly, have their scores tempered by the periods of relative quiescence. Only Indonesia remains in scale position 6, indicating that it has experienced civil war during each of the three subperiods.

Another method of profiling nations on political instability is to sum the scaled events for the entire time period without grouping the nations. The profiles yielded by this method rank countries somewhat differently than previously. Frequency of events, though weighted for intensity, is a more dominant factor than in the grouped scoring method. A final scaling method uses only violent events. The profiling of nations with these violent events (scored by the Guttman technique, see appendix) is presented in table 18-2.

It should be pointed out that all of these scaling methods show a high level of agreement, while at the same time shifting the position of specific countries in response to different emphases in the scaling criteria. The United States, for example, is at the midpoint of the 84 countries in tables 18-1A and 18-1B, but among the most unstable 25 percent of countries in table 18-2.

In subsequent sections of the study in which we analyze the relationships among measures of development, rates of change, and political instability and violence, we use these several techniques of quantifying the notion of instability and violence. In all of the studies, a consistent patterning of relationships is found, no matter which measure of instability is used. In most of the analyses, data are used from the entire time period, 1948-65. In some cases, however, a particular subperiod of time is selected because of its relationship to measures of the ecology of the system.

Table 18-1A.—National Political Instability Profiles, 1948-65

[Grouped scores, n = 84]

1	2	3	4	5	6
				France 5:435	Argentina 6:445
				Venezuela 5:429	Indonesia 6:416
				So. Africa 5:422	Bolivia 6:318
				India 5:360	Korea 6:291
				Syria 5:329	Cuba 6:283
				Guatemala 5:234	Iraq 6:274
				Lebanon 5:212	Colombia 6:244
				Brazil 5:209	Greece 6:236
				Haiti 5:205	Burma 6:213
				Peru 5:196	Dom. Rep. 6:195
				Morocco 5:194	Sudan 6:189
				Portugal 5:190	Paraguay 6:141
				Turkey 5:189	E. Germany 6:138
			United States 4:318	Poland 5:179	Laos 6:129
			Spain 4:284	Egypt 5:152	Tunisia 6:126
			Iran 4:237	Thailand 5:152	Cyprus 6:123
			Pakistan 4:231	Jordan 5:145	Hungary 6:113
			Italy 4:192	Ecuador 5:117	Honduras 6:105
			U.S.S.R. 4:165	Malaya 5:108	Panama 6:101
			Belgium 4:162	Philippines 5:105	Czech. 6:100
			Chile 4:156	Nicaragua 5:096	China (mainland) 6:086
			Ceylon 4:152	El Salvador 5:079	Costa Rica 6:058
			Japan 4:123	Cambodia 5:071	
		U.K. 3:112	Mexico 4:111	Ethiopia 5:034	
		W. Germany 3:087	Ghana 4:106		
		Canada 3:084	Uruguay 4:100		
		Libya 3:069	Yugoslavia 4:077		
		Romania 3:060	Bulgaria 4:071		
		Switzerland 3:042	Albania 4:067		
		China(Taiwan) 3:039	Israel 4:064		
	Finland 2:056	Norway 3:034	Austria 4:057		
	Australia 2:026	Ireland 3:031	Liberia 4:036		
	Netherlands 2:021	Iceland 3:026	Denmark 4:030		
	Sweden 2:020	Saudi Arabia 3:018	Afghanistan 4:029		
Luxembourg 1:012	New Zealand 2:015				

Stability _____ Instability

Table 18-1B.–Political Instability Profiles of 84 Countries (1948-65)

[Stability Score Shown for Each Country is Grouped Score, Averaged]

1	2	3	4	5	6
			France 13435		
			Union of South Africa 13422		
			Brazil 13209		
			Morocco 13194		
			Portugal 13190		
			Turkey 13189		
			Poland 13179		
			Thailand 13152		
			Jordan 13145		
			Cyprus 13123	Argentina 16445	
			Hungary 13113	Bolivia 16318	
			Philippines 13105	Cuba 16283	
			Czechoslovakia 13100	Iraq 16274	
			China (Mainland) 13086	Colombia 16244	
			Cambodia 13071	Burma 16213	
			India 12360	Venezuela 15429	
			Iran 12237	Syria 15329	
			Pakistan 12231	Korea 15291	
			Sudan 12189	Haiti 15205	
			U.S.S.R. 12165	Peru 15196	
			Ecuador 12117	Greece 14236	
		Belgium 10162	Nicaragua 12096	Guatemala 14234	
		Chile 10156	United States 11318	Lebanon 14212	
		Mexico 10111	Spain 11284	Egypt 14152	
		Uruguay 10100	Dom. Rep. 11195	Paraguay 14141	
		Israel 10064	Ceylon 11152	East Germany 14138	
		Liberia 10036	Japan 11123	Laos 14129	
		Ethiopia 10034	Malaya 11108	Tunisia 14126	
	U.K. 07112	Italy 09192	Yugoslavia 11077	Honduras 14105	
	Ghana 07106	Libya 09069	Bulgaria 11071	Panama 14101	
	Austria 07057	Romania 09060	Albania 11067	El Salvador 14079	Indonesia 18416
	Denmark 07030	Costa Rica 09058			
	Iceland 07026	Afghanistan 09029			
	W. Germany 06087	Canada 08084			
	Finland 06056	Switzerland 08042			
	China (Taiwan) 06039	Norway 08034			
	Australia 06026				
	Sweden 06020				
	Ireland 05031				
Netherland 04021	Saudi Arabia 05018				
Luxembourg 03012	New Zealand 05015				
1	2	3	4	5	6

Stability ⟶ Instability

Table 18-2.—Political Violence Profiles of 84 Countries (1948-65)
[Sources Derived from Guttman Scalogram]

Country	Score	Country	Score	Country	Score
Finland	0	Yugoslavia	27	Dominican Republic	70
Luxembourg	0	China (mainland)	28	Sudan	71
Denmark	1	El Salvador	28	Laos	72
Iceland	1	Belgium	31	Greece	73
New Zealand	1	Albania	32	Paraguay	74
Saudi Arabia	1	Japan	32	Haiti	77
Netherlands	2	Czechoslovakia	33	Pakistan	77
Norway	3	Mexico	33	Portugal	77
Sweden	3	Ghana	35	Morocco	79
Australia	4	Malaya	36	U.S.S.R.	81
Afganistan	7	Chile	38	Lebanon	83
Austria	7	East Germany	39	Burma	87
Ireland	7	Cyprus	41	France	95
Switzerland	7	Ecuador	41	Colombia	96
Israel	8	Jordan	41	United States	97
China (Taiwan)	9	Honduras	42	Guatemala	109
Canada	10	Panama	42	Syria	111
Liberia	15	Hungary	45	Iran	114
Uruguay	16	Nicaragua	48	Bolivia	120
United Kingdom	17	Ceylon	51	Iraq	120
Ethiopia	19	Philippines	51	Spain	121
Italy	19	Poland	54	Cuba	123
Romania	20	Tunisia	54	India	124
West Germany	20	Egypt	56	Korea	125
Costa Rica	21	Brazil	57	Argentina	134
Cambodia	24	Peru	64	Venezuela	153
Bulgaria	25	Thailand	65	Union of South Africa	158
Libya	25	Turkey	65	Indonesia	190

LEVEL OF DEVELOPMENT AND POLITICAL VIOLENCE

The hypotheses stated in the theoretical portion of this paper are that modern and traditional nations tend toward stability, while transition leads to political turmoil and violence. Also, the closer a country to some theoretical midpoint between tradition and modernity, the stronger the impulse to political instability. This is the logic of the conflict model of the transitional process, as well as of the exposure-to-modernity model.

In order to test these hypotheses, some cross-national measure of modernity is necessary, to compare levels of political violence. Given the complexities of the notion of modernity and the process of modernization, the measurement task is an exceedingly difficult one. Our measurement cannot embrace all aspects of modernity. It is confined to a specific set of indicators which, in combination, yield a rough indication of developmental level.

Economic Development

Let us turn first to a rather narrow definition of modernity, assuming that the difference between a modern and a traditional country lies in their relative wealth. Highly affluent modern nations are those capable of producing great quantities of goods and services and of providing their citizens with high standards of living, high incomes, adequate education, health, and other socio-economic benefits. With this approach, modernity may be measured in terms of the degree to which a nation enjoys some very specific commodity such as per capita gross national product (GNP), caloric intake, telephones, physicians, etc. These indices of modernity may be used singly, to indicate that particular aspect of modernity, or they may be combined, indicating a more comprehensive and summary view of modern development. In this study, a set of separate indicators is employed, as well as a composite modernity index. The modernity index combines GNP per capita, caloric intake, telephones, physicians, newspapers, radios, literacy, and urbanization.[17]

Level of modernity is thus assessed quantitatively: those countries scoring high on the selected indicators are judged modern, while the median range denotes the transitional group of nations. It should be pointed out that a country which is low on these indicators may be a traditional country, but not necessarily. A further criterion for distinguishing a traditional society is that it is static and unchanging. By this definition, a traditional country must not only be low in its level of development, but it must maintain this low level over time. A tendency toward improvement in economic conditions places it in the transitional group. In terms of this criterion, we have very few if any traditional countries in our sample. This lack is inevitable since a traditional country in this sense will not collect statistical data and so not be amenable to study in terms of our empirical approach. This is not to say that there are no extremely underdeveloped countries among our sample of 84. On the contrary, there are a number that are characterized by minimal industrialization, almost total dependence on agriculture or extractive industry, and a very thin stratum of educated persons within the population.

While we have predicted that very little political unrest will occur in the most traditional nations, with violence increasing with modernization to reach a peak among nations at midpoints of development, and then subsiding again among modern, industrial states, this complete pattern may not be evident in our cross-national sample. If, in the present analysis, most of the nations are either caught in the midst of transition to modernity or have achieved a high level of industrialization, we would expect the prevailing relationship to show a consistent trend of decreasing political unrest with increasing development.

Let us look first at the relationship between the composite index of modernity and political unrest. In table 18-3, countries are classified into three groups: modern, transitional, and so-called traditional states, and further subdivided into stable and unstable categories.[18] We see that the modern countries are predominantly stable (20 stable and 4 unstable). Transitional countries, on the other hand, are unstable by a ratio of 2:1. And among so-called traditional countries (which are those lowest in developmental level), instability also predominates but by a less striking ratio of 13:10. Very similar results are obtained using Russett's five-level classificatory scheme of economic development, shown in table 18-4.[19]

We may also determine socioeconomic conditions that represent critical threshold levels of political stability and instability. The possibility of finding such threshold values is illustrated in table 18-5, which presents eight tables based on environmental indicators (literacy, GNP per capita, radios, newspapers, telephones, physicians, calories, and urbanization).[20] From these empirical tables, a composite picture of the stable country emerges: it is a society

Table 18-3.—Relationship Between Modernity and Political Instability, 1948-65

[Grouped Scores]

	I. Traditional	II. Transitional	III. Modern	
Unstable (5:105–6:445)	Bolivia Burma China (mainland) Haiti India Indonesia Iraq Jordan Laos Malaya Morocco Philippines Sudan 13	Brazil Colombia Costa Rica Cuba Cyprus Dom. Rep. Ecuador Egypt Greece Guatemala Honduras Hungary Korea Lebanon Panama Paraguay Peru Poland Portugal Syria Thailand Tunisia Turkey Union of South Africa Venezuela 25	Argentina Czechoslovakia East Germany France 4	42
Stable (1:012–5:096)	Afghanistan Cambodia China (Taiwan) Ethiopia Ghana Iran Liberia Libya Pakistan Saudi Arabia 10	Albania Bulgaria Ceylon Chile El Salvador Italy Japan Mexico Nicaragua Romania Spain Yugoslavia 12	Australia Austria Belgium Canada Denmark Finland Iceland Ireland Israel Luxembourg Netherlands New Zealand Norway Sweden Switzerland United Kingdom United States Uruguay U.S.S.R. West Germany 20	42
	23	37	24	84

Table 18-4.—Relationship Between Economic Development and Political Instability, 1948-65*

	I. Traditional Primitive	II. Traditional Civilization	III. Transitional	IV. Industrial Revolution	V. High Mass Consumption	
Unstable (5:105-6:445)	Burma Laos Sudan	Bolivia China (mainland) Haiti India Thailand	Dominican Republic Ecuador Egypt Guatemala Honduras Indonesia Iraq Jordan Korea Morocco Paraguay Peru Philippines Portugal Syria Tunisia Turkey	Argentina Brazil Colombia Costa Rica Cuba Gyprus Czechoslovakia East Germany Greece Hungary Lebanon Malaya Panama Poland Union of South Africa Venezuela	France	
	3	5	17	16	1	42
Stable (1:012-5:096)	Afghanistan Ethiopia Libya	Cambodia Liberia Pakistan	Albania Ceylon China (Taiwan) El Salvador Chana Iran Nicaragua Saudi Arabia	Austria Bulgaria Chile Finland Iceland Ireland Israel Italy Japan Mexico Romania Spain Uruguay U.S.S.R. Yugoslavia	Australia Belgium Canada Denmark Luxembourg Netherlands New Zealand Norway Sudan Switzerland United Kingdom United States West Germany	
	3	3	8	15	13	31
	6	8	25	31	14	84

*These categories of economic development are from Russett et al., op. cit.

*Table 18-5.—Relationships Between the Eight Indicators of Level of
Development, 1948-55, and Degree of Political Stability, 1955-61*

A. Percent literacy

	Low (below 90%)	High (above 90%)	Total
Unstable	48	5	53
Stable	10	19	29
Total	58	24	82

Chi square = 25.93, $p < 0.001$
Yule's $Q = 0.90$

B. Radios per 1,000 population

	Low (below 65)	High (above 65)	Total
Unstable	45	6	51
Stable	9	20	29
Total	54	26	80

Chi square = 25.02, $p < 0.001$
Yule's $Q = 0.887$

C. Newspapers per 1,000 population

	Low (below 120)	High (above 120)	Total
Unstable	48	5	53
Stable	6	10	16
Total	54	15	69

Chi square = 17.34, $p < 0.001$
Yule's $Q = 0.88$

D. Percent of population owning telephones

	Low (below 2%)	High (above 2%)	Total
Unstable	35	6	41
Stable	7	18	25
Total	42	24	66

Chi square = 19.68, $p < 0.001$
Yule's $Q = 0.875$

E. Calories per capita per day

	Low (below 2525)	High (above 2525)	Total
Unstable	39	10	49
Stable	8	20	28
Total	47	30	77

Chi square = 17.43, $p < 0.001$
Yule's $Q = 0.81$

F. People per physician

	Low (below 1900)	High (above 1900)	Total
Unstable	40	13	53
Stable	6	19	25
Total	46	32	78

Chi square = 11.41, $p < 0.001$
Yule's $Q = 0.81$

G. GNP per capita (in U.S. dollars)

	Low (below 300)	High (above 300)	Total
Unstable	36	8	44
Stable	9	18	27
Total	45	26	71

Chi square = 14.92, $p < 0.001$
Yule's $Q = 0.80$

H. Percent of population living in urban centers

	Low (below 45%)	High (above 45%)	Total
Unstable	38	6	44
Stable	11	15	26
Total	49	21	70

Chi square = 13.08, $p < 0.001$
Yule's $Q = 0.79$

which is 90 percent or more literate; with 65 or more radios and 120 or more newspapers per 1,000 population; with 2 percent or more of the population having telephones; with 2,525 or more calories per day per person; with not more than 1,900 persons per physician; with a GNP of $300 or more per person per year; and with 45 percent or more of the population living in urban centers. If all of these threshold values are attained by a society, there is an extremely high probability that the country will achieve relative political stability. Conversely, to the extent that gratifications are less than these threshold values, the greater the likelihood of political instability.

To complete this picture of the relationship between economic modernization and political instability, we may look at a further set of economic, social, and political indicators of development and their relationship to the level of political violence within society.[21] The emphasis in this case is on violence, with the scoring of political unrest based solely on violent events (as illustrated in table 18-2).

The following were selected as broad indices of industralization and development in the economy: (1) percent of the population living in urban centers; (2) percent of the gross domestic product (GNP) that comes from agriculture; (3) percent of the labor force engaged in agriculture; and (4) GNP/ capita. To supplement these data, other attributes of society were also examined, such as the spread of modern communications (newspapers, radios, and mail); the distribution of social benefits (education, literacy, life expectancy); and the level of participation in politics (voting, executive stability). We find that these indicators of economic, social, and political modernization are a clue to the level of political violence within a society. Economic modernity, modern communications, health, education, and political participation are all associated with lower levels of political violence, although the relationships are not equally strong in all cases. (The correlation values for these relationships are given in the appendix.)

In combination, these analyses demonstrate some of the hypothesized relationships between level of socioeconomic development and political unrest and violence: modern countries show a lower level of political unrest, less-developed countries a higher level.

Political Development

To supplement the findings relating economic development to political instability, we sought an assessment of developmental level that would depend more on political than on socioeconomic factors. A broad framework was provided by judgments regarding democracy-authoritarianism made by Almond and Coleman for 45 nations. These authors classified nations into several groupings. Table 18-6 presents these groupings arranged to indicate increasingly concentrated authority structures.[22] If these groupings can be considered indicative of political development, as well as indicative of increasingly democratic political sturctures, one can see among them a pronounced relationship to economic and social development. Calculating the average scores on GNP per capita and on percentage of the population literate within each level of political development, a clear pattern emerges. The higher the level of political development of a society, the higher the level of the population on both income and literacy.

Table 18-6.—*Economic and Social Development, Political Violence,*
and the Political System*

Political system	GNP/capita	Percent literate	Political violence	Instability grouped-averaged	Instability grouped
Developed and/or European (n = 23)	$943	98.5	6	07116	3087
Latin American competitive (n = 5)	379	80.1	28	10156	5203
Latin American semicompetitive (n = 5)	262	55.7	37	14101	5196
Asia and Africa political democracy (n = 7)	220	47.5	43	12360	5108
Latin American authoritarian (n = 9)	189	39.4	57	14141	5429
Asia and Africa tutelary democracy (n = 4)	136	17.5	55	15169	6169
Asia and Africa modernizing oligarchy (n = 6)	119	16.4	56	13650	5241
Asia and Africa conservative oligarchy (n = 6)	99	16.2	22	12654	4604
Asia and Africa traditional oligarchy (n = 3)	92	2.5	5	09029	4029

*Median scores, 1948-65.

On the other hand, a different tendency is apparent when average scores for political violence are calculated. In table 18-6 it may be seen that conservative and traditional oligarchies are relatively stable, while significant increases in political violence are noticeable in the modernizing oligarchy, the tutelary democracy, and the Latin American authoritarian groups. Declining instability appears in the political democracy group, followed by the Latin American semicompetitive and competitive groupings. A return to relative political stability is apparent in the developed nations.

From these data one can infer that with growth in the economic and social sectors of society, the political system also undergoes change. Concomitant with these changes, there is an increasing amount of manifest conflict within society. On the other hand, once the system approaches full modernization (as indicated by almost universal adult literacy) and its economy approaches the high mass-consumption level (as indicated by a GNP per capita well above the subsistence level), political stability tends to reemerge.

Table 18-7.—Level of Coerciveness

1. Highly permissive	2. Permissive	3. Mildly coercive	4. Moderately coercive	5. Coercive	6. Highly coercive
Australia	Belgium	Austria	Bolivia	Afghanistan	Albania
Canada	Costa Rica	Brazil	Colombia	Argentina	Bulgaria
Denmark	Finland	Burma	Ecuador	Cuba	China (mainland)
Netherlands	Iceland	Cambodia	El Salvador	Egypt	China (Taiwan)
Norway	Ireland	France	Ghana	Ethiopia	Czechoslovakia
Sweden	Israel	Greece	Honduras	Haiti	Dominican Republic
Switzerland	Italy	India	Guatemala	Korea	East Germany
United Kingdom	Luxembourg	Japan	Indonesia	Morocco	Hungary
United States	Mexico	Malaya	Iran	Nicaragua	Poland
	New Zealand	Pakistan	Iraq	Paraguay	Romania
	Uruguay	Panama	Jordan	Portugal	U.S.S.R.
	West Germany	Philippines	Laos	Saudi Arabia	Yugoslavia
		Turkey	Lebanon	Spain	
			Liberia	Union of South Africa	
			Libya	Venezuela	
			Peru		
			Syria		
			Sudan		
			Thailand		
			Tunisia		

Coerciveness of Regime

A second technique for evaluating the structure of authority in the political system is to develop a typology of the coerciveness-permissiveness patterns of the regime. A six-point classification scheme was applied to the nations in this sample, rating each for level of coerciveness of regime.[23] The resultant groups are arrayed in table 18-7. As may be seen, the most coercive group of nations comprises primarily the Communist bloc and the most permissive group the Western democracies.

On the composite modernity index, the Western democracies are the most modern nations in the world. Some of the Communist nations also score relatively high in modernity, but others are closer to the midpoint on the index. If one tests for patterning of modernity within levels of coerciveness, the pattern demonstrated in table 18-8 emerges. The highly coercive nations are not as modern as the permissive or highly permissive nations, but clearly tend to be more modern that those nations at midlevels of coerciveness. The least modern nations are those that are coercive, but not at the extreme of coerciveness. The same patterning occurs between coerciveness and political violence. Violence is lowest among permissive states. It increases with increasing coerciveness of regime, but subsides to some degree with extreme coerciveness. When one compares this patterning to that in table 18-6, it is apparent that the coerciveness dimension is not identical to Almond and Coleman's typology of political development. On the latter, economic and political development go hand in hand. On the former, economic development is high among nations at both extremes of coerciveness-permissiveness. Political violence, however, shows the same relationship to both coerciveness and political development.

Table 18-8.—Modernity, Political Violence, and Coerciveness of Political Systems*

Levels of coerciveness-permissiveness	Modernity	Political violence	Instability grouped-averaged	Instability grouped
1. Highly permissive (n = 9)	1.54	4.0	07030	3083
2. Permissive (n = 12)	.70	12.0	08042	3574
3. Mildly coercive (n = 15)	−.36	51.0	13071	5108
4. Moderately coercive (n = 21)	−.49	65.0	14105	5209
5. Coercive (n = 15)	−.40	77.0	13427	5194
6. Highly coercive (n = 12)	.55	32.5	11680	4672

*Median scores.

In summary of the relationship between development and political violence, we find that with increased levels of economic modernity there is a tendency toward lower levels of political unrest. Countries in the transitional stage of economic modernization are the most beset by political turmoil.

Among the very few countries that might be characterized as yet untouched by the process of economic change, there is a tendency toward political quiescence. Regarding political development, we find in these results and others that permissive, democratic regimes, by and large, experience low levels of political unrest. This is also true of repressive, totalitarian governments that are capable of effectively suppressing the overt political expression of popular dissatisfaction. It is governments at midlevels of coerciveness and political development that experience the most political turmoil. And these governments also tend to be at a midpoint of economic modernization.

SOCIETAL CHANGE AND POLITICAL VIOLENCE

The final question, which was raised at the outset of this paper, is whether empirical relationships can be discovered between patterns of socioeconomic change within society and levels of political unrest. We now seek to go beyond an assessment of attained levels of socioeconomic development, to examine the rates at which these levels were achieved. Are countries that modernize gradually less susceptible to political violence than those in which change is rapid? Some of our hypotheses suggest this relationship, although others do not.

In order to measure rate of change, we confined ourselves to the same types of socioeconomic indicators adopted for measuring levels of development.[24] Data were gathered on these indicators for the time period 1935-62, for all of the 84 countries. An average annual percentage rate of change for each country was calculated on each indicator and a combined rate-of-change index was developed by pooling the country's separate change scores.[25] Differences in percentage change rates among countries were then compared to political instability profiles. To the procedures for measuring political violence discussed above, we added another which seemed particularly applicable to assessment of rate of change. This is a dynamic, rather than a static, scoring of political unrest, yielding a measure of change in instability level over time.[26] (See appendix.)

The results obtained from interrelating percentage rates of change on the environmental indicators and levels of political instability indicate, in general, that the faster the rate of socioeconomic change within a society, the higher the level of political unrest. The combined rate-of-change index shows a strong relationship to political instability, as do change rates on many of the indicators taken singly.[27] Looking at the dynamic instability measures, we find a similar set of relationships (see table 18-9). Countries with the lowest socioeconomic rate of change show a trend toward political stability; countries with the highest rate of socioeconomic change are beset by increasing instability; and countries experiencing intermediate rates of change toward modernization are also intermediate in instability pattern.

These general findings point to the fact that we cannot assume that modernization will bring political stability in its wake. While highly modern countries tend to be politically stable, the process of attaining modernity is one that is rife with political unrest. Furthermore, the more rapid the modernization, the greater the impact in increasing political violence. Only after certain threshold socioeconomic values have been attained may the stabilizing political benefits of modernity be experienced.

Table 18-9.—Relationship Between Mean Rate of Change on Ecological Variables, 1935-62, and Change in Stability as Measured by Variance and Slope, 1948-62

Mean rate of change on ecological variables	Stable — Low variance and either Negative slope or Zero slope		Indeterminate — Low variance/positive slope or High variance/negative slope	Unstable — High variance and either Positive slope or Zero slope		Total
	Negative slope	Zero slope		Positive slope	Zero slope	
Low change	Norway New Zealand West Germany Australia Denmark Iceland	United States Canada Sweden Switzerland Netherlands Luxembourg Israel 13	Great Britain Austria 2	Belgium	1	16
Moderately low change	Ireland Guatemala Bulgaria China (Taiwan)	Finland Italy Chile Philippines 8	France Argentina Union of South Africa Uruguay Mexico Spain Pakistan Ecuador Greece 9	Cuba Paraguay Hungary	3	20
Moderately high change		0	Thailand Costa Rica Colombia Ghana Egypt Turkey Ceylon India Poland 9	Peru Portugal Panama Brazil Haiti Iraq	Japan Yugoslavia Tunisia Burma U.S.S.R. 11	20
High change	Syria	1	Korea Malaya 2	El Salvador Bolivia Venezuela Dom. Rep.	Cambodia Morocco Honduras Indonesia 8	11
Total		22	22		23	67

The rationale for these findings may be found in the models presented in the theoretical section of this paper, particularly in figures 18-2, 18-5, 18-8, and 18-9. There it was hypothesized that rapid change will serve to increase the gap between expectations and achievements. The feedback effect of a few satisfactions will increase the demand for more accomplishments, beyond the level that can possibly be attained within the society. Also, the conflict between traditional and modern ways of life will be intensified by rapid transition between the two patterns, allowing less time for adjustment.

If we look at the socioeconomic indicators individually, however, we find that they do not all have the same impact upon society. For example, while a rapid increase in percent of the population being educated does entail a higher level of political instability, a rapid increase in percent of the population owning telephones is accompanied by more stability within the society. Similarly, rapid increase in national income brings a lessening of political unrest.[28]

Furthermore, for theoretical reasons, we are particularly interested in examining the relationships between rates of change on these various socioeconomic indicators and level of political unrest among the transitional group of countries. It was postulated at the outset of this paper that this group of countries suffers the most deleterious effects of change. Change occurring at a higher level of development presumably does not mean change in the sense of developing new patterns and new ways of life; it may simply be an intensification or logical extension of existing patterns. Moving from a low to a high level of development, however, entails conflict and discrepancies between aspirations, expectations, and attainments.

Some of the findings at this midlevel of development confirm expectations based on the wider analysis. Among transitional countries, those experiencing a faster rate of change in proportion of population receiving primary education, 1935-62, also experience a higher level of political instability at some time during 1948-65, and show a trend toward greater instability over time during this period.[29] Furthermore, if we control for the maximum value attained on ratio of population receiving primary education, we find that the relationship between an increase in this ratio and political instability is still high.[30] This is significant, since it tells us that it is actually the rate of increase in education as well as the maximum number of educated persons in the society that is important for political unrest. Using the dynamic measure of political unrest, we corroborate the tendency for change in proportion of the population receiving primary education to be positively associated with an increase in political instability over time.[31] Again, change, per se, emerges as important.

We also find that, within this group of countries, percentage change in income (gross domestic product (GDP) per capita), 1951-59, shows the opposite relationship to political unrest: the faster the increase in income, the less the political instability. This indicates that a percentage increase in GDP per capita is associated with a decrease in level of political unrest. If we control for attained level of GNP per capita within the society, we again find that rapid change in increasing incomes is important in reducing instability, apart from the impact of the absolute level of income achieved.[32]

The most detrimental combination of factors appears to be a rapid increase in proportion of the population receiving primary education, but a slow rate of percentage change in GDP per capita. This set of circumstances is most conducive to political unrest among the transitional group of countries.[33]

The relationship between these two change indicators and political instability fits a number of the models proposed at the outset of this paper. Education, like literacy, is a means of arousing awareness of modern goals and hence of raising aspirations within a society. It is also likely that education raises expectations regarding the fulfillment of these aspirations. GDP per capita, on the other hand, is an achievement indicator; it provides gratification of aroused aspirations. A society in which the trend is toward increasing numbers of educated persons within the population, without an increase in their level of income, is a society in which rates of change are widening the gap between aspirations/expectations and their satisfaction. This would appear to be particularly explosive for the transitional society.

The challenge in these findings is whether it is possible to avoid an imbalance between number of educated in the population and opportunity for increased income. Unfortunately, it would seem that the process of modernization makes this imbalance highly probable. Education is a necessary first step to infusing the society with the skills appropriate to industrialization. But the lag between this first step and the second—that of developing the industrial society—is hazardous indeed. Huntington speaks of the dangers of education in the underdeveloped society, a danger that many leaders of nonindustrialized states themselves recognize.[34] He particularly stresses the pitfalls of an increasingly educated population for a society in which political opportunity is lacking. While the political and economic aspects of society are clearly interrelated, our findings suggest that if economic opportunities were immediately available to the newly educated, the lack of political opportunities might not be so disruptive.

A second challenge in these findings relates to a proposition advanced by some economists, that widespread psychological discontent is a precondition for economic growth within society.[35] This view stresses, as a psychological antecedent for modernization, the type of discontent that certainly is fostered by increased education. Again, in this view it seems that a lag between aspiration and achievement is inevitable within societies in transition, a period of hiatus that is particularly violence prone.

The question is whether, in fact, an optimal combination of all relevant conditions is feasible: a sufficient level of psychological discontent to foster change, a sufficient level of education to supply the society with a skilled population, a sufficient level of development to provide jobs and income to match popular skill levels, and a political system sufficiently open to offer access to an educated people. To maintain an optimum balance among these factors, especially during a period of rapid change, may be difficult indeed. Typically, it is education that is expanded most rapidly in response to expressions of popular discontent, an expansion that creates the discrepancy between skill and opportunity.

CONCLUSIONS

To interpret the relationships that we have uncovered between levels of development, rates of socioeconomic change, and political violence, we must return to some of the initial questions raised in this study. The first of these concerns the meaning of social change. As has been pointed out, change is a complex concept that cannot simply be identified with increases, decreases, or fluctuations in the economic characteristics of a society. If these quantifiable ecological traits do have bearing on the question, it must be because they reflect a wide variety of other, unmeasured, qualitative societal factors. The validity of this assumption, that quantifiable economic change is a clue to other types of change, may depend upon the historical era under investigation. As discussed earlier, the prevailing insight of contemporary social science is that the process of modernization provides the pathway of change in the postwar world. This process is generally regarded as socioeconomic and amenable to quantification.

This, however, is not the only interpretation. For example, quite a different view is presented by Sorokin, from the perspective of a major portion of human history. In this light, our 20-year span of analysis is but a wave in a much larger cycle.[36] Sorokin's view of change is essentially ideological or attitudinal, not economic. Civilizations vary between an emphasis on material ("sensate") culture and an absorption in ideological ("ideational") concerns. Sensate culture is accompanied by a rise in economic conditions, which is only to be expected since such a culture deems these economic factors of importance. Ideational culture, however, is generally accompanied by a low level of material success, since material welfare is not a valued commodity and material concerns are considered of secondary importance. Sorokin traces the rates of change in the general economic situations of the ancient world of Greece and Rome from 600 B.C. to A.D. 400, of France from 800 to 1926, and of Germany from 700 to 1932. These curves show considerable fluctuation, tending to be low during eras which Sorokin identifies as ideational and high during periods of sensate culture. In this long-range view, the 20th century is the epitome of sensate culture. From this we may deduce that change is inevitable, since Sorokin's model is a cyclical one in which the penultimate realization of the goals of either type of culture inevitably breeds the conditions of its own decline. Transition then sets in, a period of social disruption and violence in which the dominant cultural theme begins to move in the opposite direction.

If this Hegelian, "poison-fruit" approach is correct, we would be led to a different investigation of change than we have pursued in this study. In the Sorokin view, disruptive change will occur at the highest levels of modernity, when sensate culture is at its peak. Some intuitive and empirical support might be found for this view in the apparently restless dissatisfaction of intelligentsia and student elements within American society, a phenomenon that Sorokin identifies as typical of the last stages of sensate culture. On the other hand, our examination of the economic situation of the postwar world certainly indicates that the economic decline of modern countries is not yet in sight. Also, it shows that the highest levels of turbulence occur at lesser levels of development.

Thus, while Sorokin's broader vision may prove to be correct in the long run, the crisis of transition in our era still seems to be tied to the effort at achieving the higher levels of economic well-being sought by members of a materially oriented culture. And it is a particular attribute of the modernization process that its quality can be indexed not only in quantitative, but specifically in socioeconomic terms. With sufficient ingenuity, other attributes of society, even ideational, could conceivably be reduced to observable, quantifiable indicators.[37] With the process of modernization, however, this effort at ingenuity is superfluous since economic levels and stages of development are well nigh synonymous.

Interest in the relationship between economic development and political violence has characterized a number of recent investigations. All begin with the common insight that the more advanced countries are less subject to political disturbances. This finding is corroborated by those who define development in political terms, as well as by those who define it in economic terms.[38] The kernel of agreement among these investigators is that the highest level of development is accompanied by a decrease in violence, while levels that fall short of modernity are more prone to political unrest. The consistency of this general relationship has been corroborated using quite different measures of violence and different samples of nations. Its stability as a finding may be due to the fact that there is a sufficient sample of identifiable modern and transitional nations in the present-day world.

It is not equally clear whether, in the relationship between development and violence, the least-developed countries show less of a tendency to violence than states at midlevels or transitional stages of development. The problem of discovering the direction of the relationship between violence and development at the low end of the modernity continuum is largely due to the fact that extremely few countries now qualify as traditional, in the sense that they are unaware of modernity. We have suggested earlier in this report, and elsewhere,[39] that such countries do not report data to the United Nations, which makes it difficult to include them in this type of empirical study. Nevertheless, if we are willing to base our assessments on a very few cases, we find that countries at the lowest levels of development are less prone to political instability than are countries at the next higher stages of modernity. Political development, in combination with economic development, shows this pattern (tables 18-6 and 18-8), as does economic development alone, but to a lesser degree (tables 18-3 and 18-4). Again, this slight tendency has been found by other researchers.[40] If it is an actual trend, it corroborates theoretical insights regarding the gap between aspirations/expectations and their achievement, the effects of uncertainty of expectations, and the occurrence of motivational conflict elaborated in the theoretical section of this study. All of these hypotheses point to the transitional stage of development as the most frustration ridden. Neither lower nor higher levels of development will be as prone to violence.

Since this study is specifically concerned with rates of change, it may be asked why so much attention has been paid to attained levels of development. The answer is twofold. On the one hand, an assessment of level of development gives a cross-sectional view of the same process that, in longitudinal perspective, is indexed by rates of change. It is true that knowledge of the present level of development of a nation cannot tell us how rapid or slow, how continuous or discontinuous was the process of attainment. But we may infer from the relationship between development and violence that as countries become more modern, they will also become more politically stable. This inference may be correct in broadest perspective, but it may also be misleading regarding the impact of change on a society that is still far removed from the threshold economic values accompanying political stability (table 18-5).

Therefore, the second point regarding the importance of attained modernity lies in the interrelationships between the static levels and rates of socioeconomic change. It is suggested that rates of change have different implications for societies that differ in modernity level. Furthermore, different indicators, and rates of change on these indicators, have varying impacts on society. There are thus three factors that must be taken into account in assessing the relationship between change and political instability: attained level of development, the nature of the specific socioeconomic indicator, and the rate of change.

This more detailed approach may help to explain some of the conflicting claims of researchers who have explored this problem. For example, in our own first investigation of the question, we found that the faster the rate of socioeconomic change, the higher the level of political unrest.[41] We also noted that rate of change, measured in percentage terms, was strongly related to attained level of development. Modern countries showed smaller percentage change rates; less-developed countries showed higher percentage change rates. At the same time, we discovered that on one indicator, national income, the relationship was reversed: the faster the rate of increase on this variable, the lower the level of political unrest. Furthermore, rate of change in national income, unlike change rates on the other indicators, was related to modernity level in such a way that modern countries showed the highest percentage change rates while underdeveloped countries showed the lowest.

A similarly complex set of findings regarding the relationship between rate of economic change and political violence occurs in the work of other researchers. Alker and Russett find that the highest annual growth rates occur at midlevels of per capita income.[42] Furthermore, the higher the level of income within a society and the greater the growth in income levels, the lower the level of political unrest. Gurr, on the other hand, finds no relationship between measures of civil violence for 119 countries, 1961-63, and growth rate in per capita income, 1953-62.[43] Using only Latin American countries, Bwy finds that the higher the rate of annual growth of GNP per capita, 1950-59, the lower the levels of both organized and anomic violence.[44] Since his study is limited to countries beyond a suggested threshold level of attained development, Bwy speculates that for countries at lower levels of modernity, the relationship may operate in the reverse direction. Finally, Tanter and Midlarsky assess the relationship between rate of increase in GNP per capita in the 7 years immediately prior to the outbreak of revolution, and the number of deaths from domestic group violence in all successful revolutions occurring between 1955 and 1960.[45] They find more revolutionary violence with higher economic growth rates in 10 revolutions occurring in the Middle East and Asia, but the opposite relationship in 4 Latin American revolutions. For all 14 cases combined, there is some indication of greater numbers of persons killed in revolutions preceded by higher annual growth rates in GNP per capita.

It is suggested that the resolution of these contradictions will be found in an approach that differentiates between rates of change on different types of indicators and among nations at different levels of development. A beginning in this direction has been made in this study and further work is intended. Our preliminary efforts have been directed toward distinguishing indicators in terms of their implications for the members of a society. This categorization is based upon the distinction between social aspirations/expectations and so-

cial achievement. Change on one type of indicator may imply greater gratification for society; change on another indicator may simply broaden aspirations and expectations.

Evidence in support of this interpretation comes from the finding that a
rapid increase in primary school enrollment is positively related to political
violence, while a rapid increase in GNP per capita is negatively related. One
change increases the level of political unrest; the other tends to decrease it.
Furthermore, the impact of both change rates was separately analyzed among
countries at the transitional stage of development. We find that for these nations, the combination of factors most closely associated with political violence is a rapid spread in society of an awakened population, combined with a
slow rise in income.

As a final application of this study, we may ask whether our findings have
any bearing on the occurrence of violence within our own society. In socioeconomic terms, the United States is the most modern nation in the world,
showing the highest attained level on almost all indicators. On the other
hand, it is not among the most politically stable societies, although neither is
it among the most violent. Using various methods of measurement for the
18-year period, 1948-65, the United States falls generally at the median position of world violence: half of the nations exceed our violence level; half do
not attain it. There is thus some discrepancy between our economic level and
our level of political unrest, given the expected form of relationship.

It should also be pointed out that the occurrence of violence in the United
States has increased during the 1960's. In the previous two decades, the internal aggression profile of the United States was lower and generally more in
line with the majority of Western democratic political systems. During
1955-61, for example, the United States was among the group of nations at
position 3 on the seven-point instability scale. It ranked 24th among 84 states,
falling within the more stable third of the sample. In the subsequent period,
however, it moved into the 4th scale position, joining nations experiencing
more severe internal turmoil. From 1961 to 1965, 12 percent of this
country's events were at scale position 4.

In terms of the factors discussed in this paper, the rise in political unrest in
the United States could be explained in several quite different general ways.
This is not to say that these explanations are necessarily contradictory or mutually exclusive. Rather, they may reinforce each other. On the one hand, if
Sorokin is correct, we may be witnessing a transitional stage which few if any
other nations have yet experienced: the passing of material culture based on
an advanced technology. It would not be surprising that the United States
should be among the first nations to enter this phase, in view of its most advanced technological standing. This probably is the most speculative, and perhaps most imaginative, among the possible explanations.

On the other hand, a different explanation is perhaps more plausible, based
as it is on familiar contemporary notions of transition. The United States, as
a large heterogeneous society, is an aggregate of subcultures not all of which
share the advanced way of life of the majority. A large portion of specific instability events in the United States arise directly from the problems of racial
and other minority cultures within the wider society. The average newspaper
reader is aware of passive resistance, demonstrations, and urban ghetto riots.

To this picture we may add that half of the 12 assassinations (successful or attempted) that occurred in this country during the 1960's can be attributed to issues of minority conflict.[46]

Nor is it simply the domain of majority-minority conflict that must be blamed. Also relevant are notions of modernity and participant, egalitarian society. Our aggregated measures are not sensitive to these internal variations, since they assign one score to an entire nation. We may nonetheless suggest that forces of tradition are now undergoing transition in our society and that we have in microcosm the processes evident in the global pattern. We can perhaps think of the current "Black Revolution" as a transition process that involves both the white and the black communities. A previously isolated, tradition-bound stratum is becoming politically significant and participant, reaching toward modern goals. This stratum is subject to the revolution of rising expectations and its consequent systemic frustration. Undoubtedly the entire society is involved in the systemic conflict that accompanies the passing of an established pattern of social relationships and institutions.

Another point is that the combination of a rapid increase in educational level and a smaller increase in per capita income may be as virulent a mixture of conditions for groups within our society that are seeking to emerge from traditionalism, as it is for so-called transitional societies. There is support for this view in some of the findings regarding the participants in recent riots in the United States.[47] Interviews with rioters in Newark and Detroit provide a picture of the rioter as young, native to the ghetto, educated, and underemployed. The interpretation proposed by the investigators is one of "blocked opportunity." It is a case of an increasing gap between education and income, between aspirations and satisfaction. Education may also serve to strengthen the sense of legitimacy of demands and expectations. The educated person feels qualified and entitled to betterment in his conditions of life.

It may further be speculated that the transitional process within our own society was intensified by the demonstration effect of the global process of transition at mid-20th century. Its most salient aspect may have been provided by the emergence of a number of nations from colonial bondage to gain independence. Perhaps an additional and powerful impetus to the transition witnessed within our society is a function of the logic of social change depicted in figures 18-2, 18-5, and 18-6. Figures 18-2 and 18-5 postulate that both abrupt and rapid improvement in social achievement may, paradoxically, bring violence in their wake. Figure 18-6 suggests that when unrealistic hopes are pinned to an occurrence, these hopes are often disappointed. The scheduled event itself takes place, but the concomitant changes foreseen as accompanying it do not occur.

Some striking developments in the 1940's and 1950's heralded the lessening of racial discrimination in this country. For example, the series of Supreme Court decisions, legislative and Federal measures, including the desegregation of the Armed Forces, may have been instrumental not only in bringing satisfaction to the Negro population but also in raising expectations for the future. Greater equality, more abundant opportunities, and social and economic betterment all may have been foreseen. When actual conditions did not provide satisfaction for these expectations, a strong sense of systemic frustration predictably followed. Note that none of these hypotheses assumes a setback in achievements. Frustration may result from the lack of realization of what prove to be exaggerated expectations. Furthermore, the greater the certainty with which fulfillment is expected, the greater the disappointment when it fails to materialize.

In the broadest view, then, much violence in the United States may be interpreted as resulting from a transitional stage of modernization characterizing specific groups within the society as a whole. During this stage of improving conditions, violence may actually rise, and this will be especially likely if increases in achievement do not keep pace with increases in aspirations and expectations. The question of whether this disparity can be avoided is particularly challenging. It may be discussed specifically in terms of a gap between increases in education and increases in income. At first glance, it would seem that this imbalance is highly likely, if not inevitable, at least in the short run, since training for skills is a necessary prerequisite to taking one's place in the industrial society. It may be, however, that the lag could be shortened.

A second, more provocative proposition discussed above is that widespread psychological discontent within a society is a necessary precondition to economic growth. At the individual level, this implies that only when his discontent has reached a certain level will the individual be motivated to seek the training and skills that eventually gain him admission to the modern way of life. This is not to ignore the fact that minority groups within our society have historically been excluded and discouraged from embarking upon this path. Rather, it is to stress that for all individuals, regardless of origin, the motivation necessary to raise one's goals arises from a dissatisfaction with present attainment. Thus discontent is a basic prerequisite for effort expended. And if the effort is not eventually rewarded, the outcome is very apt to be aggression, directed against the perceived barriers to accomplishment.[48]

As a prognosis for the future, this analogy tells us that once certain socioeconomic threshold values have been reached by relatively deprived persons within our society, violence will subside. On the other hand, the process of transition will be tumultuous, especially in the short run, as education becomes more prevalent and outstrips opportunity. It must be remembered, of course, that these insights are only suggestive, and based on cross-national studies of political violence and change. They have not been validated by an intensive or historical empirical analysis of American society.

References

1. We are grateful for the support of the National Science Foundation (Grant No. GS-1781), which made it possible to collect and analyze the data on internal political aggression as well as the underlying conditions of political instability.
   We wish to thank Rosemary J. Roth and Antonia E. Williams for their help in constructing tables for this manuscript, and Franz Jaggar for the computer analyses.
2. Cross-national quantitative analysis of political and social variables is a relatively recent development. For an overview, see Richard L. Merritt and Stein Rokkan, eds., *Comparing Nations: The Uses of Quantitative Data in Cross-National Research* (New Haven: Yale University Press, 1966). Two impressive cross-national data collections and analyses should also be mentioned: Arthur S. Banks and Robert B. Textor, *A Cross-Policy Survey* (Cambridge: MIT Press, 1963), and Bruce M. Russett, Hayward R. Alker, Jr., Karl W. Deutsch, and Harold D. Lasswell,

World Handbook of Political and Social Indicators (New Haven: Yale University Press, 1964). Among the few cross-national analyses of internal political violence we may mention: Harry Eckstein, *Internal War: The Problem of Anticipation* (a report submitted to the Research Group in Psychology and the Social Sciences, Smithsonian Institution, Washington, D.C., Jan. 15, 1962); Ted Gurr with Charles Ruttenberg, *The Conditions of Civil Violence: First Tests of a Causal Model*, Research Monograph No. 28 (Princeton: Center of International Studies, Princeton, University, Apr. 1967); Rudolph J. Rummel, "Dimensions of Conflict Behavior Within and Between Nations," *General Systems Yearbook*, vol. VIII (1963), pp. 1-50; Raymond Tanter, "Dimensions of Conflict Behavior Within and Between Nations, 1958-60," *Journal of Conflict Resolution*, vol. X (Mar. 1966), pp. 41-65; Ivo K. and Rosalind L. Feierabend, "Aggressive Behaviors Within Polities, 1948-1962: A Cross-National Study," *Journal of Conflict Resolution*, vol. X (Sept. 1966), pp. 249-271; and Betty A Nesvold, "A Scalogram Analysis of Political Violence," *Comparative Political Studies*, forthcoming, July 1969.

3. For a sample of contemporary literature using these notions, see Gabriel A. Almond and James S. Coleman, eds., *The Politics of the Developing Areas* (Princeton: Princeton University Press, 1960); David E. Apter, *The Politics of Modernization* (Chicago: University of Chicago Press, 1965); H. R. Barringer et al., *Social Change in Developing Areas* (Cambridge: Schenkman, 1965); Karl W. Deutsch, "Social Mobilization and Political Development," *American Political Science Review*, vol. LV (Sept. 1961), pp. 493-514; Samuel P. Huntington, "Political Development and Political Decay," *World Politics*, vol. XVII (Apr. 1965), pp. 386-430; Everett E. Hagen, *On the Theory of Social Change* (Homewood: Dorsey Press, 1962); Daniel Lerner, *The Passing of Traditional Society* (Glencoe: Free Press, 1958); W. W. Rostow, *The Stages of Economic Growth* (Cambridge: Cambridge University Press, 1960); Pitirim A. Sorokin, *Social and Cultural Dynamics*, vol. III: *Fluctuation of Social Relationships, War, and Revolution* (New York: The Bedminster Press, 1937, 1962); and George K. Zollschan and Walter Hirsch, eds., *Explorations in Social Change* (Boston: Houghton Mifflin, 1964).

4. The theme that social change carries with it political crisis and turmoil is commonly acknowledged in the literature, as is the contradictory insight. See the literature cited in footnote 2.

5. For the classic theoretical statement of the frustration-aggression hypothesis, see John Dollard et al., *Frustration and Aggression* (New Haven: Yale University Press, 1939). Also, there are several more recent general restatements, among them Leonard Berkowitz, *Aggression: A Social Psychological Analysis* (New York: McGraw Hill, 1962), and Arnold H. Buss, *The Psychology of Aggression* (New York: Wiley, 1961).

6. In the literature of political science, Ted Gurr systematically applies the frustration hypothesis and modifies its terms to develop a coherent empirical and multivariate theory of political violence. His use of the concept of relative deprivation comes very close to our use of systemic frustration. Also, we believe that the broad insights, hypotheses, and models presented in this section would generally be sustained by his theoretical constructs, although they might be couched in different terminology. See Ted Robert Gurr, *Why Men Rebel* (Princeton: Princeton University Press, 1969, in press), and "Psychological Factors in Civil Violence," *World Politics*, vol. XX (Jan. 1968), pp. 245-278.

7. In the most recent literature on revolution, David Schwartz uses the notion of conflict, as well as of cognitive dissonance, to build a processual model of revolution; see his "Political Alienation: A Preliminary Experiment on the Psychology of Revolution's First Stage," paper presented at the annual meeting of the American Psychological Association, Washington, D.C., 1967. The psychological literature on which these applications are based may be found in F. Heider, "Social Perception and Phenomenal Causality," *Psychological Review*, vol. LI (1944), pp. 358-374; Theodore Newcomb, "An Approach to the Study of Communicative Acts," *Psychological Review*, vol. LX (1953), pp. 393-5; and Leon Festinger, *The Theory of Cognitive Dissonance* (New York: Harper & Row, 1957).

8. See James C. Davies, "Toward a Theory of Revolution," *American Sociological Review*, vol. XXVII (Jan. 1962), pp. 5-19.

9. The notion of a marked contrast among sets of ecological conditions having a greater effect on expectations and behavior than would a continuous series can be viewed as an application of adaptation level theory. See Harry Helson, *Adaptation-Level Theory: An Experimental and Systematic Approach to Behavior* (New York: Harper & Row, 1964). According to this view, a cohesive set or series of stimulus conditions creates adaptation; a contrast within the stimulus conditions triggers response.

10. Victor LeVine, "The Trauma of Independence in French Speaking Africa," paper presented at the Midwest Conference of Political Scientists, 1967.

11. Robert LeVine observes that, in sub-Saharian Africa, those colonial powers that over the decades consistently denied self-rule to the indigenous populace, or those which consistently fostered such a goal, experienced the lowest incidence of anti-European violence. Those regimes that vacillated between the two policies of permissiveness and coerciveness were often subject to intense outbreaks of violence. See his article, "Anti-European Violence in Africa: A Comparative Analysis," *Journal of Conflict Resolution,* vol. III (Dec. 1959), pp. 420-429.

12. These models are given fuller elaboration in I. K. Feierabend, R. L. Feierabend, and B. A. Nesvold, "Political Violence and Social Discontent," in David C. Schwartz, ed., *Revolution Studies,* forthcoming.

13. For example, Lucian W. Pye, in *Aspects of Political Development* (Boston, Little, Brown, 1966), identifies six such crises that hamper smooth political processes: the identity crisis, the legitimacy crisis, the penetration crisis, the participation crisis, the integration crisis, and the distribution crisis.

14. Apter, *op. cit.*, among other authors, describes these more or less intense conflicts, especially in the African context and on the Gold Coast. Destruction of the traditional culture may ensue if the indigenous culture is entirely hostile to innovation and the acceptance of modernity. On the other hand, if the traditional culture is more instrumentally oriented, the conflict may be less intense. Apter also speaks of the appropriate political systems that may follow from these situations.

15. This is the goal-gradient hypothesis, which derives from psychological learning theory and has wide applicability to both animal and human behavior. It maintains that the impulse to action, or the strength of attraction, varies as a function of the distance (spatial or temporal) between the organism and the goal. The closer the individual comes to attaining a desired goal, the stronger the level of attraction and the greater the impulse to action. The further the individual is from a goal, the less the attraction and the weaker the impulse to action. See N. E. Miller, "Experimental Studies of Conflict Behavior," in J. McV. Hunt, ed., *Personality and the Behavior Disorders* (New York: Ronald Press, 1944), and C. L. Hull, *Principles of Behavior* (New York: Appleton-Century-Crofts, 1943).

16. Other researchers have also attempted to measure stages of development and rates of change for the purposes of cross-national study of political violence. For example, see Seymour M. Lipset, *Political Man: The Social Basis of Politics* (Garden City: Doubleday, 1960); Russett et al., *op. cit.*; Gurr with Ruttenberg, *op. cit.*; Raymond Tanter and Manus Midlarsky, "A Theory of Revolution," *Journal of Conflict Resolution*, vol. XI (Sept. 1967), pp. 264-280; Douglas Bwy, "Political Instability in Latin America: The Cross-Cultural Test of a Causal Model," *Latin American Research Review*, vol. III (Spring 1968), pp. 17-66.

17. Betty A. Nesvold, "Modernity, Social Frustration, and the Stability of Political Systems: A Cross-National Study" (San Diego: San Diego State College, Master's thesis, June 1964). Data on these indicators were collected for the 84 nations from United Nations sources. The country raw scores were converted into standard scores and a mean standard score was calculated for each country as a measure of level of development.

18. The cutting points for these three groups are to some extent arbitrary. The 24 countries that are highest on the modernity index are selected as the modern group. The traditional group is set equal in size to the modern group, while ranking at the opposite end of the modernity continuum. The remaining countries, falling between the modern and traditional groups, are designated transitional. As already pointed out, the countries designated "traditional" are simply less modern than those classed as "transitional," but they have nonetheless been exposed to modernity.

19.   Russett et al., *op. cit.* The correlation coefficient between our Modernity Index and Russett's level of development, which is based on GNP per capita, is $r = 0.90$.

20.   The cutting points on these modernity indicators were chosen in such a way as to maximize the loading of countries in one set of diagonal cells and minimize it in the other. In this way, threshold values may be determined.

21.   Data for these measures of development were taken from the compilations in Russett et al., *op. cit.*

22.   Nations were rated according to characteristics of participation in governmental and political groups and the existence of a viable legislative body and freedom of the press. The underlying assumption of the classificatory scheme was that when an agency such as the military or a political party fills a specialized role in the polity, the conditions for democracy, or pluralism, are present. If, on the other hand, a few such agencies monopolize policymaking, the conditions for elite authority structures are generated. Within this classification scheme, Latin American nations are trichotomized into competitive, semicompetitive, and authoritarian political systems. The Asian and African classifications contain seven such groupings: political democracy, tutelary democracy, modernizing oligarchy, conservative oligarchy, and traditional oligarchy. Of the remaining nations in our study that were not rated by Almond and Coleman, 23 qualify as Western European, developed nations. One can assume that these latter nations served as a model for Almond and Coleman's original typology and that it would be reasonable to classify them as highly competitive political systems. See Almond and Coleman, *op. cit.*

23.   Information regarding such matters as the competitiveness of the political system, the protection of free speech, and the degree to which police actions inhibit the freedoms of the citizenry were used to assign nations to one of the six categories. Case studies were examined for 84 nations for the time period 1948-60. See Jennifer G. Walton, "Correlates of Coerciveness and Permissiveness of National Political Systems: A Cross-National Study" (San Diego: San Diego State College, Master's thesis, 1965). Also I. K. Feierabend and R. L. Feierabend, "The Relationship of Systemic Frustration, Political Coercion, International Tension and Political Instability: A Cross-National Study," paper presented at the annual meeting of the American Psychological Association, Sept. 1966.

24.   The initial analyses using these data concentrated on nine indicators: urbanization (percent of the population living in localities of 100,000 or more inhabitants); percent of the population literate; primary education (ratio of total school enrollment to total population age 5-14); postprimary education (percentage of total population enrolled in all educational institutions beyond the primary schools); national income in local currencies; cost-of-living index; calories per capita per day; infant mortality rate; and total number of radios per 1,000 population. See Wallace W. Conroe, "A Cross-National Analysis of the Impact of Modernization Upon Political Stability" (San Diego: San Diego State College, Master's thesis, 1965), and Feierabend and Feierabend, "Aggressive Behaviors Within Polities."

25.   The yearly percent rate of change on the ecological variables was calculated by subtracting the lowest value of the variable in the 28-year period from the highest value attained, dividing by the lowest value to convert to a percentage change, and then dividing by the number of years spanned to obtain the yearly percentage change. The advantage of the combined rate of change index, assuming substitutability of indicators, is that it makes it possible to compensate for missing data. The index is based on data for six or more indicators per country.

26.   Stability scores for the 84 nations were calculated on a year-by-year basis and plotted as a function of time. To characterize the time function, two measures were used: the slope of a best-fit line, indicating the average instability trend over the time period; and amplitude of change from year to year, as estimated by variance.

27.   The correlation with the combined rate of change index is Pearson $r = 0.66$, using the seven-point scaling of political instability for the 1948-65 time period.

28.   The correlation between rate of change in primary education and scaled level of political instability is $r = 0.49$. The corresponding correlation for rate of increase in percent of the population owning telephones is $r = 0.44$, for increase in national income, $rho = -0.34$ with the static measure of stability, and -0.45 with the dynamic measure.

29. The correlation is $r=0.50$ with the static level of instability and $r=0.31$ with the dynamic measure.
30. The partial correlation technique makes it possible to assess the degree of relationship between two variables, with the influence of a third variable statistically controlled or removed. The partial correlation in this case is 0.49.
31. The partial correlation is 0.29.
32. The correlation with political instability level, 1948-65, is $r=-0.34$ and with trend in instability over time it is -0.37. Controlling for GNP per capita in 1957, the partial correlation is -0.40 with scaled instability and -0.37 with trend in instability. Growth rate in GDP per capita, 1951-59, is taken from "World Tables of Economic Growth," Economics Department, MIT, mimeographed.
33. The multiple correlation is $r=0.56$ using the static measure of instability and $r=0.44$ using trend in instability over time.
34. Samuel P. Huntington, *Political Order in Changing Societies* (New Haven: Yale University Press, 1968), especially pp. 47-49.
35. See, for example, Ronald G. Ridker, "Discontent and Economic Growth," *Economic Development and Cultural Change*, vol. XI (October 1962), pp. 1-15.
36. Sorokin, *op. cit.* Cyclical and historicist conceptions of history are, of course, not peculiar to Sorokin. They are especially current in 19th-century literature, but also span earlier and later times. Marx and Engels' conceptions are the best known and certainly the most influential. Other names that come immediately to mind are Gobineau, Hegel, Spengler, and Toynbee.
37. Efforts in this direction today are associated with the tremendous increase in awareness of the possibilities of social data. See, for example, Eugene Webb et al., *Unobstrusive Measures* (New York: Wiley, 1967).
38. See, for example, Lipset, *op. cit.*; Philip Cutright, "National Political Development: Measurement and Analysis," *American Sociological Review*, vol. XXVIII (Apr. 1963), pp. 253-264; Gurr with Ruttenburg, *op. cit.*; Hayward R. Alker, Jr., and Bruce M. Russett, "The Analyses of Trends and Patterns," in Russett et al., *op. cit.*; Feierabend and Feierabend, "Aggressive Behaviors Within Polities"; and Bwy, *op. cit.*
39. Feierabend and Feierabend, "Aggressive Behaviors Within Polities."
40. Alker and Russett, *op. cit.*; Gurr, *op. cit.*; Bwy, *op. cit.*
41. Feierabend and Feierabend, "Aggressive Behaviors Within Polities," and Conroe, *op. cit.*
42. Alker and Russett, *op. cit.*
43. Gurr with Ruttenberg, *op. cit.*
44. Bwy, *op. cit.*
45. Tanter and Midlarsky, *op. cit.*
46. See I. K. Feierabend, R. L. Feierabend, B. A. Nesvold, and F. J. Jaggar, "Political Violence and Assassination: A Cross-National Assessment," report prepared for the Task Force on Assassinations of the National Commission on the Causes and Prevention of Violence, Nov. 1968.
47. Nathan S. Caplan and Jeffery M. Paige, "A Study of Ghetto Rioters," *Scientific American*, vol. CCXIX (Aug. 1968).
48. The question of the target of aggression has received considerable attention in all psychological theories of aggression. The forces underlying displacement of aggression from one target to another are given precise formulation in Miller, *op. cit.*

POLITICAL INSTABILITY

DATA COLLECTION

The data on political instability are extracted from two sources, *Deadline Data on World Affairs* and the *Encyclopedia Britannica Yearbooks*. Events are classified into 28 nonoverlapping categories: elections, dissolution of legislature, resignation, dismissal, fall of cabinet, significant change of law, plebiscite, appointment, organization of opposition party, governmental action against specific groups, strike, demonstration, boycott, arrest, suicide of significant political persons, martial law, execution, assassination, terrorism, sabotage, guerrilla warfare, coup d'état, civil war, revolt, and exile.

Each event is coded on 16 characteristics: country, date, whether a composite or noncomposite event, whether or not event is accompanied by violence, location (capital city, urban, rural, etc.), duration, number of persons involved, number of persons injured, number of persons killed, number of persons arrested, amount of property damage, nature of tension, whether or not significant persons are involved, outcome, scale value (in terms of the intensity scale devised by the investigators), and data source. Where sufficient data are not available to characterize the event in absolute terms (e.g., absolute number of persons involved), an alternative judgmental scale is used (e.g., "few, many," etc.). Each event is recorded on a separate IBM card. The Data Bank of Political Instability Events, covering the years 1948-65, now contains some 8,000 events. A major portion of the bank, including the years 1948-62, is on file with the Inter-University Consortium for Political Research, Ann Arbor, Mich.[49]

DATA RELIABILITY

Deadline Data on World Affairs is a news abstracting service that draws its information from a variety of leading world newspapers. It is an abbreviated and hence selective source of event coverage. Data obtained from this source, therefore, may exhibit systematic biases both due to reporting in the original news source and in *Deadline Data*, as a result of press censorship and notions of newsworthiness of particular countries or regions of the world.

We have assessed the reliability of the political instability data bank, both by comparing it to similar work of other researchers and to information on particular political events drawn from other sources. Also, we have examined the empirical relationship between both press censorship and population size (the latter used as a rough indicator of country importance and hence newsworthiness) and both overall level of political instability and incidence of selected violence events. We find evidence that our data provide a representative picture of the comparative levels of instability and violence of the nations in the sample, although the bank undoubtedly does not include every single relevant event which occurred in the 84 nations over the past 18 years.

Our first comparison is with a comparable effort by Ted Gurr to assess the level of civil violence among the nations of the world from 1961-65. Gurr drew his data from the *New York Times, Newsyear, The Annual Register of World Events, Asian Recorder, Africa Diary, Africa Digest, Africa Report, East Europe,* and *Eastern Europe.* His scoring of these events is weighted for extent of participation, duration, and intensity of violence.[50] Although Gurr uses different data sources and a different scoring method, we find a correlation of $r = 0.7$ between our nation instability profiles and his nation violence scores for the same time period.

If we select a particular type of violence, assassination, and compare national profiles on this variable as drawn from *Deadline Data* and from the *New York Times,* we find a correlation of $r = 0.8$, although three times as many assassinations were reported in the latter source. We may say that the relative frequency of reported assassinations remains largely the same among nations, although absolute frequency varies with the source.[51]

Furthermore, we find a correlation of $r = 0.51$ between ratings of press censorship and levels of political violence, indicating that, contrary to expectations regarding news suppression, the higher the level of press censorship within a country, the higher the level of political violence.[52] Evidently news of major internal conflict does reach the press. This positive relationship may be explained in terms of the relationship between coerciveness of political regime (of which press censorship is one facet) and level of political violence. That is, nations with highly coercive regimes that censor the press tend to have much more political violence than less coercive, non-censoring regimes.

Finally, we find little or no evidence of relationship between population size and political violence. Across the entire sample of nations, the correlation of these variables is $r = 0.12$, indicating a lack of systematic bias in underreporting of news from smaller countries. Undoubtedly less news is included from these states, but since violence is in itself newsworthy, the events in which we are interested are likely to be reported from all states.

DATA SCALING

The seven-point intensity scale of political instability described in the text is based on construct validity and consensual validation. High consensus on the operationalization of such a complex variable as political instability is, however, only one way of validating a measuring instrument. An alternative approach is to subject the instability data to a statistical method for ordering data, such as the Guttman scaling technique. A basic assumption inherent to this method is that there is a common characteristic present to a greater or lesser degree in each of the events.[53] The common characteristic, or underlying dimension, within our data is presumed to be the intensity of violence. In applying this method, only violent events were used. These were grouped into four classes: (1) riots and demonstrations, boycotts against the government, political arrests, governmental action against specific groups, and sabotage; (2) martial law, coups d'etat, and revolt; (3) guerrilla warfare, assassination; (4) execution and civil war. These four classes were conceived as denoting sets of increasingly violent events.

Essentially, a Guttman scale is present if occurrences of events in the most extreme class are accompanied by events in each of the other classes. Similarly, if there are no events in the most extreme group, but events occur in the next most extreme class, they are expected to be accompanied by events in the two classes denoting lesser violence. This pattern should repeat itself with each step of decreasing violence. A perfect scale is perfectly reproducible from a knowledge of the most extreme event on the scale. For example, knowledge that the most extreme event experienced within a polity was among those grouped in class (2)—e.g., martial law—would also convey the knowledge that events designated in class (1) are present. No events from class (3) or (4) should be found, however. Since perfect scales are unlikely to exist in empirical data, a reasonable approximation of a perfect scale may be determined by counting the "errors" in scale position that occur within the data and calculating a coefficient of reproducibility. As a rule of thumb, if 90 percent of the behaviors are scalable and 10 percent or less constitute "errors," one may use the scaling technique to order the data and to weigh the events. This criterion was met with our violence data with a coefficient of reproducibility of 0.97, indicating that only 3 percent of the events did not fit the pattern. The profiling of nations with these violent events scored by the Guttman technique is presented in Table 18-2. These summed scores were correlated with the summed scores from the original seven-point scaling of political instability, yielding a coefficient of $r = 0.95$, an empirical validation of the scale.[54]

DEVELOPMENT AND POLITICAL INSTABILITY

Table 18-10 presents the correlation coefficients between the measures of economic, social, and political development and the summary score of political violence calculated by the Guttman scale technique. Also included are the correlations with each of the classes of events indicating increasing intensity of violence: Turmoil Events (type 1), Revolt Events (type 2), Guerrilla Warfare Events (type 3), and Civil War Events (type 4). The magnitude of the relationship between indicators of modernization and political violence is consistently the highest with frequency of Revolt Events (type 2). It is generally the lowest using Turmoil Events (type 1).[55]

MEASUREMENT OF RATE OF SOCIOECONOMIC CHANGE

The rate at which socioeconomic change appears to occur is a function of the base level attained by the society, especially if rate is calculated in percentage terms. A high value of percentage rate of change depends on a low base value, and vice versa. Thus less-developed countries, with much smaller base levels on all indicators, will show high percentage increases, while modern countries will appear to be low changers. The relationship between the rate of change index, based on percentage change, and level of development is $r = -0.82$, using our modernity index, and $r = -0.75$, using GNP per capita in U.S. dollars, 1957.

Table 18-10.–Development and political instability

A. Relationship Between Industrial Development and Political Instability

	Percent urban	Percent GDP in agriculture	Percent labor in agriculture	GNP per capita
	1	2	3	4
Summary score of instability	-0.191	0.285	0.360	-0.343
Frequency of type 1	0.044	-0.006	0.064	-0.105
Frequency of type 2	-0.273	0.352	0.368	-0.357
Frequency of type 3	-0.249	0.279	0.318	-0.259
Frequency of type 4	-0.147	0.309	0.245	-0.148

B. Relationships Between Modern Communications and Political Instability

	Newspapers per 1,000 population	Radios per 1,000 population	Domestic mail per capita
	1	2	3
Summary score of instability	-0.452	-0.288	-0.373
Frequency of type 1	-0.210	-0.064	-0.096
Frequency of type 2	-0.418	-0.325	-0.452
Frequency of type 3	-0.359	-0.285	-0.335
Frequency of type 4	-0.118	-0.056	-0.342

Table 18-10.—Development and political instability—Continued

C. Relationships Between Social Development and Political Instability

	Higher education per 1,000 population	Primary and secondary enrollment	Percent literate	Life expectancy	Death rate
	1	2	3	4	5
Summary score of instability	-0.169	-0.267	-0.306	-0.483	0.477
Frequency of type 1	0.027	-0.027	-0.080	-0.194	0.325
Frequency of type 2	-0.256	-0.351	-0.344	-0.599	0.522
Frequency of type 3	-0.134	-0.331	-0.360	-0.442	0.359
Frequency of type 4	-0.064	0.033	0.013	0.001	-0.095

D. Relationships Between Political Development and Political Instability

	Percent voting	Executive stability
	1	2
Summary score of instability	-0.297	-0.232
Frequency of type 1	-0.263	-0.034
Frequency of type 2	-0.281	-0.296
Frequency of type 3	-0.066	-0.198
Frequency of type 4	0.082	-0.108

In view of the strong inverse relationship between attained level and percentage rate of change, we sought to measure change in a different fashion. The slope of a regression line through the change points was selected as logically independent from the initial base level. This technique of measurement, which was also used to assess increases and decreases in instability over time, indicates the absolute rate of change, in contrast to the percentage rate. We find, however, that it also relates to modernity level but in two different ways, depending on whether we are dealing with ceiling or non-ceiling indicators. A ceiling indicator is one which has a logical upper limit. Indicators that are themselves percentage calculations, such as literacy level, show this characteristic. Most modern nations, for example, are around 90 percent literate, and as they approach the 100 percent ceiling, their rate of change reaches a standstill. The same is true of primary education, reported as the percentage of school-age children actually enrolled. Caloric intake also has a limit beyond which humans can no longer consume additional food.

There are other indicators, however, which have no such logical bounds or, at least, for which the saturation point is still not reached even by the most developed contemporary nations. These nonceiling indicators include such variables as radios, newspapers, telephones, and national income per capita.

On indicators with an intrinsic ceiling, an absolute measure of change yields the same pattern as a percentage rate of change. Countries low in development appear as high changers, while the reverse is true of highly modern countries. On nonceiling indicators, however, the absolute measure yields the reverse pattern: the modern countries are the high changers; the underdeveloped nations are the low changers. In effect, we have found that on nonceiling indicators modern countries continue to show large absolute gains although their percentage rate remains low. Less-developed states, with a much smaller base level on the indicators, show high percentage increases but their small absolute advancement may be interpreted to mean that they are not really moving as fast as might appear. This reversal pattern makes it apparent that change is dependent on level of modernity.

This patterning helps us to classify ceiling and nonceiling indicators. They may be identified either on the basis of the direction of relationship to level of development, or the relationship between the results obtained from percentage and absolute methods of calculating change. For example, over the whole sample of countries, both percentage and absolute rates of change in primary education are inversely related to level of development, $r = -0.61$ and -0.40, respectively. The same direction of relationship is found with calories consumed daily. Absolute change on this variable correlates $r = -0.45$ with level of development, while the correlation based on percentage rate of change is $r = -0.24$. On the other hand, the increase in radios per 1,000 population shows a positive relationship of $r = 0.66$ to modernity level, if measured in terms of absolute change rate. With percentage rate of change, the relationship to development is reversed and the correlation is $r = -0.51$. The same reversal of relationship is apparent with change rates on percentage of population owning telephones: using an absolute change measure, the correlation to modernity is $r = 0.88$, while with a percentage change measure, the correlation is $r = -0.35$.[56]

Given this patterning, the relationship between the two types of change rates and level of instability may also be predicted. Percentage change rates or rates of change on ceiling indicators will be positively related to instability, indicating that the faster the rate of change, the greater the political violence. Absolute change rates on nonceiling indicators, however, will show the reverse pattern: a rapid rate of change will be associated with political stability. In view of the relationship between change rates and developmental levels, however, it is not clear that it is change, per se, that produces political unrest. It may be the level of attained development.

To extricate rate of change from level of development, we have controlled for the influence of level of modernity through the use of the partial correlation technique. Also, we have restricted the range of development of the sample of nations used to those classed as "Transitional." This group, as mentioned earlier, was selected for theoretical reasons. An added advantage is that the countries within this group show the greatest range of rates of change, measured in either percentage or absolute terms.

References

49.   For more detailed information on the data bank, see Ivo K. Feierabend and Rosa-
       lind L. Feierabend, *Cross-National Data Bank of Political Instability Events (Code
       Index)* (San Diego: Public Affairs Research Institute, San Diego State College,
       1965).
50.   See Ted Gurr, "A Causal Model of Civil Strife: A Comparative Analysis Using
       New Indices," *American Political Science Review,* vol. LXII (Dec. 1968), pp.
       1104-1124; also *op. cit.*
51.   Feierabend, Feierabend, Nesvold, and Jaggar, *op. cit.*
52.   The press censorship ratings were based on information derived primarily from
       John C. Merrill, *A Handbook of the Foreign Press* (Baton Rouge: Louisiana
       State University Press, 1959); I.P.I. Survey, *The Press in Authoritarian Countries*
       (Zurich: The International Press Institute, 1959); and Associated Press Surveys
       of World Censorship.
53.   Louis Guttman, "The Basis for Scalogram Analysis," in Samuel A. Stouffer et al.,
       Studies in Social Psychology in World War II, Vol. IV: *Measurement and Predic-
       tion* (Princeton: Princeton University Press, 1950). For a further explanation
       of this and other techniques of scaling, see Warren S. Torgerson, *Theory and
       Methods of Scaling* (New York: Wiley, 1958).
54.   For a further elaboration of these procedures, see Nesvold, *op. cit.*
55.   See Betty A. Nesvold, *Turmoil to Civil War: A Cross-National Analysis.* Ph. D.
       dissertation, University of Minnesota, 1968.
56.   For a more detailed discussion of methods of measuring socioeconomic change,
       see Norman M. Howard, "Modernity, Rate of Change and Coerciveness of
       Political Systems: A Cross-National Study" (San Diego: San Diego State
       College, master's thesis, 1966).

PART VIII

PROCESSES OF REBELLION

We are struck by uniqueness when we examine the circumstances of a single instance of political violence. At very close hand, each riot, each revolution appears *sui generis*. When several are compared, though, we begin to detect common patterns and processes. The contributors to the preceding part compared some causes and characteristics of violence in the aggregate. The next two chapters offer parallel case studies of some processes that lead to political violence and that determine its course and outcome.

Two conventional "explanations" of rebellion and revolution have been used popularly to explain the militancy and violence of some black Americans in recent years. One is that men rebel when they are suddenly awakened, perhaps by "agitators" or "promises," to their dismal status in life. The other is that men are especially prone to violence "when things are getting better," either because the taste of progress generates exponentially increasing expectations for more progress or because they intensely resent the few remaining barriers they face. James C. Davies suggests a different and more general pattern of change preceding rebellion, one illustrated by his case studies of the French Revolution, the American Civil War, the Nazi revolution, and the uprisings of black Americans in the 1960's. In all these cases, revolt was preceded by a long period of improvement in conditions followed by a more or less sharp decline. The dynamic is that rising socioeconomic or political satisfactions generate in people expectations that improvements will continue. If such expectations are substantially frustrated for many people, group conflict is likely to increase and popular uprisings to occur.

This J-curve pattern of rising and then declining
satisfactions is reflected in the economic and political conditions of the bourgeoisie, urban workers and
peasants in France during the decades before 1789,
in the changing political and economic status of
Southerners vis-a-vis the North before the Civil War,
and in the conditions of Negro Americans after
1940. The economic condition of Negroes, compared to white Americans, increased very substantially toward equality between 1940 and the early
1950's; nearly half the relative gains of that period
had been lost by the early 1960's. At that same
time the obdurate resistance of some white Americans
to the expansion of Negro rights and opportunities, especially in the South, seemed to demonstrate that
further progress was blocked. The behavior of black
Americans would have been less explicable had they
not reacted as they did to a situation that paralleled
the situations of rebellious Frenchmen, white Southerners, and Germans in earlier eras.

The uses of public force influence strongly the
course and outcomes of riots, as Morris Janowitz
pointed out in chapter 10. It similarly influences revolutionary movements, which Edward
Gude demonstrates in his comparative study below,
of the uses of insurgent force and regime counterforce in two extreme situations: the successful
Cuban revolutionary movement of 1956-59 and the
unsuccessful Venezuelan revolutionary movement
of the early 1960's. An editorialist recently wrote
that "Force empowers its own destruction."[1] The
Cuban and Venezuelan cases demonstrate unmistak-
ably that under certain circumstances the use of
violence does indeed empower its adversaries. The
most crucial circumstance is the popular legitmacy
attributed to the use of violence, whether by governments or their opponents. In Cuba, guerrilla
activity inspired a terroristic overresponse from the
military and police that undermined middle-class
support for the Batista regime, and at the same time
strengthened popular support for the 26th of July
movement. In Venezuela, where the circumstances
of the regime and of the insurgents closely paralleled

---

1. Roy Pearson, "The Dilemma of Force," *Saturday Review*, Feb.
   10, 1968, p. 24.

those in Cuba, the Betancourt government responded cautiously to insurgent terrorism, using intensive force only after terrorism had alienated the insurgents' potential supporters and had led to increased public support for retaliatory action by the regime. In the Cuban case, governmental force engendered its own destruction. In Venezuela, insurgent force ultimately proved self-destructive.

CHAPTER 19

THE J-CURVE OF RISING AND DECLINING SATISFACTIONS AS A CAUSE OF SOME GREAT REVOLUTIONS AND A CONTAINED REBELLION

By James C. Davies*

The J-curve is this: revolution is most likely to take place when a prolonged period of rising expectations and rising gratifications is followed by a short period of sharp reversal, during which the gap between expectations and gratifications quickly widens and becomes intolerable. The frustration that develops, when it is intense and widespread in the society, seeks outlets in violent action. When the frustration becomes focused on the government, the violence becomes coherent and directional. If the frustration is sufficiently widespread, intense, and focused on government, the violence will become a revolution that displaces irrevocably the ruling government and changes markedly the power structure of the society. Or the violence will be contained within the system, which it modifies but does not displace. This latter case is rebellion. The following chart (figure 19-1) shows what happens as a society heads toward revolution.[1]

This is an assertion about the state of mind of individual people in a society who are likely to revolt. It says their state of mind, their mood, is one of high tension and rather generalized hostility, derived from the widening of the gap between what they want and what they get. They fear not just that things will no longer continue to get better but—even more crucially—that ground will be lost that they have already gained. The mood of rather generalized hostility, directed generally outward, begins to turn toward government. People so frus-

*The author is professor of political science at the University of Oregon. He is author of *Human Nature in Politics* (New York: Wiley, 1963), editor of *When Men Revolt—and Why* (New York: The Free Press, forthcoming), and has written several influential articles on collective and revolutionary behavior.

[1] I wish to note that Janice Rademaker and Hendrik van Dalen gathered most of the statistical and many of the factual data presented here. Their work was indispensable to the completion of this paper. Ted Gurr made some generous and acute comments on an earlier draft that helped the reader to get more easily to the heart of the matter.

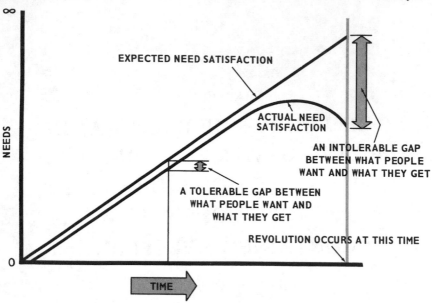

Figure 19-1.—Need satisfaction and revolution.

trated not only fight with other members of their families and their nieghbors. They also jostle one another in crowds and increase their aggressiveness as pedestrians and bus passengers and drivers of cars. When events and news media and writers and speakers encourage the direction of hostilities toward the government, the dispersed and mutual hostility becomes focused on a common target. The hostility among individuals diminishes. The dissonant energy becomes a resonant, very powerful force that heads like a great tidal wave or forest fire toward the established government, which it may then engulf.

This phenomenon of synergic unification of a public when frustration becomes widespread and deep is awesome in its tendency to erase hostility between people. It is akin to the feeling that develops in a quarrelsome household at times. A fighting family may just barely manage to hold together. The father may be unemployed and frequently drunk the mother worn to a frazzle, the children quarrelsome as they displace the tensions generated by poverty and the frustrations of their fighting parents. The father, no longer able to provide for his family, may lose his authority within the family and strike out at those nearest to him. But when the landlord knocks on the door and announces that the rent must be paid by 10 o'clock tomorrow morning on pain of eviction, the family suddenly stops its own fighting, beats up the landlord, and throws him out on the street.

Such tension within the family is a microcosm of the tension within the national community; that is, among the individual members of the political society and among its conflicting regional, religious, racial, and socioeconomic groups. When the various segments of a deeply divided society suddenly sense that they all have the same enemy, the government, they can spontaneously unite for long enough to overthrow it.

CAUSES OF REVOLUTION AND REBELLION,
PSYCHOLOGICALLY CONSIDERED

Revolutions and rebellions differ in result but have like origins. And the differences in origin are less ones of kind than of degree. Revolutions involve more segments of the population than do rebellions. The intensity of feeling in revolutions is probably greater and has taken a longer time to develop than in rebellions. The violent phase of a revolution is longer and more savage. The bitterness that lingers after the violence is likely to endure for decades or centuries after a revolution.

The difference is not in causes and the violent action or even in the long-range consequences so much as it is in the immediate result. Rebellions do not remove the established government but instead are contained, partly as the consequence of the use of violent force in large enough amounts to override the rebels' anger at the government. The rebels may choose to live with their frustrations rather than endure the blows of the police and the army and the dull, sick anguish of imprisonment. But rebellions also are contained within the established system to the extent that the government pays heed to the grievances that led to the rebellion. If the only response to extralegal violence is legal violence, then hatred of oppression becomes deeply imprinted in the minds of the momentarily silenced rebels. The hatred lingers and deepens like embers in dry tinder after firefighters have tried to beat to death a small fire.

As the American Declaration of Independence said in 1776, people do not for "light and transient causes" make a rebellion or revolution. What then are the grave and enduring conditions that produce frustrations in a broad and varied citizenry, that in turn produce the revolutionary state of mind?

The common condition appears to be the denial of satisfaction of those needs that are basic to all human beings. Not all needs (as for a new automobile) are basic, and not all basic needs are of equal revolutionary potential. Abraham Maslow has argued that man's basic needs are arranged in sequence, from the most to the least powerful. The most potent are the physical needs, which must continuously be satisfied for all people during their entire life. But when a person gains their satisfaction—as an infant, a child, and an adult—he does not then, animal-like, remain content with satisfying just these bodily needs. Soon after birth he demands affection and, if he gets it, he reciprocates affection toward others. But his physical needs persist, and if he is forced to choose, he will first satisfy his need for food and then his need for affection.

In early childhood the individual who has been regularly gratified in his physical and affectional needs does not then rest content with this mental state of affairs. He begins, usually no later than when he is 8 or 10 years old, to demand recognition as an individual who is worthy of his own regard for himself and of others' regard for him. In early childhood people begin to demand that others accord them respect. The respect of others is necessary if people are to acquire self-respect.

It is this kind of demand that lies so close to the surface of the Declaration of Independence, in the statement that all men are created equal and in the specific indictments of British rule—for example, in the great indignation expressed at the quartering of troops in private homes without the consent of the homeowners, and at the removal of trials at law from the Colonies to England.

This demand is evident in the Declaration's "decent respect to the opinions of mankind," whose approval the American rebels sought.

And once these successive needs—the physical, the social-affectional, and the equal esteem or dignity needs—are sufficiently gratified, humans are not even then content: they then begin to look for that kind of activity that is particularly suited to them as unique individuals. Whether their competence is to be a ditchdigger, a powershovel operator, a construction foreman, a civil engineer or a building contractor, an architect, a mother, a writer, or a politician—they must do these things when they have become rather sure in the gratification of their even more basic physical, social, and esteem needs.

The crucial point is this: no human being so long as he lives is ever completely gratified in the satisfaction of his needs. Up to the moment of his death, he must eat and sleep; he must be with people; he has to be acknowledged as a distinct person; and he must realize his individual potential. When he ceases to do these things, he ceases to live. All of these needs of his have got to be gratified; they ultimately can be denied only by natural or by violent death. Armies and police forces can quash these natural and irrepressible human needs only by reducing human beings to animals and then killing them. The logic of this was stated in fictional form by George Orwell, in describing what was necessary for the perpetuation of dictatorship: "a boot, stamping in a human face, forever."

The Maslow need hierarchy is a necessary part of a psychological explanation of the causes of revolution. Marx to the contrary, revolutions are made not only by economically depressed classes and their leaders but by the joint effort of large numbers of those people in all social groups who are experiencing frustration of different basic needs. People deprived of career opportunities may join in revolt with people who have suffered indignities at the hands of employers, landlords, police, or military troops. They also may join with people who have suffered no indignities but are for the moment simply hungry.

The common characteristic of potential revolutionaries is that each of them individually senses the frustration of one or more basic needs and each is able to focus his frustration on the government. After this need frustration is generated, people begin to share their discontents and to work together. But preceding this joint action, there is no more conspiracy than there is among trees when they burst into flame during a forest fire.

THE J-CURVE AND PARTICULAR REVOLUTIONS

On the level of general theory, one can say precisely the same thing—in abstract terms—about each revolution and rebellion. But in some ways each revolution is unlike every other revolution. And from the practical research standpoint, directly comparable data are not available for all revolutions, particularly when they took place decades or centuries ago. In many nations now, the seeds of revolution are sprouting. But established governments in these nations are not likely to welcome social scientists in search of data by conducting public opinion surveys inquiring about attitudes toward the government.

In the interest of arriving at some conclusions and of arriving at the understanding that they are tentative, we can profitably consider particular revolutions.

The French Revolution of 1789

The French Revolution is the first of the great modern postindustrial revolutions. It is the first grand revolution after that grandest of all modern revolutions, the 16th-century Protestant Reformation.

The position of the various major social classes in France gives a major clue as to how the revolution came about. The relationships between these classes help explain also why liberty, equality, and fraternity did not arrive on the day they were declared to be human rights. The major segments of French society in the late 18th century were the well-known three estates: the clergy, the nobility, and then everybody else, who collectively were called the third estate for lack of a more precise term.

What is less well known are the proportions that each of these estates comprised of the total French population of about 23 million. There were, according to Georges Lefebvre, perhaps the greatest historian in 20-century France of the French Revolution, about 100,000 Frenchmen in the clergy (less than half of 1 percent); about 400,000 in the nobility (about 2 percent); and over 23 million in the third estate. The third estate included the high bourgeoisie, an economically, socially, and politically active group of merchants, bankers, and manufacturers. Also in the third estate were the petty bourgeoisie—small merchants, bakers, artisans in wood and metal, and the growing body of skilled government bureaucrats. Finally, the third estate included workingmen, many of them the sons of peasants, and also the vast body of peasants. France, beginning its industrialization somewhat later than England, was still overwhelmingly an agricultural nation.

Even less well known than the proportions of each of the three estates in the total population is the proportion of land which each estate owned. Again, according to Lefebvre, the clergy owned about 10 percent of the land, the nobility somewhat less than 20 percent, the bourgeoisie about 20 percent, and the peasants all the rest. The heavy imbalance of landownership reflects only the most evident part of the land-tenure picture. Anywhere from 20 to 75 percent of the rural households in France before the revolution did not own any land. These peasants were either working as tenants to save money to buy land, or they had given up and were working as paid farm laborers. And in massive numbers they were drifting into cities to find work.

These peasants who aspired to landownership or who had achieved it saw themselves as facing an unending struggle to survive and to get a little ahead. As the industrial economy began to develop rapidly, the demand for farm products increased because so many people who once tilled and lived off the soil now worked for money in cities, which—as everywhere in developing nations undergoing industrialization—made ever-increasing, insatiable demands on the countryside to feed their people. Peasants, seeing the chance thus to move up the ladder from farm labor or land rental, were beset by a variety of inhibitors. There were the feudal dues (payment to landlords for the use of his flour mill, the exclusive right of landlords to hunt and fish, the reversion of land to a landlord if the peasant died without proper heirs, etc.); the duty to perform physical labor for public purposes (building public roads and other structures); the tithe (a 10-percent tax due to the church); and a variety of taxes payable directly to the national government through its local representatives and more specifically to the local collector, who took his lawful share of what he was able to extract from the peasant.

Peasants did not, in short, believe that they were beloved objects of solicitude of other segments of French society. Neither did their sons who went into the cities to work in factories and small shops or into mines to dig coal. Wages went up slowly in the 18th century, as we shall see later, and prices went up rather rapidly. Better off then when they left the countryside, they were nevertheless gradually getting worse off than they had been in years past in the city.

That portion of the bourgeoisie containing skilled artisans suffered some of the same taxing pains as did the landowning peasants. Their guilds were heavily taxed and so were their incomes. The high bourgeoisie, growing in wealth and power, suffered the disadvantage that the more systematically they ran their enterprises and kept record of profits and losses, the more they had to pay in taxes. And they believed the government was becoming increasingly subservient to the nobility.

The nobility saw the government as increasingly subservient to the bourgeoisie. With no respect for the dignity of inherited title, the government for a price was adding pseudonoble titles to wealthy men of no family, arrogantly designating these arrivistes as "nobles de robe" to distinguish them from the natural-born "nobles d'épée." The old nobles observed the new nobles buying country estates from increasingly vestigial but still very sworded noblemen. The nobles of the robe were enfolding, smothering, the nobles of the sword.

Old nobles, looking through dusty old documents, discovered a way to be with but not be of the modern mercantile-industrial world. They found that services and payments in kind were due them from peasants, many of whom had for centuries been free peasants. (Serfdom was first abolished, according to Tocqueville, in Normandy in the 13th century and was virtually nonexistent on the eve of the great 18th century revolution.) In short, landlords, seeing their economic advancement, their political power, and their prestige all threatened and actually diminished by the energetic and of course unhonorable bourgeoisie, began in the mid-18th century to reassert long-dead "rights" against peasants, who thereby saw not only their freedom, power, and prestige but also their economic welfare threatened and diminished.

The sworded nobles furthermore had little to do—few, if any functions in society to give their lives meaning. The government gradually was taking away—efficiently, effectively, and thoroughly—such governmental powers as nobles had possessed before kings could successfully establish national power. They were no longer needed to keep the peace, to adjudicate disputes among vassals and serfs, and most particularly to protect from violence their people, their peasants, their onetime serfs. Now the government acted, or tried or professed to act, directly in the behalf of the population at large. So the old nobles, sensing their loss of position in society as the new nobles of the robe began to emulate the sword-bearing style of life, began to emulate the new nobles in their wealth. And this meant evading such taxes as the capitation, by law payable by all people with incomes. It also meant using documents to enforce feudal dues, in many cases centuries after the reason for the dues had been reduced to legal paper, which now was hard to read and harder to justify.

The clergy, that one-half of 1 percent of the population, had a few functions to perform. They kept records of births and deaths. They baptized. They warned souls of the need for grace and invoked God's grace. And they prayed, managed estates, and bottled wine, extracted the tithe from the peasants. And, for their recordkeeping and their divine intervention, they were freed of any tax payments.

These then were the major segments of society, each of which eyed every other segment and its members with suspicion and envy. Was that a tax collector coming? Was that a secret hoard of grain which that peasant or that landlord so hurriedly covered up? Where was that set of books of the merchant that were a true report of how rich he was getting? How much did that fat father pay the government to get his bright but unprincipled son the job as secretary to the resident government commissioner?

If individuals in each estate tended to suspect and envy individuals in all other estates, they all mistrusted and condemned the government. The monarchy asserted in the mid-15th century (during the reign of Charles VII) the power to tax anyone without the consent of any estate. In the 18th century, the crown was intermittently, and more frequently, beginning to use the power. It had to. France engaged in a nearly unbroken series of expensive wars in the 18th century. Good for members of all estates, as businessmen, landowning lords and peasants and the small class of workers, the wars were bad for businessmen and peasants as taxpayers. Starting in 1781, the government increased—but with an infirm hand—its efforts to collect taxes, demanding even that the nobility actually pay the taxes nominally due from it.

The government was thus disappointing the popular expectation of continued prosperity without cost. And until the French intervention in the American War of Independence, the wars were lost. The intervention in America gave France pride in somewhat vicariously defeating England, which by 1763 had virtually knocked France out of North America except for Louisiana. The financial crisis—which threatened and actually deprived high bourgeoisie, nobles, and now even clergy of wealth they had come to expect as their due—got worse. Inflation intensified. Lefebvre has calculated the rise in cost of living thus: in about 50 years before the revolution, prices went up some 65 percent and wages went up some 22 percent. Whether rich or poor, most people had enough excuse to displace at least some of their inter-state hostility onto the government. And in addition they had reason enough also to dislike and condemn the government, which either lost its wars or was unable to pay for the one war that it assisted in winning.

These growing tensions, increasingly directed toward government, were aggravated by events that amounted to bad luck at best and gullibility at worst. In 1786 France made a trade treaty with the England it had helped to defeat 3 years earlier in America. France agreed to reduce the tariff on textiles, which helped the then more efficient and mass-market-oriented English mills. In return, England agreed to reduce tariffs on wines and brandies, which England did not produce anyhow but important from Portugal and France. The trade treaty went into effect in 1788.

In 1778, the French harvest of grain suffered from bad weather. That is, the weather was bad for grain and good for the vineyards. There was thus a nearly catastrophic shortage of grains for bread and a large surplus of wine to flood the English market after the lowering of the trade barriers. And the opening of war of Turkey against Russia and Austria diminished these countries as markets for French textiles, which now faced competition in French stores from cheap English cloth.

Unemployment rose along with the reduced demand for textiles. The abundant grape harvest dropped wine prices somewhat. Peasants who produced wine had to buy their food at higher prices. These economic dislocations chain reacted to reduce the demand for everything but jobs and bread—the two goods that were in scarcest supply. Bread had never been so expensive since the end of the reign of Louis XIV in 1715, and so bread riots broke out in the major cities, and people in the cities began restlessly roaming out into the countryside to get food. Long-term rising expectations of a prosperous and peaceful economy and effective government were quickly disappointed. In the spring of 1789 and into the summer, the growing interclass hostility and growing hostility to government quickly burst into revolution, when the fear of physical deprivation quickly became real and immediate. The 18th-century developments are shown in figure 19-2.

The J-curve helps explain the French Revolution. The growing frustration of the land expectations of peasants, of the dignity expectations of landlords who wanted the status-wealth of the high bourgeoisie, and of the dignity- and power expectations of the high bourgeoisie are all closely comparable to developments in other nations that have had revolutions. And so is the effect of sudden economic dislocation following long-term economic growth.

But the J-curve is not a total explanation of the French Revolution. At least in its intensity, the interclass hostility in France, not as such related to the J-curve, was unique. More or less independently of frustrated rising expectations in the 18th century, French society was already deeply fragmented. The internal war of all against all had already begun. The absorption of these forces, in conflict between classes and individuals, did temporarily deflect them from the government. But in the end the sheer hostility, as it became more intense, turned toward the government.

And in addition to the disappointed expectations and deflected interclass hostility, there was in France in 1789 the visible and exciting example of the successful American revolution. In 1968 French students followed the example of students in Japan, America, and elsewhere by rebelling against French universities and government. But this was only the second time the American revolutionary example had been followed: it had already been followed almost 180 years before.

The American Civil War of 1861

The difference between the terms "revolution," "rebellion," and "civil war" may be nothing more than this: revolution succeeds, rebellion fails, and civil war leaves the question open. All involve violence. In the Gettysburg Address of 1863, Lincoln referred to the ongoing conflict as "a great civil war"; at other times he called it rebellion and he never acknowledged the sovereign independence of the 11 Southern States that asserted it. It is not quite clear even a hundred years later that it was a rebellion or that it failed, but it is clear that the American Civil War did not end in Southern independence. It remains hard to characterize this most savage conflict. In proportion to the population of the time, this civil war produced the most catastrophic loss of life and property that America has ever suffered. The awesome depth of the conflict makes it important to explain.

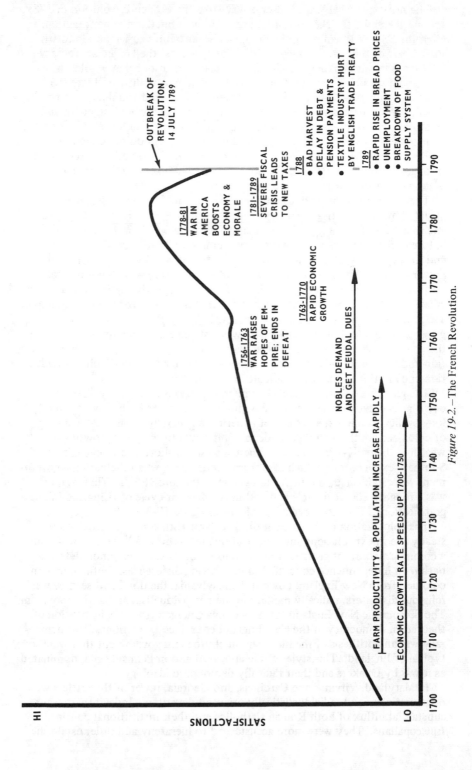

Figure 19-2.—The French Revolution.

The American Civil War is in some ways like the French Revolution of 1789, and in others like the Nazi revolution of 1933 examined in the next section. As in the French Revolution, the middle-class, entrepreneurial, and industrializing part of the nation was arrayed in battle against the landed aristocracy. Southern plantations fought a change in social institutions that would make them more suitable to the profound changes which capitalism and industrialization brought with them. But the American Civil War is unlike the French Revolution in the absence of joint action by both American bourgeoisie and landlords against the national government. If Southern landlords and Northern industrialists had combined against the government, it is quite possible the civil war would have resembled the Nazi revolution. It could have established an oligarchical dictatorship of the urban upper-middle-class and rural landlords, as in many 20th-century developing nations.

The American conflict does resemble the Nazi revolution in that it was initiated by conservative segments of society that were restive with the pace and direction of change. In both America before the Civil War and Germany before nazism, an agrarian economy was being rapidly replaced by industry, and the hegemony of landed aristocrats was threatened by the growing political power of merchants and industrialists. Industrialization was about as recent in both countries—about two generations, though its growth rate in Germany was greater. But the principal difference between America in 1861 and Germany in 1933 was in the orientation of the two revolutions: the latter was more progressive in its orientation in that there was a strong and real appeal in nazism to those people who felt they had been denied equal opportunity to acquire education and technical skills. In America the South denied the desirability of education and anything other than agricultural technology.

The gradual rise and rapid decline in gratifications in pre-Civil War America occur in two cycles, one contained within the other. There had been a very long cyclical rise in expectations of Americans generally, from the beginnings of colonization, through independence, and down to the great growth of wealth in the early-19th century. There also was a shorter term cycle in Southern expectations, which rose from about 1789, when the national government was established, and began to decline in the mid-1850's. That is, there was a roughly 200-year cycle and within it a 70-year cycle of rising and falling gratifications. The latter cycle is set forth in figure 19-3.

The colonization of America in the 17th and 18th centuries provided a steady rise in expectations and gratifications until the 1750's and 1760's. But a common pattern of growth in the various colonies and a common determination on independence concealed some growing differences. In the northern colonies, from New England down to Pennsylvania, the dominant settlers were religious dissenters, radically modern in their individualism and anticorporatism. The democratic New England town meetings emerged from the institution of theoretical democracy in the New England church congregations. This democracy was an antithesis of the hierarchy in church and government that were so typical of England. This style of rule appeared also in Pennsylvania, dominated as it was by Quakers and their radically democratic ideology.

In Maryland, Virginia, the Carolinas, and Georgia, fewer of the settlers were democratically and individualistically oriented dissenters. Indeed there was a substantial influx of both Roman Catholics and their institutional cousins, Episcopalians. They were more accustomed to hierarchy and order established

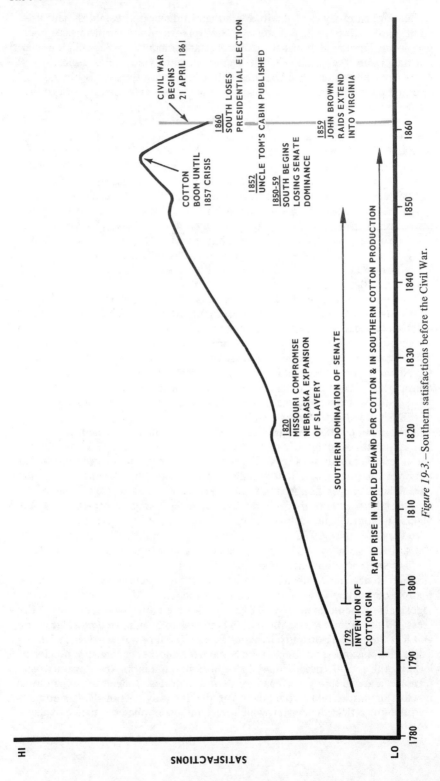

Figure 19-3. — Southern satisfactions before the Civil War.

from above and they carried with them the nondissenting, establishment orientation of their English ancestors. There were, in addition, influxes of poor people with more individualistic and less establishment-oriented religious views, but they rarely were a major influence in the South, politically or socially, at any time before the Civil War, and they shared with the establishment-oriented plantationer class a dedication to the rectitude of slavery and to the virtues of the rural life.

Differences in institutions and values if anything became greater with the passage of time. Big cities of commerce and industry grew in the North and, with the exception of the great port city of New Orleans, never developed in the South. Agrarian development in the North was typified by family-sized farms. With their highly individualistic outlook, farmers had appreciable political power in the Northern state governments from the beginning of national independence. Agrarian development in the South was on the surface of things like growth in the North. There were far more family-sized farms in the South than there were plantations, but the plantationers dominated Southern politics, using the issue of black inferiority to all white men very effectively in maintaining acquiescence by poor whites in the rule of the large landholders and slaveowners.

Inevitably, as industrialization and commerce developed in the North it began to urbanize rapidly. This process included not just a division of labor between farmers and city dwellers, but also a rapid growth in population. Correlatively and inevitably, an agrarian society like that in the South experienced a slower growth in population. The growth toward political equalitarianism in the North became more and more fundamentally opposed to the oligarchical domination of politics by the plantationers. And so began—more exactly, continued—the widening of the gulf between economic and social values and ways of life between North and South.

In national politics, the question of who should rule echoed continuously across the ever-eroding canyon between South and North. The Virginia dynasty was not a legend but a reality for a generation after independence. Excepting the brief and not very portentous administrations of John Adams (1797-1801) and his son John Quincy Adams (1825-29), there was an unbroken line of Southern Presidents of the United States, from Washington through Jefferson, Madison, Monroe, and Jackson. John Calhoun of South Carolina served as Vice President during J. Q. Adams' administration and the first term of Jackson's. From 1789 to 1837 the Presidency was almost continuously Southern.

This Southern domination became increasingly more romantic. The Southerners who became Presidents acted nationally, not sectionally. In Congress, the Missouri Compromise settled and unsettled (in 1820) the conflict over sectional representation. By this Compromise the South won the votes in Congress of the border state of Missouri, which was to be admitted as a slave state, and lost the free opportunity to expand its political power westward. The South did continue to dominate the Senate for another generation, judging at least by the 1854 Kansas-Nebraska Act, which, repudiating the Missouri Compromise, allowed slaves to come into these territories. Indeed the Senate was not just the last retreat of the South but also the only part of the government that did not reflect the ever growing social and economic dominance of the North.

The regional growth comparisons are awesome. In one decade, from 1850-60, the population of the South grew greatly—about 23 percent; in the same decade the non-Southern population increased a fantastic 43 percent. Although adequate economic trend data over time are hard to come by, in 1860 the North was producing over 90 percent by value of all manufactured goods. The proportion produced by the North had apparently been increasing rapidly as the war approached. The North was even exporting food (grains and livestock) to the agricultural South. And free farmers were saying politically that they did not want to compete, economically or socially, with plantationers whose fieldhands worked without pay.

These developments suggest, at least in hindsight, that the South was made to suppose that it could win a war against the growing industrial and commercial Yankee giant. But the South itself was enjoying, early in the 1850's, unprecedented prosperity. There was an almost insatiable world demand for cotton, of which the South had close to a world monopoly in production. The average annual production during the 1840-50 decade was 2.2 million bales; it increased to 3.4 million in the next decade. At the same time the average annual price during 1840-50 was about 8 cents per pound, rising more than 30 percent, to 10.6 cents, in the final prewar decade. Along with this—and an improvement in profit from tobacco and sugarcane production—came an increase in the price of prime field hands, the most commonly valuable category of slaves. Their price doubled during the 1850-60 decade, reaching as high as $1,500 per head, and the demand was enormous. It was not easy for Southerners to concede the rightness or the efficiency of an economy based on free labor.

But the little-diversified agrarian Southern economy was fragile. A particular weakness was the plantationers' custom of buying on credit advanced before the sale of their crops. Even before the 1775 War of Independence, it was common for Southern planters to be thus in long-range debt to English merchants. After 1783 there was on change: the creditors were now Northern merchants, mainly in New York. The South quite simply remained money-poor up to 1861 (and beyond). On a sellers' market, which the South enjoyed with some ups and downs until 1857, the system of credit worked well enough for Southern planters. And it worked even better for Northern creditors. To protect themselves from market uncertainties—and from individuals who were poor credit risks—Northern dealers would charge Southern buyers higher than normal prices. Southern buyers, when they were paid by credit paper at harvesttime, would sell the paper at a discount to pay their bills. So they paid twice at least: in the form of higher prices for the goods they bought, and lower prices for the credit paper they sold to pay off their annual debt.

This chronic low-intensity economic crisis, in the face of seemingly endless prosperity, is akin to the situation that produced the looting and burning of white-owned stores by Negroes in the 1960's—more than a century later: the Southern plantationers developed no affection for the big Yankee houses that had the goods and sold them at a price higher than a Yankee would have to pay. They were unable to set fire to the New York stores and say "Burn, Baby, Burn." But they did try to destroy the Union.

Near the end of this cycle of rising and then declining political gratifications was the more immediate and very threatening economic crisis of 1857. It was an epitome of the Southern dependence on the North, of the dependence of any raw-material-producing colony on the financial and other economic cir-

cumstances of the diversified "mother country." In 1857 the South was hit
by a panic in the New York commodity exchange market. For a time money
exchange with England virtually ceased, and so did the effective demand for
cotton in England. Although the Liverpool price was 18 or 19 cents a pound
for cotton, in contrast to 10 cents a pound in New York, Southerners for the
most part had to sell in New York. Many of them had already committed their
crop to New York buyers and so were stuck; many who had not committed
their crop needed money badly and were in virtually the same bind as those
who had already sold their crops for future delivery. A Southern Senator in
Washington saw the situation with a clear intelligence and passed his judgment:
a cotton crop that could have sold for $100 million went for $65 million. To
save irresponsible and selfish Northern speculators—who perhaps blamed the
system for producing the money crisis—the South lost $35 million.

This was the final critical downturn in the gratifications of Southerners.
They had lost political power that they had exercised so successfully in nearly
a half century of Southern but Nation-minded Presidents of the United States.
They had neared the final loss of their dominant power in the Senate, where
so often they held a veto over laws demanded by Northerners. And now, in a
process that so starkly showed their economic thralldom to the North, they had
to save their economic masters to the tune of a loss of a third of the value of
their major crop—and the nation's major export.

The growing and now enormous tensions found release in secession. The
eventual outcome of the 1854 Kansas-Nebraska Act, which in 1854 still offered
some hope of restoring the balance of sectional power in the Senate, soon became clear. An honest referendum on the slavery issue indicated an 8-to-1
majority in Kansas in favor of entering the Union as a free state. After liberat-
ing a few slaves in Kansas, that madman and self-styled liberator, John Brown,
in 1859 made a raid in search of arms on the U.S. arsenal at Harpers Ferry.
But Harpers Ferry was not in Kansas; it was in Virginia. And it was clear
where John Brown now proposed to commence the liberation of slaves.

So the South began to secede. South Carolina was the first to take the step,
on December 20, 1860. And South Carolina fired the first shot, on the federal Fort Sumter in Charleston Harbor, on April 21, 1861. The Civil War had
begun as the ever-romantic South came to the end of its neofeudal dream. Its
expectations of freedom to continue to expand its wealth and way of life were
shattered by the events of the late 1850's, in Congress and in the mercantile
houses of New York.

The Nazi Revolution of 1933

The Nazi revolution was a German and a world catastrophe. It led to the
partial destruction and the partition of a population that had been growing in
unity, civilization, and recognition since the Protestant Reformation that
Luther led, since the tremendous spurt in industrialization in the late-19th
century, and since the surge of nationalism that took the form of empire building and then, in 1914, of war.

Germany was the first to experience a successful reformation, that major
advance toward establishing the equalization and individuation of men. For
whatever reasons, it was the last major European nation to undergo that pro-
foundest of modernizers: industrialization. In one sense the first modern

popular revolution took place in Germany in the 16th century, before industrialization had developed anything like its modern factory system anywhere.
In another sense Germany never had a postindustrial revolution comparable to
the French Revolution. The German Reformation was universalist in its equalitarian principles and so was the French Revolution. There was a messianic
quality to the equalitarian beliefs of the German Reformation of the 16th century, the French Revolution of the 18th, and the Russian of the 20th. These
revolutions spawned and nurtured many popular movements in the world. But
the Nazi revolution—the nearest counterpart to the postindustrial French Revolution—was not universalist. It was particularistic, intensely nationalistic, and
imperialistic, proposing to subject and exploit both Slavic and Gallic peoples
to the control and enrichment of the Germanic. It was a kind of revenge for
the world recognition that came to France and Russia after their universalist
revolutions, renown that had stifled Germany between two peoples that felt
their own superiority to Germans.

The growth in vitality of German society and culture was relatively steady
and continuous, perhaps for centuries up to 1918. Surely it was continuous
since the tariff union (developing from 1819-1844) that intensified the trend,
under Prussian domination, toward economic unity. With the growth of an
enormous iron and steel industry, the basis was laid for building warships, ar-
tillery, and rifles. Construction of these commodities made war and expansion a euphoric dream that called for realization. In 1870, in battle, Germany
defeated the France that had been the terror of Europe just two generations
before. Within months, in January 1871, came the siege and surrender of
Paris. Within days after the surrender of Paris came the formal inauguration
of the unified German empire, when the Prussian king was crowned Emperor
William I. The curves of rising expectations and gratifications were steadily
rising, for Germans as individuals and as a nation.

In such a short analysis it is not possible to specify steps in the progress of
Germany upward to its dismaying and unacknowledged defeat in world war in
November 1918. It is clear enough that the long-range trend, accelerating
rapidly after the tariff union and the 1871 unification, was upward. It is clear
that the 1918 defeat came as a profound shock. It was suficiently stunning
and ambiguous to be regarded as only a temporary setback by those elitist individuals who believed in an imperial destiny and by those ordinary Germans
who had a deep pride in their country. All these had entrusted basic decisions
to the government. Under two emperors and such gifted paternalistic rulers as
Bismarck and the Krupp family, the government had given them economic
prosperity, social security, and world prestige.

Again, as in the analysis of the American Civil War, there was a centuries-
long J-curve and a decades-short one. For present purposes, we can commence
the analysis of the final rise and decline with the ambiguous 1918 defeat, recall-
ing only that the advances up to 1918 had been real and enormous and remained in the memories of perhaps most Germans.

Both the French and the German Nazi revolutions were preceded by military defeat. But the former nation could not so easily turn the blame outward
as could the latter. In the French case, the Seven Years' War, ending in 1763,
was a virtually total defeat by England in North America. The vicarious French
victory over England at Yorktown in 1781 produced independence for the
United States and near-bankruptcy for France. The military action was far

from France. England did not make demands intimately affecting Frenchmen in France in 1763 and the government's financial crisis in 1781 could hardly be blamed by Frenchmen on the defeated British.

With Germany after the 1918 Armistice it was different. The Allies blockaded German ports and then occupied just enough German territory to hurt pride and business badly. German Communists, exalted by the Russian example, threatened their countrymen with total destruction of the established system, already shaken by the loss of the emperor. Germans therefore could readily displace blame and thereby dissociate the glories of an ever-greater German nation from the trickeries of external and internal enemies who sought only their own aggrandizement and German degradation. This hope for restoration of recently and meanly lost greatness was a very central part of the mental outlook of perhaps most Germans in the 1920's.

The continuation of hope and of pride in being German formed a cement that kept the nation from the disintegration that France experienced in the late-18th century. There was not quite the war of all against all that characterized prerevolutionary French society. Internal hostility was less personal and the enemies were more symbolic. The Allies, the French, the Communists, the Jews, the capitalists were the enemies rather than one's neighboring peasants, one's landlord, one's boss in the shoe factory, or the arriviste wealthy bourgeois who bought one's estate.

The impersonal contacts with enemies in Germany were such as to reinforce displacement of the internal tensions of an economy that had suffered the consequences of vast military expenditure, in an all-out war from 1914 to 1918. It was easier to forget the sanctions (governmental and industrial) against industrial strife than the more comfortable fact of punitive and unrealistic reparations. It was the government that initiated currency inflation. But the effect of the inflation on the internal economy could be overshadowed in people's minds by its effect on the French enemy, especially since the inflation was an effort to defeat the French and Belgian military occupation of the Ruhr Basin, starting in January 1923, by watering down the high price of reparations. German workers, who did strike in large numbers in this period, often regarded the French and Belgian occupying forces (and their attendant business experts who took over management control of the big enterprises) as the enemy. And then they could also blame those German captialists, many of them Jews, who skillfully made fortunes out of the inflation. Because their customs made them stand out—particularly in the abstract—the Jewish capitalists were easier to blame than the German ones. And middle-class Germans could blame the Communists as agitators of the proletariat. In many such plausible ways, blame for Germany's ills could be projected outward. These plausible and sufficiently genuine external and internal enemies limited the tendency, which was never notably strong, of Germans to blame themselves for their problems, which in the 1920's indeed became severe.

The underlying optimism (a continuing heritage from the imperial and Reformation eras) and the surface displacement of responsibility for contemporary problems probably combined to encourage an irrepressible optimism in the mid-1920's. The inflation was a trauma. It began in August 1922 and ran wild for more than a year, until November 1923 when efforts at drastic monetary reform were undertaken. But the 1920's nevertheless were times of hope and progress in Germany. If the inflation wiped out private savings and insurance policies, it also wiped out internal public debt, and in April 1924 the Dawes plan promised a large influx of external capital for reconstruction. Though there were peaks of unemployment (1.5 million in January 1923, 2 million in February 1926, and 1.4 million in January 1928), the trend in jobs was generally upward. Taking the prewar year 1907 as a base of 100, by 1925 the number of gainfully employed had increased to about 127, and by 1933 had increased to 128. Again taking 1907 national population as a base of 100, by 1925 it had increased only to 102 and by 1933 to 106. In short, the proportion of the population that had jobs, roughly a decade after World War ended, was a fourth larger than a decade before the war ended.

Up to 1929, economic conditions in Germany generally improved. And then, starting in July 1929, there was a steady, unremitting increase in unemployment until some time in the first quarter of 1933—that is, until after Hitler came to power on January 30, 1933. At the peak of unemployment, sometime in 1932, between 5.6 million and 7.3 million were unemployed. This was about three times the previous peak of about 2 million in February 1926 and 10 times as high as the 560,000 people who were out of work in July 1928.

The depression hit hard in other ways. Germans, who as we noted had lost all their savings in the inflation, had begun to save again. Savings had increased by about half between 1928 and 1930. In the next year, 1931, the amount of money in savings accounts declined about 6 percent. This hurt many kinds of people, perhaps most seriously the lower middle class. And the shortage of work, statistically a cold figure, became a chilling reality, particularly for the working class. Germans on the average in 1928 worked 7.7 hours per day. By 1932, the hours worked per day had declined to 6.9—roughly by 10 percent.

What this adds up to, in summary, is that fewer people were working; those who worked were working fewer hours. And more money had to be drawn out of savings than could be put in. The sense that work and thrift would pay off, as Germany and Germans rose out of the defeat in war and the disgrace in postwar inflation and occupation, was rapidly replaced with despair. The gap between expectations and gratifications yawned wide, for perhaps a large majority of Germans. The gap was filled first with Nazi words and then with deeds as the economy was revived and geared toward war.

We have become so sensitive to the impact of ideology—perhaps as a consequence of the enormous amount of it generated and broadcast throughout the world since the 1917 Russian Revolution—that we tend to explain the success of the Nazis in terms of the racist, irrational rhetoric that stems from *Mein Kampf*. However nicely it fit the German mood in the late 1920's, the words would have found few ears if there had not been recurrent and at last catastrophic ecnomic crisis. Figure 19-4 shows the series of crises.

The physical needs of millions of people were deeply denied. The standard diet of the unemployed consisted largely of potatoes and margarine. Working-class people might have been a force to oppose the racist or at least antiproletarian appeals of the Nazis. But unemployed people, particularly when they have suffered for several years, are more inclined toward apathy than activity. Those whose physical survival was not so directly endangered—those who had enough to eat—were threatened in virtually all walks of life with a regression to the economic level of 1919-23.

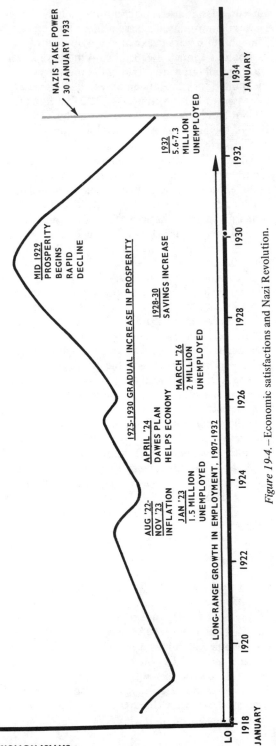

Figure 19-4. — Economic satisfactions and Nazi Revolution.

Interclass conflict took different form in pre-1933 Germany from that in pre-1789 France. In the German instance, intergroup conflict seems to have been less pronounced, at least on anything approaching the personal level of hostility that prevailed in France in the late-18th century. Nevertheless various segments of the society did show hostility toward others, however vague its form and ill defined its object. There was a high degree of symbolic hostility between labor and capital in Germany, but the number and intensity of strikes declined greatly from 1925 on. At first this decline was probably due to the rather general prosperity of the mid-1920's. Later (1920-32) it was probably due to the acuteness of unemployment, which led men to fear a strike because they would then be faced with a diet of potatoes and margarine. The conflict between labor and capital was thus more abstract and ideological than real, and took place more in politics than outside factory gates. As such it was inevitably attenuated. Its savagery diminished to a rather generalized hostility, perhaps on both sides.

The petty bourgeoisie, the *Kleinbürgertum,* is now almost fabled as the hard core of anti-Semitism. Indeed it may be that from this social group came those who formed the mobs that quite concretely smashed Jewish shops. In any case, the frustrated expectations of the petty bourgeoisie must have been compounded of the loss of their savings along with the fear that they would retrogress into the mass of pitiably poor people, whence they thought they had emerged by a combination of thrift and hard work.

One major segment of German society that saw its expectations frustrated were those who hoped for a resurgence of the nation that had fought so valiantly in the World War. This segment consisted principally of two groups—the military elite, those who were indeed Junkers or who styled themselves as such; and the returned veterans who after the war were met not with victory parades but often with contempt and derision. Even more crucially, veterans were often faced with unemployment or unemployability—the latter including many of those for whom military life had been their first successful occupation. They had no GI bill to train or retrain them for useful work. Thinking themselves heroes returned, they often found themselves drifters and bums. From this subgroup came many of the early Nazi rank and file. From the other subgroup, the officer caste, came those who first supported more traditionally nationalist political parties than the Nazis, who then stood by and observed the arrant Nazis with mingled contempt and envy, and who at last became the willing instruments of the Nazis when the glorious war clouds gathered again.

The pervasive German attitude in the late 1920's seems to have been one of bafflement rather than of active support for the Nazi movement or widespread intergroup hostility. Labor was inhibited by fear of loss of jobs. Many of the middle class were disconcerted by their recurrent failure to better themselves. Members of the upper middle class could not believe that things were getting as bad for so many people as clearly was the case. And the old aristocracy remembered only the glories of feudalism and war or of the sheltered academic life.

It is this stunned state of mind that produced a high measure of political apathy or of active contempt for the inadequate efforts of the republican, parliamentary government to govern. The Nazi revolution was not just a coup d'etat: it had broad popular support. But it did depend for its rise to power on the growing political irresoluteness of people who had hitherto been polit-

ically more self-confident (labor and the upper middle class). And it depended
on a high degree of involvement and participation on the part of those whose
frustrations—whether military or economic—coincided with the medley of
themes played by the Nazis. The Nazi revolution depended on the support of
people whose desperation and consequent dissociation from reality led them
to ignore, tolerate, and even take part in violence they would otherwise have
abhorred.

The Black Rebellion of the 1960's

The black uprisings in America in the 1960's clearly amount to a rebellion,
but they are not in any precise sense a revolution like those of France in 1789
or Russia in 1905 and 1917. However, the differences between these revolutions and the black rebellion are largely quantitative. The latter involves a
widespread joint commitment to rather fundamental change among all segments of Negro society in the country: change in the political power structure
of the country in all political units—cities, counties, states, and nation. And
these changes, involving all blacks and all parts of the political community,
have been accompanied by the violence that is a universal element of revolution.

The differences between revolution and the black rebellion derive from
several facts: Negroes constitute only about 11 percent of the national population and therefore are numerically incapable of enforcing changes to the same
degree as in a nation where a substantial majority is frustrated by the established
government. The constitutions and laws of the national and most state gover-
ments have not contained many restrictions that discriminate against people
on racial grounds—quite the contrary.

So there has been no basic change in principles. The Constitution and law
of the land have been used or developed in ways that make them instruments
to achieve changes in the nonlegal social practices and customs of discrimination. And there has been a sufficiently developed sense of commitment to
equality as a major social value to make the equalizing of opportunities for
black people a process against which most whites could not readily fight.
They could not readily deny the applicability of their principles to those who
newly have demanded equality. And that portion of the nation which frankly
accepted the principle of racial inequality lost the savage Civil War. The very
slow struggle for racial equality and human dignity for blacks commenced with
Lincoln's 1863 Emancipation Proclamation and the military defeat of the South
2 years later.

What is striking, in a comparison of this (and other) contained rebellions
with the great revolutions, is that the Negro rebellion appears to have been
preceded by the same J-curve of expectations that are at first gratified and
then frustrated. The same reaction patterns of this level of analysis appear to
have developed in the minds of American blacks as have developed in the minds
of those who have become revolutionaries in previous eras and other countries.

The difficulty in seeing this likeness relates to the vast gap between what
whites and blacks have gotten in America. This gap has made it hard to see
just what advances blacks have made and when. Those who as blacks and
whites believe in equality have emphasized the vast and continuing inequalities.
Black or white, they do not see what advances have been made. In the 1960's,

when conditions were better than in the 1860's or than in the 1930's, the expressions of discontent have been at their maximum. The new words and deeds of discontent can be understood only if one appreciates that profoundly deprived people are often incapable of expressing their discontent. In short, to understand why the black rebellion has occurred, it is necessary to see how black people had already developed.

At the end of the Civil War, Negroes were perhaps as near to minimal survival in the psychological sense, as human beings, as they had been since their initial transportation from Africa. They had lost the security of provision for food, clothing, shelter, and physical safety that had been fairly well assured them as long as they docilely accepted their position as slaves. They could no longer be sure that the master would provide for them. They had, often, to forage for themselves, like war refugees everywhere when crops have been destroyed and normal patterns of collaboration in productive work have been shattered. Overjoyed at their emancipation, they could use their freedom no more effectively than could concentration camp inmates in Germany when the doors at last swung open in early 1945. They could concern themselves really with only the satisfaction of their physical needs, which freedom is not and equality and dignity are not.

Those who must concentrate only on survival usually do not revolt: they are too hungry. This preoccupation simply with staying alive if anything strengthened in the late decades of the 19th century as the practice of lynching—the killing by mobs rather than by lawfully or other systematically employed force—continued. Between 1882, when records of lynchings were first kept, down to 1941, lynchings averaged 78 per year. The constant fear that one might be arbitrarily killed, maimed, or injured was one of the day-to-day facts of life for most blacks, particularly until the early 1920's. Lynching and physical injury could be said to have declined to a relatively minor worry—comparable perhaps to the level of worry about automobile accidents in the 1960's—in the late 1930's and the 1940's: the average for 1937-42 was five per year and for 1943-48 less than three per year. But the level of general health remained low and so did life expectancy.

The process of moving up off the even, flat plane of survival itself was of course continuous. But it was so slow that it seems best to date the first major upturn, from concern for mere survival for most blacks, as the beginning of the Second World War. Responding to the threar of a large demonstration, a repetition of something akin to the 1932 veterans' march on Washington, Franklin Roosevelt in 1941 issued an Executive order prohibiting discriminatory hiring practices in all defense industries, and establishing the Fair Employment Practices Commission (FEPC) to administer the order. Though it worked unevenly and in many cases not at all, it nevertheless was a major basis for advance above subsistence for Negroes. By war's end, some 2 million blacks were employed in war industry, and the FEPC reported that 1,300,000 of these had gotten jobs in consequence of its efforts.

What could have been a cataclysmic frustration of rising expectations for blacks at war's end turned out not to be. The successful efforts to avoid a postwar recession, which would have witnessed the old (and still common) practice of discharging Negroes first, benefited blacks as well as whites. There was no widespread and sudden drop in Negro employment. Instead, the pace of rising economic opportunity continued. In 1946 the CIO and AFL trade-union organizations undertook a drive to organize Negro workers in the South and to integrate them into existing unions. By 1948, FEPC legislation had been passed in six states, taking up some of the slack when the ending of war contracts removed the protection of the wartime FEPC. Symbolically, and a bit more, the first Negro was admitted in 1947 to major league baseball, Jackie Robinson; there were 14 major league Negro players in 1951; by 1954 all but 3 of the 16 major league teams were integrated. Racially integrated low-cost public housing after the war began the breakdown of discrimination in this basic concern of life. In 1956 all public housing in Washington, D.C., was desegregated. In 1962 President Kennedy issued an order prohibiting discrimination in any housing that was either financed or had mortgage insurance under a Government program. It was estimated that this affected a fourth of all future housing construction in the nation.

These advances relate to jobs and housing and therefore to the physical needs, but they also—notably in the case of sport participations—have overtones of equal dignity. Advances that more directly related to this profound, nonphysical need for equality included the following:

> The admission of Negroes into the category of commissioned officer: 500 Negro officers in the Army in 1943, 7,500 by war's end; and 28 officers in the Navy in 1944, 50 by war's end;

> The integration of 90 percent of all Negro army personnel into unsegregated units by 1953 and complete integration a year later;

> The first desegregation of interstate buses in 1946, of railway dining cars in 1950, and of railway passenger cars in 1952;

> The long series of steps designed to desegregate education, commencing with the court order to the University of Oklahoma in 1948 to admit on a segregated basis a graduate student who was black, to the University of Texas in 1950 to admit on a nonsegregated basis a Negro to the law school, down to and beyond the landmark 1954 case which ordered the integration of public secondary and primary schools "with all deliberate speed";

> The similarly long series of steps to end discrimination in the voting process, starting with the court invalidation in 1944 of the white primary closed to blacks and continuing with the 1954, 1964, and later civil-rights acts, which increasingly protected and enforced the right of blacks to register and vote in all elections.

The range and number of national and state legislative and judicial and administrative efforts to see that black people were accorded equal dignity is very large indeed. Repeatedly in the 1940's, 1950's, and early 1960's it gave evidence to Negroes that progress was being made. Their expectations inevitably rose from the near-ground level before the second World War to what proved increasingly to be excessivly optimistic. Acts of legislatures, court, and administrative agencies—and of private groups and citizens—to equalize life opportunities for black people have never quite fulfilled their initial purpose. This brings us to the matter of promise and performance, to assessment of the gap between the expectations aroused by legislation, Executive order, and court decision, on the one hand, and realization of equality, on the other.

The killing by lynch mobs dwindled to one case in 1947 and two in 1948. A new kind of killing of blacks began and at times something like the old lynch mob operated again. In 1952 a top state NAACP official in Florida who organized a campaign to secure the indictment of a sheriff charged with killing a Negro prisoner was killed by a bomb. After the 1954 commencement of public shcool integration, there were some 530 cases of violence (burning, bombing, and intimidation of children and their parents) in the first 4 years of integration. Schools, churches, and the homes of black leaders were bombed and many people were killed in these bombings. Federal troops were brought into Little Rock in September 1957 to integrate the high school; during the following school year (1958-59), public schools were closed in Little Rock.

In short—starting in the mid-1950's and increasing more or less steadily into the early 1960's—white violence grew against the now lawful and protected efforts of Negroes to gain integration. And so did direct action and later violence undertaken by blacks, in a reciprocal process that moved into the substantial violence of 1965-67. That 3-year period may be considered a peak, possibly the peak of the violence that constituted the black rebellion. It was violence mostly against white property and black people. It merits reemphasis that during this era of increased hostility, progress continued to be made. Indeed, the occurrence of some progress intensified both the white reaction to it and the black counteraction to the reaction, because every time a reaction impeded the progress, the apparent gap widened between expectations and gratifications.

Direct (but not violent) action by Negroes began in late 1956 with the bus boycott in Montgomery, Alabama, which endured for over a year and succeeded. It was precipitated when a Negro woman got on a city bus, sat down in a front seat, was ordered to give up her seat to a white man, and refused. The bus boycott soon came under the leadership of Dr. Martin Luther King, Jr., whose belief in nonviolent resistance—and the mild temper of blacks in Montgomery at the time—succeeded in keeping the action relatively peaceful.

Direct violent action began in April 1963 in Birmingham, Alabama, in what may be called the first full-scale concerted violent encounter of blacks and whites in recent years. Seeking integration of such facilities as lunch counters, parks, and swimming pools, the blacks in Birmingham, most of them young, were met with water hoses, police dogs, and violent acts of police and white people. The number of demonstrators increased to some 3,000 and there were 1,000 arrests. The repressiveness of the police united a hitherto-divided black community in Birmingham. And it produced perhaps the first major case since the second World War in which Southern blacks threw rocks and bottles at police. From this time on, violence deepened and spread among blacks. The Birmingham riots immediately touched off a response in other cities—according to one estimate, 758 demonstrations in the 10 weeks following the Birmingham violence. And in 6 weeks of that 1963 summer, blacks (in Birmingham and elsewhere) succeeded in getting some 200 lunch counters and other public facilities desegrated.

The combined effect of substantial, though slow, progress in employment, housing, education, and voting did not have the effect of quieting blacks or stopping the Negro rebellion of the 1960's. The full-fledged riots of Los Angeles in 1965 and Newark and Detroit in 1967 have been amply studied, at least from the descriptive viewpoint. But there is a tendency to see these events in isola-

tion. It is recognized that riots in one place will touch off riots in another or—
more likely—in several others, but the social-contagion theory (including the contagion of seeing African nations liberated after the Second World War) by no
means gets to the roots of the rebellion. And neither does the notion that
blacks are frustrated and are striking out rather blindly at the centuries of
repression. If 300 years of repression have been too much, why were 200 or
280 not enough to produce rebellion?

What is striking is the time sequence of events. As in major historic revolutions, the events relating to the 1960's rebellion consist of a rather long period
of rising expectations followed by a relatively brief period of frustration that
struck deep into the psyches of black people. And I suggest that from the 17th
to the early-20th century there has been very little development beyond mere
physical survival for virtually all black people in America (and in Africa). It is
significant to note that in the prosperous 1960's, there was no sharp or sudden
rise in unemployment of blacks. There was no marked deprivation of material
goods to which blacks had become accustomed. But there was, starting notably in 1963, not the first instance of violence against blacks but a sudden increase in it. This resurgence of violence came after, and interrupted, the slow
but steady progress since 1940. It quickly frustrated rising expectations.

This increase in violence, commencing so to speak with the firehoses and
police dogs in May 1963 in Birmingham, affronted not only the physical safety
of the demonstrators, thereby reactivating anxiety and fear of bodily harm itself—the most basic of human concerns. This increase in violence also affronted
the dignity of black people as human beings. Black people sensed that their
various and continuously rising expectations, now confronted with violence,
were to rise no more.

In addition to this violence between whites against blacks and of blacks
against whites, there has been an explosive growth of private acts of violence of
blacks against blacks. This has newly activated the fear for physical safety
itself. And the ever-growing congestion in the slums has worsened housing
conditions.

White people who fail to understand their own past and their own ever-
rising expectations (if we have one car, we must have two; if we finished 4
years of college, our son must become a doctor or a lawyer) are puzzled at the
dissatisfaction of blacks who have made such considerable progress since the
Second World War. But what would be odd about blacks, and indicate that
they indeed had some special nature, would be for them to be satisfied in present circumstances. The very rapidity of their advance makes them expect to
continue its pace. The very low point from which they started makes them
expect to reach equality within a few years or at the very most a few decades.
Their mental processes are operating in an altogether normal manner. They
would be less than human if they acted otherwise.

Figure 19-5 and Table 19-1, the latter devised by Harmon Zeigler with the
assistance of Jerry B. Jenkins, represent one striking index of the origin and
time sequence of black frustrations. He chooses, as the items to form his index,
average family income and average years of schooling. He divides the former
by the latter, for the total U.S. population and for the nonwhite population
(which is about 95 percent black), from 1940 to 1967, using U.S. Census Bureau data. The increase and decrease in the gap between what an average

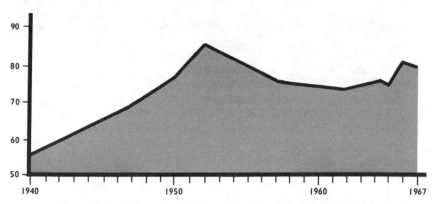

Figure 19-5.—Index of nonwhite economic satisfaction, 1940-67.[a]
[a]For data see table 19-1.

family and a nonwhite family of given educational level gets in income becomes Zeigler's measure of frustration.

If black and white workers with the same amount of education were earning the same income, there would be no difference in the indexes between the two categories of people. As the chart indicates, nonwhites were closest to earning the same amount as the total population in 1952. They rose from 58 percent in 1940 to 86 percent in 1952, but declined after 1952 to a low of 74 percent in 1962. They did not return to their relative status of 1940, but they lost substantial ground compared with where they were in 1952.

If the education-income relationship were the only one involved in producing frustration in people as their expectations and gratifications diverge, we could have expected a peak of unrest sometime in the mid-1950's. It came later—by my reckoning in 1963. This suggests that the gap formed from the increased incidence of violence on the part of police and white citizens provided the quantum of energy necessary to raise black frustrations to the point of rebellion. Figure 19-6 shows the developments.

Two ways are possible of resolving the problem that arises when the expectations-gratifications gap develops—and perhaps there are others. One way to close the growing gap is to attempt to deprive blacks in America of all the gains that they have made since at least the beginning of the Second World War. These gains have been mostly in the satisfaction of their physical needs (in jobs and housing); their social and their dignity needs are beginning to gain prominence. In George Orwell's phrase, we may call this the technique of the boot stamping in a human face forever. If white people were to attempt and even succeed in so reducing black people to a life that consisted of trying to stay alive—the life they lived under slavery and, most of them, for two to four generations after emancipation—black rebelliousness could be contained. In the process white prople would be reduced to the same animal-like behavior that they themselves were imposing on blacks, just as concentration camp guards and concentration camp inmates came to resemble each other in appearance and behavior.

A second way to resolve the problem is to recognize and help them to satisfy their expectations, which fundamentally are the expectations which degraded white people in decades and centuries long past have themselves achieved—

Table 19-1—Origin and time sequence of black frustrations.

Explanation

Col. 1: $\dfrac{\text{Social want satisfaction}}{\text{Social want formation}}$ = systemic frustration

Col. 2: $\dfrac{\text{Social want satisfaction (nonwhite)}}{\text{Social want formation (nonwhite)}}$ = frustration (nonwhite)

Col. 3: Index of satisfaction (nonwhite)   Col. 4: Index of frustration (nonwhite)

	1	2	3	4
	Average family income divided by average years of schooling for—		Nonwhite satisfaction	Nonwhite frustration
Year	Total population	Nonwhite population	Nonwhite percentage of total population frustration level (100 percent would represent equality of want satisfaction relative to want formation between nonwhites and total)	Percentage difference between nonwhite population and that of total population (derived by subtracting col. 3 from 100 percent)
1940[a]	$\dfrac{\$1,231}{8.4} = 146.3$	$\dfrac{\$489}{5.8} = 84.3$	$\dfrac{84.3}{146.3} = 57.5$	42.5
1947	$\dfrac{\$3,031}{9.0} = 336.8$	$\dfrac{\$1,614}{6.9} = 233.9$	$\dfrac{233.9}{336.8} = 69.4$	30.6
1950	$\dfrac{\$3,319}{9.3} = 356.9$	$\dfrac{\$1,869}{6.8} = 274.9$	$\dfrac{274.9}{356.9} = 77.0$	23.0
1952	$\dfrac{\$3,890}{10.1} = 385.1$	$\dfrac{\$2,338}{7.1} = 329.3$	$\dfrac{329.3}{385.1} = 85.5$	14.5
1957	$\dfrac{\$4,971}{10.6} = 469.0$	$\dfrac{\$2,764}{7.7} = 359.0$	$\dfrac{359.0}{469.0} = 76.5$	23.5
1960	$\dfrac{\$5,620}{10.6} = 530.2$	$\dfrac{\$3,233}{8.2} = 394.3$	$\dfrac{394.3}{530.2} = 74.4$	25.6
1962	$\dfrac{\$5,956}{11.4} = 522.5$	$\dfrac{\$3,330}{8.6} = 387.2$	$\dfrac{387.2}{522.5} = 74.1$	25.9
1964	$\dfrac{\$6,559}{11.7} = 560.6$	$\dfrac{\$3,839}{8.9} = 431.3$	$\dfrac{431.3}{560.6} = 77.0$	23.0
1965	$\dfrac{\$6,957}{11.8} = 589.6$	$\dfrac{\$3,994}{9.0} = 443.8$	$\dfrac{0.5740}{0.7627} = 75.3$	24.7
1966	$\dfrac{\$7,436}{12.0} = 619.7$	$\dfrac{\$4,628}{9.2} = 503.0$	$\dfrac{0.6223}{0.7666} = 81.2$	18.8
1967			79.8	20.2

[a] 1940 income figures are actually for 1939, and are for families and unrelated individuals.

   SA: 1952. (73d ed.), p. 111: median school years (1947, 1957, and 1964-67).
   SA: 1965. (86th ed.), p. 112: median school years 1960.
   SA: 1966. (87th ed.), p. 340: median family income: (1947, 1950, 1952, 1957, 1959, 1960, 1962, and 1964).

NOTE—The frustration index and tables were devised by Harmon Zeigler with the help of Jerry B. Jenkins

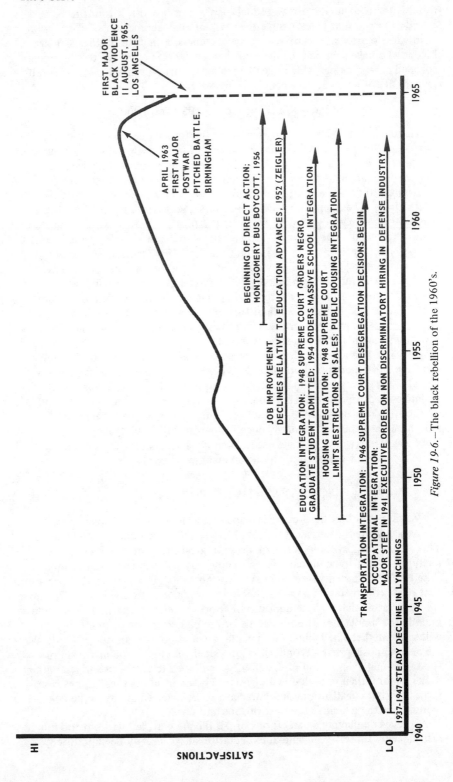

Figure 19-6. – The black rebellion of the 1960's.

notably the recognition of their equal dignity and worth. It is not to be supposed or hoped that black people then will at last become satisfied, any more than white people who achieve dignity become satisfied. But at least those blacks who have achieved dignity will then be that much closer to becoming fulfilled human beings, able at last to realize themselves in the climate of self-respect that is necessary for people to grow.

Student Rebellions of the 1950 and 1960's

These rebellions seemingly commenced first among university students in Japan and then began in the United States and in Western and Central Europe. Partly because of space limitations, it is impossible to assess the J-curve as a device for explaining these particular rebellions. Part of the reason for deferring an attempt to do so lies in the continuing complexity of related events.

It is true, for example, that living quarters and classrooms for French students were getting progressively worse as the postwar French wave of newborn children reached university age. Expectations rose and were frustrated, contributing to the May 1968 riots. It is true that the 1964 Berkeley riots followed soon after enforcement of a previously unenforced rule against on-campus fund solicitation for off-campus organizations. Expectations had risen and were frustrated. And it is true that American university students who were raised with expectations of a bright future have seen their hopes disappointed when faced with military service in Vietnam. These explanations may be the central ingredients of the rebellious mood.

But these phenomena are not quite new. Students have previously been crowded and otherwise disappointed. What is new is the occasional use of violence. The reasons for resort to this technique are not clear. The amount of violence—as distinguished from nonviolent direct action, which people tend incorrectly to read as violence—is not great but it is real. When black people, who have been the victims of violence for centuries, use violence, it is comprehensible. When white students use it, the reasons remain obscure enough to cause at least this writer to postpone an attempt to explain.

SOME TENTATIVE CONCLUSIONS

We have seen that the J-curve is a necessary though not sufficient part of the explanation of at least several revolutions and some contained rebellions. This J-curve is a psychological, not a sociological explanation. The units of analysis are individual human beings. They may fall into visible categories (like blacks or students or working men or peasants), but their mental processes that relate to frustration and aggression are fundamentally the same. That is, we are positing that anyone deprived of food—whether his normal circumstances include the simple diet of poor people or the elaborate one of rich people—will suddenly become inclined to break any social convention to get food. We are also supposing that anyone who is physically secure in the provision of food, clothing, health, and physical safety will seek to establish and strengthen social ties and then to seek equal dignity. The demand for these things is so profound that constitutions and laws have to be made to adapt to the demands—not the demands to constitutions and laws.

If the ever-emerging expectations of people are gratified without too much resistance by those whose similar expectations have already been gratified, then revolution and rebellion are unlikely. If they are not, orderly political processes are displaced by violence. It was that way with out ancestors; it is that way now. And it is that universal a phenomenon. Lawmakers as well as clerks, businessmen as well as laborers, professors as well as students would react the same if suddenly deprived of the goods and dignity they had come to expect in the normal course of life. They would be less than human if they too did not become angry.

References

References on the French Revolution

Ralph W. Greenlaw, ed., *The Economic Origins of the French Revolution,* Boston: D.C. Health, 1958. A very useful collection of essays.

Georges Lefebvre, *The Coming of the French Revolution* (1939), New York: Vintage Books, 1957. Probably the best single volume to date on the causes of the French Revolution.

Alexis de Tocqueville, *The Old Regime and the French Revolution* (1856), New York: Doubleday Anchor Books, 1955. This hundred-year-old classic is still the best starting point for studying origins of the French Revolution.

References on the Civil War

W. J. Cash, *The Mind of the South* (1941), New York: Vintage Books, 1960. A penetrating, passionate, and fairminded view of the outlook of Southerners before and after the Civil War.

M. B. Hammond, *The Cotton Industry: An Essay in American Economic History,* New York, 1897. A valuable statistical source.

Robert R. Russel, *Economic Aspects of Southern Sectionalism: 1840-1861,* Urbana: University of Illinois Press, 1924. An excellent economic analysis of the pre-Civil War South, demonstrating the very rapid growth of that economy before the war.

U.S. Bureau of the Census, *Historical Statistics of the United States: 1789-1945,* Washington, D.C.: U.S. Government Printing Office, 1949. An invaluable statistical source.

References on the Nazi Revolution

Theodore Abel, *The Nazi Movement* (1938), New York: Atherton Press, 1965. An excellent, careful explanation of the socioeconomic and psychic appeal of nazism, based on direct and systematic reports of 600 Germans who chose nazism freely.

Hadley Cantril, *The Psychology of Social Movements,* New York: Wiley, 1941. Still a classic study of why people join fascist (and other social) movements.

Statistischen Reichsamt, *Statistisches Jahrbuch für das Deutsche Reich,* Berlin. The volumes from 1920 on are an official source of a wide variety of crucial statistical data.

Gustav Stolper, *The German Economy, 1870-1940,* New York: Reynal & Hitchcock, 1940. A source of economic indexes from the imperial to the Nazi periods.

References on the Black Rebellion

There are excellent sources of bibliography in such primary sources as the *Report of the National Advisory Commission on Civil Disorders.* Data used here came from the *Encyclopaedia Britannica Book of the Year* (1938-68) and from the U.S. Census Bureau's *Current Population Reports.*

General References on Revolution and Rebellion

Crane Brinton, *The Anatomy of Revolution* (1938), New York: Vintage Books, 1955.
This oft-revised classic is the best introduction to the study of revolution.

James C. Davies, "Toward a Theory of Revolution," *American Sociological Review*, vol.
XXVII (Feb. 1962), pp. 5-19. This is the original statement of the J-curve.

James C. Davies, *Human Nature in Politics*, New York: Wiley, 1963. The first two
chapters develop a politically oriented theory of human needs; the concluding chapter
relates to growth processes that relate to revolution.

James C. Davies, "The Circumstances and Causes of Revolution," *Journal of Conflict
Resolution*, vol. XI (June 1967), pp. 247-257. A critical view of the state of knowledge about revolution in the mid-1960's.

John Dollard et al., *Frustration and Aggression*, New Haven: Yale University Press, 1939.
This is the initial and still basic statement of the frustration-aggression nexus, necessary
for understanding revolution psychologically.

Harry Eckstein, "On the Etiology of Internal Wars," in George H. Nadel, ed., *Studies in
the Philosophy of History*, New York: Harper Torchbooks, 1965, pp. 117-147.
Like the Laqueur essay below, a good brief starting point.

Frantz Fanon, *The Wretched of the Earth*, New York: Grove Press, 1968. The most inti-
mate analysis of the roots of political violence that I have seen. Based on the author's
psychiatric work with patients in Algeria who had experienced or used violence during
the final years before Algeria's independence.

Walter Laqueur, "Revolution," *International Encyclopedia of the Social Sciences*, vol.
13, New York: Macmillan, 1968, pp. 501-507. A good, brief starting place.

O. Mannoni, *Prospero and Caliban: The Psychology of Colonization*, New York: Praeger,
1964. A brilliant study of the tensions resulting from the confrontation of individuals
from an advanced cultural state with those from an undeveloped condition. The effects on both the dominant and the subordinate individuals are elegantly analyzed.

Abraham H. Maslow, "A Theory of Human Motivation," *Psychological Review*, vol. L
(July 1943), pp. 370-396. The first statement of the hierarchy of basic needs, a theory
that is very helpful in understanding how people varying from poor to rich, educated
and uneducated, can join together to overthrow a government.

Mancur Olson, Jr., "Rapid Growth as a Destabilizing Force," *Journal of Economic History*,
vol. XXIII (Dec. 1963), pp. 529-552. An economist's statement of what happens
when an economy causes people to get dislocated and less poor because the economy
is developing rapidly. Applies to some of the effects not only on American blacks but
also on developing nations.

Thomas F. Pettigrew, "Social Evaluation Theory: Consequences and Applications," in
David Levine, ed., *Nebraska Symposium on Motivation*, Lincoln: University of Nebraska
Press, 1967, pp. 241-315. A synthesis of research and theory relative to how people
see each other in the eyes of others. If self-esteem is indeed not separable from others'
esteem of self, then this is a major theoretical contribution. It applies to the black
rebellion particularly and to the mental outlook of potential revolutionaires, anywhere
and any time.

George Wada and James C. Davies, "Riots and Rioters," *Western Political Quarterly*, vol.
X (Dec. 1957) pp. 864-874. Based on riots that took place in the relocation centers
for Japanese in the United States during the Second World War, this study distinguishes
the riot participants from the nonparticipants on grounds of the social marginality of
the former.

Chapter 20

BATISTA AND BETANCOURT: ALTERNATIVE RESPONSES TO VIOLENCE

By Edward W. Gude*

Governmental response to violence is of both theoretical and practical importance. On the most obvious level, it takes two parties to generate a cycle of violence—insurgents and government forces. Police-type action in response to terrorism is at one end of the coercive response scale, military counterinsurgency at the other. All such responses interact with those of the insurgents in the revolutionary processes. On the practical level, governmental response is the side of the equation over which governments obviously have some control.

Much analysis has focused upon the strategy and tactics of revolutionaries, as a means for assessing how governments ought to respond. This focus assumes that government forces are reactive, neglecting the important effect the government forces themselves have on the course of strategy and tactics of insurgents. In actuality, revolutions are made by both insurgents and governments. Mistakes or excesses committed by government forces are as responsible for the collapse of established regimes as are the tactics of the insurgents. This essay examines one aspect of the revolutionary process—governmental responses—in two cases: Cuba under Batista and Venezuela under Betancourt.

THEORETICAL CONSIDERATIONS

It can be argued that revolutionary politics are but an extension of violent politics of less severity. Revolutionary politics exaggerates the implications of governmental actions in such a way as to make clearer the implications of this part of the equation. Some argue that violence signals the end of politics and that force becomes the sole arbiter. This military view of politics sharply differentiates the normal nonviolent processes of governing societies from those involving force. This view usually does not differentiate between means, in this case violence, and process, in this case politics. Certainly when violence

*The author is assistant professor of political science at Dartmouth College and author of "Political Violence in Venezuela: 1958-1964," in James C. Davies, ed., *When Men Revolt—and Why* (New York: The Free Press, forthcoming).

is introduced, a new form of communications and bargaining emerges on both sides. Symbols are partially displaced by violence as the means and substance of politics, but the processes of maintaining legitimacy continue to be the task of governing.

In the military view of violence in politics, the most important criterion of success is usually violent confrontation of military and paramilitary forces. When this becomes the overwhelming objective, the political implications of the use of force become lost. Kill ratios are substituted for support ratios. In the political view, conflict is basic to politics and is handled in more peaceful times by the process of allocation of resources in response to various demands in such a way that a government maintains support, a sense of legitimacy, and an adherence to these more peaceful means. This allocation of resources involves both substantive and symbolic rewards. While in these more peaceful times the allocation of symbolic and substantive rewards is accomplished by bargaining and communication whose primary content is symbols, in less peaceful times violence becomes part of this process. The goals of government, however, remain the same: to maintain support and a sense of legitimacy.

Before violence can become a factor, there must be a governmental failure to maintain support or legitimacy; otherwise there would be no basis for a serious threat to it. Even a few hundred dedicated revolutionaries would be captured in short order if no portion of the community was willing to provide them some protection. Any willingness to give such protection is an indication of decline of support and legitimacy of government. Any government in such a situation must conduct itself so as not to increase the loss of support and legitimacy. Organized violence in this sense is a signal of political trouble within regimes, not only a signal of the existence of a group dedicated to changing the means and content of the political process. It signifies that a government has failed to maintain adherence to more peaceful means.

In this perspective a government must do more than eliminate a few revolutionaries, for if there has been a decline in popular support and legitimacy, they can be easily replaced. A government so threatened by violence must continue to seek its political goals. It is potentially disastrous to lose sight of political objectives in the effort to stop violence.

Two important concepts have a bearing on this problem: legality and legitimacy. Officials naturally tend to see problems in legal perspective, in terms of the prescribed rules governing peaceful political bargaining as well as personal behavior. A legal system can function, however, only so long as there is popular consensus and legitimacy for that system of laws and rules. The introduction of violence as a means in the political process indicates that there has been at least a partial breakdown in support. To view events only in conventional legal terms at such a time is to exclude from consideration the attitudes of a significant portion of the polity. In a situation in which the legal system has partially broken down, it is important to shift the perspective from the formal legal level to the underlying sense of legitimacy. Only when legitimacy becomes the locus of concern is it possible to pursue the political objective of maintaining support.

If actions are categorized as they are in the following table, there is an inherent bias against recognizing the broader threat of violence.

The legal perspective leads to consideration only of cells I and IV in the chart: government actions are assumed to be legal, insurgent actions illegal. This is

	Acts of—	
	Government	Insurgents
Legal	I	II
Illegal	III	IV

further complicated by the fact that governments are primarily responsible for the promulgation of law.

Violence becomes a factor in politics either when some individuals recognize the illegality of their acts yet consider them legitimate, or when they recognize the legality of government acts yet consider them illegitimate. By replacing the concept of legality with legitimacy, we can more easily see the problem facing a regime:

	Acts of—	
	Government	Insurgents
Legitimate	I	II
Illegitimate	III	IV

In this formulation it is possible to define relatively peaceful political times as those in which most acts of violence are perceived to be on the I and IV axis. But the greater the number of people who attribute legitimacy to acts of insurgents and illegitimacy to acts of government, the more threatening the situation is for government. This formulation is independent of the actual level of violence; violence is significant when citizens' perceptions fall in the II-III axis. Thus a shift in popular attitudes from the I-IV axis to the II-III axis signals the introduction of violent politics. This can be summarized in a proposition: Political stability varies directly with the proportion of citizens whose perceptions fall on the governmental axis (I-IV), and inversely with the proportion whose perceptions are on the insurgent axis (II-III). The greater the rate of change from the governmental to the insurgent axis, the greater the decline in stability. It is the nature and rate of change in perceptions of legitimacy that are crucial for stability, not the absolute level of violence. This relationship may be stated more precisely, as follows: Political stability is equal to the rate of change of perceptions from the I-IV axis to the II-III axis, or

$$PS = \frac{d}{dt}\left[\frac{(I + IV)}{(II + III)}\right]$$

This formulation provides a basis for evaluating the impact of governmental and insurgent actions in the course of violent politics. It subsumes several other important factors such as outside support for either party, degree of organization of the revolutionary movement, particular ethnic or class differences within the polity, terrain, ethical tradition, and many others. For the purposes of comparative analysis, they might well be tested only as they affect the overall perceptions by significant groups of the legitimacy of the acts of governments and of insurgents. The one other factor that might be singled out for attention is the degree of revolutionary organization and skill, which is important for assessing whether a government was lucky or skillful in defeating an insurgent movement. After all, revolutionaries can make critical mistakes as well as governments.

One way to look at the impact of the organization and skill of revolutionaries is to assess the impact of this factor on the probability of successful revolution. To do this we might consider figure 20-1. The probability of successful revolution is a function of the position of the curve, which in turn is dependent on the degree of revolutionary skill and organization. At a given level of political stability (A) we have differing probabilities of successful revolution (B, C), depending on the curve for a particular level of skill and organization. The upper curve denotes a higher level of skill and organization than the lower.

As we have developed these concepts, it is obvious that a government has more control over the level of political stability than revolutionary organization. Thus it is less able to affect the position of the curve than the position of point A. Effective police and military tactics, especially intelligence, can affect the skill and organization of the revolutionaries, but the fundamental fact is that these must be carried out in such a way as to keep point A stationary or move it to the right of the chart. Governmental actions frequently do reduce the effectiveness of revolutionaries, but if this is accompanied by a shift toward governmental illegitimacy, and a consequent shift in level of political stability in the direction of D, the probability of revolutionary success is not reduced.

The primary focus of this essay, then, is to examine the political and military actions of governments under threat of violence, with reference to their effects first on the degree of political stability and on revolutionary organization and skill, and finally on the overall probability of successful revolution. This is at least as much a political problem as a military one: the determining factor, according to this analysis, is the perception of the legitimacy of acts by significant groups within the polity.

Violent politics characteristically involve only a few active participants. The number of revolutionaries is never large in comparison with the population as a whole. Similarly, the number actively involved on the governmental

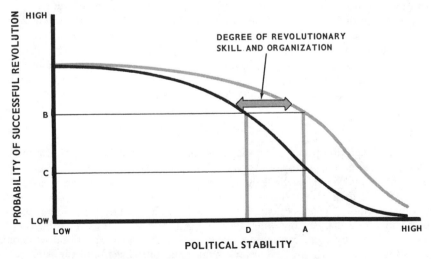

Figure 20-1.—Probability of successful revolution.

side is small. The large majority of citizens are not mobilized to the struggle. One of the primary tasks of a regime is to avoid losing further support; the goal of the insurgents is the converse. The decline in political stability that characterizes the revolutionary situation inclines many people to take a hesitant and more critical attitude toward the regime than is usually the case. They frequently develop a skeptical "wait and see" attitude, which makes the task of government that much more difficult. A regime needs positive support if it is to get the necessary intelligence and cooperation needed to weather a revolutionary situation. The insurgents, on the other hand, need only for the majority to withdraw support from the government. In the early phases they do not need positive revolutionary support.

In pursuit of these objectives, insurgents attempt through violence to demonstrate that the government cannot provide public safety. This is a relatively simple task for terrorists. A more important objective involves the attempt to induce the regime to commit acts against the uncommitted so that they will withdraw their support from the government. This involves inducing a government to overrespond and commit acts that citizens will consider illegitimate (even though they may be technically legal). In the battle for differential political mobilization, the task of the government is enormously delicate and requires political leadership of tremendous sophistication to avoid falling into the traps set by revolutionary violence.

If the assumptions that underlie this analysis are correct, then the political tasks of a government faced with revolutionary violence must determine and take precedence over the military tasks. Excessive military action can lead to a reduction in the organization and skill of an insurgent movement, but if done at the cost of increasing the number of people who perceive the acts of government as illegitimate, it is a pyrrhic victory.

The cases of Cuba under Batista and Venezuela under Betancourt provide a useful comparative test of these ideas. The analysis in this essay is of necessity incomplete, but nevertheless sheds some light on the relationship of violence to politics. The relationship of political processes dominated by largely symbolic communications and bargaining to those in which violence becomes a factor is most clearly illuminated by discussing extreme cases of revolutionary potential, which these are. Similar analysis could be used to discuss the earlier phases of violent politics, in which the shift to violent means initially occurred. The same demands, pitfalls, and opportunities exist.

CUBA UNDER BATISTA

When Fulgencio Batista seized power in the coup of March 1952, shortly before a scheduled election, he set in motion the violent processes that led to his flight on New Year's Day of 1959. Batista was an obscure sergeant when he led his first revolt in 1933, against the regime of Gerardo Machado. He dominated the government for the next 10 years, until his voluntary retirement in 1944. In 1952, during his attempt at a legal comeback, the election polls found him a poor third. This apparently motivated his trip to Camp Columbia, Cuba's most important military base, to lead his second coup. Although the popular outcry was great, little opposition immediately developed. Fidel Castro, who had been a candidate for Congress when the coup interupted the campaign, attempted to challenge the legality of the move but the courts refused to consider the issue. These events convinced many that the peaceful route to social or political change was rather a losing proposition. The attack on the Moncada barracks on July 26, 1953, was the first step in Castro's rise to power. Although the attack was an absolute failure militarily, it became the symbol of resistance and provided as well the name of Castro's organization, the July 26th Movement.

Much has been written of how Castro, after release from prison, went to the hills and organized a peasant revolution. This myth has been most recently enshrined in the writings of Regis Debray. While it is true that Castro landed with 82 men in 1956, after a period of training and organization in Mexico, only 12 of this group reached the mountains. The others were killed or captured and tortured. In the Sierra Maestra base he was able to build a group of some 180 men by the spring of 1958—certainly not a formidable band compared with the 30,000 American-trained troops at Batista's disposal. Even late in 1958 the total rural guerrilla force numbered about a thousand, with some 7,000 in the urban underground. It was this latter group that became the backbone of the revolutionary movement.

The Castro forces themselves did engage in some terrorism and raids on supply stores, but they did not constitute a serious military threat. In fact, even to the end they avoided a large-scale military confrontation with the Army. It is certainly true that Castro became an important symbol of the revolution via his frequent radio broadcasts over clandestine stations and other publicity he received both in and out of Cuba. In order to achieve even this base of support, it was necessary for the guerrila band to develop friendly relations with local peasants for logistics and intelligence. This Castro certainly did.

How could a band of several hundred, finally a thousand, guerrillas bring down a government? Clearly they did not do so alone. Operating in almost all urban areas were significant underground organizations led by numerous leaders, mostly unheralded. These forces harassed and terrorized the government, provoking the most brutal of responses. It is clear that counterterror became the strategy of the Batista government.[1] Everyone suspected of the slightest disloyalty was subjected to the threat of arrest, torture, and even death. The urban underground was not comprised solely of middleclass ex-students, the mainstay of the Castro forces. Its members included much of the political and professional elite of the country, as well as many skilled workers.

Batista's forceful accession to power had deprived him of much of the legitimacy normally associated with a constitutional government.[2] With marginal support from the start, he apparently did not think it necessary to seek a broader base of political support. Through his police he succeeded in alienating much of the middle class, who otherwise were not totally unsympathetic to the government's efforts to restore law and order. When police efforts focused on the sons of the middle class, this potential support evaporated. Batista acted as though he accepted Mao's dictum that power comes out of the barrel of a gun.

The record of the Batista police and military is impressive if only for its thoroughness. Approximately half of the government forces were tied down with the urban problem, some 15,000 troops. It has been estimated by some that as many as 20,000 civilians were tortured or killed by the government from 1956 until the end of 1958. This is a victor's figure, but even if exaggerated by a factor of 2 or 3, it represents a tremendous number for such a small country. It is not difficult to see how so many families could be affected.

Throughout this struggle the question of legality seemed to lose importance—there was little legality anywhere. The overriding consideration became the legitimacy of guerrilla terror and governmental counterterror. The rebel forces took great care to develop tactics that alienated as few people as possible. Thus, when burning sugarfields brought great hardship on the peasants as well as the landowners, it was discontinued. The government lacked this sensitivity and continued to use tactics that offended many.

The acts of the insurgents were not so much considered legitimate, as the governmental acts illegitimate. This affected the shift from the stable axis (I-IV) to the unstable axis (II-III): the political consequences of the governmental use of force significantly increased the probability of successful revolution. At the same time the rural and urban resistance groups gained experience that increased their ability to operate in a police state and their sensitivity to popular reactions and cooperation.

This process must be understood in the context of full-scale revolutionary violence. In addition to the selective raids for military supplies, the insurgents carried out numerous assassinations of particularly hated figures of the Batista regime and other serious acts of terrorism. Students made an abortive attempt on the dictator's life in March 1957 that brought particularly severe reprisals. Other acts of revolutionary terrorism were carried out to demonstrate that the government could not provide physical security for the population.

Another revolutionary stratagem was a general strike called for April 8, 1958. The strike was a debacle, since it exposed so much of the revolutionary organization to police reprisals. The refusal of Communists to cooperate in the strike insured its failure. It was not until the pact of Caracas, signed in July 1958, that the various revolutionary groups were able to agree to a degree of cooperation necessary to avoid such failures. The agreement brought the several groups under the nominal leadership of Castro, by then the best known of the leaders. The weakness of this coalition is revealed in the rapid factionalization that occurred after January 1959, in which the rural (but decidedly not peasant) faction gained tentative ascendancy.

The actions of the police during 1957 and 1958 were significant in that they served to alienate signifcant factions from the government. Because the revolution was primarily middle class in composition, counterterrorism particularly affected that class: This was particularly counterproducive because the police and military themselves were soon affected. Military morale and discipline rapidly declined to the point that the spring offensive of 1958, which pitted 10,000 or-more troops against the few hundred Castro forces in the mountains, failed completely. This failure seemed to signal to the populace that the government was no longer viable.[3]

Given its internal divisions, lack of meanful coordination, poor communications, and extremely limited numbers, it is difficult to see how the revolutionary movement succeeded except as a consequence of the ineptitude of Batista. He repeatedly fell into the trap set by the insurgents by reacting viciously with his own forces. The insurgents demonstrated that the government could not prevent violence; the police and military then proceeded to engage in counterterror perceived by many as illegitimate. In the race for differential mobilization, the regime fared badly.

Having only limited popular support after the 1952 coup, Batista tried "free" elections, amnesty, and similar moves to bolster his regime. All of these failed to attract significant popular support, however, and as a result many Cubans were uncommitted before revolutionary violence began. The significant events of the revolution were the steps by which this uncommitted group shifted increasingly to the side of the insurgents.[4] The Batista regime appeared unable to control the revolutionary violence, no matter how violent its own response, promising only civil war for the future. The popular relief at Batista's flight probably reflected as much a hope for an end to violence as it did positive support for the insurgents, but this just as surely represents the failure of government.

In summary, the Cuban revolution can be interpreted as a case in which a middle-class insurgency in both urban and rural areas, without substantial peasant or working class participation, brought down a regime. The trigger of terrorism and violence of the insurgents opened the floodgates of police and military reprisals, which alienated the significant uncommitted segment of the population. This sealed the fate of the regime by tipping the scales of political mobilization in favor of the insurgents.

VENEZUELA UNDER BETANCOURT

Romulo Betancourt gained power under the most difficult of circumstances in February 1959. The dictatorship of Perez Jimenez had brought both economic and political havoc to the country. The tens and probably hundreds of millions of dollars lost in graft had left the nation in a state of bankruptcy. Oil resources had been squandered through new concessions that never reached the national treasury, public works projects had been established to appease labor with no meaningful program of payment, and there was lavish spending on the military to maintain their support. The country was in the most serious of crises in terms of maintaining its ability to govern.[5] When students and others finally brought down the Perez regime in early 1958, the intervening junta was hesitant to act decisively since its members had programed a return to civilian rule within the year. This meant an additional year in which conditions did not improve.

In addition to the difficult economic position, the factions that had momentarily united against Jimenez reappeared. A considerable faction within the military felt threatened by the end of military rule. Throughout the immediate postcoup period there were recurrent rumors of plots and several actual attempts at overthrow. Castro Leon, almost pathologically opposed to the possibility of rule by Romulo Betancourt and the Acción Democrática (AD) Party, which won the election of December 1958, was particularly active in antigovernment activity. There were serious attempts in July and September of 1958, October of 1959, and April 1960. All of these attempts involved the classic techniques of the military coup. They did not involve the mobilization of the population; the dynamics of political violence as we have defined them were not involved. Such seizures of government, if successful, present the public with a fait accompli with little chance to intervene.

When the Acción Democrátia Party was first in power, in 1945, Betancourt was not sufficiently sensitive to support from the military and the party was thrown out in 1948. In 1959 the newly elected President was wiser, carefully courting the advice and support of the various leaders in the military. It was his success in holding the majority of the military to his side that led to the failures of some right wing military leaders.

Leftwing political violence dates from a split in the AD party. A younger faction of the party had been active in the underground during the Jimenez regime, while leaders such as Betancourt were in exile. In this period members of the faction had worked actively with the radical faction of the Communist Party. Becoming disenchanted with the pace of reform under Betancourt, this group broke with the party in 1960 and formed the Movement of the Revolutionary Left (MIR). Members of this group became convinced that violence was the only route to the type of reform they demanded.[6] Against the advice of more seasoned and older Communist leaders, the MIR almost immediately launched a campaign of urban violence, which reached its peak in November 1960. The failure of this attempt at fomenting large-scale riots and strikes resulted in a plan for developing a full revolutionary situation in 1962. The Communist leadership attacked the assumptions, timing, and general plan of the MIR insurgents, causing considerable conflict within the radical movement. Nevertheless the frequency of attacks increased during the ensuing months. The 46 reported serious attacks attributed to it in 1960 may not appear numerous, but the MIR had become a factor to be reckoned with in Venezuelan politics.[7] These early attempts were quite random, probably being used as training missions. Random terrorism takes less planning and skill than robbery or sabotage. Table 20-1 indicates the types of violence used by the MIR during the 1960-

Table 20-1—Leftwing violence in Venezuela, 1960-63.[8]

Type	Percentage distribution of reported leftwing political violence by means employed			
	1960	1961	1962	1963
Riot	17	3	13	5
Assassination	4	9	12	6
Robbery	0	6	9	12
Terrorism	63	60	50	42
Sabotage	5	7	6	2
Other	11	15	10	33
Cases reported	100%	100%	100%	100%
	46	33	120	181

[1]From *El Universal.*

63 period. Random terrorism declined in proportion over this period and more purposive violence such as robbery and sabotage increased. The initial terrorism, in addition to possibly providing training, communicated most distinctly the concerns and commitment of this group.

Throughout 1961 the government was active in attempting to capture the terrorists, though the tactics terrorists used made detection particularly difficult. However, Betancourt was careful not to employ police tactics in an indiscriminate manner so as to alienate innocent victims. During this period there was also the development of significant leftwing support within the military itself. This was manifested in June 1962 with serious risings at Carupano and Puerto Cabello. These risings were used as a pretext by the government to suspend some constitutional guarantees and ban the Communist Party and the MIR. However, the government waited to carry out large-scale public measures against the insurgents until the public had been sufficiently frightened by the seriousness of the uprisings at Carupano and Puerto Cabello. That is, Betancourt waited until the illegitimacy of the insurgent actions was well accepted before making a major move. In this manner he was able to maximize support for the government action. In addition, he did not use the opportunity of suspended constitutional guarantees to attack other political opposition. On the 31st of July 1962, the guarantees were restored.

Continued insurgent activity led, however, to a second suspension on the 7th of October. This time the government went out of its way to enlist the support of major groups within the society. The strong measures against the insurgents were accompanied by successful appeals for support from the military and groups such as labor. Betancourt accelerated action against the insurgents only as the public demands for such action warranted, and was extremely careful to maintain popular and institutional support for his use of counterforce against the insurgents. In this manner he avoided the problem of alienating the innocent who might otherwise have been affected by repression.

The Communist Party became more and more disenchanted with the program of violence, which they regarded as counterproductive.[8] The threat from the left actually increased support for the government. Many factions that might otherwise have been more vocal in opposition united under the threat of violence. In fact, Betancourt was not unmindful of this phenomenon and used it repeatedly in appeals for unity, action, and support. One of the strategies advanced by the insurgents was an attempt to stimulate a military coup against the AD government. They judged that a return to military dictatorship would make recruitment into the revolutionary ranks easier, since it would unite the moderate left with the violent left.[9]   Again, Betancourt used the existence of this plan to convince the military that they must at all costs remain loyal to avoid falling in with the plans of the insurgents themselves. Restraint again was the characteristic of the government action. Throughout the entire period of violent threat, the reported frequency of government acts of violent reactions was closely correlated with the reported acts of the insurgents. This apparently contributed to the impression of legitimacy of the police and military responses. The insurgents during 1962 did not significantly increase the base of their support and the government did not suffer significant defections.

As the elections of December 1963 approached, violence increased rapidly. The insurgents felt that it was necessary either to induce a military coup or to force the government into overreaction before there was a successful transfer of democratic power. Again Betancourt was careful not to overstep his support, and he appeared in public to be responding less forcefully than many would have wished. His was an unstable tightrope to walk, because he was exposed to failure from insufficient action as easily as from excessive action. Because the insurgents were unsuccessful in expanding their scope of operations, the threat against the government did not increase as rapidly as it did in Cuba. A vicious attack on an excursion train in September 1963 provided an opportunity for a very forceful response with large-scale popular support. Betancourt took advantage of this situation to arrest MIR and Communist Party deputies, to use regular military troops in urban areas, and to pass emergency measures. These actions were carried out with the strong support of the military and the public at large. As previously, the Betancourt response to insurgent activity appears to have been commensurate with public judgements about what was appropriate.

As in the case of Cuba, violence remained primarily a middle-class phenomenon. The labor movement, though its members had voted against the AD Party and were a potential base of insurgent support, remained neutral or progovernment during the entire period in spite of the fact that the Communist Party had gained control of the union movement during the Jimenez era.[10] The significant difference in the experience of the two countries lies in the continued support for the government from the Venezuelan middle class, including the military and police.

While the insurgents in Venezuela were probably less highly skilled than the Cubans, the government did not make their job easier by overresponding and thus alienating important middle-class support. Had the government lost the support of this important sector, it is entirely possible that the skill and success of the insurgents would have increased sufficiently to overthrow the government or stimulate a military coup.

The cadre of the insurgents was about a thousand men, more than Castro had in the mountains until the fall of 1959 but less than the combined urban and rural force of insurgents in Cuba. The split between Castro and the Communists was similar to the split in Venezuela. The revolutionary testing ground of the Jimenez period was similar to that of Batista. Given all these similarities it is difficult to assess finally the causes of the failure of the insurgents in Venezuela. It is clear that maintaining support from the middle class as well as labor and the peasants was critical for Betancourt's success. With less political adroitness and more intensive police response, this support could easily have been lost. The AD government was successful in maintaining popular perceptions that the acts of violence fell on the I-IV axis of stability rather than the II-III axis of instability. In addition, the government responses did not lead to significant defections that could have increased the skill and organization of the revolutionary movement. There is one last qualification to this analysis. It is entirely possible that Betancourt was able to minimize the factionalism of his own coalition, the moderate left opposition, and the military by the very threat of the insurgents. Had that threat not existed, Betancourt might not have been able to govern successfully. If so, it is strange irony for the insurgents.[11]

CONCLUDING COMMENTS

In this essay we have examined two cases of revolutionary violence. In one instance—Cuba—the insurgents were successful, in the other—Venezuela—unsuccessful. We have looked at the tactics of the respective governments in terms of the underlying strategy, either political or military; the perception of the legitimacy of acts of violence; and the differential political mobilization that occurs as a consequence. If this analysis is correct, it suggests that a predominately military strategy of eliminating insurgents at all costs is fraught with pitfalls that can benefit the insurgents. It suggests that primary issues for scholarly and policy analysis are popular perception of the legitimacy of the acts of violence committed by insurgents and responded to by government forces, the impact of governmental actions on the organization and skill of the insurgents, and the continuance or withdrawal of support of the largely uninvolved sectors of the population. There are, of course, other relevant factors that would be necessary for a complete comparison of these cases. Outside support, popularity of the existing regime, terrain, objective economic conditions, and others are all of importance. What is argued here is that they are not so critical to the dynamics of the political processes involving violence as the ones chosen for this analysis.

The cases selected were, in addition, ones in which the objectives of the insurgents were the complete overthrow of the regime and system in power. In such cases the dynamic relationship between the violence of both sides and the political process is clearly defined. In cases in which violence is used as a tool of reform rather than revolution, it is likely that the same dynamic relationship exists, although not so clearly evident. The argument is based on the assumption that the critical variable is the perception of the legitimacy of the act of violence, not its legality. Violence in this sense may represent a breakdown in the legal system but not necessarily of politics. No political process is as delicate as one involving significant levels of violence. To lose sight of the political implications of force and violence is to toy with dangerous consequences. Governments can no more hide behind the legality of their acts than insurgents can assume they will have large-scale support. In this dynamic relationship, the violence of governments is more amenable to control than that of insurgents. At the least a government should be able to avoid counterproductive consequences of its own actions.

References

1. David D. Burks, *Cuba Under Castro* (New York: Foreign Association, 1964), p. 8.
2. George I. Blanksten, "Fidelismo and Its Origins: Fidel Castro in Latin America," in Robert Tomasek, ed., *Latin American Politics: 24 Studies of the Contemporary Scene* (Garden City, N.Y.: Doubleday, 1966), p. 369.
3. See Federico Gil, "Antecedents of the Cuban Revolution," *The Centennial Review*, vol. VI (Summer 1962), p. 383.
4. Douglas P. Bwy, "Discerning Causal Patterns Among Conflict Models: A Comprehensive Study of Political Instability in Latin America," unpublished MS., p. 35.
5. Robert J. Alexander, *The Venezuelan Democratic Revolution* (New Brunswick: Rutgers University Press, 1964), pp. 42-43.
6. Atlantic Research Corp., *Castro-Communist Insurgency in Venezuela* (Alexandria, Va.: author, Dec. 31, 1964), pp. 39-53 (mimeo).
7. As reported in the Caracas daily, *El Universal.*
8. See Atlantic Research Corp., *op. cit.,* p. 38.
9. For an important statement of the thinking of the leftists, see Walter H. Slote, "Case Analysis of a Revolutionary," in Frank Bonilla and Jose A. Silva Michelena, *The Politics of Change in Venezuela,* vol. 1: *A Strategy for Research on Social Policy* (Cambridge: M.I.T. Press, 1967), pp. 241-311.
10. Alexander, *op. cit.*
11. See Edward W. Gude, "Political Violence in Venezuela: 1958-1964," in James C. Davies, *When Men Revolt—and Why* (New York: The Free Press, forthcoming), for a fuller treatment of this point.

PART IX
ECOLOGICAL AND ANTHROPOLOGICAL PERSPECTIVES

No scholarly discipline has a primary, much less an exclusive, claim to expertise in explaining the nature, processes, and consequences of violence. Psychiatrists, psychologists, criminologists, and sociologists have all contributed substantially to the understanding of individual violence. The analysis of collective protest and violence has proceeded from the viewpoints of these disciplines as well as those of history and political science. The inadequacy of our understanding of the phenomena of violence is only partly the result of insufficient research. In fact we know a great deal about the subject, as the contributions to this volume testify. One lack is an integrated theoretical and empirical approach to the subject in its entirety, one that overcomes the essentially arbitrary divisions of conventional academic discourse and gives unified, systematic attention to all aspects of the human dispensation to do violence to other humans. The two chapters in this section do not attempt any cross-disciplinary theoretical integration. Rather, they demonstrate the relevance—perhaps a critical relevance—of research in the supposedly more esoteric biological and social sciences for a comprehensive explanation of violence.

It is sometimes assumed that man is an infinitely adaptable being. Whether or not he has an innate disposition to aggression—a matter of dispute among psychologists and students of animal behavior—it usually is held that human aggression is socially determinable, if not entirely socially determined. What is sometimes neglected in analyses

589

based on such assumptions is that there may be a fundamental interaction between men's biological nature and ecological circumstances that increases aggressiveness. The work of Lorenz, Ardrey, and others on territoriality and aggressiveness in animal populations points to one such relationship. In the first of the following chapters, George Carstairs draws on laboratory studies of animal behavior, evidence on the incidence of mental disorder, and the history of millenarian social movements to demonstrate that overcrowding seems to have biological concomitants that heighten disruptive behavior, behavior that is reinforced but not solely caused by social disorganization. The evidence is suggestive, not definitive. It does imply some devastating social consequences of unchecked increases in the density and concentration of human populations.

How do groups respond when they experience external threat or deprivation that seems to threaten their cultural integrity? Perhaps the first answer suggested by a reading of American history is the resort to retaliatory or defensive violence. White Southerners, Northern immigrants, and American Indians all have done so in response to varied external stresses. When the threatened group is relatively powerless, however, quite a different response occurs: its members often attempt to establish and preserve their cultural identity by nonviolent defensive techniques. Bernard J. Siegel describes the nature of these defensive adaptations in the second chapter below. In the American context, examples of groups that have adapted defensively include Pueblo Indians of New Mexico, the Black Muslims, and religious bodies like the Amish, Hutterites, and Mormons. All such groups have certain characteristics in common: in response to perceived stress they develop and enforce detailes and rigorous codes for the regulation of their members' behavior, they increase cultural integration by emphasizing and elaborating a few key cultural values, and they intensify communication within the group and minimize communication with outsiders. The two most general questions raised by the study of defensive groups for the contemporary problems of the United States are these: What effects do they have on the disposition to individual and collective violence? and What are their consequences for the attainment of the American ideal of a culturally and socially integrated national society? The following anthropological analysis implies that they minimize the former but at the cost of raising serious barriers to the latter.

The disciplines represented by these contributions have given relatively little attention to questions of the etiology and consequences of violence. In view of the significance of the findings in hand, how great an increment in knowledge might we have if these and other little-studied aspects of violence were thoroughly examined?

Chapter 21

OVERCROWDING
AND HUMAN AGGRESSION

By George M. Carstairs*

When statisticians warn us about the inevitable consequences if recent population trends are allowed to continue unchecked during the next few generations, our first concern has naturally been over the basic question of survival: Will the world's resources suffice to feed all those extra billions? No sooner have we heard the arguments on this than we find ourselves facing the next question: What will be the quality of the life led by the inhabitants of an overcrowded planet? In particular, what will be the effects of overcrowding on the manifestations of aggression within and between societies?

In former centuries, disease and early death exercised so effective a form of population control that the vast majority of mankind could not indulge in the luxury of aspiring to a high standard of living. Simply to survive into late adulthood, at the same level of subsistence as one's forefathers, was good fortune enough. From the time of the earliest prehistoric civilizations to the present day, in almost every human society, only the privileged elite were in a position to cultivate their sensibilities and to expand the boundaries of human experience and understanding. In London, as recently as the beginning of the present century, the very chances of survival through early infancy were more than twice as high for the children of the rich as for the children of the poor. Throughout the contemporary world, survival has become generally attainable, for rich and poor alike; and now, for the first time in the history of mankind, education, self-awareness, and the aspiration for a meaningful and satisfying life experience are being shared by a majority of people.

Inevitably, once the killing diseases and the threat of starvation have been averted, people become increasingly aware of, and discontented with, minor forms of discomfort or unhappiness. One of the striking changes in morbidity in both highly developed and in developing countries during recent decades has been the apparent increase in neurosis and psychosomatic disorders. These functional illnesses—which some people would prefer to regard as manifestations of "problems of living" rather than of disease—have long been recognized among the privileged classes. Already in 1689, Thomas Sydenham declared that half of his nonfertile patients, that is, one-sixth of his total

*Dr. Carstairs in professor of psychological medicine at the University of Edinburgh.

practice, were hysterical; and in 1733, George Cheyne (in his book entitled *The English Disease*) stated that a third of his patients were neurotic.

Both Sydenham and Cheyne were fashionable physicians, most of whose clientele was drawn from the wealthy minority of the English society of their day. Sydenham himself observed that hysteria was commoner among women of the leisured classes than among those who had to toil. It is only in the present day that the working classes have been in a position to enjoy the luxury of being neurotic; but recent surveys, both in Asia[1] and in Manhattan,[2] have shown that the rates for almost every form of mental illness are highest among the socioeconomically underprivileged sections of contemporary societies.

It must be emphasized that the very marked increase in the "visibility" of mental disorders in most countries of the world is partly due to the better control of infections and other serious physical illnesses. Neurosis is a by-product of a raised level of expectation of the quality of life experience when these higher expectations are denied fulfillment. It can, at times, be manifested as what Charles Kingsley called "divine discontent," a spur toward the further enhancement of the standard of living—provided, of course, that steps can be taken to remedy the adverse environmental factors to which the symptoms of neurosis have drawn our attention.

There are, however, many situations in which individuals feel themselves powerless to better their state: conspicuous instances can be found in the socially disorganized slum areas of great cities, especially in periods of very rapid growth such as that experienced by Chicago and Detroit in the early decades of this century, and by such cities as Tokyo, Calcutta, Rio de Janeiro, and other conurbations after the Second World War. Here we are confronted by this vital question: What will be the consequences, for mental helath, of a continuing massive increase in human populations?

As yet, the science of human behavior is not sufficiently developed to be able to answer this question with precision, or even with confidence. Nevertheless it is possible to learn from studies of animals, both in their natural environment and under experimental conditions, and to note certain regularly occurring consequences of severe overcrowding: with due caution, one can infer some similar repercussions of overcrowding in man. There are also a number of direct observations, in human populations, on the interrelationships between overcrowding and certain indices of mental health, from which we can predict with greater confidence the likely consequences of overcrowding on a still larger scale.

STUDIES OF ANIMAL BEHAVIOR

At first sight, it might seem that much could be learned from observations on species such as lemmings or voles, which are subject to periodic fluctuations of population size. There is still a good deal of controversy among naturalists as to whether these fluctuations are essentially determined by rather gross environmental factors of food supply or infection or whether social interactions also play an important role. Films of lemmings taken during one of their mass migrations have shown that although scarcity of food may be one factor, the movement of the whole population takes on a cumulative momentum as the result of repeated, frenetic interactions, which have been described as showing a hysterical quality.

In recent years the work of ethologists has taught us a great deal about the interaction of innate, biological propensities and learning experiences in many animal species. At a relatively crude level, this can be demonstrated by a modification of the animals' adrenal size and activity. The adrenals play an essential role in an animal's response to stress, whether by fighting or by taking flight. There is a conspicuous difference between the size of the adrenals in wild rats and in rats which have been bred for generations in captivity, the latter having much smaller adrenal glands. When wild rats are caged, and allowed to breed, a diminution in adrenal size becomes apparent in a few generations. In colonies in which there is a great deal of fighting, the mean size of the rats' adrenals increases by up to 30 percent—and this is true both of the aggressors and the victims. Observations in nature have shown marked diminution in adrenal size when rat populations are depleted. For example, the rat population in the sewers of Hamburg at one time became alarmingly large. A vigorous campaign of extermination succeeded literally in decimating their numbers. It was found that the size of the adrenals (in relation to total body size) significantly diminished after the reduction in the rat population. Similar findings were observed when numbers were reduced in an overcrowded herd of deer.

Adrenal activity is stimulated by social interaction, especially by the challenge of attack and the need for counterattack in self-defense. One interesting finding is that the quality of the stress response takes on a different character for the animal that is victorious in the contest. Such an animal can go from strength to strength, able to fight one battle after another; in the intervals of fighting, its sexual potency is also at a high level. In contrast, an animal which undergoes a series of defeats becomes debilitated, even although suffering no obvious physical injury, and is sexually less active. A biologist, Anthony Barnett, has shown that prolonged exposure to even moderate hostility can lead to weakness and death. He has epitomized this reaction as follows: "evidently the bodily response to humiliation resembles, in some ways, that to danger to life or limb."[3] Usually the loser in such contests is able to survive by escaping from the scene of battle and thereafter refraining from challenging its victor; but there are situations, both in the wild and in the captive state, where animals are unable to escape, and are repeatedly confronted by the threat of a contest in which they are doomed to defeat. There are well-authenticated observations, in rats, of the weaker animal's sudden death under such circumstances, and even careful postmortem examination has failed to show any organic trauma sufficient to account for these deaths.[4]

Another instance of the interaction of biological and social factors in the response to stress can be found in observations on the toxity of amphetamine drugs, whose action is similar to that of adrenalin, the secretion of the medulla of the adrenal gland. A relatively small dose of amphetamine will prove fatal to a rat that is confined in a cage with many other rats, whereas a rat that is kept in isolation can survive doses of amphetamine up to four times greater. It is presumed that the effect of the drug is greatly enhanced, in the former situation, by the numerous stressful interations with the other rats, each of which stimulates the output of more adrenalin until complete exhaustion supervenes.

These, of course, represent extremes of overstimulation. Many species of animals and birds have evolved self-protective behavior patterns to insure that such extremes will not occur. Typical of these behavior patterns is the "peck order" or status hierarchy, by virtue of which a group of animals whose members meet each other regularly first fight each other, and then mutually agree to a rank order of ascendancy, after which the animal of inferior status invariably concedes in the face of a challenge from those above him in rank. More detailed studies have shown that status hierarchies can be either *absolute,* whereby every member of a group of animals invariably remains in the same position in relation to each of his fellows, or *relative,* in which under different circumstances of time or place, the individual's respective degrees of ascendancy over one other may change.[5] Absolute status hierarchies are most likely to be found where all the animals in a group share the same living space; they become most clearly defined when that space is a restricted one. Under such circumstances, Barnett has shown that adrenal size becomes inversely correlated with height in the social hierarchy.

Relative dominance is seen most clearly in animals that have individual territories. When on their home ground, they are often able to vanquish an intruder and compel him to retreat, whereas if they are challenged by the same individual on his home territory, they in turn will admit defeat. Many species of birds, and most mammals (including man), exhibit this kind of territorial behavior. Not only football teams, but all of us, tend to perform best on our home ground—mental as well as physical—and to resist anyone who ventures to challenge us there. Naturalists have recognized in territorial behavior, and in the varying degrees of dominance associated with the center and the periphery of the territory, a self-regulating mechanism that insures an optimal degree of dispersion of the species.[6]

When animals such as domestic cats, which customarily enjoy quite a wide range of movement, are crowded together in a limited space, there tends to emerge one particularly tyrannical "despot" who holds all the others in fear and also one or more whom Leyhausen terms "pariahs," at the bottom of the status hierarchy.[7] These unfortunate creatures, he observes, are "driven to frenzy and all kinds of neurotic behavior by continuous and pitiless attack by all the others." Although these "pariahs" bear the severest brunt, the whole community of cats held in such close confinement is seen to suffer. These cats "seldom relax, they never look at ease, and there is continuous hissing, growling and even fighting. Play stops altogether, and locomotion and exercise are reduced to a minimum."[8]

This clearly represents a pathological social situation, in which overcrowding and confinement conspire to accentuate disturbing confrontations between individuals. Another observer, studying the behavior of colonies of rats under different degrees of over-population, observed similar changes in their customary interrelationships. Where overcrowding was most marked, the enforced social interactions were seen to interfere with the satisfaction of quite basic biological needs such as feeding, nest building, and the care of their young. Normally mother rats whose nest is disturbed will carry their young, one by one, to a place of safety, but in overcrowded pens this behavior pattern was lost, and the rats' general maternal care became so faulty that in one experiment 80 percent and in another 96 percent of all the young died before reaching maturity. Among the males, some became ascendant over their fellows but others showed a number of disturbances of behavior, of which two patterns were particularly striking: some males appeared to opt out of sexual and social interaction altogether, sulking alone on the periphery of the group, while others became morbidly pensexual, mounting female rats, whether receptive or not, whenever they could do so without being attacked by one of the ascendant males. These hyperactive rats contravened many of the norms of behavior of their group, even becoming cannibal toward the young of their own kind.[9]

It has been maintained by some writers that the human species is unique in its tendency to destroy its own kind; but this is not quite true. Colonies of rats will frequently attack, and even exterminate, single newcomers or groups of "alien" rats that are introduced into their midst. On the other hand, if several rats, previously reared in separate cages, are simultaneously introduced into a strange pen, they will spend several hours exploring the confines of the pen, and each other, without showing aggression; but after a relatively short interval any additional stranger introduced into this newly formed group will be liable to be attacked and killed.

It is, of course, a far cry from the behavior of rats and cats to that of humans; but observations on the behavior of higher primates have a more immediate relevance. Recent studies of apes and monkeys in their natural habitat have greatly modified earlier preconceptions about the frequency of both fighting and sexual behavior. These beliefs were much influenced by observations made by Zuckerman upon apes in zoos, which displayed almost incessant fighting and sexual competition;[10] but this has proved to be only a travesty of their conduct in their natural surroundings. Instead, it is the product of their being confined in overcrowded conditions without the possibility of escape. In the wild state, protective mechanisms operate to control the frequency of both the above types of behavior; but when groups of primates outgrow their territory, the frequency of quarreling and fighting increases.[11]

OBSERVATIONS ON HUMANS

It is perhaps significant that Leyhausen and Lorenz, the two naturalists who have devoted more attention than almost any others to the disruptive effects of overcrowding, themselves both underwent the painful experience of being closely confined in prisoner-of-war camps for several years. Their personal observations, which have been corroborated by other medical and psychiatric witnesses (e.g., Bettelheim, Cochrane, Gibbens),[12] were that when a group of men was penned up together in close quarters for many months on end, its members tended to become hyperirritable, and to find each other's small mannerisms positively intolerable.

These, too, like the observations on caged cats and rats, were instances of extreme conditions; and yet one must realize that there are many impoverished groups in the world whose conditions of life today are scarcely better. In theory, of course, they can escape from their surroundings; but in practice the "culture of poverty" can induce a sense of despair of ever being able to escape.[13] One is tempted to draw an analogy between the rat that is subjected to a series of physical defeats, or the "pariahs" in an overcrowded colony of cats, and the members of problem families in our city slums who display a seeming inability to make a successful social adaptation. It appears that social institutions and transmitted value systems can create a sense of confinement no less demoralizing than the bars of a cage.

Many years ago, Farris and Dunham[14] drew attention to the ecological concentration of certain forms of mental illness in those parts of a large city where both overcrowding and social disorganization—or *anomie* as Durkheim[15] had earlier described it—were most marked. Subsequent research has challenged Dunham's specific contention that schizophrenia is generated by the conditions of life in a socially disorganized community; but many other studies have confirmed his finding that alcoholism, illegitimacy, divorce, delinquency, and numerous other forms of social pathology are most prevalent in such areas.

There remains, however, an interesting contrast in the social correlates of two particular manifestations of social pathology, namely, suicide and attempted suicide—at least, as they are observed in cities of the Western World. Suicide rates are highest in areas where many people live in a state of social isolation, bereft of the support of family, or of any other primary group. On the other hand, studies of attempted suicide have shown that the most important social correlate is overcrowding. Typically, the person who makes a nonfatal suicidal gesture has been harassed beyond endurance by recurrent friction within the domestic group, in cramped and overcrowded premises. Here, too, as in the instance of rats' dose resistance to amphetamine, one can see the mutual reinforcement of multiple factors. A majority of those who attempt suicide are relatively young men and women, who often have had a bad start in life with unstable or absent parent figures. These patients tend to experience great difficulty, in their turn, in forming stable interpersonal relationships: they are often at the same time demanding and inconsiderate toward others, and yet are themselves emotionally immature and dependent. Their deficiencies prompt them to seek out partners from whom they hope to derive support, but all too often the partner whom they select is handicapped in much the same way; so far from meeting each other's dependency needs, these unfortunates only suceed in making each other's state even worse than before. Often, too, they turn to drink or drugs to allay their need for dependence, and this in turn further impoverishes their ability to form rewarding personal relationships.[16]

During recent years many countries have been obliged to take stock of increasing rates of alcoholism, crimes of violence, and attempted suicide. Sociological and social-psychiatric research has shown that there are clusters of disturbances that are found most commonly in overpopulated, underprivileged sectors of large cities; but several interacting factors, in addition to that of overcrowding, are believed to contribute to their appearance. In recent years mass outbreaks of violence have quickened attention to these phenomena. It is disquieting to be reminded that even in countries that have experienced an overall improvement in their standard of living during the last quarter century, an increasing number of people feel alienated from the goals, and the rewards, to which their fellow citizens aspire—and alienated so profoundly that they despair of ever being able to get back into the mainstream of humanity.

Alienation and despair are the product of extreme situations—such as, for example, were realized in the grotesque, doomed societies of the Nazi concentration camps. Many, if not most, of the inmates of such camps found themselves surrendering their customary standards of behavior and their values, becoming completely disoriented by the inhuman conditions under which they were forced to live.[17]

There have been crises in the course of human history when quite large sectors of mankind experienced this sense of alienation from participation in the life of their fellow countrymen. Sometimes after prolonged deprivation their discontents have exploded in outbreaks of revolution, as a result of which a new social order has been created; but at other times leaderless masses of the dispossessed have shown themselves only too ready to become the dupes of mentally unstable yet charismatic demagogues, who promised them a magical deliverance from their miseries. The historian Norman Cohn has shown how often in European history periods of social and economic disruption have resulted in the demoralization of large populations. Cohn has identified a number of social circumstances in which this is liable to occur. Conspicuous among these have been occasions in which long-settled means of production and traditional occupations have been rapidly superseded by new techniques, throwing many individuals out of work; circumstances in which different sectors of a population experience widely contrasting standards of living; and situations where traditional values are weakened, and customary authorities cease to fulfill their protective function. Common to all these circumstances is an all-pervading sense of uncertainty about the future.[18]

George Kennan has epitomized the consequences of such periods of uncertainty with his customary eloquence:

> Whenever the authority of the past is too suddenly and too drastically undermined—whenever the past ceases to be the great and reliable reference book of human problems—whenever, above all, the experience of the father becomes irrelevant to the trials and searchings of the son—there the foundations of man's inner health and stability begin to crumble, insecurity and panic begin to take over, conduct becomes erratic and aggressive.[19]

Just how erratic and aggressive conduct can become in such situations is amply illustrated in Cohn's monograph. He shows that the rootless, uncertain populations who are the victims of too rapid social change tend to regress emotionally, and to clutch at magical solutions for their plight. Nor have leaders been lacking to offer them just such magical solutions, promising a millennium of effortless bliss just around the corner.

A characteristic of these millennial movements has been their tendency to begin on a note of generosity, brotherliness, and willingness to let all share equally in the plenty which is soon to be available. This was the case with the followers of Tanchelm, who inspired a vast following among the poor in Flanders in the early 12th century, and with those of Eudes de l'Etoile, who preached a millennium of universal riches to hordes of peasants in Brittany rendered landless by successive years of famine. Both of these leaders were worshiped as divine during their short heydays.

Two hundred years later, the English "Peasants' Revolt"—fundamentally a rebellion against the feudal relic of villeinage, which restricted laborers' freedom to avail themselves of new forms of employment in trades and manufacturing—found a more down-to-earth leader in John Ball, who contrasted the "natural state of man," born equal and entitled to his fair share of the world's goods, with existing social inequalities. The peroration of one of his addresses went: "Good folk, things cannot go well in England nor ever shall until all things are in common and there is neither villein nor noble, but all of us are of one condition."

The most remarkable of all the European millennial movements was the 2-year reign (1534-36) of the Anabaptist sect in the German town of Münster. Members of this sect proclaimed a universal brotherhood, and held all their possessions in common; but like all their predecessors, they met with vigorous opposition from the established authorities, and this opposition, in every case, provoked counter aggression that was all the more extreme because it was fired with righteous indignation. The benign, ascetic Tanchelm surrounded himself with a ferocious bodyguard; Eudes was executed, threatening to return " on the third day" and wreak vengeance on the oppressors; John Ball soon began to advocate the extermination of all great lords, justices, and priests as a necessary prelude to the Kingdom of the Saints; and the Anabaptists of Münster found themselves tyrannized by a fanatical leader who personally and publicly executed anyone who questioned his "divine" authority.

In parentheses, it is interesting to observe a somewhat similar sequence of events during the past 5 years of student protest. In almost every case, these protests have occurred in vast, rapidly expanded campuses (Berkeley, Columbia, Paris, Rome, Tokyo, etc.) where students felt themselves alienated both personally from their teachers and ideologically from the aims of the university courses. Typically, student protest movements have started with generous, not to say utopian ideals and have taken an ugly turn only when they were confronted with measures of control that were not merely firm, but openly violent. When this happens, the naive slogans of "Flower Power" are soon replaced by cries of "Kill the Pig."

One of Cohn's purposes, in reviewing earlier millennial cults, was to show the similarity between their origins, their magical expectations, and their decline into orgies of "highprincipled" killings and the corresponding sequence of events in Hitler's "thousand-year Reich." Similar outbreaks of unreason have occurred in recent times in less developed societies, typically in one of two social situations. The first occurs when a technologically undeveloped community is suddenly confronted with the material products of the industrialized West. This happened during both World Wars, and led to the outbreak of a series of Cargo Cults that bore a striking resemblance to the earlier European millennial movements, and that like them, began optimistically with promises of magical abundance, encountered the inevitable frustration of the hopes so aroused, and then frequently ended in bitterness and bloodshed.[20] The second situation, familiar to many of the newly liberated colonial countries, is that in which large numbers of the community have developed aspirations for a standard of living long before the economic and political institutions of their country have advanced to the point where these expectations could be fulfilled.

The common theme in all of these examples of the abrogation of commonsense, of contact with reality, and, in the face of frustration, of the unleashing of extremes of violent and destructive behavior, has been the simultaneous arousal of extravagant aspirations together with the shock of realizing that these aspirations are not going to be. The mere juxtaposition of wealth and poverty is not sufficient by itself to excite a spirit of revolt. The stimulus to develop impossible expectations seems to come from a sense of inner insecurity and hopelessness, a total loss of confidence in one's own future. During the postwar era, this has been nowhere more apparant than in the ghettos of the great cities, both in the relatively rich, highly developed societies and in the hungry half of the world. The situatior is aggravated when, as a result of uncontrolled population increase, standards of living actually begin to decline at the very time when, by marginal, vicarious participation in a "consumer culture," a people's material aspirations have been raised to new levels.

Today's underprivileged differ from those of previous generations in two respects: their actual poverty is much less severe, and their level of information about their better-off fellows is much greater, thanks to the mass media. As Dr. Sukarno put it, in a much-quoted speech:

> The motion picture industry has provided a window on the world, and the colonized nations have looked through that window and have seen the things of which they have been deprived. It is perhaps not generally realized that a refrigerator can be a revolutionary symbol—to a people who have no refrigerators. A motor car owned by a worker in one country can be a symbol of revolt to a people deprived of the necessities of life.

What he says of undeveloped societies applies with equal force to the impact of movies and television on the aspirations of the less privileged citizens of the technologically advanced countries.

In summary, it seems that overpopulation only aggravates the widespread threat to social stability presented by masses of our population who are basically unsure of their personal future, who have lost confidence in their chance of ever attaining a secure place in their community. It is imperative that we recognize the gravity of this threat because mankind today commands such destructive powers that we cannot afford to risk outbreaks of mass violence; and yet the lesson of history points to the threat of just such disasters. Unless the masses of our city poor can be persuaded that there is a future for them too in the Great Society, their morale is likely to crumble until vast human communities degenerate into the semblance of concentration camp inmates, if not even to that of Zuckerman's pathologically belligerent apes.

References

1. T. Y. Lin, "A Study of the Incidence of Mental Disorder in Chinese and Other Cultures," *Psychiatry,* vol. XVI (1953), pp. 313 ff.
2. L. Srole, T. S. Langer, S. T. Michael, M. K. Opler, and T. A. C. Rennie, *Mental Health in the Metropolis* (New York: McGraw-Hill, 1962).
3. S. A. Barnett, "The Biology of Aggression," *Lancet* (1964), p. 803.
4. *Ibid.*
5. P. Leyhausen, "The Communal Organization of Solitary Mammals," *Symposium of the Zoological Society (London),* vol. XIV (1965), pp. 249 ff., and V. C. Wynne-Edwards, *Animal Dispersion in Relation to Social Behavior* (Edinburgh and London: Oliver & Boyd, 1962).
6. See Konrad Lorenz, *On Aggression* (New York: Harcourt, Brace & World, 1966), and Robert Ardrey, *The Territorial Imperative* (New York: Atheneum, 1961).
7. P. Leyhausen, "The Sane Community—a Density Problem? *Discovery,* vol. XXVI (Sept. 1965), pp. 27 ff.
8. *Ibid.*
9. J. B. Calhoun, "Population Density and Social Pathology," in L. J. Duhl, ed., *The Urban Condition* (New York: Basic Books, 1963), p. 33.

10. S. G. Zuckerman, *The Social Life of Monkeys and Apes* (London: Kegan Paul, 1932).

11. I. DeVore, *Primate Behaviour* (New York: Treubner King, 1965).

12. Bruno Bettelheim, "Individual and Mass Behavior in Extreme Situations," *Journal of Abnormal and Social Psychology,* vol. XXXVIII (1943), p. 417 ff.; A. L. Cochrane, "Notes on the Psychology of Prisoners of War," *British Medical Journal,* vol. I (1946), pp. 282 ff.; and T. C. N. Gibbens, *The Psychology and Psychopathology of Prisoners of War,* M.D. thesis, University of London, 1947.

13. Oscar Lewis, *Five Families: Mexican Case Studies in the Culture of Poverty* (New York: Basic Books, 1959).

14. R. E. L. Farris and H. W. Dunham, *Mental Disorders in Urban Areas* (Chicago: University of Chicago Press, 1939).

15. Emile Durkheim, *Le Suicide* (Paris: Ancienne Libraire Germer Bailliere, 1897).

16. W. I. N. and J. W. McCulloch, "Repeated Acts of Self-Poisoning and Self-Injury," *Proceedings of the Royal Society of Medicine,* vol LIX (1966), pp. 89 ff.

17. L. Eitinger, *Concentration Camp Surivors in Norway and Israel* (London: Allen & Unwin, 1961).

18. Norman R. C. Cohn, *The Pursuit of the Millennium* (London: Secker & Warburg, 1957).

19. George Kennan, *Realities of American Foreign Policy* (Princeton: Princeton University Press, 1954).

20. Peter Worsley, *The Trumpet Shall Sound* (London: MacGibbon & Kee, 1957).

Chapter 22

DEFENSIVE
CULTURAL ADAPTATION

By Bernard J. Siegel*

In this paper I explore the essential features of a class of societies whose members attempt to establish and preserve a cultural identity in the face of what they perceive to be threats to that identity from the environment. The paper considers groups under stress, but departs from the general theme of this symposium in that it deals with a strategy of coping with stress that is basically nonviolent in nature. Such groups are of interest in the present context because they demonstrate that violence is only one among several strategies of social response to environmental threat. Members of all the defensive societies with which I am familiar see their surrounding environment as hostile, and the people in it as prepared to engage at any time in destructive or depriving actions against them. Such groups have been difficult for the disinterested investigator to penetrate as an observer. Willing informants are few in number and are often subject to reprisal and disciplinary action; individuals in defensive societies who do not readily submit to authority figures are likely to lose their membership in the group and to be physically rejected.

This analysis is mainly paradigmatic, in that it is primarily concerned with specifying the structure of defensive adaptation, its elements, and their relationship. This is an inductive task, though its aim is to generate some casual explanations about a variety of questions. What dimensions of stress and prior conditions of the group are likely to have a defensive or some other outcome? Will groups that have adopted a defensive strategy in relation to the larger society have, because of their very nature, less likelihood of responding violently than those that have not? At present no definitive answers can be given to these kinds of questions, but it is possible to provide some informed speculation.[1]

For purposes of exemplification I have confined myself to certain groups in the United States that appear to exhibit this pattern. Investigations at Taos and Picuris Indian pueblos of eastern New Mexico first provided insights into

---

*Professor Siegel is professor of anthropology at Stanford University. Some of his extensive fieldwork and theoretical analysis of group adaptations to stress are summarized in his study, written with Alan R. Beals, of *Divisiveness and Social Conflict: An Anthropological Approach* (Stanford: Stanford University Press, 1966). Among his many articles are "Cultural Integration and High Anxiety Levels: Notes on a Psycho-Cultural Hypothesis," *Social Forces,* 1955, and "Conflict and Factionalist Dispute," *Journal of the Royal Anthropological Institute,* 1960.

the nature of the phenomenon; further confirmation was provided by studies of religious and ethnic enclaves like the Amish, Hutterites, and Mormons, and of the Black Muslims. The roster of societies for which the defensive paradigm is relevant includes many other historically unrelated groups: viz, Jews who lived, prior to World War II, in compact villages called "shtetls" in eastern Europe; certain villages of Japan and southeastern Asia; the Egyptian Copts; and village communities in the Alpine region of Europe.

THE STRUCTURE OF DEFENSIVENESS

Behavioral Controls and Training for Self-Restraint

Defensive groups have few and carefully controlled avenues for self-expression appropriate to the life situations usually encountered by their members. Rules of conduct tend to be very explicit, so that the individual must exercise great restraint over his own behavior, which in turn is closely supervised by an authoritative elite. The controls, therefore, are twofold, consisting in (1) the nurturance of self-discipline in the individual beginning very early (usually by the end of the second year), and (2) the allocation of authority or power at the broadest level to a small number of designated persons. The legitimation of political control is circular: it is derived from the imputed wisdom of the elite in interpreting cultural values; the values are, in turn, often elevated to sacred status, thus conferring additional authority upon the leaders.

One manifestation of control is the maintenance of a high level of anxiety, sometimes evidence in a low incidence of heavy drinking or the use of strong disapproval and swift application of sanctions against offending individuals. As Hallowell put it, we find—

> a conscious strict control or even rejection of available anxiety-reducing patterns and concomitant elaboration of in-group symbols of identification. . . . certain anxieties may be inculcated in individuals as part of the socialization process] in order to motivate them in the performance of patterns of behavior that are socially approved.[2]

In such groups there are many occasions for intensive interaction among all members in communal ceremonials and other collective enterprises. As part of their approved repertoire for coping with others, they also sanction various kinds of malevolent accusations—witchcraft or other forms of denunciation— that wax and wane in frequency of expression.

In the past we have loosely and commonly assumed that, in the absence of other outlets, both these types of institutionalized behaviors—i.e., intensive interaction and displacement—tended to give comfort to individuals, to relieve tensions or to dispel them temporarily. Actually there is no real evidence for this assertion. Stated in this way, the assumption is very difficult to prove or disprove. Are the real and supposed dangers of individuals removed, at least in part, by the comfort of common participation in group-centered activities? Is their tension (however we may propose to measure it) relieved by displacement of aggression upon others? To the extent that studies of authoritarianism and relevant psychoanalytic theory made sense to the student of behavior, he tended to accept such statements rather uncritically. The most we can say in the present context is that these behaviors are prominent and that they coexist with other structural features of defensiveness.

In the defensive group there thus appears to be a conscious attempt to maintain comparatively intense anxiety states among members by requiring constant exercise of control over behavior potentially destructive to the group in relation to external threats. Real and perceived threats to continued existence require continual emphasis upon and renewal of social cohesion; latent conflict or cleavage demands both internal and external controls. I would propose that, in comparison with nondefensive societies, brawling, overt domestic quarreling, and excesses in aggressive behaviors that disrupt ongoing activities or call attention to dissension within the group occur infrequently and endure briefly in defensive groups before they are suppressed. Although the evidence at present is meager, I would also hypothesize that the suicides that do occur are of the kind that Durkheim spoke of as "suicide altruists," for the reasons that he maintains.[3] For the individual, the gains of adaptive behavior are measured in a high degree of security (in the form of continual support and approval from all others, and his confident knowledge of norms). The corresponding losses are the comparatively great effort he must make in self-discipline as well as the submission he must always display over much of his adult life in the face of authoritative decisionmakers.

To provide examples, among pueblo Indians the early training for control of impulses, and particularly of direct forms of aggression, is almost proverbial. It is interesting to note the same emphasis among Black Muslims, in view of a popular image by nonmembers that portrays them as advocates of violence.[4] In the ideology of the movement, the black man is of vastly different metal from the white man and therefore must live in a way that is appropriate to that superiority, throwing off the vices taught his people by the malicious white man: tobacco, alcohol, gambling, gluttony, jealousy, father-absent families, several foods associated with the diet of the southern Negro, and the like. In other words, he must cast aside the entire stereotype of the "so-called Negro" and lead a new life of strict morality and devotion to the welfare and development of his people and of the institutions of the Nation of Islam. To remain a member in good standing, he must conform essentially to a puritanical moral code.

The temples of Islam carry out active recruiting programs in the black slums of a large number of American cities, but they try to be selective by retaining only those who are likely to respond positively to the rigid retraining process. The initial step seems to be the isolation of the individual from his former identity and his identification with a new role. Isolation from white men is particularly imperative in view of their corrupting influence. Ties with members of the non-Muslim Negro community obviously cannot be cut in all cases, nor is it always desirable that they should be. However, one's family and friends must recognize the change, or they too are liable to be cast aside, with however much regret. Training for submission to authority is continuous, and takes place in many domains of behavior simultaneously. Resocialization takes place over a long period of time, in the form of lessons. The aim is a transformation so sweeping that it affects every part of a man's life and of his self-conception, reinforced in every conceivable way.

Cultural Integration

A central characteristic of defensive adaptation is the presence of a few key values. This lends a keen sense of cultural integrity to the group, in the sense of being complete or whole. As commonly used, the term "cultural integration" refers essentially to the degree of interrelatedness, interdependence, or linkage to be found among the elements of a culture.[5] In turn, these linkages seem to reflect the operation of values or underlying principles common to more than one activity. A tightly integrated system is characterized by a strong centralization of values; that is, the tendency for broad sectors of custom to be related to a few key values.[6] Under these circumstances a person who might otherwise favor a given innovation will often discard the idea because he knows that substitution for one custom that he no longer values will mean the loss of others which he does value.[7]

A central value of all defensive groups appears to be subordination of the individual to the welfare of the group. This is reflected in the generalization of cooperative effort in many in-group activities, the settlement of disputes by knowledgeable authorities before they become unregulated, and the emphasis upon steady goal-oriented work habits.

Symbols and Identity

However varied the content of these values, they are reflected in supporting symbols. By means of these symbols a given aggregate of individuals develops an intensive sense of group identification. They state, in effect: "I am a Taos," "I am a shtetl member," and so forth, and this identification is supported by a few badges which members are emotionally reluctant to discard. The latter commonly include language and special colloquialisms (ordinary discourse among members is carried on in one language, another being employed in conversations with nonmembers). They may also include special customs of deference, punctilious observance of particular rituals, and, when encountered in the form of natural communities, selection of marriage partners from within the group and a particular territory.[8] Acceptance of and conformity to behavior consonant with these symbols is not open to discussion; alternative means of coping with social situations are either prevented from coming to the attention of the groups, or, if individuals learn about them and propose them for adoption, they are carefully screened.

Insofar as supporting symbols assume the significance we impute to them, one would expect as a corollary that identity problems that currently preoccupy so many students of personality development in our own society would be largely absent in groups with tightly integrated cultures. If such identity is originally weak, ambiguous, largely absent, or in a formative state, it will, under stress and as a group, become increasingly defensive, be invented and buttressed with available symbols from the past or present. In the process of emerging from the multimillion aggregate of American Negroes, the Black Muslims very deliberately developed a social identity by means of certain symbols to which they assigned special meanings. To gain and retain membership, for example, Black Muslims are expected to assume a Mohammedan name. They are exhorted to dress in a manner that will not betray lower-class origins and to eat certain foods and to avoid others. They, of course, attend distinctive temples and learn a ritual language associated with a special version of the Koran.[9]

Members of defensive societies tend to interact with nonmembers in conventional ways. When interrogated on issues they consider sensitive—and they are usually many and pervasive—members will respond with readymade answers which are meant to deceive. Potential innovations, as we have seen, are carefully screened by legitimate authorities. A special humor contains allusions deliberately confined to insiders. In general, social intercourse with nonmembers is of limited duration. Where enduring relations do occur (viz), between friends or godparents, between a patron or merchant and client or customer) they tend to be specific and established only with individuals who are known to be discrete and with whom there exists some implicit agreement to avoid all sensitive matters in conversation.[10]

Communication and Interaction Patterns

The net effect of such controlled intercourse and communication between members and nonmembers is to make the nonmember often want membership but to be kept at a distance, and to lead the member to reinforce emotionally the beliefs and behaviors which symbolize continuity of the group. To maintain this kind of solidarity requires continuous surveillance and some culturally available techniques that facilitate rapid communication and mobilization of public opinion. Most commonly these conditions are met by a dense or nucleated settlement pattern in which dwellings are located very close to, sometimes literally on top of, one another (as in pueblo societies and ghetto communities). Some numerically large and broadly dispersed groups that exhibit defensive structuring, like the Egyptian Copts, the Mormons, or the Black Muslims, have solved this problem by combining strong centralized authoritarian control at the top with the allocation of decisionmaking power in most daily affairs to highly autonomous neighborhood temples, church schools, and missions.[11] In the case of the latter, modern transport and communication techniques make possible continual links of the local groups to national leadership.

The Black Muslim group (the Nation of Islam) was founded in Detroit in the summer of 1930 by W. D. Fard Muhammad. At first, Fard simply went from house to house bringing people his message. As followers accumulated he secured a temple and instituted formal meetings. An organization was established to administer the cult both in ritual and in the recruitment of members. The group subsequently founded a parochial elementary and secondary school (the University of Islam); a minister, trained personally by the founder and assisted by junior ministers, was appointed to run the organization. In the early days all of these activities took place within a restricted district of Detroit. Headquarters were subsequently transferred to Chicago; the movement flourished and diffused to other cities where ministers, always subject to the overriding word of Elijah Muhammad, the present patriarch, were appointed to the local temples.

Perhaps because the central feature of any meeting is the sermon (or more precisely, the exhortation), there is a great deal of exchange preaching done between temples, and Elijah Muhammad himself travels all over the country to speak at gatherings. The establishment of a new tradition and the development

of an orthodox commitment to it owe their success in large measure to mutually reinforcing communication networks: the acquaintance and interchange of
ministers from diverse regions and the education of teachers on the school staffs
at a single training center.[12]

Elites and Centralization of Authority

This pattern of shared understandings could not persist without the regular
provision of strong centralized authorities for the group. Training individuals
so that they will exert a considerable measure of control over their own behavior
is characteristic of all defensive societies, but it does not work at all times.
When cultural survival is thought to be at stake, the matter of regulation cannot be left exclusively to self-control. It is buttressed formally by a relatively
small number of authoritarian powerholders. What is more, the legitimation of
centralized authority stems from the urgent and apprehensive need for solutions to daily problems; the resource that confers power upon these offices is
special knowledge. In most cases, therefore, the men who make decisions act
in a sacred or quasi-sacred capacity. In some groups they may inherit their
offices, but in all cases they must constantly validate their right to exercise the
functions associated with them.

Thus the Catholic priests of Quebec villages and Coptic priests of Egypt,
respectively, control ritual performances of the church and church-related
education which, in each case, is primarily a manifestation of group autonomy.[13]
In the case of Hutterites or Mormons, clergy are elected from among all male
members in good standing. The priesthood or its equivalent is therefore very
broadly based. The highest authority, however, is vested in a few individuals
whose qualifications involve the ability to interpret the basic and traditional
experiences and sacred texts of the group into living doctrine. The Hutterites
sanctify their own history, using it as a sacred record for the interpretation
of present problems and the presentation of appropriate solutions within the
Hutterite tradition.[14] The Mormons similarly use the *Doctrine and Covenants,*
which consists of instructions to the early Church and the establishment of
precedents for church administration. Throughout the period of his leadership
of the movement, Joseph Smith continued to receive divine guidance in times
of difficulty, and the instructions given him at those times are regarded as valid
for present difficulties as well. Mormon doctrine indeed awards the president
of the church the power to receive additional revelation in order to supplement
the recorded guidance of the past.[15]

A significant attribute of many defensive groups is the implementing role
of women. It appears that in all such communities, at least, women provide a
basis for cultural maintenance but are essentially ignorant of the symbolism
that expresses the particular goals of the group in a particular way. They learn
that certain symbolic behaviors or places are important to defend, but they
may not know connotations that such behaviors, things, or places actually have
in the ideology of the group. Being in this sense nonrationally committed to
cultural values, they may seek, even more stringently and less discriminately
than men, to prevent strangers from having access to knowledge about them.
By the same token, males also tend to screen the kind of communication available to females within the group. Therefore, however much special knowledge
of the outside world the former may acquire, traditional defensive attitudes will

be transmitted anew to each generation by virtue of the important role of women in early curtural transmission and socialization.

EXTERNAL PRESSURES AND GROUP STRUCTURE

Groups develop the properties we outlined above in response to external pressures or stress that, at a certain point, are felt to be a threat to continued existence. The stresses most commonly identified in the anthropological literature are encounters with alien people who interfere with the conventional modes of utilization of the environment. Alien contact may render ambiguous or useless some of the customary rules for regulating human relations and satisfying emergent wants, or they may call into question the viability of the group's universal values, upon which its very continuity depends. To more narrowly defined acculturation studies we should add a variety of other environmental transformations: urbanization, industrialization, urban-rural interaction, and the like.

Taos and Picuris Pueblos: A Controlled Comparison

Defensive adaptation, then, is a response to environmental pressures and changes, and more particularly to certain dimensions or variables of these pressures. As a prototype of this interaction between group and environment, we consider briefly the experiences of Taos pueblo and compare them with the experiences of a close neighbor, the pueblo of Picuris. The two societies are especially valuable for our purpose because they share a long history of settlement and tradition in the area out of a common past.[16]

Archeological evidence suggests that, prior to contact with agents of Western society, the ancestors of these peoples defended themselves against the encroachments of other Indian tribes that invaded their territories. In the past 400 years they engaged, first, in a number of hostile encounters with Spanish colonists and, later, in their relations with Anglos, had to compromise in many ways over land rights. When Coronado first visited them shortly after 1540, he estimated that they had roughly comparable populations. His estimate was around 3,000 inhabitants for each. Recent investigations at Picuris indicate this community (and Taos by implication) in fact had around 2,000 inhabitants. From his description and from more systematic investigation, we have every reason to believe that they shared a very similar social structure and culture. For reasons that are not entirely clear, both suffered dramatic population decreases at least through the middle of the 18th century, probably in part through the introduction of new diseases and in part through defections to the Spanish settlements. The Census for 1890 lists, in round numbers, 400 and 300 persons for Taos and Picuris, respectively. From that time onward there was a steady increase in the former and a slight reduction in the latter, both suffering from the influenza epidemic after World War I. Today, however, Picuris has barely 100 persons, while Taos has over 1,200. As we shall see, these figures are closely related to corresponding differences in cultural vigor.

At this point—the turn of the century—environmental stresses on the two communities begin to diverge in what turn out to be important ways. Consider certain salient events at Taos during the periods of Mexican and Anglo

political control: Boundaries were fixed (a process that has been in adjudica-
tion until very recently), thus stabilizing the ratio of people to resources among
a traditionally agricultural people. A new community, part Spanish-American
and increasingly Anglo in composition, was located only a mile from the Indian
pueblo. Over the past 50 years it has attracted a variety of settlers and visi-
tors, notably merchants, traders, teachers, builders, service persons, artists, and
tourists. Pressure on the land was thus accompanied by the opening of new alternatives for employment—catering to the tourist trade, jobs as domestics,
hotel aids and dancers, service station attendants and skilled workers.

This entire configuration of events was seen as a problem, or better perhaps
as a set of problems. People continued to think of Taos citizenship as a good
thing, but continuation of that entity is bound up with an agrarian adaptation,
a supporting belief system about man's relation to nature, and related ceremonial activities. Increasing numbers of uncontrolled nonmembers in their midst,
new jobs, and a conflicting set of rules regulating work habits may and do interfere unpredictably with pueblo expectations and demands. To render services
and participate in activities of central concern to the village, one must leave
work in which he is engaged elsewhere. Farming, by contrast, has traditionally
been articulated with such demands. We can think of the new situation as a
complication in patterns of communication. The settlement has become, as it
were, encircled, and Taos leadership confronted with the problem of cultural
survival. If we add (1) the presence of the United Pueblo Agency in Albu-
querque and constantly changing, imperfectly understood policies toward
Indians originating in Washington; and (2) modern transport that enables dissident individuals to leave the village for urban employment, often some distance away, the return to it in an indeterminant manner, we can see how complex the environment must now appear to the great majority of the group
that is committed to continuity of its cultural system.[17]

During the same period many of the stresses observed at Taos have confronted Picurenses, but in a different way. Children attend Indian schools on
and off the reservation (boarding school at Santa Fe) where the curriculum is
established and teaching done by aliens. Picuris is a few miles removed from
the main highway that passes hard by Taos and is within walking distance
only to a Spanish-American village that provides no regular job opportunities.
To opt for employment off the pueblo means residing in towns or cities, the
closest of which is 24 miles away (Taos). Individuals who do so must rely almost exclusively upon secondary languages, English and Spanish, and forego
many of the emotional gratifications associated with the use of the native language (especially participation in pueblo-centered activities like the ceremonial
calendar and household rituals, which make use of intensive social interaction
to which Picurenses are socialized very early in life).

Elsewhere I have summarized the contrasting nature of pressures and outcomes in the two communities as follows:

> Perhaps the single most important factor that distinguishes the recent
> history of Picuris and Taos is the different impact of stress created by
> environmental changes. The proliferation of alternatives created in the
> immediate vicinity of Taos challenged the conventional power system,
> but in so doing strengthened it. The community as a whole began to
> take the shape of a nativistic movement. We might say that what hap-
> pened in the process of this confrontation was the development of a keen

sense of urgency in adapting to a perceived threat to cultural survival. In Picuris, by contrast, it is just this sense of urgency that is lacking. Being removed from the centers of development there is, so to speak, leisure in the contemplation of alternatives, perhaps too much leisure to confirm themselves in their beliefs. Disassociation from the pueblo, on the other hand, has seldom been a possible alternative except for those who have been incompletely socialized. The net result has been a classic example of pervasive anomie in the generation of young adult males (ages 16-38), partial integration in the next older generation (ages 40-58), and an integrated generation of elders (age 60).[18]

Dimensions of Perceived Stress

Examination of certain classes of historical events at Taos and Picuris will facilitate analysis of environmental pressures as people see them. From these cases perceived stress appears to vary according to its direction, intensity, complexity, ambiguity, control, and effect on group image. Until approximately the end of the 19th century, members of both groups might well have perceived the alteration of their environment by the intrusion of others in very similar ways on all of these dimensions. Clearly this stress-inducing intrusion was of long duration; each group had to contend increasingly with agents of Spanish and Anglo tradition for over 350 years. It was unambiguous (the "others" are clearly different and threatening), controlling over their actions, and depreciating to themselves, as was explicit in the colonizing, missionizing, and politically defining efforts of first one of the dominant groups and then the other. If we think of intensity in terms of frequency of interaction, their experiences probably differed little in this regard as well.

After 1900, however, some of these features began to vary in magnitude. Duration, control, and effect on group image remained roughly the same. The construction of a new road and motor transport, on the other hand, left Picuris relatively isolated but generated a very pronounced increase in rate of interaction between Taosenos and nonmembers. Not only were there many new occasions for rubbing shoulders at Taos—curious or interested outsiders and artists, new enterprises, amusements, and the like—but they confronted the pueblo dweller almost continuously in everyday life. Individuals and the group as a whole were faced with the problem of how to cope with these interactions. As one alternative, individuals might have been left free to make their own decisions at will: to remain traditionally occupied within the pueblo, communicating to a very limited degree with outsiders; to divide their time between both worlds; or physically to detach themselves from the group, either permanently by emigration or by leaving for indefinite periods and returning when emotionally or otherwise disposed to do so.

The strategy actually employed was to reinforce the value of group membership by selectively emphasizing traditional symbols. In the process Taosenos simplified the environmental context of their earlier life by redefining its complexity simply as threat, and they controlled the level of intensity of intercultural interaction by specifying the kinds, frequency, and content of relations that were permitted. The result was an affirmative defensive adaption that had revealed all the properties of this phenomenon described above.

At Picuris the aspects, but not the magnitudes, of environmental change were very similar to those at Taos. No such increase in stress intensity occurred; the environment to Picurenses remained very complex in terms of models and ambiguous concerning the messages they received. We observe, also, no such monolithic interpretation of such pressures. Some defined the situation as threat and emphasized a traditional solution; others, as new opportunities and new wants. An increasing majority, however, came to be confused by multiple choices of both valued goals and means of achieving them, to the point of immobilization of any effort and normlessness.

Interaction Between Group and Environment

It should be clear from this discussion that we must assume a continuing interaction between environmental pressures (as interpreted by an outside observer, or as perceived by members of some social entity) and the structure of groups in order to predict subsequent responses that the latter will make to environmental transformations.[19] Some previous tendency in the direction of centralized sociopolitical organization is probably necessary, in order to mobilize efforts of individuals to cope collectively with urgently felt needs for a more or less satisfying way of life in the face of forces that are perceived to be opposed to such an effort. The necessity for controlling the use of water in irrigation-based agriculture, it has been suggested, very possibly led to centralized community leadership among the eastern pueblos well before the Spanish contact period.[20] Another pattern sometimes occurs in a mass or aggregate of individuals with minimal organization structure. A social appeal to a felt need for value-oriented identity may attract a segment of such a population to a new, centralized structure. The Black Muslims are an outcome of such appeals among the northern urban Negroes of the United States.

By the same token, if the group-environment interaction process in the past had stabilized in a structure that was ill equipped to cope with new and traumatic perceived stress, we might predict an outcome other than defensive adaptation, no matter how closely the stress values approximated those described for Taos pueblo. I am not familiar personally with such a case from the annals of American history, but they are encountered in the anthropological literature.[21] I would hypothesize that a successful defensive reaction requires either a centralized prior structure or a loose one—viz, the earlier urban Negro ghetto community in its initial phase.

DISCUSSION AND IMPLICATIONS

Defensive Adaptation and Theories of Social Movements

The theory of defensive adaptation builds upon certain important lines of cultural theory and work on the problem of social movements. Several ethnic enclaves in the United States had their origins in social movements: the Menonnites, Amish, and Hutterites, for example, began as sectarian movements in Europe and the Mormons in America.

Smelser makes a distinction between a norm-oriented movement and a value-oriented movement.[22] The NAACP is an example of the former. In its attempt to advance desegregation in the United States, the NAACP is critical of certain practices in society but not of its fundamental democratic values. It proposes reforms as a more adequate realization of those values but does not advocate a far-reaching cultural transformation. A value-oriented movement, on the other hand, criticizes values; the Black Muslim movement is said to be value oriented and to advocate change at the core of society. "God is Black," their leaders assert, and thereby challenge the assumption that "God is White" with all that it connotes. In a very large sense, however, setting forth this dogma is simply a dramatic way of establishing a symbolic basis for identity and consensual commitment among individuals drawn from a distinctive but relatively unorganized social aggregate. Actually, in its efforts to socialize new members, the Black Muslims clearly stress central values of middle-class whites. The challenge to values of the larger society lies in the further assertion that the means by which this can be achieved is by complete segregation and new nationhood rather than by desegregation and increased meaningful inter-action. The contrast with the NAACP in this respect is in means and not in goals. There is nevertheless a real difference in strategy; one is defensive, the other is not.[23]

Many defensive societies bear a close resemblance to a certain stage in the development of what Wallace, in a stimulating paper, has termed "revitalization movements," which are efforts to create a more satisfying culture from cumulative dissatisfactions.[24] Such movements emerge well along in the defensive process, after adherents have overcome hostility from the dominant community and a new cultural state, if suitably stress reducing, has become routinized and expressed through a new organization.

By far the most impressive scholarly contribution to the study of social movements is Aberle's analysis of the Peyote religion among the Navaho.[25] In this work Aberle has succeeded specifically in making an exhaustive and convincing evaluation of all the factors that differentiate those who are attracted and committed in varying degrees to the Peyote cult from those who are opposed to it. After examining all internal variables of Navaho society—viz, age, sex, education, livelihood, health, education, church membership, kin relations, participation in the tribal council, and degree of acculturation—he was forced to conclude that the only factor that was significantly associated with cult membership was the livestock reduction program initiated in 1933 by the national government, in an effort to control progressive erosion. This process he invites us to think of in terms of relative deprivation. Individuals who became members of the cult were not necessarily poorer than those who did not, but relative to others they lost a significantly greater amount of wealth.[26]

In a subsequent chapter[27] the author attempts to place the Peyote cult in the wider context of a theory of social movements that is full of useful insights. He arrives at some four types of such movements:

(1) Transformative movements that aim at total social-cultural change (comparable to Smelser's value-oriented movements and including millenarian movements and revolutions).

(2) Reformative movements that aim at a partial social-cultural change (comparable to Smelser's norm-oriented movements and including fluoridation movements, child-labor-law movements, and peasant rebellions).

(3) Redemptive movements that aim at a total change in individuals (the Peyote cult falls in this class, as would probably Jewish ghetto and shtetl communities, early Christianity, Mormonism, and the Black Muslims).

(4) Alternative movements that aim at a partial change in individuals (birth control movements).

He then proceeds to identify constant and variable features of each and to indicate the significance of realtive deprivation, reference groups, and environmental contexts in relation to choice of one or another type of movement. Aberle's observations are broad ranging and repay careful reading, although he makes no effort to construct an exhaustive theory of the phenomenon. By concentrating on process, this analysis understandably fails to indicate common structural characteristics of defensive adaptation that cut across several types of movements. Among the possible alternative reactions to status deprivation, however, the author does include a "defensive insistence on the rightness of its behavior in the face of known, or imagined, opposition." And, in discussing the context of social movements, he hypothesizes that ". . . transformative goals are most likely when a deprived group is segregated spatially or socially and when its involvement with the larger social order is either slight or decreasing or both" [as when confronted with a superior technology or physical enclosure].[28] He would, I suspect, put Taos pueblo in this category. One might as well or better argue, on the other hand, that Taos leadership has mobilized its efforts to prevent transformation or even redemption through changed behavior, by a process of involution or turning in upon itself.

In brief, theories of social movements share, as elements in their analysis, a number of behavioral and environmental characteristics with a paradigm of defensive adaptation. Not all instances of the latter, however, are subsets of the former. In particular, defensive adaptations never take the form of revolution by violent means.

Defensive Adaptation and Culture

Defensive coping in the first place is a response to stress and perceived threat to continuities of, or barriers to, a meaningful way of life. It is a strategy that occurs when protagonists have limited resources for direct and possibly violent confrontation with the source(s) of frustration. Nevertheless, there are many instances of aggressive collective confrontation in the face of limited resources. Activist and so-called militant groups in America today are cases in point. This suggests that it is necessary to take into account something more than either of these factors in order to predict a defensive outcome.

An understanding of defensive adaptation ultimately is derived from the single most fundamental attribute of culture. This can be stated simply: culture is (symbolic) communication. People who respond positively but defensively to perceived threat from whatever exogenous source—subjugation, exploitation, urbanization, industrialization, urban-rural interaction, and the like—must either have a tradition or, out of a felt need, succeed in creating one. In either case, sharing at least core values over the long haul requires the means for sustaining regular and frequent communication. Minority ethnic enclaves, whether composed of immigrant groups or small-scale societies that came to be surrounded by dominant others in the course of settlement in American history, meet this requirement. In addition to groups specifically mentioned in this essay, we should include the Spanish-Americans in the southwest and Mexican Americans in the west, Chinese, Italians, Irish, and so forth.

Not all of these groups perceived a danger to their cultural integrity, hence made a defensive adaptation. An interesting example of cognitive change in an altered social context is described in a sociology dissertation. The data for this study involved aspects of adjustment patterns of a small minority of Catholics in relation to a preponderantly Mormon majority (about 93 percent of the total) in a small Idaho city (total population about 8,000). The Catholic enclave, instead of losing elements of value identification in their relations with the Mormons, which they would according to a theory of social marginality, actually exhibited considerably more cohesion and support of communal values than did Mormons. In this situation the church authorities exercised greater control over the individual's behavior than was true in comparable urban parishes from which immigrants came. For example, the Irish Catholic element, comprising about 30 percent of the total within this group, revealed almost none of the traditional pattern of drinking, which in this community came to be severely frowned upon. Family-centered internalized control in other areas of overt behavior was similarly reinforced by the same external authorities. These conditions obtained despite amiable relations between Catholics and Mormons generally. Leaders of the Catholic enclave perceived danger of group extinction as a distinctive entity. They were also able to communicate the reality of this threat to members and to enforce latent control over individual behavior to emphasize collective goals.[29]

The Jews, with such a long historical tradition, are a special case. It would be possible and useful to investigate response patterns at various peak periods of stress in the trajectory of their experiences from classical to modern times. More directly relevant, perhaps, it would also be instructive to study comparatively the immigrant population of eastern European shtetl Jews in relation to second- and third-generation American-born Jews. Both orthodox Jewish and Mormon traditions stress the value of formal learning. In so doing they embrace a paradox within the context of the larger society; namely, the alienation of the young who are exposed to important conflicts between school and home and church by virtue of the content of what is learned and to what purpose. This paradox is only partly resolved by the establishment of parochial schools. It would be interesting to study Jewish university leadership roles in the current, seemingly anarchistic element of Students for a Democratic Society, and to compare this phenomenon with their goal-oriented activism of a generation ago (in Trotskyite and Stalinist movements) in relation to cultural commitment.

Shared value commitment need not restrict itself to societies in the conventional sense of the word. To pull together and to hold members in some kind of long-range organization with a sense of shared urgency, however, requires rapid communication that approximates face-to-face interaction. These are precisely the conditions that, in contemporary America, enable the creation of viable defensive groups, like the Black Muslims, from broadly distributed sectors of society.

In a personal communication, Dr. William S. Madsen, then engaged in a field study of Alcoholics Anonymous in the San Francisco Bay area, informed me that this group—and probably all Anonymous groups, like Heroins Anonymous and Gamblers Anonymous—pinpoints precisely the structural elements we have identified with defensive adaptations (including the stress values, derived in this instance from the perception of hostile norms of non-Alcoholics of the established society). Alcoholics Anonymous, of course, is not an enclave and does not recruit members from married group members. However, it does have rather explicit criteria for "citizenship" in the sense of minimal conformance with a set of standards of behavior. Nonconformists are rigidly excluded, leaving a residual group strongly committed to these standards and to the authoritative controls of a small elite.

People who participate in defensive organizations are, in a sociological sense, minorities in that they feel deprived in relation to dominant institutions. They exist at the sufferance of other who have the means, should they wish to employ them, to suppress completely their efforts at independent cultural identity. Dependency behavior and subordination of decisionmaking to powerful centralized leadership develops out of a necessity to cope rapidly with day-to-day situations with which the group may be confronted. So, too, training for impulse control has strategic value in these groups because they possess limited resources and in the long run cannot hope to succeed by violent means.[30] They might, of course, attempt to do so by coopting large numbers of the dominant society to their cause, but in this way they run the risk of losing or weakening their identity. The early Christians, themselves a defensive society, succeeded admirably in missionary efforts, but ultimately gave rise to a rash of schisms and sectarian movements. I would invite more knowledgeable students about the subject than I to speculate in this vein about the defensive nature of the trade-union movement at the time of its early florescence under Samuel Gompers, and perhaps even in the early phase of the CIO. Most of the violence associated with some strike activities in the 1930's was, after all, initiated by suppressive elements of the dominant society. The coopting of powerful members of the latter through the political process led to successful efforts at achieving the cultural goals of the labor movement—and in the end to its transformation and integration with the establishment. It is instructive to observe the conservative tendency of labor unionism today and the loss of the ideological persuasion that attended its earlier phases.

A final note. By inference, people who are organized defensively are less likely than members of weakly organized groups or persons who participate in temporary collectivities (viz, ad hoc confrontations) to engage in violence. This is so because they have come to share a sense of cultural purpose that, in the social context in which they find themselves, can only be maintained by discipline and subordination of the individual to the larger entity. Crowds and assemblages are hard to discipline, given the nature of the communication process and unfiltered selection of participants. When defensive adaptation does occur, it always displays the same structure. Perhaps it is replicated in its essential features because for any group, category, or aggregate of people, it is the most economical and efficient means for coping with the problem of perceived severe stress applied over a long period of time.

Some of the remarks in this concluding section are more firmly wedded to the central analysis than others. I have engaged in a certain amount of speculation about selected problems of relevance to the nature of violence in America that clearly demand detailed, expert investigation. All of the comments, however, are shaped by a general paradigmatic theory of defensive adaptation.

References

1. Detailed historical analysis of the emergence of defensive societies—a history of the Mormons, of the Jews, at least from the 19th-century ghetto period through second-generation American Jewry, of Taos and other Indian pueblos, and of the Black Muslims—would provide some of the best evidence for the solution of these kinds of problems. Systematic comparison of culturally related groups, which vary only with respect to specified dimensions of environmental changes, is another method of predicting alternative strategies of adaptation. For want of space both of these methods can be applied only in a limited way in this essay.

2. A. I. Hallowell, "The Social Psychology of Acculturation," in Ralph Linton, ed., *The Science of Man in the World Crisis* (New York: Columbia University Press, 1945). See also Barnard J. Siegel, "High Anxiety Levels and Cultural Integration: Notes on a Psychocultural Hypothesis," *Social Forces* (Oct. 1955).

3. Emile Durkheim, *Le Suicide* (Paris: Ancienne Libraire Germer Bailliere, 1897), ch. IV. See also the discussion of "institutional suicide" in Ruth Shonle Cavan, *Suicide* (Chicago: University of Chicago Press, 1927), pp. 69 ff.

4. Observations about the Black Muslims are derived primarily from two sources: C. Eric Lincoln, *The Black Muslims in America* (Boston: Beacon Press, 1961); and E. U. Essien-Udom, *Black Nationalism* (New York: Dell Press, 1962).

5. Or, as Ward Goodenough has expressed it, the "limiting effect [of each custom] on the forms that other customs can conveniently take." *Cooperation in Change* (New York: Russell Sage Foundation, 1963), p. 68. Hence, where there is a high degree of integration in this sense we would expect a continual scrutiny of inconsistencies and ambiguities among beliefs.

6. It is perhaps not accidental that the holistic approach to the concept of culture, an emphasis upon the functional interdependence of custom and belief, came early to dominate the thinking of anthropologists, as a consequence until recently of their almost exclusive concern with the study of small-scale, relatively isolated and discrete primitive societies. The communication network of defensive societies tends to approximate that of primitive isolated groups, and is indeed intended to foster isolation in the complex environments of the modern world.

7. Not all so-called tribal and peasant societies exhibit this reluctance to accept innovations and proliferate alternatives, a view once commonly assumed by Western advocates of technological innovation who encountered so many negative experiences. Quite the contrary, as many postwar studies vividly reveal. This characterization, an artifact of oversimplified classification of human groups by many anthropologists, often masked their variability in this respect. The error was compounded by failing to consider as part of social theory the continuous interaction of group and environment. See, for example, Raymond Firth, *Elements of Social Organization* (London: Watts, 1951), p. 109.

8. The high degree of endogamy among orthodox Pueblo Indians, Jews, and Mormons is well documented. Among Black Muslims marriage with a white is emphatically prohibited. Less well known is the fact that, in comparison with blacks as a whole, marriage is strongly preferential within the group. When a member does marry a non-Muslim, great pressure is put on non-muslin spouses to join the nation.

9. See Essien-Udom, *op cit.*, p. 199.

10. To the investigator this wall of seclusion is both frustrating and challenging. The gates seldom open wide, and then for short intervals, always attended by vigilant gatekeepers—to use Kurt Lewin's graphic simile. This is why some of the best ethnographies are the products of members or former members who have become behavioral scientists and retain an entree into the group.

11. See Edward Wakin, *A Lonely Minority: The Modern Story of Egypt's Copts* (New York: Morrow, 1963), pp. 141 and 147 ff.; also Lincoln, *op. cit.*, pp. 15 ff. and 199. For many years the Copts had a strong central political organization. Its influence over the past few years had progressively weakened as they identified their own welfare in Egyptian colonial days with dominant European Christians. With the virtual elimination of other non-Moslem minority groups during the Nasser regime (Jews and non-Coptic Christian groups), they once more lived in a world

in which they perceived the threat of being absorbed into the general population and of economic and social deprivation. It is interesting to note, as they recall with increasing alarm the belligerence of the Moslem Brotherhood and Egyptian nationalism, unmistakable evidence of increased Coptic nationalism.

12. Other dispersed defensive societies, like Mormons and shtetl Jews, similarly evolved mechanisms for frequent communication of active members both within and between communities.

13. Wakin, *ibid.*, Walter A. Riddle, "The Rise of Ecclesiastical Control in Quebec," doctoral dissertation, Faculty of Political Science, Columbia University, 1916, pp. 94 ff.; Everett Cherrington Hughes, *French Canada in Transition* (Chicago: University of Chicago Press, 1962), p. 9.

14. Lee Emerson Deets, "The Hutterites: A Study in Social Cohesion," doctoral dissertation, Faculty of Political Science, Columbia University, 1939, p. 17.

15. Thomas F. O'Dea, *The Mormons* (Chicago: University of Chicago Press, 1957) pp. 49, 130, and 143. See also Gaylon L. Caldwell, "Mormon Conceptions of Individual Rights and Political Organization," doctoral dissertation, Department of Political Science, Stanford University, 1952, p. 234. Both the Hutterites and Mormons initiate virtually all adolescent males into the Church's esoteric matters and responsibilities. From late adolescence on, they constitute a reservoir of potential members of the priesthood.

We do find defensive societies in which the ultimate source of power is apparently not derived from a special religious knowledge. A Japanese sociologist informs us, for example, of a fishing hamlet in northeastern Honshu, so removed in modern times from communication with neighboring hamlets that it remains as isolated as one can possibly imagine under present conditions. This isolation, moreover, is preferred and controlled. Only a few households receive newpapers or magazines, or listen to a radio. This is in great contrast to the reading habits among Japanese as a whole. Eighty-five percent of men and 75 percent of women are natives of the hamlet. Local endogamy, in other words, is the role for all but a small percentage of members; the latter in turn select marriage partners from neighboring hamlets. The scope of life is so narrow that people rarely visit other hamlets that comprise the village, and they still continue an old practice of shopping as a community twice a year at the neighboring town.

Traditionally strong patriarchal control had long been exerted by family heads and by a village council consisting of older males, in conformance with Confucian values that defined desirable properties of family life. These values provide the moral basis for action but cannot be said to constitute part of a religious system, in the sense of being codified in sacred literature, oral or written. In another sense, however, they might be thought of as belonging to the realm of the sacred, in that they necessitate acting out, with almost punctilious ritual, conformity to detail and a deeply felt reluctance to change. Today the custodians of this tradition suppress even more stringently on the part of the young any relaxation of the etiquette that symbolizes these authoritarian relations: the use of respectful language, seating customs at meals and during visits, the subservience of a man's wife to his mother, and the stern emphasis on hard work imposed upon the young. See Yoshio Saito, "On the Structural Analysis of a Fishing Village: The Case of Miyagi-Ken, Ojurugun, Onagawa-Machi," *Japanese Sociological Review,* vol. V (1955), pp. 24-46.

16. See, e.g., Fred Eggan, *Social Organization of the Western Pueblos* (Chicago: University of Chicago Press, 1950), pp. 291-324

17. For a more detailed analysis of stress and social process in Taos pueblo, see Alan R. Beals and Bernard J. Siegel, *Divisiveness and Social Conflict: An Anthropological Approach* (Stanford: Stanford University Press, 1965), chs. 3 and 4.

18. Bernard J. Siegel, "Social Disorganization in Picuris Pueblo," *International Journal of Comparative Sociology,* vol. VI (1965), p. 205.

19. This point of view, and indeed most anthropological conceptions of society and culture, however inductively arrived at, is consistent with modern systems theory. In the interest of clarity, I have tried to avoid the introduction of unnecessary jargon. For an introduction to a systems outlook, the reader is referred to Walter Buckley, ed., *Modern Systems Research for the Behavioral Scientist* (Chicago: Aldine, 1968).

20. See Esther S. Goldfrank, "Irrigation Agriculture and Navaho Community Leadership: Case Material on Environment and Culture," *American Anthropologist,* XLVII (No. 2, 1945), pp. 262-277. Although she deals principally with the Navaho, Dr. Goldfrank considers also data relating to the pueblos.

21. See, for example, the excellent analysis of such a case among Yiryiront, a society of Australian Aboriginese, as recounted by Lauriston Sharp, "Steel Axes for Stone Age Australians," in E. H. Spicer, ed., *Human Problems in Technological Change* (New York: Russell Sage, 1952), pp. 69-90. The evidence that Sharp provides suggests, among other things, that sporadic stress encounters, however traumatic, will not lead to social change either in the direction of defensive structuring, other than disorganization, or in any other direction away from the status quo ante.

22. Neil J. Smelser, *Theory of Collective Behavior* (New York: The Free Press, 1963).

23. It is interesting in this regard to note the general detachment of American Indians from active involvement in and support of the civil rights movement. What the blacks are struggling for, they feel they already have and are not about to jeopardize their cultural vitality by participation in a larger incorporative organization.

24. A. F. C. Wallace, "Revitalization Movements," *American Anthropologist,* vol. LVIII (No. 2, 1956), pp. 264-281.

25. David F. Aberle, *The Peyote Religion Among the Navaho* (New York: Wenner-Gren Foundation for Anthropological Research, 1966).

26. This is a gross simplification of a much more sophisticated argument.

27. Aberle, *op. cit.,* ch. 19.

28. *Ibid.,* pp. 327, 330.

29. See Jack Homer Curtis, "Group Marginality and Adherence to Religious Doctrine in an American Community," doctoral dissertation, Department of Sociology, Stanford University, 1954.

30. If we were to inquire further, we would probably see that dispersed defensive associations tend to attract and to hold within the central core persons characterized by strong dependency needs, however varied their social and cultural backgrounds (substantial numbers of dissidents are sloughed off or removed in one way or another), and then to weld them into a novel organization.

CONCLUSION

I. THE COMMONALITY OF COLLECTIVE VIOLENCE IN THE WESTERN TRADITION

Future historians may marvel at the ostensible "rediscovery" of violence that has both fascinated and bemused contemporary observers. That the recent resurgence of collective nonmilitary violence in Western society is widely regarded as anomalous probably reflects both a cultural and a contemporary bias. We have tended to assume, perhaps unconsciously, that such violence was an uncivilized practice of more primitive societies that the civilized and affluent West had largely outgrown. Our historians have themselves been guilty of contributing to this popular illusion; while they have retained their fascination for military exploits, they have tended either to ignore the persistence of domestic turmoil except when it reached revolutionary proportions, or to minimize its significance by viewing it from the perspective of established authority. When viewed from the top down, violence was understandably regarded as an abnormal and undesirable breach of the public order.

On the contrary, Tilly concludes, "collective violence is normal."

> Historically, collective violence has flowed regularly out of the central, political processes of western countries. Men seeking to seize, hold, or realign the levers of power have continually engaged in collective violence as part of their struggles. The oppressed have struck in the name of justice, the privileged in the name of order, those in between in the name of fear.

In Tilly's analysis, collective violence in the European experience was fundamentally transformed but not foredoomed by the processes of industrialization and urbanization. The old "primitive" forms of violence in feudal Europe—such as communal feuds and religious persecutions—were characterized by small scale, local scope, communal group participation, and inexplicit and unpolitical objectives. The subsequent evolution of the nation-state prompted such "reactionary" disturbances as food riots, Luddite destruction, tax revolts, and anticonscription rebellions. Although industrialization and urbanization muted such disorders by disrupting their cohesive communal base, the metropolitan society these forces forged gave rise to "modern" forms of protest—such as demonstrations and strikes—which involved relatively large and specialized associations with relatively well-defined and "forward-looking" objectives and which were explicitly organized for political or economic action.

Tilly's model suggests that modern collective protest, owing to its broader associational base, is more likely to occur on a large scale. But modern protest is less likely to become violent because the associational form gives the group a surer control over its own actions, and thus permits shows of force without concomitant damage or bloodshed. Moreover, the historic shift from communal to associational bases for collective protest brought into being a number of modern nonviolent mechanisms for the regulation of conflicts: the strike, the demonstration, the parliament, and the political campaign. Collective violence, then, historically belongs to political life, and changes in its form tell us that something important is happening to the political system itself.

What is happening to the political system in contemporary America? Preliminary to such an inquiry is the historical task of surveying the patterns of group violence that have accompanied the development of the United States. Brown has traced an overview of American collective violence, and his organizational categories of "negative" and "positive" violence in some ways parallel Tilly's analytical distinctions between reactionary disturbances, which center on rights once enjoyed but now threatened, and modern disturbances, which center on rights not yet enjoyed but now within reach. It might be more appropriate in this conclusion to discuss the American historical legacy of violence in relation to the contemporary relevance of the various categories Brown employed. Brown catalogued as "negative" forms of American violence that associated with feuds, lynching, political assassination, free-lance multiple murder, crime, ethnic and racial prejudice, and urban rioting. "Positive" forms were associated with the American Revolution and Civil War, agrarian uprisings, labor protests, vigilantism, Indian wars, and police violence.

Perhaps the historically violent episode that is least relevant to our contemporary concerns is the family feud. The famous and colorful clan feuding seems to have been triggered by the Civil War in border areas where loyalties were sharply divided and where the large extended family of the 19th century provided both a locus for intense loyalties and a ready instrument of aggression. But this tradition has waned with the fading of the circumstances that conditioned its birth. It is arguable, however, that the brutalizing traditions associated with the Indian wars have left their callous imprint on our national character long after the estimated 850,000 American Indians had been ruthlessly reduced by 1950 to 400,000. Similarly, the violence associated with the American Revolution, the Civil War, and Reconstruction has surely reinforced the ancient notion that the ends justify the means, and clearly the defeat of the Confederacy and the failure of Reconstruction has convinced generations of white Southerners that Negro political participation and Federal efforts at reform are irrevocably linked with corruption and subversion.

Whether the long association with violence of agrarian uprisings and the labor movement has permanently faded with changing modern circumstances is fervently to be hoped, but by no means certain. Employer acceptance of unions during and after the New Deal suggests that that long and bloody conflict is largely behind us. But the stubborn persistence of rural poverty constitutes a latent invitation to a resurgence of latter-day populism.

Two other sordid American traditions that have largely waned but that recently have shown some signs of revival are vigilantism and lynching. Although vigilantism is associated in the popular mind with such frontier and rural practices as antirustler and antihorsethief popular "justice" in areas largely devoid of regular enforcement agencies, the largest local American vigilance committee was organized in San Francisco in 1856. If vigilantism is defined more broadly to include regional and even national movements as well as local organizations, then America's preeminent vigilante movement has been the Ku Klux Klan—or rather, the Ku Klux Klans, for there have essentially been three of them. The original Klan arose in the South in response to radical Reconstruction, and through terror and intimidation was instrumental in the "redemption" of the Southern state governments by white conservatives. The second Klan, by far the largest, was resurrected in Atlanta in 1915 and boomed nationally in the 1920's. Strong in the Midwest and Far West as well as the South, and making inroads even in the cities, the Klan of the 1920's—despite its traditional racist and xenophobic rhetoric—focused its chastisement less upon Negroes, Catholics, and Jews than upon local white Protestants who were adjudged guilty of violating smalltown America's Victorian moral code. The third Klan represented a proliferation of competing Klans in the South in response to the civil rights movement of the 1950's. Generally lacking the prestige and organizational strength of the earlier Klans, these groups engaged in a period of unrestrained terrorism in the rural and smalltown Black Belt South in the 1950's and early 1960's, but have belatedly been brought under greater control.

Lynching, vigilantism's supreme instrument of terror and summary "justice," has been widely practiced in America certainly since the Revolutionary era, when miscreant Tories were tarred and feathered, and worse. Although lynching is popularly associated with racial mob murder, this pattern is a relatively recent one, for prior to the late 19 century, white Americans perforce lynched one another—Negro slaves being far too valuable to squander at the stake. But lynching became predominantly racial from 1882 to 1903, when 1,985 Negroes were murdered in the tragic but successful effort of those years to forge a rigid system of biracial caste, most brutal and explicit in the South but generally reflective of national attitudes. Once the point—that this was a white man's country—was made, lynching gradually declined. Its recent resurgence in response to the civil rights movement is notorious, but it nowhere approximates its scale at the turn of the century.

The contemporary relevance of political assassination and freelance multiple murder needs no documentation to a nation that has so recently witnessed the murders of John and Robert Kennedy, Dr. Martin Luther King, and, on television, Lee Harvey Oswald—in addition to the chilling mass slaughtering sprees of Charles Whitman in Austin, Texas, and Richard Speck in Chicago. Historically, political assassination has become a recurrent feature of the political system only in the South during (the first) Reconstruction and in New Mexico Territory. Although four American Presidents have been assassinated since 1865, prominent politicans and civil servants occupying the myriad lesser levels of government have been largely immune. Whether the current spate of public murder is an endemic symptom of a new social malaise is a crucial question that history cannot yet answer, other than to observe that precedents in our past are minimal.

Similarly, historical precedents are few regarding massive student and antiwar protests. American students have historically succumbed to the annual spring throes of the panty-raid syndrome, but the current wave of campus confrontations is essentially an unprecedented phenomenon—as is the massive and prolonged opposition to the war in Vietnam. As Professor Brooks has observed, "unfortunately the past does not have much to tell us; we will have to make our own history along uncharted and frightening ways."

But the past has much to tell us about the rioting and crime that have gripped our cities. Urban mobs are as old as the city itself. Colonial seaports frequently were rocked for days by roving mobs—groups of unruly and often drunken men whose energies were shrewdly put to political purpose as Liberty Boys in the American Revolution. Indeed, our two principal instruments of physical control evolved directly in response to 19th-century urban turmoil. The professional city police system replaced the inadequate constabulary and watch-and-ward in response to the rioting of the 1840's and 1850's, largely in the Northeast. Similarly, the national guard was organized in order to control the labor violence—or more appropriately, the antilabor violence—of the 1880's and 1890's.

Probably all nations are given to a kind of historical amnesia or selective recollection that masks unpleasant traumas of the past. Certainly Americans since the Puritans have historically regarded themselves as a latter-day "Chosen People" sent on a holy errand to the wilderness, there to create a New Jerusalem. One beneficent side effect of our current turmoil may be to force a harder and more candid look at our past and at our behavior in comparison with other peoples and nations.

II. CONTEMPORARY AMERICAN VIOLENCE IN HISTORICAL PERSPECTIVE

Our current eruption of violence must appear paradoxical to a generation of Americans who witnessed the successful emergence from depression to unparalleled affluence of a nation they regarded as the world's moral leader in defense of freedom. Only a decade ago America's historians were celebrating the emergence of a unique society, sustained by a burgeoning prosperity and solidly grounded on a broad political consensus.[1] We were told—and the implications were reassuring—that our uniqueness was derived from at least half a dozen historical sources which, mutually reinforcing one another, had joined to propel us toward a manifestly benevolent destiny. We were a nation of immigrants, culturally enriched by the variety of mankind. Sons of the frontier, our national character has grown to reflect the democratic individualism and pragmatic ingenuity that had conquered the wilderness. Our new nation was born in anticolonial revolution and in its crucible was forged a democratic republic of unparalleled vitality and longevity. Lacking a feudal past, our political spectrum was so truncated about the consensual liberal center that, unlike Europe, divisive radicalism of the left or right had found no sizable constituency. Finally, we had both created and survived the great transformation from agrarian frontier to industrial metropolis, to become the richest nation of all time.

It was a justly proud legacy, one which seemed to make sense in the relatively tranquil 1950's. But with the 1960's came shock and frustration. It was a decade against itself: the students of affluence were marching in the streets; middle-class matrons were besieging the Pentagon; and Negro Americans were responding to victories in civil rights and to their collectively unprecedented prosperity with a paradoxical venting of outrage. In a fundamental sense, history—the ancient human encounter with poverty, defeat, and guilt as well as with affluence, victory, and innocence—had finally caught up with America. Or at least it had caught up with white America.

Historical analysis of our national experience and character would suggest that the seeds of our contemporary discontent were to a large extent deeply embedded in those same ostensibly benevolent forces which contributed to our uniqueness. First, we are a nation of immigrants, but one in which the original dominant immigrant group, the so-called Anglo-Saxons, effectively preempted the crucial levers of economic and political power in government, commerce, and the professions. This elite group has tenaciously resisted the upward strivings of successive "ethnic" immigrant waves. The resultant competitive hierarchy of immigrants has always been highly conducive to violence, but this violence has taken different forms. The Anglo-Americans have used their access to the levers of power to maintain their dominance, using legal force surrounded by an aura of legitimacy for such ends as economic exploitation; the restriction of immigration by a national-origin quota system which clearly branded later immigrants as culturally undesirable; the confinement of the original Indian immigrants largely to barren reservations; and the restriction of blacks to a degraded caste. But the system was also conducive to violence among the latter groups themselves— when, for instance, Irish-Americans rioted against Afro-American "scabs." Given America's unprecedented ethnic pluralism, simply being born American conferred no automatic and equal citizenship in the eyes of the larger society. In the face of such reservations, ethnic minorities had constantly to affirm ⟋ their Americanism through a kind of patriotic ritual which intensified the ethnic competition for status. As a fragment culture based on bourgeois-liberal values, as Hartz has observed, yet one populated by an unprecedented variety of immigrant stock, America's tightened consensus on what properly constituted "Americanism" prompted status rivalries among the ethnic minorities which, when combined with economic rivalries, invited severe and abiding conflict.

Most distinctive among the immigrant minorities was the Negro. The eternal exception in American history, Afro-Americans were among the first to arrive and the last to emerge. To them, America meant slavery, and manumission meant elevation to the caste of black pariah. Comer has seen in the psychological legacy of slavery and caste a psychically crippling Negro dependency and even self-hatred which is largely immune to mere economic advance. The contemporary black awareness of this tenacious legacy of racial shame is abundantly reflected in the radical rhetoric of black power and "Black-is-Beautiful," and goes far toward resolving the paradox of black rebellion against a backdrop of general—albeit uneve, as Davies suggests— economic improvement. Meier and Rudwick have charted the transformation of racial violence from white pogrom to black aggression—or, in the analysis of Janowtiz, from "communal" to "commodity" rioting. While emphasizing that the transformation has led to violent black assault less against white persons than against white property, and while Janowitz speculates that the summer of 1968 may have been yet another turning point, we are reminded that history, even very recent history, is an imperfect guide to the future.

The second major formative historical experience was America's uniquely prolonged encounter with the frontier. While the frontier experience indubitably strengthened the mettle of the American character, it witnessed the brutal and brutalizing ousting of the Indians and the forceful incorporation of Mexican and other original inhabitants, as Frantz has so graphically portrayed. Further, it concomitantly created an environment in which, owing to the paucity of law enforcement agencies, a tradition of vigilante "justice" was legitimized. The longevity of the Ku Klux Klan and the vitality both of contemporary urban rioting and of the stiffening resistance to it owe much to this tradition. As Brown has observed, vigilantism has persisted as a socially malleable instrument long after the disappearance of the frontier environment that gave it birth, and it has proved quite congenial to an urban setting.

Similarly, the revolutionary doctrine that our Declaration of Independence proudly proclaims stands as a tempting model of legitimate violence to be emulated by contemporary groups, such as militant Negroes and radical students who confront a system of both public and private government that they regard as contemptuous of their consent. Entranced by the resurgence of revolution in the underdeveloped world and of international university unrest, radical students and blacks naturally seize upon our historically sacrosanct doctrine of the inherent right of revolution and self-determination to justify their rebellion. That their analogies are fatefully problematical in no way dilutes the majesty of our own proud Declaration.

The fourth historic legacy, our consensual political philosophy of Lockean-Jeffersonian liberalism, was premised upon a pervasive fear of governmental power and has reinforced the tendency to define freedom negatively as freedom *from*. As a consequence, conservatives have been able paradoxically to invoke the doctrines of Jefferson in resistance to legislative reforms, and the Sumnerian imperative that "stateways cannot change folkways" has historically enjoyed a wide and not altogether unjustified allegiance in the public eye (witness the debacle of the first Reconstruction, and the dilemma of our contemporary second attempt). Its implicit corollary has been that forceful and, if necessary, violent local and state resistance to unpopular federal stateways is a legitimate response; both Calhoun and Wallace could confidently repair to a strict construction of the same document invoked by Lincoln and the Warren court.

A fifth historic source both of our modern society and our current plight is our industrial revolution and the great internal migration from the countryside to the city. Yet the process occurred with such astonishing rapidity that it produced widespread socioeconomic dislocation in an environment in which the internal controls of the American social structure were loose and the external controls were weak. Urban historian Richard Wade has observed that—

> The cities inherited no system of police control adequate to the numbers or to the rapid increase of the urban centers. The modern police force is the creation of the 20th century; the establishment of genuinely professional systems is historically a very recent thing.

> Throughout the 18th and 19th century, the force was small, untrained, poorly paid, and part of the political system. In case of any sizeable disorder, it was hopelessly inadequate; and rioters sometimes routed the constabulary in the first confrontation.[2]

Organized labor's protracted and bloody battles for recognition and power occurred during these years of minimal control and maximal social upheaval. The violence of workers' confrontations with their employers, Taft and Ross concluded, was partly the result of a lack of consensus on the legitimacy of workers' protests, partly the result of the lack of means of social control. Workers used force to press their grievances, employers organized violent resistance, and repeatedly state or federal troops had to be summoned to restore order.

The final distinctive characteristic—in many ways perhaps our most distinctive—has been our unmatched prosperity; we have been, in the words of David Potter, most characteristically a "people of plenty." Ranked celestially with life and liberty in the sacrosanct Lockean trilogy, property has generated a quest and prompted a devotion in the American character that has matched our devotion to equality and, in a fundamental sense, has transformed it from the radical leveling of the European democratic tradition into a typically American insistence upon equality of opportunity. In an acquisitive society of individuals with unequal talents and groups with unequal advantages, this had resulted in an unequal distribution of the rapid accumulation of abundance that, especially since World War II, has promised widespread participation in the affluent society to a degree unprecedented in history. Central to the notion of "revolutions of rising expectations," and to Davies' J-curve hypothesis as well, is the assumption that unproved economic rewards can coincide with and often obscure a degree of relative deprivation that generates frustration and can prompt men toward violent protest despite measurable gains.

Our historical evolution, then, has given our national character a dual nature: we strive, paradoxically, for both liberty and equality, which can be and often in practice are quite contradictory goals. This is not to suggest that American society is grounded in a fatal contradiction. For all the conflict inherent in a simultaneous quest for liberty and equality, American history is replete with dramatic instances of the successful adjustment of "the system" to the demands of disparate protesting groups. An historical appraisal of these genuine achievements should give pause to contemporary Cassandras who bemoan in selfflagellation how hopelessly wretched we all are. These radically disillusioned social critics can find abundant evil in our historical legacy: centuries of Negro slavery, the cultural deracination and near extinction of the Indians, our initiation of atomic destruction—ad infinitum. Much as the contemporary literary Jeremiahs have, in Lynn's view, libeled the American character by extrapolating violence from its literary context, these social critics in their overcompensations have distorted the American experience in much the same fashion, although in an opposite direction, as have the more familiar superpatriotic celebrants of American virtuosity. While a careful and honest historical appraisal should remind us that violence has been far more intrinsic to our past than we should like to think—Brooks reminds us, for example, that the New York Draft Riot of 1863 vastly exceeded the destruction of Watts—our assessment of the origins and dimen-

sions of contemporary American violence must embrace the experience of
other societies.

III. COMPARISONS OF PROTEST AND VIOLENCE

Whether the United States is now a "violent society" can be answered not
in the abstract but only by comparison, either with the American past or with
other nations. The historical evidence, above, suggests that we were somewhat
more violent toward one another in this decade than we have been in most
others, but probably less violent in total magnitude of civil strife than in the
latter 19th century, when the turmoil of Reconstruction was followed by
massive racial and labor violence. Even so, in contemporary comparison with
other nations, acts of collective violence by private citizens in the United States
in the last 20 years have been extraordinarily numerous, and this is true also of
peaceful demonstrations. In numbers of political assassinations, riots, politically
relevant armed group attacks, and demonstrations, the United States since
1948 has been among the half-dozen most tumultuous nations in the
world.[3] When such events are evaluated in terms of their relative severity,
however, the rank of the United States is somewhat lower. The Feierabends
and Nesvold have used ranking scales to weigh the severity and numbers of
such events during the years from 1948 to 1965, rating peaceful demonstrations as having the least serious impact, civil wars the most serious impact
on political systems. In a comparison that gives greatest weight to the frequency of violent events, the United States ranks 14th among 84 nations.
In another comparison, based mainly on the severity of all manifestations of
political instability, violent or not, the United States stands below the midpoint,
46th among 84 nations. In other words, the United States up to 1965 had
much political violence by comparison with other nations but relative stability
of its political institutions in spite of it. Paradoxically, we have been a turbulent
people but a relatively stable republic.
Some more detailed comparisons are provided by a study of the characteristics of civil strife in 114 nations and colonies in the 1960's. The information
on "civil strife" includes all reported acts of collective violence involving 100
or more people; organized private attacks on political targets, whatever the
number of participants; and antigovernment demonstrations involving 100 or
more people. Three general kinds of civil strife are distinguished: (1) *Turmoil*
is relatively spontaneous, partially organized or unorganized strife with substantial popular participation and limited objectives. (2) *Conspiracy* is intensively organized strife with limited participation but with terroristic or
revolutionary objectives. (3) *Internal war* is intensively organized strife with
widespread participation, always accompanied by extensive and intensive
violence and usually directed at the overthrow of political regimes.
The comparisons of the strife study are proportional to population rather
than absolute, on grounds that a demonstration by 10,000 of Portugal's 9
million citizens, for example, is more consequential for that nation than a
demonstration by the same number of the United States' 200 million citizens
is for ours. About 11 of every 1,000 Americans took part in civil strife, almost
all of it turmoil, between mid-1963 and mid-1968, compared with an
average of 7 per thousand in 17 other Western democracies during the
1961-65 period. Six of these 17 had higher rates of participation than the

United States, including Belgium, France, and Italy. About 9,500 reported casualties resulted from American strife, most of them the result of police action. This is a rate of 48 per million population, compared with an average of 12 per million in other Western nations, but American casualties are almost certain to be overreported by comparison with casualties elsewhere. Strife was also of longer duration in the United States than in all but a handful of countries in the world. In total magnitude of strife, taking these three factors into account, the United States ranks first among the 17 Western democracies.

Despite its frequency, civil strife in the United States has taken much less disruptive forms than in many non-Western and some Western countries. More than a million citizens participated in 370 reported civil-rights demonstrations and marches in the 5-year period; almost all of them were peacefully organized and conducted. Of 170 reported antiwar demonstrations, which involved a total of about 700,000 people, the participants initiated violence in about 20: The most extensive violence occurred in 239 recorded hostile outbreaks by Negroes, which resulted in more than 8,000 casualties and 191 deaths. Yet the nation has experienced no internal wars since the Civil War and almost none of the chronic revolutionary conspiracy and terrorism that plague dozens of other nations. The most consequential conspiratorial violence has been white terrorism against blacks and civil-rights workers, which caused some 20 deaths between 1963 and 1968, and black terrorism against whites, mostly the police, which began in 1968.

Although about 220 Americans died in violent civil strife in the 5 years before mid-1968, the rate of 1.1 per million population was infinitesimal compared with the average of all nations of 238 deaths per million, and less than the European average of 2.4 per million. These differences reflect the comparative evidence that, from a worldwide perspective, Americans have seldom organized for violence. Most demonstrators and rioters are protesting, not rebelling. If there were many serious revolutionaries in the United States, or effective revolutionary organizations, levels of violence would be much higher than they have been.

These comparisons afford little comfort when the tumult of the United States is contrasted with the relative domestic tranquillity of developed democratic nations like Sweden, Great Britain, and Australia, or with the comparable current tranquillity of nations as diverse as Yugoslavia, Turkey, Jamaica, or Malaysia. In total magnitude of strife, the United States ranks 24th among the 114 larger nations and colonies of the world. In magnitude of turmoil alone, it ranks sixth.

Though greater in magnitude, civil strife in the United States is about the same in kind as strife in other Western nations. The antigovernment demonstration and riot, violent clashes of political or ethnic groups, and student protests are pervasive forms of conflict in modern democracies. Some such public protest has occurred in every Western nation in the past decade. People in non-Western countries also resort to these limited forms of public protest, but they are much more likely to organize serious conspiratorial and revolutionary movements as well. Strife in the United States and other European countries is quite likely to mobilize members of both the working class and middle classes, but rarely members of the political establishment such as military officers, civil servants, and disaffected political leaders, who so often organize conspiracies and internal wars in non-European nations. Strife also is likely to occur within or on the periphery of the normal political process in Western nations, rather than being organized by clandestine revolutionary movements or cells of plotters. If some overt strife is an inevitable accompaniment of organized social existence, as all our comparative evidence suggests it is, it seems socially preferable that it take the form of open political protest, even violent protest, rather than concerted, intensively violent attempts to seize political power.

One evident characteristic of civil strife in the United States in recent years is the extent to which it is an outgrowth of ethnic tensions. Much of the civil protest and collective violence in the United States has been directly related to the nation's racial problems. Comparative studies show evidence of parallel though not identical situations in other developed, European, and democratic nations. The unsatisfied demands of regional, ethnic, and linguistic groups for greater rights and socioeconomic benefits are more common sources of civil strife in Western nations than in almost any other group of countries. These problems have persisted long after the resolution of fundamental questions about the nature of the state, the terms of political power and who should hold it, and economic development. It seems ironical that nations that have been missionaries of technology and political organization to the rest of the world apparently have failed to provide satisfactory conditions of life for all the groups within their midst.

IV. THE SOURCES OF VIOLENCE

Is man violent by nature or by circumstance? In the Hobbesian view, the inescapable legacy of human nature is a "life of man solitary, poor, nasty, brutish, and short." This ancient pessimistic view is given recent credence by the ethologists, whose study of animals in their natural habitats had led them to conclude that the aggressive drive in animals is innate, ranking with the instinctive trilogy of hunger, sex, and fear or flight.[4] But most psychologists and social scientists do not regard aggression as fundamentally spontaneous or instinctive, nor does the weight of their evidence support such a view. Rather they regard most aggression, including violence, as sometimes an emotional response to socially induced frustrations, and sometimes a dispassionate, learned response evoked by specific situations.[5] This assumption underlies almost all the studies in this volume: nature provides us only with the capacity for violence; it is social circumstance that determines whether and how we exercise that capacity.

Man's cultural diversity offers concrete evidence that this essentially optimistic view of human nature is justified. Man can through his intelligence so construct his cultural traditions and institutions as to minimize violence and encourage the realization of his humanistic goals. Cultural anthropologists have identified societies, such as four contiguous language groups in the remote Eastern Highlands of New Guinea, in which the rhythms of life were focused on a deadly and institutionally permanent game of rape and cannibalism. But they have also studied such gentle societies as those of the Arapesh of New Guinea, the Lepchas of Sikkim, and the pygmies of the Congo rain forest, cultures in which an appetite for aggression has been replaced by an "enormous gusto for concrete physical pleasures—eating, drinking, sex, and laughter." Revealingly, these gentle societies generally lack the cultural model of brave, aggressive masculinity, a pervasive model that seems so conducive to violence. Evidence that culture is a powerful if not omnipotent determinant of man's propensity for violence is the melancholy contemporary fact that Manhattan Island (population 1.7 million) has more murders per year than all of England and Wales (population 49 million). We need not resolve the interminable hen-and-egg debate over the primacy of nature versus nurture to conclude that man has the cultural capacity to minimize his recourse to violence.

One general approach to the explanation of the nature and extent of collective violence, supported by considerable evidence in this report, begins with the assumption that men's frustration over some of the material and social circumstances of their lives is a necessary precondition of group protest and collective violence. The more intense and widespread frustration-induced discontent is among a people, the more intense and widespread collective violence is likely to be. Several general attitudinal and social conditions determine the extent and form of consequent violence. People are most strongly disposed to act violently on their discontent if they believe that violence is justifiable and likely of success; they are likely to take violent political action to the extent that they regard their government as illegitimate and responsible for their frustrations. The extent, intensity, and organization of civil strife is finally determined by characteristics of the social system: the degree and consistency of social control, and the extent to which institutions afford peaceful alternatives to violent protest.[7]

If discontent is a root cause of violence within the political community, what kinds of conditions give rise to the widespread discontents that lead to collective violence? All societies generate some discontent because organized social life by its very nature frustrates all human beings, by inhibiting some of their natural impulses. Socialized inhibitions and outlets for such discontents are provided by every society, though their relative effectiveness is certainly an underlying factor in national differences in rates of aggressive crimes. Another fundamental factor may be the ecological one. Carstairs summarizes evidence that overcrowding of human populations may lead to aggressiveness. On the other hand, Tilly shows that high rates of immigration to French cities in the 18th and 19th centuries was, if anything, associated with civil peace rather than rising disorder. Lane also finds that increasing urbanization in 19th-century Massachusetts was accompanied by a decline in violent crime rates. Neither culture stress nor population concentrations per se seem to be consequential causes of upsurges in collective violence, though they probably contribute to the "background noise" of violence common to almost all cultures. Probably the most important cause of major increases in group violence is the widespread frustration of socially deprived expectations about the goods and conditions of life men believe theirs by right. These frustratable expectations relate not only to material well-being but to more intangible conditions such as security, status, freedom to manage one's own affairs, and satisfying personal relations with others. Men's rightful expectations have many sources, among them their past experience of gain or loss, ideologies of scarcity or abundance, and the condition of groups with which they identify. In any case, men feel

satisfactions and frustrations with reference to what they think they ought
to have, not according to some absolute standard.

New expectations and new frustrations are more likely to be generated in
times of social change than social stasis. The quantitative comparisons of
the Feierabends and Nesvold suggest, for example, that nations undergoing
the most rapid socioeconomic change also are likely to experience the
highest levels of collective violence. Large-scale socioeconomic change is
ordinarily accompanied by changes in peoples' values, by institutional dislocations that affect people on top as much as people "on the way up,"
and even by the temporary breakdown of some social institutions. Rapid
social change is thus likely to add to the discontents of many groups at
the same time that it improves the conditions of some. In addition, it may
contribute to the partial breakdown of systems of normative control, to
the collapse of old institutions through which some groups were once able
to satisfy their expectations, and to the creation of new organizations of
the discontented. Under these conditions the motivational and institutional
potential for collective violence is high.

Some specific patterns of social change are directly indicted as causes of
collective violence. One is a pattern of rising expectations among people
so situated that lack of opportunity or the obdurate resistance of others
precludes their attainment of those expectations. American society is
especially vulnerable to the frustration of disappointed expectations, for we
have proclaimed ourselves the harbinger of a New Jerusalem and invited
millions of destitute immigrants to our shores to partake of its fulfillment.
"Progressive" demands by such groups that have felt themselves unjustifiably
excluded from a fair share of the social, economic, and political privileges
of the majority have repeatedly provided motivation and justification for
group conflict in our past, as they have in the history of Western Europe.
Demands of workers for economic recognition and political participation
were pervasive and chronic sources of turmoil in the United States and
Europe. The aspirations of the Irish, Italians, Slavs, and—far most consequentially—Negroes have also provided repeated occasion for violence
in America. Demands for an end to discriminatory privilege have not
been confined to minorities or ethnic strata either. The struggle for
women's suffrage in the United States was not peaceful, and America
has not heard the last of women's claims for effective socioeconomic
equality with men. Although the current resurgence of protest by many
groups testifies to the continued inequity in the distribution of rewards,
it also reflects the self-sustaining nature of social adjustment in this most
pluralistic of nations. The same process through which Americans have
made successive accommodations to demands for equity encourages the
regeneration of new demands.

Protective resistance to undesirable change has been a more common
source of collective violence in America than "revolutions of rising
expectations," however. For example, most ethnic and religious violence
in American history has been retaliatory violence by groups farther up
the socioeconomic ladder who felt threatened by the prospect of the
"new immigrant" and the Negro getting both "too big" and "too close."
As Taft and Ross have demonstrated, most labor violence in American
history was not a deliberate tactic of workingclass organization but a

result of forceful employer resistance to worker organization and demands. Companies repeatedly resorted to coercive and sometimes terroristic activities against union organizers and to violent strikebreaking tactics. The violence of employers often provided both model and impetus to counterviolence by workers, leading in many situations to an escalating spiral of violent conflict to the point of military intervention or mutual exhaustion.

Aggressive vigilantism has been a recurrent response of middle- and working-class Americans to perceived threats by outsiders or lesser classes to their status, security, and cultural integrity. The most widely known manifestations have been the frontier tradition of citizens' enforcement of the law and Ku Klux Klan efforts to maintain class lines and the moral code by taking their version of the law into their own hands. Brown has traced the emergence of such vigilante groups as the "Regulators" of pre-Revolutionary South Carolina and the Bald Knobbers of the Missouri Ozarks in the late 1800's. There are many other manifestations of aggressive vigilantism as well; no regions and few historical eras have been free of it, including the present. A contemporary one is the sporadic harassment of "hippie" and "peacenik" settlements in rural and smalltown America, and the neovigilante organizations of urban Americans, white and black, for "group defense" that often have aggressive overtones. There also is a vigilantism of a somewhat different sort, an aggressive and active suppression of deviancy within an otherwise-cohesive group. An historical example was the White Cap movement of the 1880's and 1890's, a spontaneous movement for the moral regulation of the poor whites and ne'er-do-wells of rural America. Such vigilantism also is apparent in the internecine strife of defensive black organizations, which have occasionally used violence to rid themselves of innovative "traitors" like Malcolm X.

Agrarian protests and uprisings have characterized both frontier and settled regions of the United States since before the Revolution. They have reflected both progressive and protective sentiments, including demands for land reform, defense against more powerful economic interests, and relief from onerous political restrictions. Among them have been Shays' Rebellion in Massachusetts, 1786-87; Fries' Rebellion in eastern Pennsylvania, 1799; some of the activities of the Grangers, Greenbackers, and Farmers' Alliance after the Civil War; and the "Green Corn Rebellion" of Oklahoma farmers during World War I.

Antiwar protest in American history also has a predominantly protective quality. The nation's 19th-century wars, especially the Civil War, led often to violent resistance to military conscription and the economic impositions of war. The 20th century has seen the development of a strong, indigenous strain of pacifism in the United States. The goals of those who have promoted the cause of peace, during both the First World War and the Vietnam war, have been protective in this sense: they adhere to a set of humanitarian values that are embodied in the basic social contract of American life, and see that contract threatened by those who regard force as the solution to American and foreign problems. The evidence of American history and comparative studies suggests no exact relationship between the occurrence of war and domestic protest against it, however. In the United States it appears to be

the pervasive sense that a particular war and its demands are unjust or illegitimate that leads to protest and, occasionally, to violent resistance.

Davies identifies a third general pattern of change that is frequently associated with the outbreak of rebellion and revolution: the occurrence of a
short period of sharp relative decline in socioeconomic or political conditions
after a prolonged period of improving conditions. A period of steady progress
generates expectations that progress will continue. If it does not continue, a
pervasive sense of frustration develops which, if focused on the government,
is likely to lead to widespread political violence. It is not only economic reversal in this pattern that leads to violence. People whose dignity, career expectations, or political ambitions are so frustrated are as likely to rebel as
those whose pocketbooks are being emptied.

This specific pattern is identified in Davies' studies of socioeconomic and
political changes affecting various groups before the outbreak of the French
Revolution, the American Civil War, and the Nazi revolution. It may also be
present in data on relative rates of white and Negro socioeconomic progress
in the United States during the last several decades. From 1940 to 1952,
nonwhite family income relative to educational attainment appears to have
increased steadily and substantially in comparison with white income. In
1940 the average Negro with a high school education was likely to receive 55
percent of the earnings of a white worker with comparable education. This
figure increased to 85 percent in 1952—but then declined to a low of 74
percent by 1962. These data call into question simplistic notions to the effect
that unsatisfied expectations of black Americans increased to the point of
violence simply because of "agitation," or because of unfulfilled promises.
Rather it may have been real progress, judged by the firsthand experience of
the 1940's and early 1950's, and probably also by reference to the rise of the
black bourgeoisie, which generated expectations that were substantially
frustrated by events of the late 1950's and early 1960's.

Discontent is only the initial condition of collective violence, which raises
the question of the extent to which the actualization of violence is determined by popular attitudes and institutional patterns. A cross-national
study by Gurr was designed to provide preliminary answers to this question,
by relating differences among nations in economic and political discontent,
apparent justifications for violence, and institutional strength to differences
in magnitudes and forms of civil strife. The results are that more than a
third of the differences among contemporary nations in magnitudes of strife
are accounted for by differences in the extent and intensity of their citizens'
discontent, even though measured imprecisely. Attitudes about politics and
violence are almost as important. Nations whose political systems have low
legitimacy are likely to have extensive strife; nations with a violent past—
and, by implication, popular attitudes that support violence—are likely to
have a violent present, and future. Institutional patterns can meliorate or
magnify these dispositions to violence. If physical controls are weak, and
especially if they are inconsistent in application, strife is likely to be high.
Similarly the weakness of conventional institutions, and the availability of
material and organizational support for rebellion, lead to high levels of strife,
particularly in its most intensive and violent forms.

The experience of the United States is consistent with this general pattern.
For all our rhetoric, we have never been a very law-abiding nation, and illegal

violence has sometimes been abundantly rewarded. Hence there have developed broad normative sanctions for the expression or acting out of discontent, somewhat limited inhibitions, and—owing to Jeffersonian liberalism's legacy of fear of central public authority—very circumscribed physical controls. Public sympathy has often been with the lawbreaker—sometimes with the nightrider who punished the transgressor of community mores, sometimes with the integrationists who refused to obey racial segregation laws. Lack of full respect for law and support for violence in one's own interest have both contributed to the justifications for private violence, justifications that in turn have helped make the United States historically and at present a tumultuous society.

On the other hand, the United States also has characteristics that in other countries appear to minimize intense revolutionary conspiracies and internal wars. Thus far in our history the American political system has maintained a relatively high degree of legitimacy in the eyes of most of its citizens. American political and economic institutions are generally strong. They are not pervasive enough to provide adequate opportunities for some regional and minority groups to satisfy their expectations, but sufficiently pervasive and egalitarian that the most ambitious and talented men—if not women—can pursue the "American dream" with some chance of success. These are conditions that minimize the prospects of revolutionary movements: a majoritarian consensus on the legitimacy of government, and provision of opportunity for men of talent who, if intensely alienated, might otherwise provide revolutionary cadres. But if such a system is open to the majority yet partly closed to a minority, or legitimate for the majority but illegitimate for a minority, the minority is likely to create chronic tumult even though it cannot organize effective revolutionary movements.

Some consequences of patterns of social control, legitimacy, and institutional development for the processes of collective violence are examined more fully below.

V. SOME CONSEQUENCES OF VIOLENCE

Does violence succeed? The inheritors of the doctrines of Frantz Fanon and "Ché" Guevara assert that if those who use it are sufficiently dedicated, revolution can always be accomplished. Many vehement advocates of civil order and strategists of counterinsurgency hold essentially the same faith: that sufficient use of public violence will deter private violence. This fundamental agreement of "left" and "right" on the effectiveness of force for modifying others' behavior is striking. But to what extent is it supported by theory and by historical evidence?

The two most fundamental human responses to the use of force are to flee or to fight. This assertion rests on rather good psychological and ethological evidence about human and animal aggression. Force threatens and angers men, especially if they believe it to be illegitimate or unjust. Threatened, they will defend themselves if they can, flee if they cannot. Angered, they have an innate disposition to retaliate in kind. Thus men who fear assault attempt to arm themselves, and two-thirds or more of white Americans think that black looters and arsonists should be shot. Governments facing violent protest often regard compromise as evidence of weakness and devote additional resources to counterforce. Yet if a government responds to the threat or use of violence with greater force, its effects in many circumstances are identical with the effects that dictated its actions: its opponents will if they can resort to greater force.

There are only two inherent limitations on such an escalating spiral of force and counterforce: the exhaustion of one side's resources for force, or the attainment by one of the capacity for genocidal victory. There are societal and psychological limitations as well, but they require tacit bonds between opponents: one's acceptance of the ultimate authority of the other, arbitration of the conflict by neutral authority, recognition of mutual interest that makes bargaining possible, or the perception that acquiesence to a powerful opponent will have less harmful consequences than resisting to certain death. In the absence of such bases for cooperation, regimes and their opponents are likely to engage in violent conflict to the limit of their respective abilities.[8]

To the extent that this argument is accurate, it suggests one kind of circumstance in which violence succeeds: that in which one group so overpowers its opponents that they have no choice short of death but to desist. When they do resist to the death, the result is a Carthaginian peace. History records many instances of successful uses of overpowering force. Not surprisingly, the list of successful governmental uses of force against opponents is much longer than the list of dissident successes against government, because most governments have much greater capacities for force, provided they keep the loyalty of their generals and soldiers. Some dissident successes discussed in this volume include the French, American, Nazi, and Cuban Revolutions. Some governmental successes include, in Britain, the suppression of the violent phases of the Luddite and Chartist movements in the 19th century; in Venezuela the Betancourt regime's elimination of revolutionary terrorism; in the United States the North's victory in the Civil War, and the quelling of riots and local rebellions, from the Whiskey Rebellion of 1794 to the ghetto riots of the 1960's.

Governmental uses of force are likely to be successful in quelling specific outbreaks of private violence except in those rare circumstances when the balance of force favors its opponents, or the military defects. But the historical evidence also suggests that governmental violence often succeeds only in the short run. The government of Imperial Russia quelled the revolution of 1905, but in doing so intensified the hostilities of its opponents, who mounted a successful revolution 12 years later, after the government was weakened by a protracted and unsuccessful war. The North "won" the Civil War, but in its very triumph created hostilities that contributed to one of the greatest and most successful waves of vigilante violence in our history. The 17,000 Klansmen of the South today are neither peaceable nor content with the outcome of the "War of Northern Aggression."[9] State or federal troops have been dispatched to quell violent or near-violent labor conflict in more than 160 recorded instances in American history; they were immediately successful in almost every case yet did not significantly deter subsequent labor violence.

The long-range effectiveness of governmental force in maintaining civil peace seems to depend on three conditions identified by the papers in this volume: public belief that governmental use of force is legitimate, consistent

use of that force, and remedial action for the grievance that give rise to
private violence. The decline of violent working-class protest in 19th century
England was predicated on an almost universal popular acceptance of the
legitimacy of the government, accompanied by the development of an effective police system—whose popular acceptance was enhanced by its minimal
reliance on violence—and by gradual resolution of working class grievances.
The Cuban case was quite the opposite: the governmental response to private
violence was terroristic, inconsistent public violence that alienated most
Cubans from the Batista regime, with no significant attempts to reduce the
grievances, mostly political, that gave rise to rebellion.

We have assumed that private violence is "successful" in those extreme
cases in which a government capitulates in the face of the superiority of its
opponents. This is not the only or necessarily the best criterion of "success,"
though. A better criterion is the extent to which the grievances that give rise
to collective protest and violence are resolved. Even revolutionary victories
do not necessarily lead to complete success in these terms. The American
Revolution returned effective political control to the hands of the colonists,
but eventually led to an expansion of state and federal authority that diminished local autonomy to the point that new rebellions broke out in many
frontier areas over essentially the same kinds of grievances that had caused
the revolution. The Bolshevik revolution ended Russia's participation in
World War I, which was perhaps the greatest immediate grievance of the
Russian people, and in the long run brought great economic and social benefits; but the contingent costs of the subsequent civil war, famine, and totalitarian political control were enormous. The middle-class political discontents
that fueled the Cuban revolutionary movement, far from being remedied,
were intensified when the revolutionary leaders used their power to effect a
basic socioeconomic reconstruction of society that favored themselves and
the rural working classes.

If revolutionary victory is unlikely in the modern state, and uncertain of
resolving the grievances that give rise to revolutionary movements, are there
any circumstances in which less intensive private violence is successful? We
said above that the legitimacy of governmental force is one of the determinants of its effectiveness. The same principle applies to private violence: It
can succeed when it is widely regarded as legitimate. The vigilante movements
of the American frontier had widespread public support as a means for establishing order in the absence of adequate law enforcement agencies, and
were generally successful. The Ku Klux Klan of the Reconstruction era
similarly had the sympathy of most white Southerners and was largely effective in reestablishing and maintaining the prewar social and political status
quo. The chronicles of American labor violence, however, suggest that violence was almost always ineffective for the workers involved. In a very few
instances there was popular and state governmental support for the grievances of workers that had led to violent confrontations with employers, and
in several of these cases state authority was used to impose solutions that
favored the workers. But in the great majority of cases the public and officials did not accept the legitimacy of labor demands, and the more violent
was conflict, the more disastrous were the consequences for the workers who
took part. Union organizations involved in violent conflict seldom gained
recognition, their supporters were harassed and often lost their jobs, and tens

of thousands of workers and their families were forcibly deported from their homes and communities.

The same principle applies, with two qualifications, to peaceful public protest. If demonstrations are regarded as a legitimate way to express grievances, and if the grievances themselves are widely held to be justified, protest is likely to have positive effects. One of the qualifications is that if public opinion is neutral on an issue, protest demonstrations can have favorable effects. This appears to have been an initial consequence of the civil-rights demonstrations of the early 1960's in the North. If public opinion is negative, however, demonstrations are likely to exacerbate popular hostility. During World War I, for example, pacifist demonstrators were repeatedly attacked, beaten, and in some cases lynched, with widespread public approval and sometimes official sanction. Contemporary civil-rights demonstrations and activities in the South and in some northern cities have attracted similar responses.

The second qualification is that when violence occurs during protest activities, it is rather likely to alienate groups that are not fundamentally in sympathy with the protesters. We mentioned above the unfavorable consequences of labor violence for unions and their members, despite the fact that violence was more often initiated by employers than by workers. In the long run, federally enforced recognition and bargaining procedures were established, but this occurred only after labor violence had passed its climacteric, and moreover in circumstances in which no union leaders advocated violence. In England, comparably, basic political reforms were implemented not in direct response to Chartist protest, but long after its violent phase had passed.

The evidence supports one basic principle: Force and violence can be successful techniques of social control and persuasion when they have extensive popular support. If they do not, their advocacy and use are ultimately self-destructive, either as techniques of government or of opposition. The historical and contemporary evidence of the United States suggests that popular support tends to sanction violence in support of the status quo: the use of public violence to maintain public order, the use of private violence to maintain popular conceptions of social order when government cannot or will not. If these assertions are true—and not much evidence contradicts them—the prolonged use of force or violence to advance the interests of any segmental group may impede and quite possibly preclude reform. This conclusion should not be taken as an ethical judgement, despite its apparent correspondence with the "establishmentarian" viewpoint. It represents a fundamental trait of American and probably all mankind's character, one which is ignored by advocates of any political orientation at the risk of broken hopes, institutions, and lives.

To draw this conclusion is not to indict public force or all private violence as absolute social evils. In brief and obvious defense of public force, reforms cannot be made if order is wholly lacking, and reforms will not be made if those who have the means to make them feel their security constantly in jeopardy. And as for private violence, though it may bring out the worst in both its practitioners and its victims, it need not do so. Collective violence is after all a symptom of social malaise. It can be so regarded and the malaise treated as such, provided public-spirited men diagnose it correctly and have the will and means to work for a cure rather than to retaliate out of anger.

Americans may be quick to self-righteous anger, but they also have retained some of the English genius for accommodation. Grudgingly and with much tumult, the dominant groups in American society have moved over enough to give the immigrant, the worker, the suffragette better—not the best—seats at the American feast of freedom and plenty. Many of them think the feast is bounteous enough for the dissatisfied students, the poor, the Indians, the blacks. Whether there is a place for the young militants who think the feast has gone rotten, no historical or comparative evidence we know of can answer, because absolute, revolutionary alienation from society has been very rare in the American past and no less rare in other pluralistic and abundant nations.

VI. SOME ALTERNATIVES TO VIOLENCE

Political leaders faced with outbreaks or threats of collective violence can respond in the two general ways that we discussed above: they can strengthen systems of forceful social control, or they can exert public effort and encourage private efforts to alleviate conditions leading to discontent. Primary reliance on force has indeterminate outcomes at best. If popularly supported, public force will contain specific outbreaks of private violence, but is unlikely to prevent their recurrence. At worst, public force will so alienate a people that terrorist and revolutionary movements will arise to challenge and ultimately overthrow the regime. The teaching of comparative studies is that governments must be cautious in their reliance on force to maintain order, and consistent in the exercise of the modicum of force they choose to use. These are policies that require both appropriate leadership and well-trained, highly disciplined, and loyal military and police forces.

The effort to eliminate the conditions that lead to collective violence may tax the resources of a society, but it poses less serious problems than increased resort to force. American labor violence has been mitigated in the past 25 years partly by growing prosperity, but more consequentially because employers now have almost universally recognized unions and will negotiate wage issues and other grievances with them rather than retaliate against them. The movement toward recognition and negotiation was strongly reinforced when workers in most occupations were guaranteed the right to organize and bargain collectively in the National Labor Relations Act of 1935. Taft and Ross judge the act to have been effective not just because it established procedures but because of the concerted effort to enforce them by the National Labor Relations Board and the willingness of both employers and unions to recognize the Board's authority. Their willingness may be a testimony also to their own and public dismay at the destructiveness of earlier conflicts. It is worth emphasizing that in this situation the long-range consequences of conciliatory response was a decrease not increase in violent conflict. In fact, violence was chronic so long as union recognition was denied. The outcome suggests the inadequacy of arguments that concessions necessarily breed greater violence.

The history of English working-class protest supports these interpretations. In the 19th century, when England was tranformed by an industrial revolution in which a highly competitive, laissez faire market economy disrupted traditional employment patterns and led to sweatshop conditions for many urban workers, violent public protest then became chronic. Several conditions averted to what many Englishmen then feared as a threat of working-class revolt. One was economic growth itself, which led to a significant improvement in the standard of living of urban workers and to hopeful prospects shared by all classes. A second was the acceptance by upper-class political leaders of demands for political reform, and acceptance dictated by both principle and practicality that led to the enfranchisement and assimilation of the working classes into the English body politic. A third was a trend toward grudging toleration of, and ultimately the acceptance and encouragement, of working-class organization. Recognition of the right of workers to organize and bargain led to a flourishing not only of unions but of self-help organizations, cooperatives, and religious and educational groups, all of which together provided British workers with means to work toward the resolution of their discontents.

There were and are characteristics of English society that had no direct American parallels. Expectations of English workers were less high than those of ambitious immigrants to the United States. The English class structure, though more stratified and complex than the American, was generally accepted by all classes, seldom directly challenged. The laissez faire sentiments of British employers were tempered by an acceptance of civic responsibilities that developed more quickly than it did in the United States, and as one consequence English labor violence never reached the intensity that it did in the United States. Working-class demands for political reform were predicated on the common assumption that governments could be changed and the power of the state used to ameliorate the economic grievances of workers. Though the parallels are not exact, the English experience seems to suggest some general lessons for the contemporary United States: civil peace was established through a judicious, perhaps fortuitous, combination of governmental and political reform, and institutional development among the aggrieved classes of society.

Intensely discontented men are not will-less pawns in a game of social chess. They also have alternatives, of which violence is usually the last, the most desperate, and in most circumstances least likely of success. Peaceful protest, conducted publicly and through conventional political channels, is a traditional American option. As one of the world's most pluralistic societies, we have repeatedly albeit reluctantly accommodated ourselves to discontented groups using interest and pressure-group tactics within the political process as a means of leverage for change. But it also is an American characteristic to resist demonstrative demands, however legal and peaceful, if they seem to challenge our basic beliefs and personal positions. Public protest in the United States is a slow and unwieldy instrument of social change that sometimes inspires more obdurate resistance than favorable change.[10]

Another kind of group response to intense stresses and discontents is called "defensive adaptation" by Bernard Siegel. It is essentially an inward-turning, nonviolent response motivated by a desire to build and maintain a group's cultural integrity in the face of hostile pressures. The defensive group is characterized by centralization of authority; attempts to set the group apart by emphasizing symbols of group identity; and minimization of members' contacts with other groups. It is an especially common reaction among ethnic and religious groups whose members see their social environments as permanently hostile, depreciating, and powerful. Such adaptations are apparent, for example, among some Pueblo Indians, Black Muslims, and Amish, and

many minority groups in other nations. This kind of defensive withdrawal
may lead to violence when outside groups press too closely in on the defensive
group, but it is typically a response that minimizes violent conflict. Although
the defensive group provides its members some, essentially social and psychological, satisfactions, it seldom can provide them with substantial economic
benefits or political means by which they can promote their causes vis-a-vis
hostile external groups.

A third general kind of response is the development of discontented groups
of positive, socially integrative means for the satisfaction of their members'
unsatisfied expectations. This response has characterized most discontented
groups throughout Western history. In England, social protest was institutionalized through the trade unions, cooperative societies, and other self-help
activities. In continental Europe, the discontent of the urban workers and
petit bourgeoisie led to the organization of fraternal societies, unions, and
political parties, which provided some intrinsic satisfactions for their members
and which could channel demands more or less effectively to employers and
into the political system. In the United States the chronic local uprisings of
the late-18th, the 19th, and the early-20th century—such as the Shay, Whiskey,
Dorr, and Green Corn Rebellions—have been largely superseded by organized,
conventional political manifestations of local and regional interests. Labor
violence similarly declined in the United States and England once trade unions
were organized and recognized.

The contemporary efforts of black Americans to develop effective community organizations, and their demands for greater control of community
affairs, seem to be squarely in this tradition. So are demands of student
protesters for greater participation in university affairs, attempts of white
urban citizens to create new neighorhood organizations, and the impulse of
middle-class Americans to move to the suburbs where they can exercise
greater control over the local government.

The initial effects of the organization of functional and community groups
for self-help may be increased conflict, especially if the economic and political establishments attempt to subvert their efforts. But if these new organizations receive public and private cooperation and sufficient resources to carry
out their activities, the prospects for violence are likely to be reduced. The
social costs of this kind of group response seem much less than those of public
and private violence. The human benefits are likely to be far greater than
those attained through private violence or defensive withdrawal.

VII. THE ADEQUACY OF PRESENT KNOWLEDGE

Do we know enough about the sources, processes, and consequences of
collective violence, or about its forms and participants, its relations to social
change, or its remedies and alternatives? The preceding conclusions may imply that we know a good deal. We do not. Many, perhaps most, of these
conclusions are educated guesses or conjecture. This volume seems to be the
first attempt to link the historical and comparative dimensions of research on
the subject or group violence in America, and all we have proposed is a tentative, partial synthesis. To use an analogy, this volume is not an accurate atlas
to well-mapped terrain; rather, it is equivalent to a 16th-century map of the

New World, replete with sea serpents and expanses of terra incognita, its purported ranges and rivers based on reports of lone explorers.

Consider how new and little verified some of the information in this volume is. It includes the first general, empirically based commentary on the precise nature of violent protest over the long span of Western European history (by Charles Tilly). It includes the first comprehensive roster of American vigilante movements (by Richard Maxwell Brown) and the first general survey of American labor violence (by Philip Taft and Philip Ross). It reports, as an appendix, some results of the first attempt ever made to collect systematic data on the incidence and types of individual and collective political violence over a substantial period of American history (by Sheldon Levy). It reports the first crude effort to categorize and count the types, motives, and objectives of participants in collective violence in all nations, for the contemporary or any other era (by Ted Robert Gurr). It includes a pioneering analysis of defensive withdrawal, a common, nonviolent kind of group response to severe stress (by Bernard Siegel).

The conclusions offer other examples. We can speculate about, but do not know with any certainty, what the relative importance is among the historical forces that have contributed to our relatively high American levels of violence. We do not even know with any exactitude how high those levels were, or the details of their causation, variation, or resolution. We have speculated on the relative importance of discontent, attitudes about violence, and institutional patterns as causes of collective violence. These causal questions have been examined systematically in only a handful of comparative studies, and rarely at any depth in the historical dimension for the United States or any other society. Evidence hints that Americans are and have been more willing to take the law in their own hands, and to use violence, than citizens of many other Western societies. But no one has done the survey and depth interview studies necessary to test this speculation or to identify the circumstances under which violence is thought to be justified. Nor have popular attitudes toward violence in most historical eras been thoroughly studied, though they could be either on the basis of what people did or what they wrote. We have speculated on the efficacy of public force in maintaining order and the uses of private violence in effecting change. Relatively few cases can be cited in support of the conclusions because few cases have been studied in this light; those few may be exceptional rather than typical, and only the examination of many cases representing different types of societies and situations can test the adequacy of our conclusions.

There are other uncharted regions. Something is known about the phases through which riots and some revolutions develop and decay. Not much is known about the precesses of linked series of events, like the chronic labor violence or vigilante movements of the American past. What accounts for their establishment as a mode of action, and for their persistence or decline. Why, for instance, did the Ku Klux Klan of the 1920s collapse and disappear so suddenly, whereas rightist citizen groups in Europe evolved toward fascist regimes? Which groups took their cues from others, and how did they learn of others? Vigilante violence was often successful, and persisted; labor violence was seldom successful yet it too persisted; protest by suffragettes was successful and it ended. What accounts for such differences, both in outcome and duration? There are educated guesses, but no conclusions based on examination of many movements. Nor do we know much of the long-range consequences of violence. The farther removed we are in time from a major rebellion, revolution, or civil war, the less we know about its economic and social consequences. For riots and local uprisings we often know nothing of their aftermaths even a year later. Did the frontier rebellions of America leave any destructive and abiding traces in the attitudes or institutions or politics of the regions where they occurred? What has happened in the black ghettos wracked by riots between 1965 through 1968? Who is analyzing the consequences of different kinds of student tactics in the campus protests and rebellions of the last 4 years?

Alternatives to violence are little studied. More precisely, the peaceful processes by which most social conflicts are resolved have been studied in great detail in many Western societies, but we know of very few studies that have compared groups under similar kinds of stress, or with similar kinds of demands, to determine the options open to them and the consequences of their choice of those alternatives. On this kind of knowledge a crucial policy issue depends: whether it is necessary for groups seeking reforms to resort to limited violence to dramatize their demands, despite the dangers of creating "backlash." Presumably the answers vary, depending on the society in which reforms are sought, the nature of the reforms, and the groups making and resisting them. And with regard to the backlash, does it necessarily occur, and if so among what people, when, and with what immediate and persisting consequences? What backlashes can be identified in American history, and in the histories of other Western societies? Backlashes almost certainly occur even when demands are made peacefully, but do they inhibit reform just as much as the backlash to violence? Then there are the critical questions about the resolution of violence. Probably foremost in the minds of most public and private officials who deal with public protest and violence is: What are the relative merits of concessions and coercion for maintaining an orderly and reasonably contented community? A case can be made for the desirability of either policy approach and any combination of them, by selective choice of examples. The careful study of comparable cases, historically and comparatively, needed for a judicious answer has scarcely been started.

One of our most optimistic conclusions is that we know enough to say what some of the important but unanswered questions about American violence are. The studies in this volume demonstrate that the procedures of historical and comparative research are adequate to the task of seeking further and more precise knowledge, though we lack enough men and women with the requisite training and skills, and adequate support, to do so in the near future. This report provides substantial insights into the causes and character of violence in America; we have yet to understand fully how civil peace is created and maintained in these circumstances. But at least we know that it is possible, for Americans and other people have done so before.

References

1. Exemplary of the "consensus school" of American historians are Daniel Boorstin, *The Genius of American Politics* (Chicago: University of Chicago Press, 1953); David Potter, *People of Plenty* (Chicago: University of Chicago Press, 1954); and Louis Hartz, *The Liberal Tradition in America* (New York: Harcourt, Brace & World, 1955). These scholars did not deny that the American past was replete with violence. Rather, they emphasized that America lacked the feudal past that had led to acute class animosity in Europe, that virtually all Americans shared the liberal ideology of Locke and Jefferson, and that Americans were highly pragmatic and did not take any ideology seriously enough to be fundamentally divided by it.

2. See Richard Wade, "Violence in the Cities: An Historical View," *Urban Violence* (Chicago: University of Chicago Press, 1969), pp. 7-26.

3. These absolute comparisons are from Michael Hudson, "Violence and Political Institutionalization in the United States: A Comparative Analysis," a working paper prepared for the National Commission on the Causes and Prevention of Violence, 1968.

4. See Konrad Lorenz, *On Aggression* (New York: Harcourt, Brace & World, 1966), and Robert Ardrey, *The Territorial Imperative* (New York: Dell, 1966).

5. See Leonard Berkowitz, *Aggression: A Social Psychological Analysis* (New York: McGraw-Hill, 1962), and Ashley Montagu, ed., *Man and Aggression* (New York: Oxford University Press, 1968).

6. See Geoffrey Gorer, "Man has No 'Killer' Instinct," *The New York Times Magazine,* Nov. 17, 1966.

7. "Frustration" interpretations of the impetus to collective violence are proposed by Davies, the Feierabends, and Nesvold, and, in somewhat different guises, by Comer and Carstairs. Gude considers some effects of legitimacy and force, Janowitz social control generally. Gurr's analysis deals with motivational, attitudinal, and institutional variables that lead to violence. Siegel examines the kinds of external stresses on a group and group attitudes that lead it to defensive institutional responses which minimize external violence.

8. This discussion is drawn from arguments and evidence in Ted Robert Gurr, *Why Men Rebel* (Princeton: Princeton University Press, in press), ch. 8. The survey datum is from Hazel Erskine, "The Polls: Demonstrations and Race Riots," *Public Opinion Quarterly* (Winter 1967-68), pp. 655-677.

9. On Klan membership in 1967, see U.S. Congress, House Un-American Activities Committee, *The Present-Day Ku Klux Klan Movement* (Washington, D.C.: Government Printing Office, 1967), p. 62.

10. Kenneth E. Boulding makes the same point in a discussion of the possible consequences of antiwar protest, in "Reflections on Protest," *Bulletin of the Atom Scientists,* vol. XXI (Oct. 1965), pp. 18-20.